A TRAVELER'S GUIDE to the
GALAPAGOS ISLANDS

Third Edition

Barry Boyce

GALAPAGOS travel

APTOS, CALIFORNIA

A TRAVELER'S GUIDE TO THE GALAPAGOS ISLANDS

Third Edition

Published by:

GALAPAGOS TRAVEL
783 Rio Del Mar Boulevard
Suite #47
Aptos, CA 95003
(800) 969-9014
E-Mail: galapagostravel@compuserve.com
http://www.galapagostravel.com

HUNTER PUBLISHING
130 Campus Drive
Edison, NJ 08818
(800) 255-2343
htttp://www.hunterpublishing.com

Printing: **COLORCRAFT LTD.,** Hong Kong
Typesetting/Interior & Cover Design: **Holmes Typography,** San Jose, CA
Maps: **Kathleen Neault**
      Authorized use by the *Instituto Geografico Militar,* Quito, Ecuador
      (Permit #890509-IGM-g-62561, November 7, 1989).
Photos #16 & #46: **Dr. Elaine Heron**
Photo #7: Original Artwork by **Edgar Vargas,** Naturalist Guide, Galápagos
Photo of Author on Back Cover: **Mark Grantham**
All Uncredited Photos: **Barry Boyce**
Front Cover: A Giant Tortoise in Slow Motion Pursuit
Back Cover: A Squadron of Frigatebirds in Piratical Pursuit

Library of Congress Catalog Number: 98-072535

ISBN: 1-55650-850-6

CONTENTS

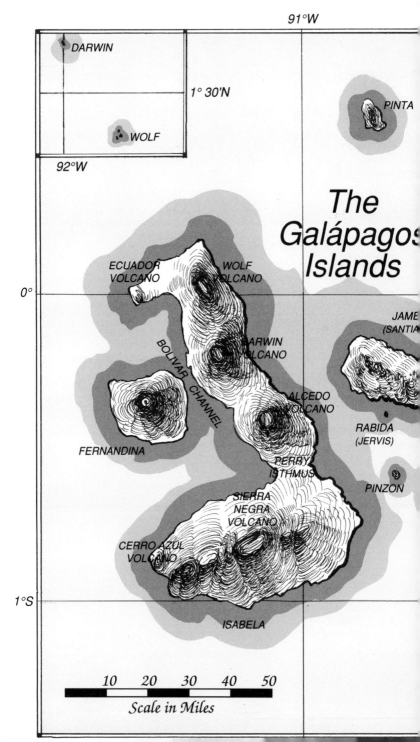

91°W

DARWIN

1° 30'N

WOLF

92°W

PINTA

The
Galápagos
Islands

ECUADOR
VOLCANO

WOLF
VOLCANO

0°

JAMES
(SANTIAGO)

BOLIVAR CHANNEL

DARWIN
VOLCANO

ALCEDO
VOLCANO

RABIDA
(JERVIS)

FERNANDINA

PERRY
ISTHMUS

PINZON

SIERRA
NEGRA
VOLCANO

CERRO AZUL
VOLCANO

1°S

ISABELA

10   20   30   40   50

Scale in Miles

90°W

MARCHENA

TOWER (GENOVESA)

The Galápagos Islands

Ecuador

0°

N

RTOLOME

MBRERO CHINO

APHNES

SEYMOUR

BALTRA

S. PLAZA IS.

ANTA CRUZ

SANTA FE

SAN CRISTOBAL

1°S

FLOREANA

ESPANOLA (HOOD)

ACKNOWLEDGEMENTS

This is the section of the book we tend to skip over. To the reader, it's a series of names and "thank yous." True enough, and yet it should be understood that many of the "acknowledged" are volunteers, giving their time and energy to help a stranger who's nosing around while "working on a book."

Many people have answered my questions and provided information. Others have gone beyond that. Among the Tour Operators, Dolores & Eduardo Diez of QUASAR NAUTICA introduced me to Quito and provided continual assistance in solving the difficult logistics of getting around the Galápagos. Jacinto Hojas provided me my second home – the yacht SAN JACINTO. Among the Guides who shared their time, a special thanks to Ernesto Vaca who has rediscovered the Galápagos with me numerous times; there were many exciting chapters in the "Adventures of Pancho & Lefty." The arranging of interviews in the Galápagos was aided tremendously by the efforts of Daniel Geller and Alexandra Bahamonde of the Hotel Galápagos in Puerto Ayora.

Finally, for background information, I want to thank Johannah Barry of the *Charles Darwin Foundation*, Dr. Robert Bensted-Smith, Director of the *Charles Darwin Research Station,* and former Director, Dr. Chantal Blanton. A special thanks to Dr. Linda Cayot of the Darwin Station for the thorough background on the herpetology programs of the C.D.R.S.

This section would not complete if I didn't say, "Thank you!" to my mother Evelyn Johnson, for understanding "why I didn't call or write" for 6 months.

To Rosemaria

CHAPTER I

THE ENCHANTED ISLES

October 8th – The natural history of these islands is eminently curious, and well deserves attention. Most of the organic productions are aboriginal creations [endemic species] found nowhere else; there is even a difference between the inhabitants of the different islands; yet all show a marked relationship with those of [South] America, though separated from that continent by an open space of ocean, between 500 and 600 miles in length. Considering the small size of these islands, we feel the more astonished at the number of their aboriginal [endemic] beings, and at their confined range. Seeing every height crowned with its crater, and the boundaries of most of the lava streams still distinct, we are led to believe that within a period, geologically recent, the unbroken ocean was here spread out. Hence, both in space and time, we seem to be brought somewhat near to that great fact, that mystery of mysteries – the first appearance of new beings on this earth.

Charles Darwin, 1845

Darwin's astute observations were to set the stage for the development of the theory of evolution by natural selection as formulated in his famous publication, **THE ORIGIN OF SPECIES.** The ideas set forth in this work remain today as one of the major breakthroughs in scientific thought, and led the way for over 150 years of biological research. In the world of science, Charles Darwin and the Galápagos Islands share a prominent location!

There are several facts about Darwin's historic journey and findings that probably come as a surprise to many of us:

1. We picture Darwin in the Galápagos sitting under a tree, scratching his white beard and carefully observing the finches that would eventually bear his name. He may well have done just that, but his beard wasn't white; when Charles Darwin visited the Galápagos Islands, he was but 26 years old.

2. We think of Darwin as one of England's "big muckity-muck" scientists, sent by England to head up an important expedition. While Darwin was des-

tined to become a "very big muckity-muck," when he left England on board the H.M.S. BEAGLE in 1831 at the tender age of 22, his credentials to date were not overly impressive – a drop-out of the Medical School at Edinburgh University and a noticeably uninspired divinity student. His father, Dr. Robert Darwin, clearly underwhelmed by young Charles' progress, lashed out at him on one occasion, "You care for nothing but shooting, dogs and rat-catching, and you will be a disgrace to yourself and all your family." Darwin's capacity on the BEAGLE was that of an unpaid observer. At that, he was a second choice for the position that Captain FitzRoy described as available to someone who would simply "... profit by the opportunity of visiting different countries yet little known."

3. We envision Darwin making copious notes of his observations, conducting research studies, and spending a considerable period of time on each of the major islands. The notes were copious and some research was conducted, but Charles Darwin's length of stay on the Galápagos Islands was a very brief 5 weeks (September-October, 1835). Prior to visiting the Galápagos, the crew of the BEAGLE had already spent more than 3 years surveying the shores of South America and would spend another year asea after visiting the islands.

4. We tend to picture historic spots (such as the Galápagos) as just that – an empty stadium, a bare stage, the ruins that once flourished. "Close your eyes," we say to ourselves, "and imagine the way that it was, for it was right here that it all happened." The amazing thing about the Galápagos Islands is that it's still happening. You can still see what Darwin saw, for the Galápagos is quite young and is still in the early stages of formation; the western islands (Fernandina and Isabela) are a geologically brief 100,000-200,000 years old. This is indeed a very rare opportunity, containing an element of going back in time.

This is precisely the feeling you get while touring the Galápagos Islands, located on the equator and about 600 miles off the coast of Ecuador. It begins with the misty, volcanic land-and-seascapes. The Galápagos archipelago consists of thirteen major islands and six smaller islets; in addition, it has about fifty named minor islets and rock formations protruding from its waters. From the time when they first literally broke through the ocean floor, some 3-5 million years ago, the Galápagos Islands have remained a very active site of volcanic activity; as of this writing, the most recent eruption occurred in 1995 (on Fernandina Island). While touring the Galápagos and gazing at the rugged terrain from the bow of your ship, the term "moonscape" may seem more appropriate than "landscape." Indeed, with all the black, porous volcanic rock, jagged cliff formations, fragmented boulders, lava fields, spatter cones, pit craters, and columns of gas-driven steam, as you put your feet ashore your mind echoes, "That's one small step...." It was probably this somewhat surreal view that led the early Spanish explorers to give the islands their first name, *Las Islas Encantadas* – The Enchanted Islands.

It's not only the geology of these Enchanted Islands that is timeless, but the wildlife as well. You are immediately overwhelmed by the extraordinary nature and diversity of the animals – the same wildlife that so fascinated and inspired Darwin. In terms of the giant land tortoises, some as large as 500-600 lbs., there is a possibility (granted, a very small one) that you are looking at quite literally the same animal that Darwin saw; it is generally thought that these gentle giants live upwards of 125 years! With the facial features that were actually used to create the visage of **E.T.**, the giant tortoises themselves seem to be of another world. Watching their careful, slow motion crash-steps does little to diminish this feeling.

Another Galápagos creature seemingly of another time (some would say prehistoric) is the marine iguana. Often seen in a most curious (some would say bizarre) frozen pose atop lava rocks, the marine iguana is actually sun bathing to raise its body temperature after a dive in the Pacific Ocean. The marine iguana is a competent diver and swimmer, the only lizard to have achieved this ability. While warming itself, it will frequently spout forth or sneeze (some would say spit) brine out of efficient salt-excreting glands located in the nostrils.

The oddities of Galápagos wildlife are not limited to the reptiles; the birds have their share of interesting characters as well. Here you will see penguins on the equator and the flightless cormorants, who have traded their ability to fly for a streamlined body to assist their swimming prowess. You will see courting blue-footed boobies elaborately gather nesting materials only to apparently ignore such niceties, as the eggs are laid and incubated directly on the ground.

As you've gathered, things are a little different in the Galápagos. With isolation comes change, and on these islands, both the isolation and the adaptations have been extreme and therefore quite noticeable. This is what caught Darwin's eye so quickly and will catch yours as well.

Isolation has several interesting aspects to it, which will be discussed throughout this book. One truly fascinating aspect is the isolation from predators, including that noteworthy predator, man himself. As a result, the animals in the Galápagos have not learned or adapted themselves to flee or shy away when approached. One can get to within arms length distance of many of the Galápagos animals, and amazingly they will not dash or fly off. This experience is a constant source of pleasure and amazement, and it's one that is very difficult for many of us to get used to. We are very accustomed to slowly approaching an animal, camera in hand, using very powerful telephoto lenses to cut down the distance. It is not necessary to do this in the Galápagos, and the picture-taking opportunities are unbelievable – to the point that you will shoot 2-3 times more than your usual daily quota (see Chapter V, PHOTOGRAPHING THE GALAPAGOS ISLANDS).

Some animals will not wait for you to approach them; they will approach you! I will never forget my first swim in the Galápagos, when I felt something zoom past me in the water. I quickly turned, and through my snorkel mask saw a huge black fin swerve and come back straight at me! After I audibly shuddered and took in a mouthful of water, I realized it was a sea lion. From that time on, I had my little yellow underwater camera ready, and the naturally playful Galápagos sea lions did not fail to perform; they would continuously be streaking by, sometimes two at a time (see Photo #15), almost but not quite touching me. This endless performance is awaiting your arrival.

Another animal that will approach, but not as predictably, is the bottlenosed dolphin. Before describing this encounter, however, it would be worthwhile to point out how your Galápagos adventure will be spent. You will be touring the islands for 1-2 weeks on-board a boat with a full crew, including a Guide who has been trained at the *Charles Darwin Research Station* in the Galápagos. These boats will do the bulk of their travel at night, so your valuable daylight hours are actually spent on the islands with your Guide, exploring and photographing the wildlife. There is a wide range of boats to choose from – 4-6 passenger sailing yachts, 6-16 passenger motor yachts, and 34-90 passenger Cruise Ships (see Chapter IV, CHOOSING A TOUR).

You will often visit two islands (or two distinct parts of the same island) per day, so there is usually about a 1-2 hour cruise right after lunch. This time of day would usually find me lying on deck, up close to the bow, digesting lunch, reading up on the wildlife to be seen that afternoon, and catching a cool spray. On one such occasion, I became aware of a splashing sound close by. I turned my head, and there was a bottle-nosed dolphin leaping through the water right alongside the boat. Then I heard another splash, turned, and sure enough, there was another dolphin on the opposite side of the boat. When I stood up and looked around, there were dolphins in the distance in almost every direction, leaping towards the boat from a distance as if dashing homeward on the run after hearing the dinner bell. Eventually several of the dolphins would get alongside the boat and keep up with us, taking turns leaping (although there were several pairs that seemed to leap in tandem). If that wasn't enough excitement, I looked down right in front of the bow and there were two dolphins leading the way for our boat; I found out later that this activity is called "piloting" or "riding the bow wave."

The first time this happened, I didn't have my camera on deck; fortunately I had two other chances (see Photo #6). In fact, from that time on, I kept my camera handy, even when eating meals, and was rewarded for doing so. In the Galápagos, your curiosity is almost always rewarded!

If the cartographers on board the BEAGLE actually surveyed the archipelago, it was Charles Darwin that put the Galápagos Islands on the map! After Darwin's historic visit and his subsequent published observations, a great deal of scientific research has been conducted on the Galápagos. For the general public, however, the Galápagos was virtually inaccessible – difficult and expensive to get to, and (until the late 1960s) with no real facilities and means by which the tourist could comfortably see the islands. Also, the interest in the natural universe and issues such as wildlife conservation were not as widespread as they are today. Such issues were certainly not foremost in the minds of many of the early visitors to the Galápagos – the pirates and whalers; more about them later (in the History section of the next chapter).

The Galápagos will inspire you in many of the same ways as it did Darwin, and your understanding of the natural world will take on a different perspective once you have visited these Enchanted Islands. When you get back home, you will be obliged to creatively express these thoughts and feelings. You will show your photos time and again, carefully explaining each shot. You may wind up writing songs (how about *The Sea Lion Serenade*), come up with new recipes (perhaps *Fettuccine Alcedo*), maybe even write a book! Whatever you do, your attitude about vacations and how to spend them will be forever changed.

CHAPTER II

ABOUT
THE GALÁPAGOS ISLANDS

Before we begin a discussion of the climate, origin, and history of the Galápagos Islands, it would be worthwhile to point out a subject of some confusion – the names of the islands themselves. As we shall see when the history of the islands is discussed, the Galápagos were used as a haven of refuge by English buccaneers long before the islands were annexed by Ecuador in 1832. These nautical soldiers of fortunes were patriotic and named the islands after British nobility – kings, dukes, earls, lords, admirals, captains, etc. In one case, Indefatigable (Santa Cruz), an island was named after a British ship. After the 1832 annexation, the islands were given Spanish names of like origin. Then in 1892, the islands were officially renamed in honor of the 400th anniversary of Columbus' first voyage and discovery of the Americas (he didn't just discover North America). To make matters worse, there have been other names given to the islands by the British, Spanish, and United States Navies. Some of these names have stuck. The result is that several of the islands have at least three names and some as many as eight!

Actually it's not that bad. For the purposes of touring the Galápagos, nine of the fifteen islands and islets you are likely to visit are commonly referred to by only one name. Of the remaining six, only two names are generally used. The confusion will come from reading some of the literature which tries to "help" the tourist by referring to the English-sounding names. Thus, you may read about Albemarle Island, even though it is almost always referred to as Isabela. I will attempt to use the most common name of an island throughout this book. This could be either a Spanish or English name. As an example, I will refer to Santa Cruz Island and not to the English name, Indefatigable. When two versions are commonly used, I will refer to the most common name first, occasionally followed by the second name in parenthesis. Thus, I will refer to Española (Hood) Island. If an island is mentioned several times in a particular section, the name in parenthesis will be omitted after the first reference.

CLIMATE

Considering that these islands are placed directly under the equator, the climate is far from being excessively hot; this seems chiefly caused by the singularly low temperature of the surrounding water, brought here by the great southern Polar current. Excepting during one short season, very little rain falls, and even then it is irregular; but the clouds generally hang low. Hence, whilst the lower parts of the islands are very sterile, the upper parts, at a height of a thousand feet and upwards, possess a damp climate and a tolerable luxuriant vegetation. This is especially the case on the windward sides of the islands, which first receive and condense the moisture from the atmosphere....
Charles Darwin, 1845

Darwin said it all. One of the keys to understanding the Galápagos is the climate. The islands are isolated (by several hundred miles of ocean), so the climate is determined almost entirely by the ocean currents, which in turn are influenced by the trade winds which push the currents. The Galápagos is a major intersection of several currents, which vary in intensity during the year as their driving trade winds blow and then weaken in a cycle that gives two distinct seasons to the islands. These currents also control the pattern and variety of Galápagos plant and animal life. Let's see how it works and fits together.

We'll start with the chain of food. Many of the Galápagos animals depend on the ocean for food. Several birds, the sea lions, and fur seals eat a variety of small fish and squid, which in turn, feed on plant life near the surface. The question is, "How do all these plants grow near the ocean surface, well out from shore?" The answer is that in most places in the world, they don't. For plants to grow, they of course need sunlight and nutrients (fertilizer material – phosphates and nitrates). In the natural state, these nutrients are produced by decomposition of organic materials (as in a compost pile or a forest floor). The problem is that in the ocean, these organic materials sink to the bottom. So you have an ocean floor that is rich in nutrients, but where there is little or no light. On the surface, you have plenty of light but no nutrients. Consequently, there's not much plant growth, unless somehow the waters are churned up, effectively pumping the nutrients to the surface. As long as this pump was left on, there would be constant plant growth at the surface, providing the fish and squid with a continuous supply of food – plankton. There are actually a few places in the world where nature has engineered such a pumping system. This system is called the process of upwelling, and it occurs in the waters of the Galápagos for a good part of most years. Upwelling frequently occurs when two or more current systems converge in the proximity of land, thus agitating the waters and bringing the rich nutrients to the surface. There are many such current systems intersecting in the Galápagos, and a complete analysis is quite complex.

Let's simplify it a bit, starting with the Humboldt Current (sometimes referred to as the "Peru"). For most of the year, the cold Humboldt sweeps northward from the waters of the Antarctic, hugging the coast of South America. While the coastline changes contour at the northern tip of Peru, the Humboldt (pushed by trade winds from the southeast) keeps on its original northwesterly course, arching its way across the Pacific, heading right for the Galápagos Islands, and washing the archipelago with cool water (about 68 Deg F).

The mass of cold water cools the air as well, and an inversion layer is formed. What's an inversion layer? Normally, the higher the elevation, the colder the air. But here you have this huge body of cold water that's going to cool the air directly above it. The result is that you have warm air sitting on top of the cooled surface air – an inversion. This process continues until an equilibrium is reached; in the Galápagos, this occurs at 1000-2000 ft above sea level, the height of the inversion layer where the warm air is trapped.

The inversion layer does a couple of things. First, it contains a heavy concentration of moisture droplets that have evaporated from the ocean. Some of the islands have highland areas that intercept the inversion layer and condense this moisture. A continuous mist is formed, called a *garúa*.

The inversion layer also upsets the usual weather pattern associated with the tropics – blue skies and afternoon showers. Thus, while the highland areas are kept lush and green by the *garúa* mist, the lowland areas of these islands (as well as entire low elevation islands) are bone dry. This then is the dry (or cool) season; oddly enough, it is called the *garúa* season, even though *garúa* itself is a form of precipitation.

The *garúa* season usually lasts from June to December; it is around December when the southeast trade winds slacken, no longer driving the Humboldt Current toward the Galápagos. This allows the warm waters of the Panama Current, flowing south and once again heading right at the Galápagos, to be dominant. Thus, the island waters are warmed (to about 78 Deg F), no longer cooling the air to a significant degree, and the inversion layer breaks up. This phenomenon is called an *El Niño,* which is Spanish for "the child" because the condition begins around Christmas. The tropical weather pattern now asserts itself with rain cloud formation and daily shower activity. This is the rainy (or warm) season, typically lasting from January-May. The oddity here is that the highland areas receive more moisture from the *garúa* during the dry season than they do from rainfall during the wet season.

That's the way things usually work. Some years, however, the southeast trade winds are a "no show," causing the Panama Current to drastically warm the waters of the Galápagos. This phenomenon is also called an *El Niño,* which is confusing because most *El Niños* are normal – they occur every year with minimal negative effects. People tend to get alarmed when they hear the term *"El Niño,"* because they associate it with an abnormal, catastrophic-like weather system. To help clarify this, I guess we can say that there are different types of *El Niños* – periodically more intense ones, and occasionally severe *El Niño* events, associated with higher sea surface temperatures and more rainfall.

The most severe *El Niño* condition is now called an ENSO (*El Niño / Southern Oscillation*), a world-wide weather anomaly with dramatic reversals between the eastern Pacific and western Pacific/Indian Oceans in oceanic circulation patterns, sea & air temperatures, rainfall, and barometric pressure. The results are typically catastrophic, with severe droughts in India and Australia and torrential rain in the normally-arid eastern Pacific. Occurring at irregular intervals, the destructive force of ENSO events have been studied since 1726, with scientists still searching for clues that will enable them to predict future ENSOs. The worst ENSO ever recorded occurred in 1982-83. Since this event was so recent and so dramatic, it is understandable that whenever the term *El*

Niño is spoken or written, the images of the 1982-83 ENSO come to mind. In the Galápagos, a very critical part of the food chain was broken, due to the lack of upwelling activity and the very warm waters (over 84 Deg F). The food shortage had a serious impact on several Galápagos animals. The fur seals were hit very hard; almost all animals 1-4 years of age died off, and large male bulls also died (not being able to recover weight lost in territorial defense). The sea lions, able to dive deeper for their food, fared a bit better, but also recorded significant losses. Many sea birds of the Galápagos were adversely affected by the ENSO, especially the flightless cormorants and the Galápagos penguins, who could not attempt a winged escape from the food shortage. The marine iguanas switched to a diet of a different type of algae, but unfortunately the new food source had little digestible nutrient value. The result was that they literally starved on a full stomach of food. To us humans, nature does not always appear to be kind.

FORMATION

Seeing every height crowned with its crater, and the boundaries of most of the lava streams still distinct, we are led to believe that within a period, geologically recent, the unbroken ocean was here spread out.

Charles Darwin, 1845

The Galápagos Islands are volcanic in origin and appear to have been formed about 3-5 million years ago, geologically very recent. These volcanoes formed under the sea, broke through the ocean floor, grew in size, and eventually emerged, rising from the surface of the water and becoming islands. Each island formed from a single volcano with the exception of Isabela, a lava welded union of six volcanoes. The eastern islands (the oldest is Española) seem to be significantly older than those on the west, with the rocks on Isabela and Fernandina islands being less than 200,000 years old. This is consistent with the "hot spot" theory of Galápagos Island formation.

In this case, the term "hot spot" doesn't refer to the popularity of the islands. Almost all the world's volcanic areas are over the boundary lines (called margins) between the relatively thin plates that make up the surface crust of the earth. Not so for the Galápagos, which instead seems to be directly over a "hot spot," a region of intense heat in the earth's mantle (the transition zone between the inner core and the outer crust), which is hot enough to burn through the crust, forming a volcano. As the plates are moving at a fixed rate (about 3 inches per year), a string of volcanoes is formed. Because of their underwater origin, the material forming the volcano builds and accumulates, spreading out like a sand hill. This gives rise to a gentle sloping shape with a central vent, which is characteristic (and the name origin) of what is called a *shield volcano.*

Today, the Galápagos are among the world's most active volcanic areas; there have been over fifty eruptions in the last 200 years, some quite recently. These events have been on the two westernmost islands, Isabela and Fernandina; their six active volcanoes are still being fed by the "hot spot" (only the Ecuador Volcano on Isabela Island is no longer active). That these are active volcanoes is evidenced by the columns of steam and gas (*fumaroles*) which the western island visitor can see rising from the Alcedo and Sierra Negra Volcanoes on Isabela.

Part of what makes visiting the islands so fascinating is that they are in the early phase of their development. Aside from the eruptions, the recent activity list is long and continues to grow. In 1954, almost 4 miles of the coastal seabed of Urvina Bay, Isabela Island were dramatically and suddenly uplifted about 15 ft. These *uplifts,* as they are called, occur frequently, but not as dramatically. Many of the islands themselves are uplifts, formed by the flow of molten rock inside the earth (*magma*) through a subsurface geological fissure (or fault). The magma exits the fissure as lava, hardening and gradually lifting the "land" mass through and past the ocean surface. Uplifts are typically associated with a previous or impending eruption. As the magma beneath the summit of a volcano cools and contracts, the entire peak may collapse inward to form a large, bowl-like depression called a *caldera.* In 1968, the Fernandina Island caldera collapsed, dropping about 1000 ft in 2 weeks, an event accompanied by hundreds of earthquakes.

The volcanic features are fascinating. On James (Santiago) Island, two distinct lava patterns can be seen – the smooth, rope-like *pahoehoe* (Hawaiian for "ropey" and pronounced pa-hoy-hoy), and the rough, broken *aa* (pronounced "ah-ah"). Also, across from James, on Bartolomé Island, is probably the most famous (and most photographed) landmark in the Galápagos, Pinnacle Rock, a remnant of what is known as a *tuff cone.* Tuff cones are interesting vertical rock formations of volcanic origin which are a consolidation of hardened ash particles (*tuff*). During an eruption, as the hot lava poured into the cold water, explosions would occur. Pockets and fragments would be sent flying in all directions and come spattering down to the ground, hardening into a cone shape. Not surprisingly, some of these formations are termed cinder cones and spatter cones.

Often, as the lava flowed, the exterior portion cooled and hardened even as the molten material continued to flow in the interior. When the lava flow abated, there was not enough liquid to fill the inner cavity, and a tunnel was formed (called a *lava tube* or *lava tunnel*). Several excellent examples exist in the Highlands of Santa Cruz Island, where a "climb down and walk through" tour is available; miner's lanterns are provided for these excursions (see the section on Santa Cruz Island in Chapter IX). When a lava flow subsides, the surface features that are directly over pockets of magma are somewhat unstable, causing depressions called *pit craters*; these are formed in the same fashion as a caldera, but are not located over a central vent. Most visitors to the Santa Cruz Highlands see the pair of giant pit craters called *Los Gemelos* (The Twins).

For a closer look at a volcano, special tours are offered (on 2 week Galápagos trips) to the rim of the Sierra Negra Volcano, with spectacular views of the caldera (4 miles by 5 miles across), the sulfur fumarole (vent), and the combined land/seascapes. Hikes to the Alcedo Volcano may be once again offered (depending on the success of the introduced mammal eradication program), featuring the largest population of giant tortoises in the wild. (See the section on Isabela Island in Chapter IX).

As harsh and rough as this volcanic terrain may appear, it is also very fragile; the weight of a single tourist stepping off the trail to "get a better shot" can break apart the low density, crusty-looking rock. It is not a matter of administration and procedures that requires visitors to stay on the trails with their Guide; it's a matter of preservation.

THE ARRIVAL OF LIFE

As you tour the Galápagos, noting the richness of the wildlife, the question arises, "How did they get there?" Indeed, 600 miles is along way to swim, fly or even just to "hang on, baby!" Actually, some of these voyages may have been made from Central America, which puts the distance closer to 1000 miles. In either case, transportation was a formidable obstacle, and only a very small number of mainland plant and animal species were able to make this journey.

Initially there were only the bacteria, algae, and fungi, providing the beginnings of an organic base for the higher species. The next generation of flora consisted largely of plants with small, lightweight seeds and spores which could be wind-borne over long distances or digested intact and carried aloft by sea birds. Some seeds would actually stick to the feathers and wings of the sea birds. Having reached the Galápagos, the next problem was short-term survival. To be successful, the first plants had to have the ability to take root and grow without a lot of organic material. These *pioneers* or *colonizers,* as they are called, include lichens and mosses, followed by ferns and grasses – flora that not only would survive, but also provide the humus for future species of plant life in the Galápagos. On several islands, principally the more-recent Isabela and Fernandina, certain locations are still in the "pioneering" stage.

Some seedlings could be transported by the ocean, being steered to the archipelago by the currents. You may remember from our discussion of the climate that the currents are driven by trade winds in the direction of the Galápagos. Thus (as the recorded history well documents), unpowered vessels and their passengers, willing or not, are carried from the mainland to the Galápagos Islands, a voyage lasting about 2 weeks (4 weeks from Central America). Several such vessels were seedlings of the red mangrove, with the ability to float in the ocean, root in the mud, immediately take hold, and grow. In addition, the red mangrove has a root system that filters out salt, allowing the leaves to receive fresh water.

Other ocean passengers making the voyage from Central and South America to the Galápagos were animals. Reptiles, whose vessels were rafts of tangled vegetation, were able to survive the journey due to their ability to fast for long periods of time. No amphibians or land mammals, with the exception of a few species of rats, were able to survive the rigors of such an ocean passage; they are thus noticeably absent from the list of species indigenous (native) to the Galápagos.

There were those that could cross the ocean on their own power. Aside from the fish that swim the waters of the Galápagos, this group includes the sea turtles, penguins, and marine mammals – the sea lions, fur seals, and dolphins.

Not everyone had to take the ocean route; sea birds and shore birds had the ability to arrive by air. Land birds would either have to get caught up in a gust and be borne along by an exceptionally strong tail wind or take the ocean crossing, perched on a branch or perhaps in a tree hollow.

SHORT-TERM SURVIVAL

Now isolated, the struggle for survival began. For the early arrivals, it was a long shot. On islands comprised of volcanic rock, the odds certainly were not very high that a seed would land or be dropped in a crevice or other precise location in which there was a bit of soil and moisture sufficient for germination. And what if it were a flowering plant that depended on insects for pollination? Well, those insects weren't on the islands at that time (for the most part they still aren't), so that plant species wouldn't make it past the first generation.

It wasn't much easier for the animals, especially for the terrestrial species. If there wasn't any food to eat, they couldn't swim or fly away. Even if they were fortunate enough to find food, they still had to perpetuate their own kind for their species to survive in the islands. Remember, these animals didn't arrive on Noah's Ark. There was no voluntary decision on their part to improve their lot in life, pack their bags, and head for the Galápagos. They were most likely caught up in a storm or flood; perhaps the piece of land beneath them broke off and fell into the waters. One second they were on land, and the next they were on an organic raft, just hanging on. Considering these circumstances, it's not too likely that a male and female of the same species would arrive together on such a raft, or even arrive at the same island during each other's fertile lifetime. There just aren't that many floods per lifetime. Rafts of tangled vegetation are rarely around when you really need them, and, in general, they tend not to be very seaworthy. Finally, the currents and prevailing trade winds are not anywhere near precise enough to get many rafts to the same island.

Even for the sea birds, who can fly where they will, conditions must be ideal for them to colonize a particular island – conditions such as vegetation, proximity to and abundance of food, availability of nesting materials, as well as climate. One island will be selected, and the neighboring islands avoided. Even today, nearly the entire world population of waved albatrosses nests on Española (Hood) Island.

The odds weren't high for any particular plant or animal species surviving the first generation of arrivees, but the factor of time enters into the equation. If the odds are one in a million, all you have to do is take a million chances. Drop a seed a day for a million days; eventually a seed is deposited in the perfect location, germinates, and grows. Land a tortoise a year on a given island for a million years; eventually, you'll get a mating pair, or a pregnant female will arrive. Future generations will eventually germinate, hatch, or be born. Sooner or later, the process of immediate survival is won. The process of long-term survival, however, is just beginning.

EVOLUTION AND NATURAL SELECTION

The long-term future outlook for a plant in the Galápagos is a lot brighter if the original seed happens to be that of a tolerant weed. A newly-arrived animal species is more likely to stay around for a few thousand years if it can stand the arid climactic conditions of the islands. Those plants and animals that were naturally well-suited for their new home had a greater chance of surviving, and those that survived the longest had more opportunities to reproduce their own kind. A look at the distribution of species in the Galápagos shows a high proportion of salt-tolerant plants and drought-resistant animals.

Some of these species had these desirable traits on arrival. Others, however, acquired these characteristics over many generations. This required a change or differentiation from the mainland parent population.

Some changes occurred quite rapidly. First, remember that we're talking about small numbers of arrivees, which greatly increases the chances of a nonrepresentative population to begin with. The traits we're discussing are those such as strength, aggressiveness, fertility, pigmentation, intelligence, etc. Breeding will reproduce these traits, genetically transmitting the nonrepresentative characteristics to future generations, causing an immediate significant differentiation from the mainland population. Second, genetic mutations will also have a greater chance of impacting a small population, causing further differentiation. Finally, bear in mind that thus far we're talking about short-term random differences in that these traits may not necessarily be for better or for worse from a long-term survival point of view.

Now here's where it begins to get interesting. If "survival of the fittest" was certainly true in terms of one species of plant or animal being more likely to survive versus another, wasn't it also true for individuals within a species? If a male lava lizard just happened to have the same coloration as the dark lava on which he lived, he probably would live longer and thus mate more often. As a result, his pigmentation gene would be transmitted more often. His progeny would multiply this effect, with those that had his protective coloring living longer, mating more often, etc. It seems basic to us now, but remember that in Darwin's day, the laws of Mendelian genetics had not been formally proposed to the scientific community. It wasn't until 1900, some 16 years after Gregor Mendel's death, that the relevance of his work was widely recognized.

Darwin's genius was in understanding that the variations he observed were non-random positive adaptations to the environment that could somehow be passed on through inheritance.

> *If variations useful to any being do occur, assuredly individuals thus characterized will have the best chance of being preserved in the struggle for life; and from the strong principle of inheritance, they will tend to produce offspring similarly characterized. This principle of preservation, I have called, for the sake of brevity, Natural Selection.*
> Charles Darwin, 1859

One species eventually becomes another; in evolutionary language, this is termed descent with modification. The marine iguana, once a land dweller, is now the world's only seagoing lizard, complete with specialized nasal glands that excrete (sneeze) salt. The flightless cormorants gradually exchanged their ability to fly for a streamlined body to assist their swimming prowess. These are not random changes of minimal importance that die out after a few generations; these are long-term adaptive modifications and can truly be termed as evolution at work.

Darwin called the Galápagos Islands a "living laboratory of evolution," a term often used today to describe the archipelago. What he meant was that the isolation, confined habitats, and the comparatively small number of species combine to give the observer a clear view of the adaptive processes. Our understanding of the laws of genetics, of the ways in which isolation statistically stuffs the genetic ballot box, makes Darwin's phrase all the more appropriate.

ADAPTIVE RADIATION

Darwin saw many examples in the Galápagos of one species eventually becoming another. What was especially surprising to him, and led him to the inescapable conclusion that adaptive processes were at work, was that one species eventually became several, based on their habitat. The term used to describe this phenomena is adaptive radiation, and the most famous examples are the Galápagos finches. As a result of Darwin's work, these birds now bear his name and are called Darwin's Finches. What Darwin saw were thirteen distinct finch species, each closely resembling each other in most ways, yet each had a characteristic beak structure well suited to a particular (specialized) food source. There were those with long, pointed beaks for feeding on cactus flowers (the cactus finch), stout beaks for breaking hard seeds (medium and large ground finches), parrot-shaped beaks for breaking up twigs to get at insect larvae (the large tree finch), and small sharp beaks for removing ticks from tortoises and iguanas (the small ground finch). The woodpecker and mangrove finches seemingly couldn't wait to develop a beak large and pointed enough to poke for grubs through decayed and dead wood; a beak extension was borrowed in the form of a twig or cactus spine. This is a very rare instance where tool-using skills have actually evolved.

It was the finches that clinched it for Darwin. They obviously were of the same parent population and yet they were distinct in a way that was inarguably purposeful and adaptive.

> *The most curious fact is the perfect gradation in the size of the beaks in the different species. One might really fancy that from an original paucity of birds in this archipelago, one species had been taken and modified for different ends.*
>
> *Charles Darwin, 1845*

What was remarkable was the relatively short time that these evolved changes took place. Researchers Peter & Rosemary Grant have actually seen and documented evolution in Darwin's finches. For a fascinating account of their observations, read **THE BEAK OF THE FINCH** (see the Literature section). Equally remarkable to Darwin was the fact that many of the islands, though often within just a few miles of each other, had their own unique species of the same type of plant or animal.

> *The distribution of the tenants of this archipelago would not be nearly so wonderful, if for instance, one island had a mocking-thrush and a second island some other quite distinct species; – if one island had its genus of lizard and a second island another distinct genus, or none whatever. But it is the circumstance, that several of the islands possess their own species of the tortoise, mocking-thrush, finches, and numerous plants, these species having the same general habits, occupying analogous situations, and obviously filling the same place in the natural economy of this archipelago, that strikes me with wonder.*
>
> *Charles Darwin, 1845*

Thus, the finch is not the only example of adaptive radiation on the Galápagos. The giant tortoise had evolved into fourteen subspecies (of which eleven remain), many with differences in the shape of the shell (called a *carapace*). These differences were most useful and therefore adaptive in nature. The saddle-back tortoises have a carapace with an elevated front end; this, combined with their long necks and ability to stand on their hind legs, enables them to reach for branches and cactus pads on the drier islands with no grasses – Española, for example. Other tortoises have dome-shaped carapaces, giving them a shorter profile and blunt front end, useful for pushing through the dense brush often found on islands with lush highlands, such as Santa Cruz and Isabela.

Other examples of adaptive radiation include the iguana (forming a land and marine species) and the fourteen taxa of prickly pear cactus (*opuntia*), with some actually evolving into tall trees to better compete for the sunlight and partially avoid being munched on by hungry tortoises and land iguanas.

ENDEMISM

Due to the serious transportation and short-term survival problems discussed earlier, there are relatively few species of plants and animals in the Galápagos. There are less than 600 species of plants on the islands, compared to the 20,000 or so on mainland Ecuador. There are but twenty-two species of reptiles, less than 100 bird species (including migrants), about 400 species of fish, and strikingly, only six *indigenous* (native or non-introduced) mammals (dolphins not included).

Not surprisingly, the evolutionary process has resulted in a large percentage of plant and animal species found nowhere else in the world, termed by the scientific community as a high rate of *endemism*. Thus, of the 600 species of plants, fully one-third are endemic to the islands. Of the fish, about 20 percent of the inshore species are endemic to the waters of the archipelago. Most noteworthy is that of all the landbased animals, including reptiles, mammals, and land birds, over 80 percent are endemic to the Galápagos Islands.

Not only are many of the plant and animal species endemic to the Galápagos, but many are only found on particular islands of the archipelago. This fact was not lost on Darwin:

> *By far the most remarkable feature in the natural history of this archipelago ... is, that the different islands to a considerable extent are inhabited by a different set of beings. I never dreamed that islands, about fifty or sixty miles apart, and most of them in sight of each other, formed of precisely the same rocks, placed under a quite similar climate, rising to a nearly equal height, would have been differently tenanted....*

Charles Darwin, 1845

An interesting concept in the evolutionary process is that of the niche, defined as a functional role in a bio-community. Since the Galápagos is species poor, certain roles are assumed by unlikely players. Take the case of the saddleback tortoise. It is said that this reptilian species evolved to fill an available niche (an opportunity or open position) for a "reacher," as the usual niche–holders, tall mammals, did not exist in the Galápagos. In a similar fashion, the absence of a bona fide woodpecker left open a niche, which was filled rather quickly and interestingly by the woodpecker finch.

If the niche concept seems a bit anthropomorphic, think of it in genetic terms. The first trace of a saddle-back on a tortoise was most likely a mutation, a chance occurrence. The features were probably not very pronounced, although it did enable the tortoise to get at food that the others couldn't. Thus, the animal was more likely to survive, live longer, mate more often, and as a result, have a higher probability of transmitting this mutated trait. In the same manner, the saddle-back features would tend to become more enhanced in successive generations.

The key here was that the food was available. If the tall mammals were present, and/or an abundance of the particular food supply wasn't, the chance saddle-back feature would not have had the enhanced (statistical) opportunities of appearing in future generations.

HISTORY

Even a casual study of the history of the Galápagos archipelago reveals several dominant themes; as a point of orientation, they are worthy of mention.

1. Isolation. There are almost no other islands off the western coast of South America and no easy means of rapid communication with the outside world.

2. Strong currents. Many underpowered vessels (generally due to light wind conditions) were carried from the Central or South American coastal waters to the Galápagos.

3. Inaccessibility. Despite the natural tendency of a boat to drift in the direction of the Galápagos, access to the islands has been for the most part difficult due to their remote location.

4. Strategic location. The Galápagos Islands are an ideally-located supply port and lie directly in the entrance path of the Panama Canal. These facts were not lost on the major international powers.

5. Arid conditions. Many visitors arrived in search of water; most of the early arrivals failed in this quest. A seemingly disproportionate number came to Floreana Island, due to the known water supply.

6. Sanctuary. The Galápagos was thought of and used as a haven by many; most were disappointed with the reality of the harsh life.

7. Exploitation. The influence of man has brought several wildlife species, most notably the giant tortoise, sperm whale, and fur seal, to the point of extinction.

8. Unprofitability. Repeated attempts at commercial use of the islands have met with failure. Tourism is proving to be the sole exception.

9. Surrealistic image. The islands have always been perceived as a blend of the angelic and the demonic. Some have literally translated *Las Islas Encantadas* to mean "the Bewitched Islands."

The Galápagos Islands are often referred to as Darwin's "living laboratory of evolution." Thus, one is likely to imagine a history filled with scientific observation and experimentation with a little quiet contemplation thrown in. While this has been the recent emphasis, the history of the Galápagos reads more like a combined swashbuckling tale of the high seas, a story of men behind bars, and a murder mystery (unsolved to this very day). Let's take a look back in time and see how these seemingly disparate pieces fit together.

EARLY HISTORY

According to historians, the Galápagos Islands were probably first discovered by the Incas in the 1400s. Despite their refined culture, industrious nature, architectural knowledge, and craftsmanly skills, the Incas did not have a written language; documentation is therefore lacking. In terms of recorded history, the Galápagos were officially and accidentally discovered in 1535 by the Bishop of Panama, Fray Tomás de Berlanga. This was at the time of the Spanish conquest of South America, and word had gotten back to King Charles V of Spain that his conquistadors were, to be kind, overzealous in their behavior. Ruthless, barbarous, and brutal are words more commonly used to describe the actions of Francisco Pizarro and his men. At any rate, the Bishop was dispatched to Peru from Panama to look into the situation. Though a safe route was chosen, hugging the coast of South America, the ship began to drift out to sea when a calm descended. Almost out of drinking water, they finally sighted land. The crew dropped anchor and went ashore. Later, in a letter written to the King, Bishop Berlanga described in some detail the sea lions, iguanas, and, in particular, the vast quantity of giant tortoises that they came upon. But they didn't find what they were looking for – water. They finally gave up the search and, thinking they were within 100 miles of Peru, sailed back to the mainland, blending the remaining water into the supply of wine. Despite their thirst, they reached the mainland in not altogether bad spirits. The islands that they encountered were described as uninhabitable, incapable of sustaining life. In was in this manner then, that the Galápagos Islands were officially discovered.

The Bishop's report was relayed to a Flemish cartographer, Abraham Ortelius, who included the islands in his atlas, **ORBIS TERRARUM**, published in 1574. The islands were called *Insulae de los Galápagos*, the "Islands of the Tortoises." The Galápagos Islands could now be called as such.

The islands had another name as well. In 1546, a group of Spanish soldiers, at odds with Pizarro and his harsh ways, were forced to flee South America. Having no charts to guide them, they went with the currents which, of course, led them to the Galápagos. Several of their landing attempts were thwarted by the swirling currents, pushing them out of sight of the island. These soldiers had little, if any, scientific or nautical training; peering through the mist and losing sight of the eerie-looking volcanic land, they concluded that the island was drifting. Surely, they thought, the islands were bewitched (enchanted); these must be *Las Islas Encantadas*.

The Galápagos were eventually to receive a third name. In 1892, the 400th anniversary of the first voyage of Christopher Columbus (*Cristóbal Colón* in Spanish), the Galápagos Islands were officially renamed by the *National Assembly of Ecuador* as the *Archipelago de Colón*. The "official" name, for all practical purposes, is not used.

THE BUCCANEERS

Columbus' discovery had a more immediate effect. In 1493, influenced by the knowledge of the New World to the west, the Spanish Pope Alexander VI granted to Spain what amounted to the entire western hemisphere. This Papal Bull, as it was called, was understandably not met with overwhelming approval (and its name, therefore, had another interpretation) in Great Britain, the

Netherlands, and France. While an act of war was not declared, the word was that these countries would not punish any of their citizens who took private action against Spain. At sea, such citizens were called buccaneers, sometimes referred to as pirates.

The difference between a buccaneer and a pirate is not all that obvious and depends on the circumstances. In times of cold war, as between Great Britain and Spain during a good portion of the 1500s and 1600s, if you robbed a Spanish ship, the British said you were a buccaneer; if you captured a British ship, however, they accused you of being a pirate. During times of war, some of the buccaneers were pressed into service as privateers.

The western coast of South America was buccaneer territory. The prizes sought after were Spanish treasure ships carrying the vast sums of money (from Spain) required to purchase supplies and meet payroll for the forces and staff in South America. In between attacks, the buccaneers made for the haven of the Galápagos, recuperated, and fed on the giant tortoises. One of these British buccaneers, William Ambrose Cowley, drew the first navigational charts of the Galápagos. Cowley, the patriot that he was, also named several islands after British royalty at the time, including [King] Charles (Floreana), [King] James (Santiago), [the Duke of] Albemarle (Isabela), and [Admiral] Narborough (Fernandina).

This is not to say that the majority of the buccaneers were cartographers, quietly enjoying a cup of coffee while trying to decide which English duke or admiral should be honored with an island bearing his name. Many of these guys were pretty ruthless, and in general they were a tough lot. They didn't just seek out treasure ships either; many a port city, including Guayaquil on the coast of mainland Ecuador, was regularly sacked by this bunch.

When the buccaneers didn't have anyone else to fight, they fought each other. Many such battles, including mutinies, are well documented. The vanquished party, if still alive, was usually marooned. One such castaway was Alexander Selkirk, marooned for over 4 years on Juan Fernandez Island (off the coast of Chile). Upon his rescue by a British buccaneering ship, Selkirk took part in a raid on Guayaquil and retreated with the crew to the Galápagos. There he instructed his mates on the finer points of living off the land. The ship's captain, Woodes Rogers, was intrigued by the man, and included the story of Selkik's solitary existence in **A CRUISING VOYAGE ROUND THE WORLD**, published in 1712. Based on this account, Selkirk became the model for **ROBINSON CRUSOE**, written by Daniel Defoe.

THE WHALERS

As the nineteenth century began, Spain's world power was declining. South America began to trade with England and France; buccaneers were now considered pirates and no longer welcome. In their place, the waters were soon filled with boats of another kind – whaling ships.

This was the age of the Industrial Revolution, and oil was in short supply. The oil that was used at this time did not come from under the ground; it came from the ocean, courtesy of the whale. After hearing several buccaneers describe the vast quantity of sperm whales off the western coast of South America, the British sent a ship into these waters in 1792 to explore the whaling potential. The captain, James Colnett, spent a considerable time in the Galápagos, making up-to-date charts and naming several islands, including [Lord] Chatham (San Cristóbal), [Admiral] Hood (Española), [Admiral]

Barrington (Santa Fé), and [Admiral] Jervis (Rábida). Floreana Island was described by Captain Colnett as a good resting spot for whaling crews, providing good anchorage, shelter, a known, dependable water supply, and a seemingly inexhaustible supply of fresh meat – the giant tortoises.

Colnett also started the first postal system in the Galápagos, a system that, although unofficial, is still in use today. It is the Barrel Post Office on Floreana Island, and it was used extensively by the whaling ships, which were often at sea for a year or two at a time. The crew of an outward-bound whaler, having rounded Cape Horn, would drop letters into the barrel; the letters would then be picked up by homeward-bound ships and ultimately delivered.

The main purpose of Captain Colnett's visit was to confirm that there was a sufficient supply of whales in the area to justify the development of the industry. Which he did, citing the upwelling activity of the currents that made these waters superb feeding grounds for the sperm whale.

Whaling, by the way, was not easy work. It required the small whaling hunt boats to get close enough to the whale so that the man in the bow, the whaling captain, could spear the chest. It took daring, skill, and a fair amount of luck to drive the harpoon between the ribs and pierce the lung, thereby mortally wounding the whale. And it didn't end there. Once killed, the whale was brought alongside the ship, whereupon the layer of blubber was stripped from the animal while it was pitching and rolling on the open seas. The blubber was hauled on-board, boiled, and the extracted oil was stored below in casks. Many of the ships sailed from New England and, as described above, were often gone for over a year before the casks were full.

As with most industries that tend to make men wealthy, whaling was poorly regulated. What transpired was short-sighted, even from a selfish whaling-oriented point of view. Things got out of hand, with the owners not willing or afraid to control the tough captains and crews required for such dangerous work. As a result, the sperm whales were killed to the point of near-extinction, also killing the very source of income upon which the industry depended. The whalers were soon gone from the archipelago.

The same scenario befell the sealers. The fur seals possess a two-layered coat, providing excellent insulation, and were therefore in great demand. Many thousands of fur seals were killed for their skins, and by 1900 the species was almost extinct.

The whalers and sealers not only decimated the very animal that supported their business, but the animal that fed them as well. Giant tortoises were easily caught, carted on board, and stacked upside-down in the ship's hold. They could be kept alive in this fashion without food or water for several months to a year. The crews thus had a supply of fresh meat, a delicacy in its own right and several times over when compared to the standard fare of salt pork and hardtack. Each ship would take between 500-600 tortoises at a time. When you consider that in the first half of the 1800s there were several hundred whaling ships operating in the general area, in addition to sealing vessels, the number of animals taken are astounding. Reports indicate that over 15,000 tortoises were taken from Floreana alone, resulting in the extinction of the subspecies found only on that island. A similar fate befell the subspecies on Santa Fé and Fernandina. In all, it is estimated that over 200,000 tortoises were taken.

The whalers and sealers also helped make life difficult for those animals that were left, as well as for future generations of tortoises. From their ships descended the black rat, an introduced mammal most effective at eating tortoise hatchlings. Too effective! Even today, the *Galápagos National Park Service* Wardens must hike through the brush and get to the tortoise eggs before the rats get to the hatchlings. The eggs are carried back to the *Charles Darwin Research Station* on Santa Cruz Island where they are incubated; the hatched tortoises are then raised in pens for about 5 years and then taken back to their native island. This is but one fight against many introduced animals, including feral dogs, cats, goats, pigs, and donkeys.

One whaler who left something good behind was Herman Melville. Melville spent several years on New England whaling ships, and the rich narrative expressed in **MOBY DICK** was acquired firsthand. Never one to hold back an opinion, Melville was decidedly underwhelmed by the Galápagos Islands. In a Melville anthology called the **PIAZZA TALES**, there is a short story set in the Galápagos entitled **THE ENCANTADAS**, which begins as follows:

Take five-and-twenty heaps of cinders dumped here and there in an outside city lot; imagine some of them magnified into mountains, and the vacant lot the sea; and you will have a fit idea of the general aspect of the Encantadas, or Enchanted Isles.

Herman Melville, 1854

THE SCIENTISTS

Melville may not have been very impressed by the Enchanted Isles, but there was a group that certainly was – the scientists. Darwin's publications, which voiced the theory of evolution and chronicled his visit to the Galápagos, were very timely. It was as if the world of science was waiting for someone to speak up. Several scientific expeditions soon made their way to the Galápagos to see the evidence first-hand.

The problem was that they took too much of the evidence back with them. In the midst of the whaling era, when the tortoise populations were hovering on the brink of extinction, the scientists took hundreds more. Many actually killed the animal first, so their museum would have a good specimen of the species "before it was too late."

THE STRATEGISTS

In 1859, the first commercial-scale petroleum was discovered beneath the ground in Pennsylvania, making available a less expensive source of oil, and whaling quickly declined throughout the world. During the rise and fall of the whaling industry, other ships were at sea in search of a different kind of prey. For most of the world, 1812 was a year of war. And England was in the thick of it, fighting Napoleon-led European forces on one hand and the United States on the other. While the hub of naval battle was in the Atlantic, there were some noteworthy exchanges in the waters off South America as well. U.S. Captain David Porter, in command of the warship U.S.S. ESSEX, created havoc among the scattered British ships in this area. Upon reaching the archipelago, Porter first headed for Floreana and inspected the letters in the Barrel Post Office. What he read helped him deduce the whereabouts of several British whalers, which he was able to intercept and capture. This was a time of war, in which commercial shipping plays a key part; in this case, it was a supply of much needed oil.

In addition to his skills in naval battle, Captain Porter had the curious mind of the explorer, and wrote detailed accounts of the Galápagos. He noted the strategic importance (owing primarily to the location) as well as the notable absence of water on most of the islands. This written report would, over the years, stimulate serious U.S. interest in acquiring the Galápagos Islands.

With peace coming to much of the world in the 1820s, and the liberation of South America from Spanish rule in the 1830s, the strategic importance of the Galápagos was, for the time being, diminished. Ecuador's sovereignty, fully-achieved in 1830, was soon followed by their formal annexing of the Galápagos Islands in 1832. At that time Charles Island was renamed as Floreana (after General Flores, the first President of the Republic of Ecuador).

A settlement was soon started on Floreana under the direction of the first Governor General of the Galápagos, José Villamil. Owing to the desolate reputation of the islands, few of the original "settlers" actually volunteered for relocation; the "settlement" was more of a penal colony. Originally, it consisted of Ecuadorian soldiers who had been sentenced to death for mutiny and given a reprieve in return for deportation to the Galápagos. Soon they were joined by political prisoners and then by common criminals, including prostitutes.

The quality of the labor force, which numbered about 200-300 in the 1830s, did not deter the enterprising ambitions of Villamil, a man who today would be called an entrepreneur. Not content with the successful, if modest, farming achievements of the settlement (with the produce being sold to the whaling and sealing vessels), Villamil attempted to commercially harvest orchil, a lichen that grows freely on the island. At that time, orchil was used as a purple dye (mostly in the printing industry) and was commonly referred to as dyer's moss. As it turned out, the sale of orchil was not very profitable, and it was soon back to farming.

By 1840, the whalers and sealers had just about wiped out the tortoise population on Floreana, and the settlement disbanded, moving to other islands in the archipelago. Villamil's next enterprise was to mine coal on San Cristóbal Island. What possessed him to think there would be coal (formed from prehistoric plant life) on an island obviously of volcanic origin is difficult to imagine. Perhaps it was the black rocks, but at any rate, this attempt also failed. Undaunted and ever the optimist, he became convinced that there were vast (commercial-scale) amounts of guano in the Galápagos (from the sea birds, mostly the boobies). At that time, guano was the main source of nitrates (used in fertilizers and explosives), and the United States was interested, as the only guano available was from Peru, and that at a very high price. The negotiations intensified when Villamil was appointed to a diplomatic position (to the U.S.). These talks soon broke off, however, when investigations showed that the vastness of the deposits were not in the Galápagos but in the mind of Villamil.

These negotiations did have the effect of once again stirring up foreign interest in gaining title to the Galápagos. The interest grew as plans were finalized for digging through the isthmus of Panama and building a canal. This would significantly open up trade between South America and Europe as well as with North America. The strategic location of the Galápagos with regard to Panama was recognized by all the world powers. Including the United States.

 # 1

Your Galápagos adventure will take you to Ecuador. Its beautiful capital Quito (#1), at 9300 feet, is located almost directly on the equator. If 'almost'' isn't good enough, you can be right on the equator by visiting the equatorial monument (#2), called **La Mitad del Mundo** (the Center of the World).

 # 2

3

Soon you'll be in the center of another world, as your plane lands in the Galápagos Islands (#3) and is met by a representative of the bio-community, a marine iguana (#4).

4

#5

A few of the boats that cruise the waters of the Galápagos archipelago are seen anchored in Academy Bay, Santa Cruz Island (notice the port guardian in the foreground — #5). These waters are also cruised by the bottle-nosed dolphin (#6).

#6

SUNDAY 12 RABIDA (JERVIS) 8:00

wet landing
short & easy trail - sandals
red beach, sea lions, flamingo lagoon,
pintail ducks, pelicans, galapagos doves
swimming & snorkelling

SOMBRERO CHINO 3:00 P.M.

wet landing
short but rocky trail - good shoes
fresh lava flows, lava tubes
marine iguanas
swimming & snorkelling.

#7

After a briefing from your Guide (often achieved with audio-visual aids — #7), you'll be off to Visitor Sites such as South Plaza Island (#8) and Kicker Rock (#9).

#8

#9

#10

Entertainment will be provided on your Galápagos Island adventure, courtesy of the sea lions. These playful aquatic mammals will swim with you (#10) and serenade you in the morning (and the rest of the day for that matter — #11).

#11

#12

Barking (#12), playing (#13), sleeping (#14), and swimming (#15), the sea lions will provide you with an endless supply of photographic opportunities. Often they'll emerge from a quick cooling dip in the water, with the wet portion of their fur a shiny jet black and the dry portion a golden tan (#16).

#14

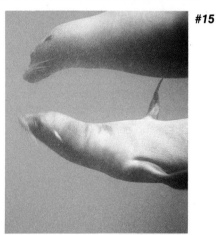

#15

#16

E. Heron

#17

A resident bull will actively protect a territory of up to 70 feet of shoreline day and night against any and all challengers (see #12) and common enemies, such as the white-tipped shark (#17). In Photo #18, two bulls are seen "defining" the limits of their adjoining territories.

#18

Around the turn of the century, the U.S. made several offers for a long-term lease of San Cristóbal, which it intended to use as a refueling station. The negotiations went on for several years but, for one reason or another, stalemated.

This interest was based almost entirely on strategic location and was not at all influenced by the resource potential. Or the governmental management responsibility. After all, there had been several detailed reports in the world press describing the various revolts and uprisings by the workers in the Galápagos settlements. Apparently these were protests against the cruel working conditions. With a work population made up largely of criminals, and a decided lack of control from the remote mainland, these insurrections often got way out of hand, with murder being the rule rather than the exception.

One of the victims was a man named Manuel Cobos, probably the most successful, as well as the most ruthless, developers in the Galápagos. Cobos established a sugar plantation and milling operation around the turn of the century on San Cristóbal. The settlement he formed, called El Progreso, was tenanted and worked by convicts. They were treated harshly, basically as slave laborers. Eventually there was mass mutiny, and Cobos paid for his cruelty with his life. El Progreso is still the center of an agricultural community on San Cristóbal.

Not all developers were tyrants. In 1897, Antonio Gil formed two settlements on Isabela Island, one called Villamil on the coast and the other one a few miles inland called Santo Tomás. These settlements are now small towns, with a combined population of less than 1000 people. Santo Tomás was named after the volcano it adjoined (now generally called Sierra Negra), the oldest and widest volcano on the island. The town was founded to start a small-scale sulfur operation, mined from the crater. A coffee plantation was also established. On the coast at Villamil, lime was produced by burning coral. These ventures were somewhat successful, but on a small scale due to the very limited water supply.

Meanwhile back in Panama, after observing a long and gruelling but failed attempt to construct the canal, the United States intervened. The newly formed Republic of Panama was persuaded to sign a treaty creating an international Canal Zone under U.S. administration. A renewed construction effort was soon underway, and with what is considered a major engineering achievement, the canal was successfully completed.

The Panama Canal was opened in 1914, just in time for World War I. As it turned out, the war was fought "Over There," with virtually no activity in the South Pacific. After the war, however, came the buildup of the Japanese presence in the Pacific, and now the full strategic role of the Galápagos was clearly seen. It guarded the entrance to the Panama Canal, which the Japanese Navy could either attack (to break an important supply line) or use to enter the Atlantic. The Galápagos was also an area to defend, lest the Japanese forces occupy the islands, from where an assault on the U.S. could be launched. As the build-up to war in the Pacific escalated, the U.S. Navy conducted several training exercises in the Galápagos.

Another transition period for the islands began in 1924 with the publication of Willaim Beebe's **GALAPAGOS: WORLD'S END**. Beebe, a renowned biologist and explorer, led a scientific expedition to the archipelago sponsored by the *New York Zoological Society*. His book paints a romantic account of this voyage; without sacrificing technical accuracy, Beebe expertly blended popular science and adventure travel. **GALAPAGOS: WORLD'S END** quickly became a best seller, inspiring many to follow in Beebe's footsteps.

Many of the early followers were wealthy and fancied themselves as amateur scientists. They traveled in their private luxury vessels, which were actually well-equipped floating laboratories, with a recruited team of professionals. The Galápagos was still inaccessible to most people, owing to the remote location, the limitations of the traveling possibilities, and the length of time required for such a trip.

Others who were likewise influenced by Beebe were visionaries, believing that the Galápagos would provide their particular "answer," be it health, wealth, or eternal peace. In 1927, a group of Norwegians, captivated by Beebe's book and by a slick promoter as well, put up their life savings for the opportunity to establish a profitable colony on Floreana. They tried everything from farming to a fish cannery operation, but as many others before them, their attempts ended in failure, disappointment, and for some, death. After 2 years, those that could, returned home. Others departed for the South American mainland. Only two Norwegians remained, making what money they could by selling dried fish. Finally, illness overtook them, and they abandoned their dwelling, their work, and their hopes for commercial success in the Galápagos. Today, the traveler can see the legacy of the community, including the remains of a corrugated-iron-and-wood structure near the beach at Post Office Bay, as well as bits and pieces of a narrow-gauge rail system (used for transport to and from shore).

FLOREANA – THE ISLE OF MYSTERY

> *It tempts no wise man to pull off and see what's the matter, but bids him steer small and keep off shore – that is Charles' Island; brace up, Mr. Mate, and keep the light astern.*
>
> Herman Melville, 1854

Another group of visionaries soon arrived that would forever shroud the island of Floreana in a real-life Agatha Christie mystery that could easily carry the title of "Death in Paradise." During your tour of the islands, you may visit the location of this fascinating tale and possibly get to meet a key player as well. Let's set the scene and follow the action.

The first set of characters are Dr. Friedrich Ritter and Dore Strauch who arrived in Floreana from Berlin in 1929. Dr. Ritter was very fond of wildlife, disliked hunting intensely, and was a vegetarian (although not a strict one – his dietary habits were to play a key part in the mystery that was to unfold). Although he was a medical doctor, Dr. Ritter strongly believed in the ability of the mind to control the body and to cure many physical ailments; he practiced what is now referred to as holistic medicine. Dore, one of his patients, was taken by the magnetic personality of Dr. Ritter, who were soon expounding that the powers of the mind were so great that they could even cure the multiple sclerosis that she was suffering from. The relationship expanded, and soon Dr. Ritter was sharing his dream for going off to a land of great solitude and freedom. Like many dreams however, there were the everyday realities of life that stood in the way, not the least of which was that they were both already married, although unhappily.

The plan they hit on was truly remarkable, mainly because, despite its absurdity, it worked. What they did was to bring their respective spouses together by convincing them that, to keep up appearances once they left, it would be best if Frau Ritter took over the household management for Herr Koerwin (Dore's husband). Owing perhaps to a ready-made way of dealing with an embarrassing situation in a very proper bourgeois society, everyone went for the idea. Dr. Ritter and Dore were thus free to set off for their utopia.

Upon arrival in the Galápagos, they settled in Floreana, once again owing to the known, reliable source of water and its agricultural potential. Their home site, which they named Freido (a contraction of Friedrich and Dore), was located at an extinct volcanic crater. Aside from providing a great view, it formed a natural basin full of lush tropical vegetation and included a clear spring. Their vast gardening activities were extremely successful. Given the fact that the land which they worked was their psychic center, it was only natural that they eventually located their house at the center of the garden. The shape was octagonal, in the best geodesic dome tradition.

The solitude that Friedrich and Dore strived so desperately for would prove to be short-lived. Their journey was well-documented (ironically by Dr. Ritter's own letters), and they were now labeled by the world press as notorious lovers, an Adam and Eve in a real Garden of Eden. Soon they were playing hosts to an increasing number of curious visitors. A series of would-be inhabitants also arrived, looking for a new way of life. Most, however, were not up to the rigors of life on Floreana, and their visits were for the most part brief in duration.

Some would stay on, however. September of 1932 marked the arrival of the Wittmer family – Heinz, his pregnant wife Margret, and Heinz' 12 year old son Harry (via a previous marriage). The Wittmer's life in inflation-torn Germany had not been easy, and the romantic magazine article descriptions of the idyllic life of Friedrich and Dore gathered their interest, as did William Beebe's book.

The reception the Wittmer's received can be best described as cool. Margret and Heinz Wittmer were down-to-earth types, and the only purpose Dr. Ritter saw in socializing was an opportunity to preach his philosophic rhetoric, which was in his estimation above the level of these new arrivals. Thus, as it was apparent that the two couples did not have that much in common (aside from their common desire to be free of the problems of pre-World War II Germany) they basically kept to themselves.

While the Wittmers and Friedrich & Dore were not fast friends, they were not enemies either, and helped each other out as common problems arose. Another group of settlers were to arrive in November, 1932, however, that would cause absolute mayhem. An Austrian woman calling herself the "Baroness" landed with a retinue of three men; they established themselves in the abandoned Norwegian buildings on the shore at Post Office Bay. Her entourage consisted of two Germans, Rudolf Lorenz and Robert Philippson, as well as an Ecuadorian, Felipe Valdivieso. The Baroness claimed to be of Austrian royalty, using the formal name of Eloise Baroness Wagner de Bosquet. She was apparently quite the sight, with a get-up right out of an S&M magazine, complete with riding britches, black boots, whip, and revolver. The two Germans were apparently her love-slaves, while the Ecuadorian was under some sort of work contract to the group, but he took his orders directly from the Baroness. Her stated intentions were to build a grandiose luxury hotel, which she already had named Hacienda Paradiso.

Soon after the arrival of the Baroness and her party, trouble started brewing between the three groups of settlers. There were reports of theft, tampering with the mail, mostly leveled against the Baroness. Most of this was related to the increasing number of luxury yachts that were arriving at Floreana, with the visitors anxious to have a look at the bohemian existence of the by now well-known inhabitants. Often, on a prior visit, the owners of these yachts had promised to bring one or more of the settlers some longed-for items. On the return trip, these items were sometimes handed to a settler who promised and failed to deliver them to the intended recipient; this "settler" was usually the Baroness. One can imagine the frustration that built up from these situations and the hostile feelings that developed.

In January of 1933, the Island of Floreana was to have its first native; Margret Wittmer gave birth to a son, Rolf. Later on that year, the Governor of the Galápagos Islands arrived to look into the now-open dispute between the various inhabitants of the island. Also, by this time there were all sorts of rumors and reports about the "strange" behavior and goings on, and he felt compelled to investigate the situation. Probably not wanting to upset any of the inhabitants, an attempt was made to pacify everyone. The fact that the Baroness intended to build a luxury hotel was not lost on the Governor, who was no doubt intrigued by the prospect of a vast tourist trade and did not want to risk losing the expected revenues. This, combined with the allure that the Baroness was said to possess, resulted in the Governor actually offering her an invitation to his residence.

The relationship between Dore and Friedrich was beginning to take a turn for the worse. This is not surprising since Dr. Ritter was in the extreme sense a follower of Nietzsche; contempt for women is in keeping with this "higher" culture, whereby the noble man is devoid of sympathy and is seen as ruthless, cruel, and violent. Ritter went so far as to forbid Dore from planting flowers, condemning this activity as frivolous.

And then it all happened – a strange and bizarre sequence of events that to this day has no entirely clear explanation. Lots of interpretation and lots of theories. No doubt, after visiting Floreana, you'll have one too! Once again, we'll set the scene. It is March, 1934 and a severe drought has hit the Galápagos. Many of the springs have dried up, and water is generally scarce. The daily business of managing the land has become a major challenge. The tension level has increased, and hostility is beginning to surface.

For some time, the Baroness has paired off with Robert Philippson, with both of them treating the now-out-of-favor Rudolf Lorenz as a slave. He is reportedly over-worked, beaten, and starved. Photographs taken around this time show a very emaciated "holocaust-genre" portrait of Lorenz. The drought has made his situation desperate, and he becomes a frequent guest of the Wittmers, seeking food, shelter, and perhaps a bit of sympathy. Often, he is just escaping from the harsh treatment. In somewhat of a daily ritual, the Baroness and Philippson would show up at the Wittmers and take Lorenz back with them; for his part, Lorenz didn't seem to protest returning with his tormentors.

The domestic problems of Dr. Ritter and Dore Strauch have escalated and are now obvious to those around them. Ritter's treatment of Dore is described as very cruel, while she stoically defends him in public. Dore goes so far as to glorify his philosophy – the very same idealistic dogma that has led to his insensitive behavior and lack of respect for her.

With this emotional overtone and the background of a severe drought, here's what happens next:

One afternoon, the Baroness shows up at the Wittmers and announces (to Margret) that she and Philippson are leaving right away for Tahiti on a boat anchored in the bay and waiting for them. There is no evidence that there was any such boat. As it turns out, they are never seen or heard from again. Not a trace. They left behind almost all of their possessions, some of which would have been taken on even a short voyage.

Within a short time, Rudolf Lorenz finds passage out of Floreana on-board a vessel named the DINAMITA. Having sailed from Academy Bay on Santa Cruz Island, and ultimately bound for Guayaquil, the DINAMITA is reported missing. Several months later, Lorenz's mummified body is found on the beach of Marchena Island along with the body of the captain of the vessel. Both have died of thirst and starvation.

In December of the same year, Friedrich Ritter, the vegetarian, takes critically ill and dies from eating spoiled chicken. It is said by Margret Wittmer, who was at Ritter's bedside when he died, that he cursed Dore Strauch with his dying breath.

And that's the mystery of Floreana. Unsolved. A lot of speculation, but never anything conclusive. Soon after the death of Dr. Ritter, Dore Strauch returned to Germany. Margret Wittmer continues to live on Floreana with her daughter Floreanita and grandchildren. Rolf Wittmer, Margret's son and the first native of Floreana, is owner-operator and sometimes captain of two Galápagos touring yachts, the TIP TOP II and TIP TOP III (see the section, Boats of the Galápagos, in CHAPTER IV). When arranged in advance, tour groups visiting Floreana are taken to Margret's cafe, where one can sometimes have a taste of the family's orange-fermented wine, browse at the small assortment of souvenirs that are offered for sale, have post cards cancel-stamped with the official emblems of the Barrel Post Office, and generally let the mind wander back in time. After visiting the Wittmer Pension (rooms are actually let out), the after-dinner conversations on-board the boat are usually very stimulating; most of the Guides and Tour Leaders will discuss the various theories pertaining to these mysterious events that transpired all those many years ago. Many questions are raised by the passengers, most of which are rhetorical in nature.

A few final comments. A complete and fascinating account of this who-done-it is offered in a book by John Treherne entitled **THE GALAPAGOS AFFAIR**. Unfortunately, this book is out of print, but is available at many libraries. Margret Wittmer has written her own version of the story as well as a complete chronicle of her 60+ years on Floreana Island; the name of the book, quite simply, is **FLOREANA** (see the Literature section for details on these books). A third account of these events is in the offing, as there is talk of a movie being made. "That," says Margret, "depends on the up-front money." Mrs. Wittmer will eternally be known and remembered as a survivor.

By the way, the story isn't quite over. Over the years, there have been other mysterious occurrences on Floreana. One event in the 1960s involved an elderly visitor who disappeared while hiking. An extensive search turned up nil. The solution and the body were found almost 20 years later; it was determined that the person apparently wandered off the trail, got lost, and was overcome by exposure to the elements. Two other situations directly involved the Wittmer family once again. The first was related to the drowning of Harry Wittmer in a

1951 boat accident. The second incident occurred in 1969 when the husband of Floreanita, Margret's daughter, also disappeared. In light of the events that transpired back in the 1930s, this last episode was investigated in some detail; while no formal conclusion was reached, some locals do offer their own "unofficial" version of the story.

GROWTH, TOURISM, AND CONSERVATION

Not all of the Galápagos settlers made the front pages of the international press. For most of them, it should be stated, notoriety is the last thing they wanted. Mostly, they wished to be left in peace while they provided for themselves. This includes some of the original Norwegian settlers who eventually relocated to Santa Cruz Island; there they began farming activities in the Highlands, a lush, fertile area owing to the *garúa* mist that blankets the high elevations for a considerable part of the year. These pioneers were joined by a few Americans and several Europeans, many from Germany. Probably the most famous of this group (again, not that they have sought fame, and somewhat resent the lack of privacy that tourism has brought) are the Angermeyers. As chronicled by Johanna Angermeyer in her beautifully written book, **MY FATHER'S ISLAND**, four Angermeyer brothers, Carl, Fritz, Gus, and Hans sailed for the Galápagos in 1935, leaving the politics of Germany behind them. The offspring of the Angermeyer family now rank among the best captains of the touring yachts that sail the waters of the Galápagos archipelago.

When World War II broke out, the Ecuadorian government agreed to let the United States construct an Air Force base on Baltra Island. The U.S. Sixth Air Force, stationed on Baltra as well as several other islands in the Galápagos, patrolled the approach to the Panama Canal and monitored enemy submarine activity in the South Pacific. The 29th Bomber Squadron, Sixth Air Force, still holds annual reunions, an event usually attended by noted Galápagos historian John Woram. John takes many authors to task for inaccurately writing that the U.S. servicemen were responsible for the extinction of the land iguana on Baltra Island. Mr. Woram's statements, which cite the sensitivity of the soldiers to the local wildlife, are adamantly supported and seconded by scientists at the Darwin Station.

After the war, the air base was given to Ecuador and still serves as one of the two main airports in the Galápagos (the other is on San Cristóbal Island), the point of arrival for planeloads of tourists 7 days a week, every week of the year. Tourism is the latest and the only large-scale commercial endeavor in the history of the Galápagos. Some of the more contemporary break-even ventures include fishing and a salt mine operation on James (Santiago) Island. For tourism to succeed where other industries have failed, it is vitally important not to commit the same sins of greed perpetrated by the whalers and sealers, that is killing the proverbial goose that laid the golden egg. The Galápagos wildlife must be preserved!

Conservation of the Galápagos sounds logical to many of us, but it is also expensive. And for the third-world economy of Ecuador, it has been a luxury that, prior to tourism, it simply couldn't afford. Raising the standard of living for Ecuadorians by developing world trade has been the first priority, and rightfully so. Even adequate administration of the Galápagos has been more expensive than the country could afford. And difficult to achieve, especially with the remote location of, and lack of communications with, the islands. There is also politics to consider. For an administration to succeed, it must first survive, and through the years, "saving the Galápagos" was not high on the list of critical issues.

This is not to say that conservation has been overlooked. The legacy of Darwin's voyage and subsequent writings have generated international support for a Galápagos conservation effort. The year 1935 was the 100th anniversary of Darwin's visit. This was a noteworthy occasion in the scientific community. In anticipation thereof, the *National Assembly of Ecuador* had passed protective legislation in 1934, creating wildlife sanctuaries on some of the islands. However, this was largely a matter of form rather than substance. The need for effective controls as well as a nature preserve was made apparent as a result of a Darwin centennial event, the *Galápagos Memorial Expedition*, led by Dr. Victor von Hagen. The establishment of a research station was proposed by Dr. von Hagen. Unfortunately, before the practical considerations of this idea could be sorted out, the world went to war once again.

There was another Galápagos centennial in 1959, this one marking the publication of Darwin's **THE ORIGIN OF SPECIES**. This event formed the impetus to put in effect some of the conservation recommendations made as a result of a *UNESCO* expedition 2 years earlier. One of these recommendations was, once again, the establishment of a research station. This effort required international cooperation and funding, and in July, 1959 an organization of renowned scientists and Ecuadorian conservationists was formally established, the *Charles Darwin Foundation for the Galápagos Islands.*

Later that year, the Ecuadorian government passed legislation aimed at preserving the Galápagos. Through guidelines set by the Darwin Foundation, all land in the archipelago not already settled by man was declared a National Park, and strict regulations were enacted. This time the laws could be enforced, because plans were being formed to develop two administrative infrastructures one scientific and the other regulatory.

First, the *Charles Darwin Research Station,* located on Academy Bay in the town of Puerto Ayora, was established in 1961 and officially opened in 1964. Four years later, the *Galápagos National Park Service* was formed. The role of the Research Station was to coordinate all scientific work in the islands, gather essential baseline data on endangered species, establish conservation goals based on the data, and recommend programs to support those goals (such as the eradication of certain introduced species – rats, feral pigs, etc). The role of the Park Service was to implement these programs.

The growing interest in the Galápagos as a tourist attraction was recognized, as was the potential revenue this industry could produce. Owing partially to the location of the Darwin Station, the town of Puerto Ayora was selected as the "center of tourism." A road was built linking the town to the Baltra Airport, where the runway was also resurfaced. A Tour Operator based in Quito, METROPOLITAN TOURING, began offering island cruises in 1970. Soon, the industry and the number of boats began to grow. From a little over 4000 tourists per year in 1970 to about 60,000 per year in 1997.

This growth was somewhat unique. In accordance with the National Park regulations, facilities could not be constructed on over 90 percent of the land not already colonized, meaning zero development on all but four islands (not including Baltra, which is operated as a military base). Thus, the tour boat assumed the roles of both hotel and restaurant. As an added control, in 1986 the *Galápagos National Park* was extended to the waters surrounding the islands with the signing into law of the *Galápagos Marine Resources Reserve.* In November, 1996, *The Galápagos National Park Service* changed the status of the *Marine Resources Reserve* into a *Biological Reserve,* making it an integral part of the national system of protected areas. A 15 nautical mile boundary zone was established; now the waters and marine wildlife of the Galápagos could also be protected.

The problem is that the protection is only in writing; for the most part, it isn't enforced. Currently, there is only one patrol boat in the Galápagos. Illegal fishing boats (including large commercial vessels of both Ecuadorian and foreign registry) are spotted on many tours, especially those that visit the western islands of Fernandina and Isabela. The illegal fishing activities include the taking of sharks (for shark fin soup, an Asian delicacy) and purse seining for tuna (and, inadvertently, sea turtles, dolphins, and manta rays). One of the most harmful fisheries is long-lining, with the seemingly endless hooks taking their toll on a very significant number of sea lions and sea birds; albatrosses in particular are being "hooked" by the long-lines, and their numbers are alarmingly decreasing throughout the world.

The latest fishery to "open" has been the taking of sea cucumbers (another Asian delight, richly coveted for the reputed aphrodisiac qualities). Starting in 1992 and continuing into 1998, literally hundreds of illegal sea cucumber fishermen (*pepineros,* as they are called) have been spotted (and occasionally apprehended) as they dive for and process (by boiling) the echinoderms. The sea cucumber requires a dense population to maintain its numbers (due to its method of external fertilization). They release their gametes (sperm and eggs) externally, and if a member of the opposite sex isn't close by, fertilization doesn't happen. As an analogy, you need a solid block of corn plants (not just a plant here and there) to ensure a good stand of corn. At any rate, the numbers of sea cucumbers are rapidly dwindling, and there's not a lot being done about it. Being slow movers, the sea cucumbers cannot defend themselves. And it's not just the sea cucumbers. Most of us have finally learned that a broken food chain is just that. To make matters worse, the *pepineros* are introducing plants and animals in a very sensitive area. There are rumors to the effect that the once pristine island of Fernandina now has introduced animals (perhaps including rats).

So the question is, "Why doesn't someone do something about it?" And the answer is – you guessed it, money! It talks loud everywhere, especially to a third-world economy and government. Is anyone fighting back? The *Charles Darwin Research Station* certainly wants to, but their hands are tied. Basically the Darwin Station and current Director, Dr. Robert Bensted-Smith, report to the *Charles Darwin Foundation for the Galápagos Islands,* an international organization created, in part, under the auspices of the Government of Ecuador. Since the responsibility of effectively patrolling the Galápagos falls squarely on the shoulders of the Ecuadorian government, it is very awkward politically for the Darwin Station to publicly complain about the very government that allows them to exist and function. Thus the tied hands and still lips. The result is no outcry forcing political action, and the word does not get out on the world press. Even when it does, very few people want to read (or write) that there are serious problems in the Land of Darwin.

It actually gets more complicated. As the tourist industry grows, so does the required support infrastructure and the population of the islands. In 1950, there were less than 1500 residents in the Galápagos. By 1974, the population was over 4000, with about 1000 residents on Santa Cruz Island. In 1998, the Galápagos population exceeded 16,000 people, with over 6000 living in the town of Puerto Ayora. The estimated growth rate is approximately 12 percent per year. This growth rate is exactly the heart of the problem. More and more people are moving to the islands because of the perceived opportunities. But not everyone is qualified for and/or able to find a job. One consequence is the beginning of "city problems," such as crime, drugs, etc. Another end product is the rising number of plants and animals that the residents are introducing to the Galápagos, an alarming situation that needs to be dealt with. Finally, getting back to the problem discussed earlier, there are a growing number of residents trying to earn a living through fishing – even illegal fishing, such as the taking of sharks and sea cucumbers. Unlike the Darwin Station (who they also dislike), this group is very vocal in their efforts to influence the government. "You let us move here," they say, "and now you have to let us earn a living here." During the mid 1990s there were well-publicized confrontations, including strikes (that closed one of the major airports), take-overs of the *Charles Darwin Research Station* and *Galápagos National Park Service,* killing of tortoises, threats to Darwin Station & National Park officials, and a shooting of a Park Warden. Talk about trouble in paradise.

The situation is very complex, and some fair share of the blame can go to the lack of effective control by the Ecuadorian government. The growing population turned to populist leaders, such as their Congressman, Eduardo Veliz, who fueled their belief that the forces of conservation were their enemy. The fight was for an open economy, with less restrictions on fishing. The voiced attitude was that the conservationists were mostly foreigners "who cared more about tortoises than about the lives of the people" that lived on the islands. At one point during the second strike, the Congressman (who organized and led the strike) actually threatened (in writing) the security of tourists. Empty as the threat was, it probably was a turning point of sorts.

Many of the locals, except for the militant fishermen who live in Isabela, very recently have woken up to the fact that overfishing would destroy the very resource that was bringing all the tourists dollars to the Galápagos. In addition, many of the local fishermen (who make their incomes from traditional, legal fishing) are now beginning to point out that many of the illegal commercial fishing boats are not owned or operated by locals *(Galápagueños),* but rather by outsiders – mainland Ecuadorians or foreigners. So, the scenario that the locals are now seeing is one in which the commercial fishing activities are directly depleting the fishing stocks and indirectly depleting the number of tourists who might have wanted to see the wildlife that are dependent on those fish. And, oh yes, as a result, their incomes were also being depleted.

At the same time, the Ecuadorian government is taking more of a direct role. While the third edition of this book was going to press, a Special Galápagos Law was about to be passed. Among the many provisions of this comprehensive legislation was a restriction on the number of people allowed to migrate from mainland Ecuador to the Galápagos.

So things are hopeful. In addition, the Darwin Station and the Park Service have worked together on several successful conservation programs. They have saved three populations of land iguanas from extinction, raising several hundred animals in the Darwin Station and returning them to their native islands. In a similar fashion, eight tortoise subspecies were also saved; about 2000 tortoises have already been repatriated. Slowly, and one by one, battles against the introduced species of animals are being won. Goats have been eliminated from several of the smaller islands, wild dogs from Isabela, and rats from Bartolomé. Some battles are longer than others. The survival of the dark-rumped (Hawaiian) petrel, once on the verge of extinction due to rat predation, now looks promising, and the population of goats on James (Santiago) Island has been reduced from 100,000 to less than 60,000. But both of these programs have been tedious, have depended on dedication by a few as well as timely outside funding, and have taken 15 years to get this far.

Much more needs to be done, and money is the limiting factor. The Darwin Station has a very small budget which is used primarily on administrative matters (including the operation of a Visitor's Center which is an important part of every Galápagos tour), the wildlife conservation programs cited above, and gathering essential baseline data on endangered species. Thus, the operations are limited, and the scope of the programs undertaken must, by necessity, be quite narrow. The budget for basic research doesn't exist; thus, most scientific research in the Galápagos is conducted by visiting scientists (although the Darwin Station coordinates and gives logistical support to such research).

Aside from the Republic of Ecuador, funding is provided entirely by contributions – private donations, endowments, and from a variety of foundations, institutions, and organizations. You (or your organization) are encouraged to make a personal (or corporate) contribution; use the following address:

Charles Darwin Foundation, Inc.
Dept. 0553
Washington, D.C., 20073-0053

Your contribution would be greatly appreciated and should typically meet tax-deductible guidelines; you may want to verify this with your tax accountant. Make your check payable to the **Charles Darwin Foundation, Inc.** All contributors of more than U.S. $25 will become members of the *Friends of the Galápagos* and receive a one year's subscription to **NOTICIAS DE GALAPAGOS,** the journal containing articles on Galápagos science and conservation, and four issues of **GALAPAGOS BULLETIN,** a quarterly news publication from the *Charles Darwin Research Station.* Subsequent annual contributions will extend the subscription to both publications.

Donations often go towards immediate conservation projects. For long-term support, an endowment fund called the *Darwin Scientific Foundation* has been set up. If you, your organization, or corporation wish to contribute to this fund, send a check payable to the *Darwin Scientific Foundation* to the following address:

Darwin Scientific Foundation
100 N. Washington St., Ste 311
Falls Church, VA 22046

For those "high-techers" in the reading audience, the Darwin Station needs equipment – computers (desktop publishing systems) and electronic instrumentation, preferably with a battery-backup system, as the generating stations of the town and the Station are unreliable. All such "in kind contributions," as they are called, should be discussed with the office of:

Johannah Barry
Executive Director
CHARLES DARWIN FOUNDATION, INC.
100 N. Washington St., Ste. 311
Falls Church, VA 22046
PHONE: (703) 538-6833   **FAX:** 703-538-6835

Lastly, if this book serves its purpose, you will tour the Galápagos Islands. On your visit to the *Charles Darwin Research Station,* show your support and leave a donation.

In a sense, you will be making a donation by visiting the Galápagos and pumping money into the local economy. Hopefully, the revenue generated by the tourist industry may actually stimulate a perceived need by the Ecuadorian government to allocate more funds to wildlife conservation.

This brings us to a sensitive topic – the effect of tourism. "Surely," some say, "you cannot continue to increase tourism without an adverse impact." I tend to agree, but feel that the problem has a two-fold solution:

1. Responsible tourism – For the most part, those that tour the Galápagos are conservation-oriented and tend to follow the regulations of the National Park. As tourism increases, this responsibility will become greater. There is something to be said for keeping the number of "pleasure boats" with nightly live entertainment to a minimum. While the Cruise Ships have their place, especially for the elderly, it will be important for these boats to fully develop their orientation to a "natural history excursion." This criticism, by the way, is also leveled at some of the small yachts where a "party" atmosphere prevails at night. The Galápagos should continue to be an adventure, not an "exotic cruise" destination. Have fun, but keep the orientation focused.

2. Controlled tourism – This is already in effect with the Guide program, the National Park regulations, the paperwork necessary for a tour boat to leave port (including a list of passengers, passport numbers, and a detailed itinerary), as well as the sanctions against private vessels entering the waters of the Galápagos. Enforcement is another matter. As stated above, this will require more patrol boats operated by the *Galápagos National Park Service* and funded by the Ecuadorian government.

In conclusion, it's the quality more than the quantity that will make the difference. Those that are interested in seriously exploring the natural world of the Galápagos and have a healthy respect for conservation are, and will continue to be, a very valuable resource for the islands.

CHAPTER III

ABOUT
THE GALAPAGOS
WILDLIFE

The fascinating wildlife of the Galápagos is extremely well documented in Michael Jackson's **GALAPAGOS: A NATURAL HISTORY GUIDE** (see the Literature section). It's not likely that you'll find this Michael Jackson moon-walking on MTV; Professor Jackson (a more appropriate designation) currently teaches at the University of Calgary. His **GUIDE** is most thorough in its discussions of the flora and fauna of the Galápagos, and it is strongly recommended that you take the book with you to the islands, where you will use it as a daily reference source. The Jackson **GUIDE** is available in mainland Ecuador, but my advice is to start looking for a copy well before you depart for the islands. The **GUIDE** is becoming a little easier to find in the U.S., especially in travel-oriented bookstores, but there is still a chance that your local, friendly book-shop may have to order it for you; it is also available through GALAPAGOS TRAVEL, the publisher of the book you are reading.

The purpose of this chapter is to augment the material found in the Jackson **GUIDE**, and to key in on certain anatomical, physiological, and more often, behavioral traits. In a sub-section called Photo Opportunities, a few suggestions for interesting shots will be briefly presented. As a point of reference, Spanish names for the animals will be cited; it may prove useful to learn them, as some of the Guides refer to certain animals by their Spanish name.

Note: Terrestrial invertebrates will not be discussed.

REPTILES

As mentioned in Chapter II (in the section, "The Arrival of Life"), reptiles were able to survive the long ocean passage to the Galápagos due to their ability to tolerate arid conditions and a salt water environment; they can also fast for long periods of time. An interesting point regarding the reptiles' arduous trip to the Galápagos was that it was a one-way voyage. The currents were not about to carry them back to the mainland! If they were going to survive, they had to adapt to the local conditions. Thus, it is not surprising that the number of reptile species is small (twenty-two in all), and of these twenty-two, twenty are endemic to the Galápagos.

The reptiles not only arrived, but they survived, reproduced, and assumed several of the niche roles typically filled by mammals. A key point is that land mammals were not able to make the ocean voyage on their own. It is for this reason that, along with amphibians, land mammals are noticeably absent from the list of indigenous species (with the exception of three species of rice rats). As evidenced by several introduced mammalian species proliferating to the point of detriment to native species, the Galápagos environment is fit for more than just prehistoric-looking reptiles. An "unfit environment" viewpoint was at one time held by many, including Herman Melville (in **THE ENCANTADAS**):

> Another feature of these isles is their emphatic uninhabitableness. It is deemed fit [for]…he jackal itself, …but the Encantadas refuse to harbor even the outcasts of the beasts. Man and wolf alike disown them. Little but reptile life is here found; tortoises, lizards, …and that strangest anomaly of outlandish nature, the iguana. No voice, no low, no howl is heard; the chief sound of life here is a hiss.
>
> Herman Melville, 1854

Being cold-blooded, the behavior cycle of the reptiles is governed by their body temperature, which they cannot control physiologically; they utilize sun and shade for this purpose. Even with such a strict limitation, they have managed to adapt (through evolution) in a remarkably efficient and most noticeable fashion to the harsh environment of the Galápagos as well as to the various microclimates of particular islands.

Note: Geckos will not be discussed.

GIANT TORTOISES – (GALAPAGOS)

> I will describe the habits of the tortoise. Some grow to an immense size; the old males are the largest, the females rarely growing to so great a size: the male can be readily distinguished from the female by the greater length of its tail. They frequent in preference the high damp parts, but they likewise live in the lower and arid districts.
>
> The tortoise is very fond of water, drinking large quantities and wallowing in the mud. The larger islands alone possess springs, and these are always situated toward the central parts, and at a considerable height. The tortoises, therefore, which frequent the lower districts, when thirsty, are obliged to travel from a long distance. Hence broad and well-beaten paths branch off in every direction from the wells down to the sea-coast; and the Spaniards, by following them up, first discovered the watering-places. When the tortoise arrives at the spring, quite regardless of any spectator, he buries his head in the water above his eyes, and greedily swallows great mouthfuls, at the rate of about ten in a minute. I believe it is well ascertained that the

bladder of the frog acts as a reservoir for the moisture necessary to its existence; such seems to be the case with the tortoise.

The tortoises, when purposely moving towards any point, travel by night and day and arrive at their journey's end much sooner than would be expected. One large tortoise, which I watched, walked at the rate of sixty yards in ten minutes, that is … four miles a day – allowing a little time for it to eat on the road.

During the breeding season, when the male and female are together, the male utters a hoarse roar or bellowing, which, it is said, can be heard at the distance of more than a hundred yards. The female never uses her voice, and the male only at these times; so that when the people hear this noise they can know that the two are together.

Charles Darwin, 1845

Of all the wildlife, it is the tortoise that most symbolizes the Galápagos Islands. The tortoise has given the Galápagos its name. It is the face of the tortoise that appears on the official insignia of the islands and is stamped on the passport of the visitor.

The tortoise is a vegetarian, well known for its ability to fast for long periods of time. This ability proved to be a great asset, enabling the giant tortoise to make the long voyage to the Galápagos on rafts of tangled vegetation and to survive the arid conditions on many of the islands. This attribute became a liability as the buccaneers and whalers carted off over 200,000 tortoises, knowing the animals would stay alive in the ship's hold without food or water, thereby providing fresh meat to the crew for several months. Some, like Melville, thought the tortoise's fate was self-predestined.

Lasting sorrow and penal hopelessness are in no animal form so suppliantly expressed as in theirs. They are strangely self-condemned. Their crowning curse is their drudging impulse to straightforwardness in a belittered world.

Herman Melville, 1854

Indeed, Melville's shipmates believed that wicked sea officers were punished by being transformed into giant tortoises. The truth be known, the Galápagos giant tortoises have proven to be very adaptive, a fact not lost on Darwin (see the section in Chapter 11 on Adaptive Radiation). Starting as a single species, fourteen subspecies evolved (now reduced to eleven), each adapting to the vegetation of the particular island on which they settled. In the case of Isabela, five subspecies evolved (one for each major volcanic region). The method of adaptation is based on several variations in the shape of their carapace (shell). At one extreme is the saddle-back tortoise with an elevated, arched front end and long neck, able to reach for the tall vegetation on the drier islands. At the other extreme is the dome-shaped tortoise, with a shorter profile and blunt front end for pushing through the dense brush often found on islands with lush highlands.

By virtue of its great mass (up to 550 pounds), the giant tortoise is better equipped than most reptiles to keep an even body temperature. Actually, weight is another subspecies variation. The saddle-back tortoises are smaller because they live on drier islands, which naturally have less food available.

Thus, being a large saddle-back (and requiring more food than the island can provide) is not a great adaptive mechanism.

While longevity estimates are about 150 years (based on a few historical records), there is at present no precise method of determining the age of older tortoises. There are markings on the shell called growth rings, which occur between the plates (see Photos #27-28), but after about 10 years of age the growth slows and the rings are too close together to accurately count. Eventually the rings erode, and age determination becomes impossible. The tortoises reared at the Darwin Station are being tagged, so that future generations of scientists can keep score.

Photo Opportunities: The tortoise pens at the *Charles Darwin Research Station* present a great picture-taking opportunity. You definitely want to get a close-up of the timeless face – an **E.T.** shot (see Photo #19). In fact, it was the facial features of the giant tortoise that were actually used to create the visage of **E.T.** Make sure you take a light meter reading off the face, so you don't lose the detail. If you're photographing the entire animal, there are often reflections bouncing off the age-worn, smooth carapace; use a polarizer to knock out the glare and get more definition.

You'll also be able to capture the aggressive male "posturing" behavior, two or three tortoises stretching their necks skyward and at each other, mouths agape, seeing who will back down and who will reign supreme – the umpire in a jaw-down with the wrinkled manager (see Photo #22). And if you want to "posture" with them, there are pens where you can pose right next to one of these friendly giants.

The best time to go tortoise shooting at the Darwin Station is early in the morning or in the evening, before and after the large Cruise Ships bring their passengers through. Once the tours start coming in, you can't really set up your shots, and someone's usually in the way. You can actually make two visits to the Darwin Station – once with your tour, when you can plan your shots, and once on your own, as most tours give you some "free time" in town. You **are** allowed to visit the Darwin Station without a Guide.

For those who see the tortoises in the wild, there may be good "water hole mud-wallowing" opportunities. The water holes are often dew ponds that form as a result of the *garúa* mist. In the Highlands of Santa Cruz Island, these ponds are often coated with duckweed, providing a beautiful green background (see Photo #25).

Where To See Them: For most visitors, the Darwin Station presents the only opportunity to view the giant tortoise. Perhaps the breeding, incubation, rearing, and repatriating programs carried on at the Darwin Station will enable future generations of visitors to see the various species of tortoises on their native islands. But it won't happen quickly, especially when you consider that it takes 40 years for a tortoise to become sexually mature! So for now, most of us must be content with viewing the giant tortoises at the Darwin Station.

Actually, there are some alternatives. During the dry season, you can see giant tortoises in the wild by taking a trip to the Tortoise Reserve (or nearby farms) in the Highlands on Santa Cruz Island; several Galápagos tours provide such an opportunity (see the section on the Santa Cruz Highlands in Chapter IX). For those of you that choose longer (2 week) Galápagos trips, there are several locations on Isabela Island to see tortoises. On the way to the rim of the Sierra Negra Volcano, there is time for a stop at the very well-designed tortoise rearing center just outside the town of Villamil. The intrepid visitors that brave the "long trail" at the Urvina Bay Visitor Site are usually able to spot a few saddle-back tortoises in the wild. Finally, those that make the arduous climb to the top of the Alcedo Volcano will be rewarded with constant sightings, as Alcedo is home to the largest population of giant tortoises in the islands, estimated at over 4000.

Note: The Visitor Site at the Alcedo Volcano has been closed since 1995, as the National Park and Darwin Station have been conducting an intensive introduced mammal eradication program. Depending on the success of this program, the Site may be reopened in the future. (See the section on Isabela Island in Chapter IX).

MARINE IGUANAS – *(IGUANAS MARINAS)*

The rocks on the coast abounded with great black lizards ... a hideous looking creature, of a dirty black colour, stupid, and sluggish in its movements. The usual length of a full-grown one is about a yard, but there are some even four feet long; a large one weighed twenty pounds. Their tails are flattened sideways, and all four feet partially webbed. When in the water this lizard swims with perfect ease and quickness, by a serpentine movement of its body and flattened tail – the legs being motionless and closely collapsed on its sides. Their limbs and strong claws are admirably adapted for crawling over the rugged and fissured masses of lava which everywhere form the coast.

It is ... most remarkable, because it is the only existing lizard which lives on marine vegetable productions.... We must admit that there is no other quarter of the world where this Order replaces the herbivorous mammalia in so extraordinary a manner.

Charles Darwin, 1845

Your introduction to the reptilian wildlife of the Galápagos will probably be the marine iguana. Your first encounter may be a bit shocking. It certainly was for me. My first evening in the islands, while lining up a sunset shot, I crouched down near a rock. Only after quite some time did I turn my head and become suddenly aware that I was eye-to-eye with a 3 ft long marine iguana. It takes a while to get past their prehistoric looks, especially meeting this way for the first time. Somehow you forget that these creatures are vegetarians, because your mind has somehow flashed-back to **GODZILLA** reruns. The crest of spines running down the back (of the male) and claw-like talons don't exactly ease these initial feelings. But, of course, they're harmless, and after a few days in the Galápagos, they start looking kind of cute. No, the sun isn't getting to you, and it's not closing time. You've simply gotten hooked on the Galápagos!

It's easy to walk right up to a few marine iguanas without noticing them at first. The dark coloring blends perfectly with the lava rocks, and they can keep their frozen pose for hours at a time. The coloring seems to serve a dual purpose. First, it offers a degree of protection to the juveniles from their only natural predator, the Galápagos hawk. Second, the dark color is better able to absorb the heat from the sun's rays. The marine iguana spends much of its day sunbathing in an elevated position, angling its body toward and facing the sun, as if searching the skies. When you encounter an entire colony in the same frozen pose, it seems as if they're worshiping the sun god, which in a way they are.

The marine iguana spends more time in the sun than other lizards, for it is the only seafaring member of the Order; it may lose as much as 20 Deg F during its daily excursion into the water, and it takes much of the day to restore its body temperature to normal (about 96 Deg F) as well as to repay its oxygen debt.

The marine iguana is not a casual surface swimmer; it is a strong diver, descending to depths of 35 ft. The dives are generally of brief duration (5-10 minutes) but if need be, the animal can slow its metabolism sufficiently to remain submerged for up to an hour. Typically, the divers are the larger males, possessing the swimming strength to make it through the breakers. The other members of the colony feed intertidally on the exposed lower portions of the rocks. Their diet consists almost exclusively of red or green algae-type seaweed.

The first impression of a marine iguana is not much improved when it appears to spit in your direction every so often. Actually, the animal is sneezing, expelling the excess salt from its system through a special gland connected to the nostrils. Yet another interesting adaptation, although for some people not a very pretty one to behold. Until they get hooked on the Galápagos!

Photo Opportunities: The frequent salt-sneezing gives the marine iguana a white-crusted forehead; it makes for a great close-up, especially early in the evening when there's less glare and a better chance of getting facial detail. Some are more white than others, giving the appearance of sneezing into the wind once or twice too often. You might want to document the blunt snout, useful for nibbling the thin layer of algae off the rocks. Remember to use your polarizing filter if you're shooting in bright sunlight. The same is true when you encounter a male in his bright breeding colors, which (in addition to animal size) vary from island to island. The males on Española (Hood) Island are colorful year-round; they are a very bright red and green (see Photos #32-33), and you will want to capture this image of "Beauty on the Beast."

The breeding season, which also varies between islands, presents the opportunity to witness the aggressive male territorial behavior. This "head-bobbing" activity goes on throughout the year but is intensified during the breeding months, as is actual conflict, which consists mostly of head-butting. All this makes for ideal footage for those with a video camera. For photographers, the action is a bit hard to capture, but a close-up of the scarred face of the vanquished iguana is very vivid.

You'll also want to get a few pictures of the entire body, making sure the focus is tight on the scales. Don't accidentally cut out the forelimb and talon from the foreground. An interesting shot is to have the iguana silhouetted against the sky and a breaking wave. Again, this is a great evening opportunity as they try to catch the last warm rays of sunlight.

Those with an underwater camera may be fortunate enough to get a shot of the marine iguana feeding on the algae beneath the surface. As the waters are not very clear (due to upwelling), for good results you may have to find a shooting opportunity in a pocket of sunlight; this is often easier said than done.

Where To See Them: While marine iguanas may seem to be everywhere, especially on the lava rock shores, their numbers (estimated at over 200,000) are in fact declining, and the distribution is patchy. In the extreme *El Niño/* Southern Oscillation (ENSO) weather phenomenon of 1982-83, the cold Humboldt Current failed, thus reducing the upwelling of nutrients from the ocean floor. The marine iguanas were thus forced to feed on algae containing little nutrient value; many perished that year, actually starving on a full stomach of food.

The marine iguana can overcome natural disasters much easier than the ones that are man-made – specifically the hard-to-control feral cats that prey on young marine iguanas, as well as on the eggs and hatchlings.

LAND IGUANAS – *(IGUANAS TERRESTRES)*

> *The terrestrial species ... is confined to the central part of the Archipelago. Like their brothers the sea-kind, they are ugly animals, of a yellowish-orange beneath, and of a brownish-red colour above: from their low facial angle they have a singularly stupid appearance. When not frightened, they slowly crawl along with their tails and bellies dragging on the ground. They often stop and doze for a minute or two, with closed eyes and hind legs spread out on the parched soil.*
> *Charles Darwin, 1845*

Just as its seafaring cousin, the land iguana is a vegetarian (although juveniles, with immature digestive systems, are known to eat insects as well). But the similarity in diet ends right there, for the land iguana dines mostly on prickly pear cactus. The pads as well as the fruit. Spines and all! It has been known to roll the cactus pads on the ground, thus knocking the tips off the spines, but the land iguana usually lies flat on the ground and munches away on the cactus with the tough spines intact.

The cactus provides both food and water to the land iguana, who, living in the drier parts of the archipelago, goes without fresh water for much of the year. Part of the adaptation to the drier environment is the conservation of energy. While capable of great speed, these 3 ft long creatures typically move quite slowly, and give the appearance of being lazy, as Darwin hinted at in his comments above.

Land iguanas are burrowing animals, and their shallow tunnels provide shelter at night, shade from the sun, a nesting place, and a temporary home for the hatchlings.

Photo Opportunities: The beautiful yellow coloring will really pop out if you can possibly shoot the land iguana in the shade of the cactus tree. It will also help to underexpose by a half to one stop. Watching the land iguana chomp away on a cactus pad will give you ample opportunity to snap off a good series. Every now and then while dining, the cute little beast will stick its tongue off to one side, as if licking its lips in exclamation of just how wonderful the meal really was. If you're using a telephoto, focus carefully on the intricate scales, which are similar in appearance to a knight's mail (see Photo #36). When you're facing the animal head-on, you won't be able to hold focus of both head and tail, so you'll have to make a decision. One answer is to shoot a bit slower and stoop down as much as possible, giving a greater depth of field (which will work if you're using fast film). If you have time, and your camera is so equipped, use the depth of field preview button.

Land iguanas have the same sort of symbiotic relationship as the tortoises with the birds that remove ticks and other parasites. You may be fortunate enough to get a shot of this behavior. Also, on South Plaza Island, you may see male aggressive activity, with head-butting and all the rest.

Where To See Them: There are two endemic species of land iguanas living in the arid zones of six central and western islands. One species is found only on Santa Fé, and though there are few to be seen, some tours ascend into the plateau area that they frequent. The other species will be viewed on your tour of South Plaza Island as you pass through a small cactus forest; here, the quantities of land iguanas are much larger.

When Darwin visited the Galápagos, the land iguana was most plentiful, as evidenced by the following statement:

I cannot give a more forceful proof of their numbers, than by stating that when we left at James Island, we could not for some time find a spot free from their burrows on which to pitch our single tent.
Charles Darwin, 1845

Unfortunately, the land iguana has drastically declined in numbers since Darwin's day and is now an endangered species. Although the adults have no natural predators, they were reportedly considered quite tasty when roasted, and many have come to such a fate at the hands of man through the years. The greatest damage, however, has once again been caused by the introduced animals that have preyed on the young land iguanas and raided their nests. While the feral animal eradication programs have been started, it has become necessary to breed and raise land iguanas at the Darwin Station (where they are off-limits to visitors in order to maintain their naturally skittish behavior). Eventually the adults are repatriated to their home island. As with the giant tortoise program, the results will be long-term, for the land iguana, with a 60 year life span, takes about 10 years to sexually mature.

MARINE (PACIFIC GREEN) TURTLES – *(TORTUGAS)*

I was on-deck as the yacht ORCA prepared to lay anchor when I heard the captain call out to the Guide, "*¡Mire, mire, copulación!*" This isn't exactly what you would expect to hear on a Galápagos Island tour. As curious as the next person, I walked over to the side of the boat they were on and looked down in the water where the captain was pointing. He was absolutely right! I started taking what turned out to be a great series of pictures of mating sea turtles.

It's quite a show, a tiring one for the female, as there's often a second male onlooker waiting his chance. She also does the swimming for both of them, as his flippers are busy just holding on.

The fascination of the marine turtle goes a lot further than their mating behavior. They can hold their breath for hours at a time, a process not well understood, but amazing nonetheless. Even more amazing is the growing evidence suggesting that the females return to the very beach on which they were hatched to nest and lay their eggs.

The marine turtle weighs 100-200 lbs and is a vegetarian, feeding on similar algae as the marine iguana, although the turtle's diet is not as narrowly restricted.

Photo Opportunities: If your tour occurs during the mating season, you'll get several shots of mating couples and threesomes. Your best photo opportunity will occur as you drift through the mangroves of Black Turtle Cove in the *panga,* the motor off to keep *"tourist interruptus"* to a minimum. The thick mangrove forest blocks out a lot of the sunlight, so you want to be shooting high speed film. In or out of mating season, marine turtles will swim past the *panga,* just under the surface of the water. Make sure your polarizing filter is on, and rotate the front filter until you can clearly see underwater with a minimum of reflection. This will also enable you to get some shots of the white-tipped reef shark (*tintorera*), which also swims these waters, as well as spotted eagle rays and cow-nosed rays.

As you're drifting along, keep alert in all directions. On shore, you will occasionally see a female resting between rounds. In the water, the head of a marine turtle will break the surface from time to time, mouth agape, to catch a breath of air, accompanied by a loud exhale. If you catch this shot just right, you can convince your friends you visited Loch Ness South when you show them the photos. The white-tipped sharks and rays will suddenly come into view, and just as quickly be gone. You have to be ready and fast to catch the action here, but it's worth the effort. This is also a great video opportunity.

Where To See Them: The marine turtle can be seen mating during the later part of the year in several beach locations just offshore and primarily in the secluded lagoons. Their favorite location is appropriately called Black Turtle Cove (Caleta Tortuga Negra) on the northern end of Santa Cruz Island; *tortuga negra,* by the way, is another local name for the Pacific green turtle. For those on 2 week Galápagos tours, there will be another opportunity to view sea turtles (as well as penguins) up close in the lagoon at Elizabeth Bay on Isabela Island.

Despite the extremely high mortality rate of the hatchlings, due to natural and introduced predators, the number of marine turtles continues to remain high in the Galápagos.

LAVA LIZARDS – *(LAGARTIJAS DE LAVA)*

These lizards, from four to eight inches in length, were marked with colours which I was beginning to expect in these islands, grey and black and scarlet-ash, and lava and flame – appropriate for a land where every hill was a volcano, every path a flow of lava, and with the plants growing from tufa beds and ash heaps. The male lizards were grey and brown above, mottled and banded with black, with the throat and underparts a mixture of pink, red and contrasting black. The females were usually more of a monochrome brown, with a brilliant slash of fiery scarlet over face, shoulders and sides. They ran and frolicked about, running in and out of the lava crevices, with always a lookout for marauding birds. Of course they were absolutely tame and investigated all our luggage. When pursued, they would impudently pause until almost within reach, at the last moment going through a great show of intimidation, nodding the whole head and body violently up and down, and expanding the scarlet and black throat pouch to its fullest.

William Beebe, 1924

Beebe's accurate descriptions of the lava lizard appeared in the best-selling **GALAPAGOS: WORLD'S END** (see the Literature section at the end of this book). The narrative account of adaptive radiation is most graphic.

In all, the lava lizard has evolved to form seven endemic species in the Galápagos, with differences in size, color, and behavior. They all have many of the intriguing characteristics typical of lizards, such as the ability to regenerate a tail sacrificed in exchange for freedom and to change color as a function of mood and/or temperature. What is unusual is the advanced development of color vision in the lava lizard, which is said to play a role in the courtship process, as the females have bright red throats during the mating season.

Lava lizards live up to 10 years, a relatively long time for such little beasts. They are omnivores, but dine mostly on insects.

Photo Opportunities: A close-up on the rocks is in order, especially a few shots of the red-throated female. For documentation, it would be great to shoot one while it was "tiptoeing" (to help regulate its body temperature by reducing the heat exchange potential).

Where To See Them: On most islands. While lava lizards are not the most exciting animals to watch, you may want to observe their territorial "push-up" behavior, which is said to vary from island to island.

SNAKES – *(CULEBRAS)*

While not high on the "photo-op" list or even on the "want to see" list for most tourists, the Galápagos snakes are first of all harmless to us and secondly quite fascinating. Slender and about a yard long, the 3 endemic species are technically constrictors. As with many of the Galápagos wildlife, there's more to it than that. While they will coil about an object, they actually kill their prey (lava lizards, painted locusts, etc.) with their rear fangs as it is being swallowed. The evil-looking forked tongue flicking through the air is actually detecting scent particles and conveying them (in stereo, for relative location information) to the mouth where the tongue is drawn past specialized sensory structures called Jacobson's Organs (found in all reptiles but especially well-developed in snakes and lizards).

Where to See Them: You're probably still more interested in not seeing them, and you probably won't. They are very cryptic, and sightings are typically on the upper beach transition areas, such as the Visitor Sites at North Seymour and Santa Fé Islands.

SEA BIRDS

Of all the animals that call the Galápagos archipelago their home, only the aquatic birds (sea birds and shore birds) can come and go as they please. Thus, it is not surprising that the rate of endemism is low. Of the land-based animals, including reptiles, mammals, and land birds, over 80 percent are endemic to the Galápagos; of the nineteen species of sea birds, only five are endemic to the islands. Two of those five, the penguin and flightless cormorant, do not have the ability to leave via the air and are thus also captive endemic species.

While having the ability to leave, sea birds have obviously chosen to call the Galápagos their home. They were among the early settlers of the archipelago, as there were fish in the ocean well before there were plants and insects ashore to form the food supply for the land-based animals. In fact, it is the sea birds themselves who carried most of the pioneer plant seeds to the Galápagos, stuck to their wings and feet as well as in their digestive systems.

In the ocean-dominated environment of the archipelago, the sea birds play a most important role. Many of your hours in the Galápagos will be spent observing their behavior in flight, on the ground, along the surface of the ocean, and under the water. Their low rate of endemism does not take away from the fascination of observing these marvelous birds. For those of you that are non-birders or feel that our winged friends are "nice, but dull," you're in for a most pleasant surprise, for the members of the nesting sea bird community of the Galápagos Islands are most unusual, visually and behaviorally interesting, as well as extremely entertaining.

Note: Most all the sea birds feed on surface fish and squid who in turn depend on a continuous supply of algae for their food. For the algae to grow, nutrients are required. It is the current-generated upwelling activity that brings these nutrients to the surface. In the extreme *El Niño*/Southern Oscillation (ENSO) of 1982-83, the Humboldt Current (responsible for upwelling) failed, and the food chain was broken. With most of the algae gone, there were significantly fewer fish that swam near the surface, thus drastically reducing the sea birds' food supply. While the adults were able to survive with little impact to the overall population, as we'll see later on, this wasn't true of the ground-based penguin and flightless cormorant. Also, in many cases the hatchling mortality rate was extremely high.

Migrant species will not be discussed.

WAVED ALBATROSSES – *(ALBATROS DE GALAPAGOS)*

While most albatrosses are found in cool, southern waters, a species endemic to the Galápagos has evolved – the waved albatross. The largest bird in the islands, weighing about 10 lb with a wing span approaching 8 ft, the waved albatross is named for the wavy grey lines on its white undercarriage. Starting early in April, virtually the entire nation of waved albatross adults (over 10,000 couples) arrives at Española (Hood) Island to nest and breed, where they remain until the end of the year.

Upon arrival, the first order of business is breeding, followed by egg laying, hatching, and rearing. There is no time to waste, as the young albatross (or "bird of the year," in ornithologist talk) needs to be fledged by December, when the southern current slackens, significantly reducing the upwelling and the resultant food supply. The fact that time is short is further understood when the 60 day incubation period and the 167 days to fledge are factored in.

That only a single egg is laid is understandable, given its weight of about 1/2 lb. That the parents roll the egg around each day, despite the obvious risk of it cracking, is less understandable. This activity increases the hatching potential, but to date the reason for this has not been documented. After the 2 month incubation period, the chick is hatched and a unique feeding process begins. Many sea birds travel great distances to find food for their family, and on the return flights must guard their catch of fish and/or squid from the piratical frigatebirds. The waved albatross digests and stores its catch as an oily blend; it does not return to base until the supply room is full, thus ensuring much larger portions than it could otherwise carry as well as an incident-free journey.

The courtship behavior, at its peak in October, is quite the ritual, an elaborately choreographed set of moves. It is by no means a quiet celebration; as their long bills circle each other, they make loud, castanet-like clicking sounds and high-pitched vocalizations, most appropriate background music for the dance, which ornithologists have elaborately notated.

After the last dance is done, a strange thing happens – nothing! The marriage is not consummated; breeding behavior does not happen – at least not yet. For now, the couple have formed (or reformed, as these beautiful birds mate for life) what is termed a "pair bond." Breeding will wait for the following spring (as explained above), when the pair will return to Española.

The serious *El Niño*/Southern Oscillation (ENSO) of 1982-83 resulted in a complete breeding failure; not a single egg hatched! Fortunately, for a couple of reasons, this doesn't seem to have affected the population. First is their relatively long life span, about 40-50 years; thus, one bad year has minimal effect. Second, the waved albatross tends to only breed about every other year on the average, so the ENSO seems to have altered the schedule rather than the overall population.

Photo Opportunities: The colors of the waved albatross are very rich and will provide you with some beautiful pictures. A telephoto lens is recommended. If you arrive in the fall, the courtship ritual is a must, which is said to be more pronounced towards evening. Great for video cameras too! The feeding behavior is somewhat humorous as the oversized, downy juveniles are the ultimate "Baby Huey" look-alikes (see Photo #41).

Where To See Them: On Española (Hood) Island. If you want to see the waved albatross, plan your visit to the Galápagos between April and the beginning of December.

BLUE-FOOTED BOOBIES – *(PIQUEROS PATAS AZULES)*

Of all the birds in the Galápagos, none is more famous than the blue-footed booby. Boobies are well represented in the islands, with three resident species. The derivation of their name most likely comes from Spanish sailors, who, between the birds' silly behavior and funny-colored feet, decided they truly were clowns (bobos). The birds would perch on raised hatches near the bow of British ships; this, as you can guess, is the origin of the term "booby hatch," which today has another uncomplimentary meaning, similar to "loony bin." There are, by the way, no loons in the Galápagos – none with wings at any rate.

While we're on the subject of names, the Spanish call boobies *piqueros* (lances), referring to the shape of their beaks. All three species dive steeply into the water, hitting the surface with tremendous force. Air sacs located in the skull serve as built-in shock absorbers, yet another interesting piece of evolutionary work. In addition, the blue-foots have proportionally longer tails than the other two species, which act as a rudder and allow them to make bullet-like dives in less than 2 ft of water and thus feed closer to shore. The male has a somewhat longer tail, although the difference is not readily apparent to most visitors. And you can't tell he from she by who's sitting on the "pseudo-nest," because they share the brooding chore.

There are other ways in which male and female blue-footed boobies are easily distinguished – via sight and sound. The male's eye pupil appears to be smaller than the female's; in reality, the pupils are the same size, with the female's pupil surrounded by pigmentation. Also, in a bit of a role reversal, he is a whistling soprano while she is a honking tenor.

Aside from the color of their feet, it is their courtship dance for which the blue-footed boobies are so well known. After watching a few performances, I seriously wondered whether the choreographers of **OKLAHOMA** ever visited the Galápagos. It's easy to imagine a Broadway-style western dance while watching these little creatures looking up at the sky with wings behind their backs, tilting their heads to one side and then the other, while the feet are lifted in sequence, pointed out at a 45 degree angle.

The nest-building behavior of the blue-footed booby can be described as vestigial; twigs and other nesting materials are dutifully gathered but are never used, as the eggs are laid and incubated on the bare ground. This reminds me of a dog trying to bury a bone in the house by pawing at the carpet, going through the inbred motions.

During incubation, both parents take turns brooding, sitting out in the heat of the sun. At this time, a couple of interesting temperature-regulatory systems are put to work. The first, called gular fluttering, is characteristic of many sea birds, and it is an easily-observed behavior of the boobies. They look like they're gargling, while the function is closer to panting. What flutters and does the cooling is the gular sac, a loose flap of skin in the throat area. Another built-in temperature control device is the webbed foot, which, owing to its heavy vasculature, is an excellent heat exchanger. Thus, to provide warmth, blue-footed boobies gently place their webbed feet directly under the egg or chick.

An average of two chicks are hatched a few days apart. Rarely will more than one survive (the exceptions being in years of plentiful food). Typically the older chick, with its superior strength, will out-compete for the available food from the parents, eventually starving out the younger one. Another technique is for the older chick to force the younger one out of the nesting ring (a circle of guano), sort of a miniature sumo wrestling match, with the consequences here much more dire for the loser; once outside the ring, it is outside the family and no longer cared for. This kind of behavior seems cruel to us, especially when we see a dead or dying youngster lying just off the trail. This is a natural insurance policy, however; if something tragic were to happen to the older chick, the younger one would be raised. This guarantees a survival factor for each generation and guards against mass-starvation in the event of a major food shortage. Given the unpredictable nature of the environment, including the availability of food, this is a very practical system.

Photo Opportunities: Many of the blue-footed boobies choose a nesting site 1-2 ft off the trail, and as is the case with so many of the animals in the Galápagos, they do not move away when approached. Thus, you will have the chance at some great close-ups, especially of their pretty blue feet. The blue coloring will really jump out on a hazy day, early in the morning, or late in the afternoon. If you're shooting in direct sunlight, use a polarizing filter to get rid of the reflected glare coming off their feet, and you'll get deeper blue coloring. Also, if you're patient and look closely, you'll see one with the egg(s) and/or the chick(s) underneath. Occasionally, you'll see a recently-hatched chick and the broken shell, which together with the blue-footed background, makes for a great shot. This will often occur in the shade of the parent, so make sure your light meter isn't picking up ambient light. A spot meter would be useful in this tricky situation; if you increase the exposure to get the detail on the chick, you may wash out the blue coloring on the feet. The best is to bracket.

If you're lucky enough to see some landings during the breeding season, they come in with their feet up and forward, using them like flaps on an airplane. It's an excellent opportunity to get an outstanding blue-footed photo. The whole landing scene is great for video cameras as well.

The courtship dance is another wonderful opportunity, both for still and video photography. It's not a continuous dance, so you have to scan the colony carefully and anticipate the next likely dance partners.

Where To See Them: You are likely to see large colonies of blue-footed boobies on Española and Seymour Islands most times of the year. Another large colony exists on Daphne Major, an islet which is not included in most tours due to restrictions on the number of visitors set by the National Park.

MASKED BOOBIES – (*PIQUEROS ENMASCARADOS*)

Owing to their large size, masked boobies need a bit of takeoff assistance from the wind, and thus nest on high locations near the coast. They feed further out at sea but otherwise have many of the same behavioral patterns as the blue-foots, although less pronounced. This includes the somewhat vestigial nesting behavior, whereby twigs and other materials are offered to the mate as part of the courtship ritual (see Photo #45). A behavioral pattern that is decidedly more pronounced is the siblicide (older chick to younger) that almost always occurs when both eggs hatch (not that frequently). This isn't simply an outcompeting for food or a nudging out of the nest area, but a bloody, frontal attack. Why such a seemingly-brutal behavior has evolved is yet another mystery for future generations of biologists to solve.

Photo Opportunities: Masked boobies are extremely photogenic, with brilliant white coloring and a black face mask. They are frequently seen by the edge of a cliff, posed on a rock. A soft focus on the sea and sky adds to the dignity of this profile shot. The juveniles, with their downy, half-feathered appearance, are the ultimate boobs, and will no doubt provide you with some amusing photos.

Where To See Them: On the steep slopes of Tower (Genovesa) and Española (Hood) Islands. Unlike the other boobies, the masked has a fixed breeding cycle, although it varies from island to island. Thus, you are likely to see courtship/nesting behavior on Tower from May to February, and on Española from September to May.

RED-FOOTED BOOBIES – *(PIQUEROS PATAS ROJAS)*

Feeding on flying fish far out at sea, the red-footed booby tends to nest on the outer islands of the archipelago. Unlike the other boobies, the red-foot nests in trees; it has little claws at the end of its webbed feet that are suitable for perching. It also builds real nests which, although nothing more than a fragile looking arrangement of a few twigs, is a marked departure from the other boobies, who nest on the open ground.

Photo Opportunities: The photogenic qualities of the red-footed boobies were noted in detail by the famous zoologist, William Beebe, in the following vivid description; Beebe takes the opportunity to point out that these boobies truly were *bobos* (clowns):

> *When one of them looked down its long beak at me it reminded me more than anything else of a circus clown in full regalia. The bill was greenish-yellow shading into blue at the tip, the base of the bill and narrow forehead pink, set off by jet black pigment behind. The skin around the eye was bright blue grey, the eye itself cadmium-yellow, framed by eyelids of clear forget-me-not blue. When the bright red feet were added to this, the harlequin effect was most striking. And with it all, the bird wore an air of anxious sobriety which heightened the bizarreness of the colour scheme.*
>
> *William Beebe, 1924*

Where To See Them: While the red foot has the highest population of all the boobies in the Galápagos, it spends much of its time on the open seas and thus appears to be more scarce than the others. While scattered colonies exist on the outer fringes of the Galápagos, the red-footed booby can best be seen by visitors on Tower (Genovesa) Island, where well over 100,000 pairs come to nest. A colony also exists on Punta Pitt, San Cristóbal Island.

FLIGHTLESS CORMORANTS – *(CORMORANS NO VOLADOR)*

The flightless cormorant is endemic to the Galápagos Islands and is the only grounded cormorant species (out of about thirty species overall) in the world. This is yet another fascinating example of evolution to fill a niche. In this case, the niche was the lack of competition for an available food source (bottomfish, eels, and octopuses) close to shore. At the same time, there was a lack of predators, thus reducing the need to flee on the wing. What took place was a slow, gradual evolution to a streamlined body (for swimming speed) and strong legs (for powerful diving ability), while the wings and supporting musculature atrophied through the generations. The sparsely-feathered wings are now considered vestigial.

Not only does the flightless cormorants swim as a means of hunting, but for romantic purposes as well. In a courtship display reminiscent of an Esther Williams movie, both male and female engage in an aquatic dance. Nesting takes place on the beaches of the western islands, just above the high water line; the nests are made of flotsam and jetsam, held together by seaweed.

In behavior uncharacteristic of Galápagos sea birds, flightless cormorants do not mate for life. In fact, after the eggs are hatched and the chicks partially raised, the female often takes up with another male, leaving dad to continue raising the young on his own.

Photo Opportunities: Although the wings are no longer used for flying purposes, the flightless cormorant still stretches its wings wide to dry them, which makes for a great photographic opportunity (see Photo #57). You may be lucky enough to get a chance at a sunrise or sunset shot, where the cormorant can be silhouetted against the golden twilight colors. Also, look for the beautiful turquoise eye, which may take some patience, as they often seem to have their eyes closed. It's worth the wait; with the right lighting, the shot will be amongst your best.

Where To See Them: Only on the western islands of Fernandina and Isabela, due to the high level of upwelling activity; there they can be found nesting on the beaches throughout the year.

The flightless cormorant is a vulnerable species. During a prolonged famine, it can not simply leave the islands in search of food elsewhere. Consequently, the already fragile number of 800 pairs was reduced by about 50 percent during the severe 1982-83 *El Niño*/Southern Oscillation (ENSO), from which there has fortunately been a recovery. A larger danger to survival is in attack from wild dogs. The flightless cormorant gave up its wings partially because there were no natural predators on land. Now, with introduced feral animals, the population could be threatened.

FRIGATEBIRDS – *(FRAGATAS)*

The frigates were war ships, commonly used by pirates; frigatebirds are the pirate ships of the air, a name earned by reputation and habit. They are built for and look the part. Adult frigatebirds are large, black birds with long wingspans and deeply forked tails, which combine to give them exceptional aerial maneuverability. They have excellent vision and are fast, being extremely lightweight for their size. Their weapon is a long hooked-tip beak. They chase after other ocean birds returning home from fishing trips, harassing them in midair until the food is disgorged and dropped. The frigatebird then quickly and expertly swoops down and plucks the food out of the air. The most common victims of this aerial piracy are the boobies and red-billed tropicbird.

The outlaw ways of the frigatebird are described in several texts as cleptoparasitic feeding patterns! Despite the terminology, this is not an aberrant behavioral pattern which formed as a result of an underprivileged youth; it is an evolved trait, formed out of necessity. The frigatebird does not have a large enough preen gland to supply the amount of oil required to effectively waterproof its wings. Since it easily can become waterlogged, it cannot dive into the water after spotting a fish in the manner of the other sea birds. This is not to say, however, that it is incapable of directly catching its own food. On the contrary, it flies low over the water and uses the tip of its beak to expertly pluck a fish or squid from the surface. The limitation of this system is the availability of food near the surface, which is seasonal at best (due to the upwelling patterns), and not at all during a bad *El Niño* year. Thus, piracy evolved as a way of survival.

Frigatebirds nest in trees and bushes. When the single egg is hatched, the parental responsibilities have just begun; it takes the juveniles about 6 months to learn to fly and over a year to learn the world-class stunt flying skills required to survive on its own.

Photo Opportunities: One of the most sought-after photographs in the Galápagos is the bright red inflated balloon-like sac of the male frigatebird. During courtship, a group of males "on display" is seated in trees or shrubs, sacs inflated. When a female passes by overhead, they turn skyward, shake, and loudly call attention to themselves. Not very subtle, but an effective technique, as the female soon accepts an offer and lands next to her chosen mate. Occasionally the males will take to the air with their sacs still inflated, which makes for a great photo opportunity. Telephoto lenses are required.

Part of your daily diet at sea will be fresh fish. When the cook (*cocinero*) cleans the fish, a squadron of frigatebirds will soon be overhead, seeming to glide without effort by moving their forked tails in and out. This makes for a wonderful opportunity for some great on-the-wing shots, and if you can convince the cook to do this towards late afternoon, you'll have excellent back lighting (see the back cover and Photo #37).

Where To See Them: There are 2 species of frigatebirds in the Galápagos – the "great" and the "magnificent" (sounds like a spaghetti western). While they can be physically distinguished from each other we'll take the easy road and do it by geographic location. The "great" is more ocean going, and thus tends to be an outer island bird; a large colony can be seen displaying on Darwin Bay, Tower (Genovesa) Island during the first half of the year. There is also a colony on Punta Pitt, San Cristóbal Island. The "magnificent" are more central in their distribution; just about all the tours visit their colony on N. Seymour Island, where they can be seen displaying throughout the year.

Individuals from both species are distributed throughout the islands and everywhere at sea on their piratical journeys.

SWALLOW-TAILED GULLS – *(GAVIOTAS DE COLA BIFURCADA)*

Forming the night-shift of the working class sea birds, swallowed-tailed gulls are endemic to the Galápagos Islands. Every evening they fly out to sea, feeding on surface fish and squid. They are aided in their nocturnal hunting by extraordinary night vision as well as by the luminescent microorganisms that often "light up" these waters. Night hunting appears to be a form of adaptive behavior for the swallow-tailed gull, evolving from the necessity of bringing back food safely (as frigatebirds are not nocturnal) and/or the greater abundance of fish and squid on the surface at night. The latter is another form of adaptive survival behavior on the part of fish and squid – feeding on the surface at night and staying in deep waters during daylight to avoid predators.

The swallow-tailed gull is noted for its vocal repertoire, including its alarm call, a "shake, rattle, and scream" alerting other members of the colony to the presence of an intruder.

Photo Opportunities: The swallow-tailed gull is a beautiful bird. It will be the first to greet you on dry landings along rocky shorelines, as you step out of the *panga* onto the steppingstone pier. Surprisingly, it won't fly off as you approach within a couple of feet. The coloring is so perfect, you can't pass up the shot. Its bright red eye-rings are set off against large dark eyes and a charcoal head, while the red feet are contrasted with its pink legs, and grey and white plumage.

Where To See Them: Along the sea cliff of most of the central and northern islands, where excellent in-flight and landing shots can be taken. There are major colonies on South Plaza, Tower (Genovesa) and N. Seymour. In all, there are an estimated 10,000-15,000 pairs of swallow-tailed gulls in the Galápagos.

LAVA GULLS – *(GAVIOTAS DE LAVA)*

The lava gull, endemic to the Galápagos Islands, is somewhat enigmatic. Though it is quite scarce, with only about 400 pairs, it doesn't seem to be in any danger of extinction. In fact, there's no evidence to suggest that the population was ever any greater. Considering their small numbers, lava gulls are quite casual in their nesting habits; the first nest wasn't found until the 1960s.

They may not have sound breeding patterns, but they are very protective when they do breed and are known for their dive-bombing attacks on intruders. From the rest of their habits, one can either classify lava gulls as lazy ne'er-do-wells or as filling the niche of the scavenger. They do scavenge, hanging around boat harbors and the fringes of coastal towns. They beg, permanently borrow, steal, and when they have to, hunt food. The loud laugh-like call supports their non-industrious image.

Photo Opportunities: Lava gulls, true to their name, blend in perfectly with the coastal lava rocks. You may want to get a close-up documentation shot; their white eye-ring makes a good focal point. If you can get a shot while they are "laughing," you can capture the beautiful deep red color in the inside of the open-gaped mouth. The entire laugh sequence is great on video.

Where To See Them: Here and there, on the coastal areas of the central islands. They can also be found on Tower (Genovesa) Island. The only significant numbers are found in the bays and lagoons of Puerto Ayora on Santa Cruz Island, owing to the scavenging potential offered by the touring and fishing boats as well as the large human population.

BROWN NODDIES – *(GAVIOTINES)*

These tern-like birds are in fact classified as terns, and they are sometimes called noddy terns or brown noddy terns. They are very delicate-looking dark brown birds with a greyish-white cap. They actually do "nod" to each other as part of the courtship ritual.

Photo Opportunities: You can sometimes get close to noddies during cliffside *panga* rides as they nest on narrow ledges on sheer walls. Make sure to get the greyish-white cap in the photo. Due to an underdeveloped preen (waterproofing) gland, noddies can not land in the ocean, lest they get waterlogged. Perhaps for this reason, they are often seen landing on the head of pelicans and feeding off the side of the pelican's bill. Whatever the reason, it is a predictable scene that makes for a great shot or video sequence.

Where to See Them: Throughout the islands (in the same locations as brown pelicans), and specifically at Tagus Cove (Isabela Island), Floreana (at various locations), and Rábida.

BROWN PELICANS – *(PELICANOS)*

Often seen flying in formation, their wings alternately beating and gliding in synch, pelicans are one of the few familiar vacation landmarks that you'll see in the Galápagos – an old friend, and nice to have around.

Photo Opportunities: Here are a few more pelican scenes to add to your collection. If you're an early riser, go on-deck and check out the *panga* (towed behind the yacht). Once in a while, there will be a pelican seated at the helm, which makes for an interesting caption shot. This opportunity might also occur when the cook casts the dinner scraps overboard. A dramatic sequence of pictures can be taken at sunset, when one plunge-diving pelican after another is silhouetted against the glowing orange and red of the evening sky. During courtship, pelicans often intertwine their necks (brown-naped in breeding plumage) and bills in an interesting pattern, which makes for another good photo opportunity (see Photo #58). Also, if you can get the sun behind a parent feeding a chick, the head of the chick can be seen inside the parent's back-lit pouch; it's quite an image if you can capture it.

Where To See Them: As in many parts of the world, brown pelicans are seen on just about every coast, dock, harbor, and anchorage in the Galápagos. There is often a nesting colony on the beach at Rábida Island.

GALAPAGOS PENGUINS – *(PINGUINOS DE GALAPAGOS)*

What would possess a penguin to live on the equator? These flightless sea birds (they do technically fly, but only underwater) seem much more at home on an ice floe and/or the waters of the Antarctic. Once again the answer lies in the Humboldt Current, owing both to its direction and the cold waters it brings from the South Polar region.

This is not to say that the first penguins to arrive at the archipelago started their journey in the Antarctic Ocean; rather, the endemic Galápagos species originated in the extreme southern part of South America – the cold, stormy region known as Chilean Patagonia. One scenario is that they arrived during an Ice Age and were subsequently stranded as the earth warmed and the ice melted.

Penguins feed on small fish and crustaceans, using their swimming speed to advantage. As is true of several species of the sea birds, they mate for life.

Photo Opportunities: If you are fortunate enough to visit the western islands, have your camera ready as you ride in the *panga*. Scan the bases of the rocky cliffs, where penguins are often seen standing outside the lava caves in which they nest. For most of you, this opportunity may occur on Bartolomé Island, but the colonies here are much smaller and the sightings are infrequent. When you do see them, notice how their "arms" are out at an angle, as if carrying a pair of invisible suitcases. This is a penguin heat exchange system, facing into the breeze and using the blood vessels in their wings as cooling fins. The photography is tricky, due to the dark background. While it may be necessary to underexpose the shot by a full stop (to negate the effect of the dark rocks and shadows on your light meter), the underexposure time may be significantly less than 1/60th of a second (especially if you have a telephoto lens on). The key is to use fast film (ASA 400) and to bracket the shot.

Snorkeling in these waters may give you the rare opportunity of getting a few underwater penguin photos. It's a real difficult shot because of their blazing underwater speed. The trick is to stop moving once you see them, and try to hang out near a school of small, sardine-like fish that are often in the area. The penguins will often return (for the fish, primarily), and they are extremely curious; I have often had them swim up to my underwater still or video camera and actually peck at it. If you try to follow or chase them, however, they're gone!

Where To See Them: As pointed out above, the Galápagos penguin has a natural nesting and feeding preference for the cooler waters of the western islands, Fernandina, and Isabela. There is also a small colony on Bartolomé, near the famous Pinnacle Rock. Occasionally penguins are also seen off the coast of Floreana, swimming close to the beach.

The Galápagos penguin was severely affected by the 1982-83 *El Niño/ Southern Oscillation* (ENSO), with losses estimated at over 75 percent! They are very slowly recovering, too slowly according to some. Population figures widely vary from a few thousand to less than a thousand individuals.

HAWAIIAN (DARK-RUMPED) PETRELS – *(PATAS PEGADAS)*

Almost extinct in Hawaii, this large, graceful sea bird is making a comeback in the Galápagos from "endangered" status (due to rat predation of chicks, as they nest in highland burrows). The Hawaiian petrel has the appearance of an Audubon's shearwater, but it is much larger. As it soars at a very steep angle on wave-generated currents, it shows off its gleaming white undersurface.

Photo Opportunities: Slim to none, as the sightings are on the wing at sea and usually at considerable distance.

Where to See Them: While cruising off elevated islands, such as Santa Cruz, Floreana, and most often, Isabela.

AUDUBON'S SHEARWATERS – *(PUFINOS)*

These countershaded sea birds (having typical, cryptic coloration with black on top and white underneath) are often seen in large aggregations on the surface of the ocean. They literally do shear the water as they soar back and forth, just grazing the wave crests.

Photo Opportunities: The best opportunities are during *panga* rides. If a flock is resting on the ocean, they will sometimes take off *en masse* as the *panga* approaches. Depending on the background and the lighting, it could be an excellent wide-angle shot.

Where to See Them: Throughout the islands. They are particularly enjoyable to watch on South Plaza Island, as they approach the cliffs in formation at top speed, seemingly on a destruction run. They are actually trying to locate (through a heightened sense of smell) their cliff-side dwellings.

STORM PETRELS – *(GOLONDRINAS DE TORMENTA)*

These are the tiny black-and-white (countershaded) birds often seen flitting on the surface of the ocean. Named after St. Peter, they do seem to walk on water as their feet are stirring up plankton (their food). As the story goes, if you see them approaching shore, it is indicative of an approaching storm. To carry it further, the term "stormy petrel" refers to a person who generally only shows up to bring bad news. There are 3 resident species in the Galápagos – the white-vented (or Elliot's), the wedge-rumped (or Galápagos), and the white-banded (or Maderian). As their names imply, identification, at least in part, is made by sorting out the tail markings.

Photo Opportunities: Too small and too far. If you have a long, fast lens and you really want it, you can get a good shot of a storm petrel "walking on water."

Where to See Them: Around the boat, here and there. Storm petrels are good indicators of a productive ocean, and you often see them while cruising off the western islands of Fernandina and Isabela.

Occasionally, there are tens of thousands of wedge-rumped storm petrels "swarming" in bat-like flight, trying to smell-locate their lava tube dwellings on Tower Island (Prince Philip's Steps).

RED-BILLED TROPICBIRDS – *(PAJAROS TROPICALES or PILOTOS)*

The red-billed tropicbird is one of the most beautiful and graceful birds in the Galápagos. Hearing their piercing cries as they fly back and forth near the steep cliffs, your eyes are drawn upwards, riveted by the long, kite-like streaming tails (see Photos #26-27). Occasionally, one will swoop down and disappear from view; when you look down over the ledge, you can sometimes spot the white tail-feathers blowing in the strong off-shore winds, protruding out of a crevice in the lava rocks. This is the nest, ideally located for protection and takeoffs, but a most difficult landing target in the swirling winds.

Despite their beauty and grace, the red-billed tropicbirds seem to lead a somewhat dangerous life. The desired nesting locations are limited and frequently fought over. Once a site is settled and the single egg is laid and hatched, getting food back to the precarious nest isn't easy. It's a long journey, for they feed far out at sea (primarily on flying fish). On the return flight, the frigatebirds are ever on the ready for mid-air piracy. Thus, there is an iffy food supply, and many hatchlings do not survive.

Photo Opportunities: Once again, a telephoto lens is required. Panning will produce several exciting shots, and often some surreal images, as they are trying to land, their wings beat furiously against the wind in a stalemate (see Photo #28). They will sometimes remain suspended in the air less than 50 ft away, hovering close to their nest, their wings a blur. Another great opportunity for a video camera!

To get your best shots of the red-billed tropicbird requires patience, as they seem to be doing endless laps up and down the coast. Eventually they will make a landing attempt. Follow them in with your eyes, and eventually you'll find a nesting area on an overhanging ledge, where you can get some shots without danger of falling. These nesting shots can be beautiful, as you have a white streaming tail and scarlet red bill against the dark background of the crevice in which they dwell.

Where To See Them: Several locations throughout the Galápagos. Your best views will be on Española (Hood), Tower (Genovesa), and South Plaza Islands, where the trail follows the vertical cliffs. Afternoons are best, when they return from their fishing trips.

COASTAL BIRDS

This section is a fairly diverse group of shore birds, waders, waterfowl, and lagoon birds. While these birds are capable of long distance flight and are often migratory, they do not feed out at sea. Instead, they find their food between the tides, in coastal lagoons, and in runoff ponds around the Highlands.

Note: Several migrant species will not be discussed.

PAINT BILLED CRAKES – *(GALLARETAS)*

While this little rail-like bird is somewhat colorful (red/yellow bill and red legs), it isn't seen that often. It is a resident, and most sightings are in the Highlands.

EGRETS – *(GARZAS BLANCAS)*

These large white wading birds are seen in mangrove lagoons throughout the Galápagos. The great (or American) egret is the largest, with the snowy egret one size smaller. Aside from size, the great egret has a yellow bill (the snowy's is black) and black legs & feet (the snowy has black legs with yellow feet, called "golden slippers" in birder talk). The cattle egret, found in the Highlands, is smaller yet. It is a recent arrival and feeds primarily on insects and other invertebrates associated with cattle and tortoises. Its markings are similar to the great egret, although the cattle egret has greenish-yellow legs for most of the year (pink when breeding) and some degree of buff coloration around the breast, crown, and back (more intense when breeding).

GREAT BLUE HERONS – *(GARZAS MORENAS)*

The name "great blue heron" is a bit of a misnomer. While it is certainly the largest heron in the Galápagos, the great blue is actually grey in appearance; this explains the adjectival portion of its Spanish name, *morena,* meaning dark or dusky. The great blue heron has the long legs and bill typical of wading birds. With its overall size, long legs, dark color, head usually hunched on shoulders, and cowlick-looking head plumes, the "great blue" is readily identifiable. It feeds intertidally, primarily on small fish (occasionally on turtle and iguana hatchlings), waiting patiently and then suddenly stabbing the prey with a quick thrust of the beak.

LAVA HERONS – *(GARZAS DE LAVA)*

The lava heron is the only endemic heron species in the Galápagos. With its dark coloring and small hunched appearance, it is hardly noticeable against the lava rock background as it slinks along in search of food (mostly small fish and Sally Lightfoot crabs).

Note: While now recognized as a separate species, the striated heron is closely related to the lava heron. Identification can be tricky, as the breast area is not always well striated.

YELLOW-CROWNED NIGHT HERONS – *(GARZAS NOCTURNAS)*

This large resident shore bird has more of what appears to be a white crown (head plumes) than a yellow one. Other identification marks include white cheek patches, orange eyes, and yellow feet. As its name implies, it is mostly nocturnal in its feeding habits. During the day, the yellow-crowned night heron is often seen at rest, typically on a ledge.

GREATER FLAMINGOS – *(FLAMENCOS)*

There are about 500 greater flamingos inhabiting the many hypersalinic (saltier than the ocean) lagoons of the Galápagos. The salts are concentrated due to evaporation of the relatively shallow water (which filters in from the ocean), providing the ideal habitat for the flamingo's main food – a pink shrimp called *"artemia."* The flamingo digest the shrimp, but not the pink pigment, which it "picks up" as its own beautiful coloring.

The greater flamingo is a filter feeder (in the manner of a baleen whale), stirring up the oozy lagoon bottom by shaking its submerged head back and forth. The agitated sediment is then ingested and sifted through rows of filter plates (called lamellae) lining its bill. What makes this behavior even more fascinating is that the flamingo's head is upside-down while feeding. The physiology is a bit upside-down as well, with the upper jaw free to move up and down during feeding (instead of being fixed to the skull as it is in almost all other birds and mammals).

Flamingos, as their name implies, are the consummate *flamenco* dancers, featuring several birds pacing in synchrony, honking loudly, their necks stretched high, and their heads turning back & forth. A scene worth waiting for.

AMERICAN OYSTERCATCHERS – *(OSTREROS)*

These beautiful countershaded waders catch a lot more than oysters. Their distinctive, bright reddish-orange beak is both a hammer and a knife. Using this stout, structurally-reinforced tool, the oystercatcher can stab a bivalve between the shells and quickly slice the strong adductor muscles to get at the meat inside, or hammer away at the shell of a sea urchin, crab, or mollusk.

It seems that the oystercatchers are more approachable now than, say 10 years ago. Actually, they approach you or seem to, as they patrol the beaches for food. My theory is that the chicks (they are residents, nesting just back of the high tide line) get used to tourists being around during their "imprinting" stage of development. Unlike the sea bird chicks that are dependent on their parents for food for quite a long time (termed altricial), the little "oysterettes" are precocial (typical of shore birds), and they are often seen trying to get their own food when just a few weeks old. You often hear oystercatchers (they usually travel in pairs) before you see them; their on-the-wing call is a loud, high-pitched "kleep, kleep, kleep."

WHITE-CHEEKED (BAHAMA) PINTAIL DUCKS – *(PATILLOS)*

Yes, there are ducks in the Galápagos. Aside from the white cheeks, they have a beautiful red marking on the base of the bill (more intense in males). You can only see the "pintail" when they are in flight. As you're viewing them through binoculars, look for the green speculum (a glossy patch on their secondary wings, located amidship). Be patient and wait for movement of the wing, because the speculum is usually hidden by the primary wing feathers.

White-cheeked pintails feed on lagoon and pond vegetation.

SEMIPALMATED PLOVERS – *(CHORLITEJOS)*

Semipalmated is quite a handle for this little shore bird, but the expression becomes more friendly if you think of it as semi- or partially palmed. In this case, palmed means webbed. Basically, they're equipped for amphibious travel. Several sea birds have totally webbed feet (e.g., the boobies, pelicans, cormorants, frigates); they are given another wonderful name – totipalmate.

We'll continue in bird talk, and point out that the semipalms have a dark breast band which provides disruptive coloration (the dark band breaks up their body contour to a potential predator). A larger version of the semipalmated plover (with a double breast band) seen in many parks and grasslands in the U.S. is the killdeer.

SANDPIPERS – *(PLAYEROS)*

Often referred to collectively as "peeps," these are the little whitish birds that patrol the water's edge. They are generally migrant species which breed up north (as far as the Arctic region). One of the most common peeps found in the Galápagos is the sanderling; you see them in groups running up and down the beach like a wind-up toy. Also common is the western sandpiper, with its long black bill (longer than its head, which may not be saying much) and black legs. If you see a peep with greenish-yellow legs, it is probably at least a sandpiper.

COMMON (BLACK-NECKED) STILTS – *(TEROS REALES)*

They really do look like they're wearing stilts, with their long pinkish-red legs. The slender, pointed bill is very elegant. This easy to identify resident lagoon wader is another one of those countershaded birds (black on top and white underneath).

COMMON GALLINULES (MOORHENS) – *(GALLINULAS)*

To the inexperienced eye, the moorhen appears to be something between a chicken, a duck, and a shore bird, but it is actually a fully aquatic coot-like rail. The bright red bill and red forehead shield are very striking on this resident lagoon bird.

GALAPAGOS RAILS – *(PACHAYES)*

Endemic to the Galápagos, this tiny brown bird is quite difficult to spot, although birders try to call them out by clapping their hands in vegetated Highland areas.

WANDERING TATTLERS – *(ERRANTES)*

If you see a medium sized, yellow-legged, mostly grey shore bird walking along the rocks and bouncing its butt up and down (teetering is more bird-correct), it's most likely a wandering tattler. It is skittish and does call out a warning as it wanders off – I guess that's tattling.

RUDDY TURNSTONES – *(VUELVE PIEDRAS)*

They are reddish (and white), and in fact they do turn over stones, looking for food (invertebrates). The reddish color intensifies in the spring & fall, and they develop a black breast band as well; they are migrants which breed in the north, and this is their breeding plumage.

Ruddy turnstones are about the same size as plovers, just a bit larger than the sandpipers.

WHIMBRELS – (ZARAPITOS)

You won't confuse the whimbrel with any other bird in the islands. It is quite large and the only non-vagrant (regularly-seen) shore bird in the Galápagos with a very long, down-curved bill. With your binoculars, you can also see the characteristic brown eye-stripes and crown-stripe. The call of the whimbrel is very high-pitched and repetitive; it sounds a bit like an oystercatcher.

Photo Opportunities: Many of the coastal birds are too small and too far away for photography. Many of them are migrants, and as such did not get used to people being around when they were chicks. Thus, they tend to be skittish. This is true for the sandpipers, semipalmated plover, ruddy turnstone, whimbrel, and wandering tattler.

You will have opportunities to photograph the flamingo, but it usually takes a long lens (300mm) that isn't usually necessary for much else in the islands, although the black-necked stilt and white-cheeked pintail duck also fall into this category. With their rich pink coloring, flamingos are great subjects for a variety of photographs. On a calm day, you can capture shots of a single bird of a group of flamingos as well as the reflection in the water. Their running-flapping-splashing takeoffs are quite spectacular, both for still and video cameras. So are on-the-wing shots, with their long neck and legs outstretched.

Good oystercatcher shots are easier to get these days as they are not as skittish as they used to be. In the right light, the long, red bill is very beautiful. Wet, black lava rocks tend to make a perfect background. If you're patient, you can sometimes find them stabbing an invertebrate (sea urchins seem to be one of their favorites), carrying it to its "dining room," and then pecking out a morsel at a time.

Patience also pays off when photographing lava herons. If your group is tide-pooling, just have a seat and wait. There will often be a lava heron in the area, most likely so intent on "fishing" that it will get close enough for a good shot. The yellow-crowned night heron is even more obliging, as it is generally inactive in the daytime, allowing for a close-up or two while it's posed against the rocks.

The great blue heron is a great subject, as it is everywhere. I especially like to take shots of them while they're in the tops of mangroves with the golden lighting you often get during early morning or late afternoon *panga* rides.

Where to See Them: Along shorelines and in lagoon areas everywhere in the islands. Two of the best spot for shore birds are James Bay, James Island and Punta Espinosa, Fernandina Island. Surprisingly, you will find some of the waders (and the white-cheeked pintail duck) near ponds in the Highlands of Santa Cruz. You will see the greater flamingo and the black-necked stilt (as well as the pintail) at Punta Cormorán, Floreana Island, and (if you're on a 2 week trip) the lagoons at Villamil, Isabela Island. Villamil will also be the best opportunity for seeing the common gallinule.

There are some that you probably won't see, due to their secretive behavior; the Galápagos rail and paint-billed crake certainly fall into this category.

LAND BIRDS

*Of land-birds, I obtained twenty-six kinds, all peculiar to the group
and found nowhere else, with the exception of one lark-like finch
from North America.*

Charles Darwin, 1845

Most land birds are medium to small size perching birds with feet well adapted for this purpose – three toes in front and one long toe behind. Land birds do not have the ability of long distance flight. Thus, the only way they could have reached the Galápagos was by chance storms with extremely high winds, carrying the birds across 600 miles of ocean. Owing to the rarity of such conditions, there are very few species of land birds in the Galápagos. Also, those that did arrive and survive couldn't leave. Thus, it is not surprising that out of the twenty-six species of land birds in the islands, twenty-two of them are endemic to the Galápagos. Darwin's count (see above) was right on; not bad for a brief 5 week visit. Speaking of Darwin, the high rate of endemism of the land birds speaks very loudly for the process of evolution. This evidence was not lost on Darwin, as we'll see later on in this section.

The degree of endemism is related to the niche factor once again. Since land birds remain on one island, the degree of evolved specialization varies from island to island as a function of the number of Vegetation Zones. The greater the number of Vegetation Zones on a particular island, the greater the variety of food and the number of niches that are available to be filled, which in turn results in a greater number of specialized evolved land birds on that island.

The degree of specialization is thus ultimately related to food preference. Some of the land birds are vegetarians, relying on green vegetation for their food supply. Another group feeds on insects, while others are seed eaters. Each type has adapted itself, usually in bill structure, to its food preference. This is strikingly noticeable in the finch, a point that became central in Darwin's arguments for natural adaptation and evolutionary processes.

Colorful plumage does not play an important part in the courting habits of the Galápagos land birds. With notable exceptions, such as the vermillion flycatcher and yellow warbler, most are dull-colored.

As a group, land birds are surprisingly tame and can usually be approached for close-up photos.

SMOOTH-BILLED ANIS – *(GARRAPATEROS)*

It's an old story. They were introduced to eat the ticks off cattle and now they are a pest, possibly outcompeting tree finches for food. The ani is a crow-sized black bird with a large, drooping tail and thick black bill. It actually has a very beautiful, distinctive high-pitched call.

Photo Opportunities: I've never known anyone who wanted to take a picture of this introduced bird.

Where to See Them: The Highlands of Santa Cruz, Black Turtle Cove on Santa Cruz, and the inland trail at James Bay, James Island.

DARK-BILLED CUCKOOS – *(CUCLILLOS)*

The dark-billed cuckoo looks like the mockingbird at first, at least until you see the sulfur-yellow breast. And then you realize that the tail is longer and the bill is decidedly shorter than that of the mockingbird. Unlike the European cuckoo, the dark-billed does not make a "cuckoo-like" call nor is it a brood parasite; in other words, it does not lay its eggs in the nests of other bird species, depending on the other (parasitized) birds to incubate the egg(s) and raise the chick(s).

Photo Opportunities: Not many. Usually you are lucky if you an see them at all, and even then it will be at binoculars distance.

Where to See Them: The best spot seems to be the Highlands of Isabela on the way to the Sierra Negra Volcano (on 2 weeks trip). Other locations include the inland trail at James Bay, James Island, and Punta Cormarán, Floreana Island.

GALAPAGOS DOVES – *(PALOMAS)*

Endemic to the islands, the Galápagos dove is the only resident member of the pigeon family (the head-bobbers). It lives in the dry zones, feeding largely on prickly pear (*Opuntia*) cactus seeds and pulp. During courtship, mating pairs occasionally bow to each other, Japanese-style.

Photo Opportunities: The Galápagos dove is a beautiful subject, with its spectacular blue eye-ring as the focal point. It is often half-hidden under shrubs, and your patience will be rewarded with an unobstructed shot.

Where To See Them: On the drier portions of several islands, including Española (Hood), Tower (Genovesa), James, Rábida (Jervis), and Santa Fé.
    In the past, many Galápagos doves were hunted for food. Now protected, and not in immediate danger of extinction, there is still concern over their reduced numbers in areas with feral cat populations.

DARWIN'S FINCHES – *(PINZONES DE DARWIN)*

> *A most singular group of finches, related to each other in the structure of their beaks, short tails, form of body, and plumage. There are 13 species ... peculiar to this archipelago. The most curious fact is the perfect gradation in the size of the beaks in the different species. One might really fancy that from an original paucity of birds in this archipelago, one species had been taken and modified for different ends.*
>
> *Charles Darwin, 1845*

Mighty important words and subject matter, especially when you consider the subject – a small, drab-colored, inconspicuous bird called the Galápagos finch. These birds were so central to Darwin's (r)evolutionary theory that they were given the name "Darwin's finches" in the 1930s. Members of this group include four species of ground finches, two cactus finches, three tree finches, a vegetarian finch, woodpecker finch, mangrove finch, and war-bler finch.

What fascinated Darwin was not only the diversity of what were inar-guably thirteen unique species, but how quickly and purposefully they evolved from a common ancestor (see the section on Adaptive Radiation in Chapter 11). The "purpose" was to adapt (which they did through modifica-tions in beak structure) to the local food supply, which varied tremendously from island to island and even within an island, based on the Vegetation Zone(s). Thus, modifications in beak shape and size facilitated the special-ized diets, including soft seeds, hard seeds, twigs, leaves, cacti, insects, ticks (removed from tortoises and iguanas), and even booby blood (in the case of the sharp-beaked "vampire" ground finch). There are two species (the wood-pecker and mangrove finches) which actually use tools (twigs or cactus spines) to extract insect larvae from holes in the dead branches of trees. These specialized adaptations are textbook examples of niche-filling, purposeful adaptation to exploit an available food source for which there is a minimum of competition. Researchers Peter and Rosemary Grant have actually seen and documented evolution in the Darwin's finches. For a fascinating account of their observations, read **THE BEAK OF THE FINCH** (see the Literature section).

Unlike other animals in the Galápagos that have filled an available niche in the ecosystem, Darwin's finches have maintained a degree of gen-eralization. Thus, while the flightless cormorant has lost the ability to fly, the Darwin's finches can and will change their diet in a time of shortage, such as during a drought. Perhaps this is a purposeful fallback, and some specu-late that over-specialization never developed owing to all the bad years for a particular food supply. Such are the forces of survival and competition.

The competition among males during courtship is not quite as subtle but nonetheless socially interesting. The male builds several side-entrance nests which are used to help attract the female. It's easy to envision several rich men competing for the sweet young thing by impressing her with their accu-mulated land holdings. After selecting a mate, the female may want a house of their own, and yet another nest is built. To carry his devotion even further, the male feeds the female prior to egg laying and after incubation.

Photo Opportunities: Darwin's finches look very similar; it is the varia-tions in beak structure which set them apart. As with the mockingbird, you may want to take a few finch pictures on several islands and compare them after you get back. In this case, you'll also want to take some shots in the dif-ferent Vegetation Zones within the same island, specifically on Santa Cruz. Remember to note down the frame numbers and respective locations. For any kind of success, you'll need a telephoto lens.

Where To See Them: Just about everywhere. Very few casual and begin-ning birders can make positive identifications of all thirteen species, but you can narrow the possibilities based on the island and Vegetation Zone. Even here, there are annual variations based on the availability of a particular food source. Only the medium tree finch is endemic to a particular island – Floreana. Several tours offer an afternoon in the Highlands of Santa Cruz. This is an excellent area to find tree finches as well as the woodpecker finch.

GALAPAGOS (LARGE-BILLED) FLYCATCHERS – (*PAPAMOSCAS*)

True to their name, flycatchers feed on insects, usually chased through the air and caught with a snap of the beak. This beautiful little bird is endemic to the Galápagos. The male and female are virtually identical with a brown back, grey breast and sulfury-yellow belly.

Photo Opportunites: Surprisingly, you can often get fairly close to Galápagos flycatchers. Even then, it is better to use manual focus, as their relatively small size (to the background) will often cause the autofocus feature to "hunt" (alternately try to focus on a branch or the bird). Try to get a gleam of reflected sunlight in the eye.

Where To See Them: They are found on several of the islands you will visit.

VERMILLION FLYCATCHERS — (*PAJAROS BRUJOS*)

There are those who feel that land birds are mostly dull-looking "LBJs" ("little brown jobs"). If that's the rule, the vermillion flycatcher is certainly an exception. The male is a brilliant, bright red with black upperparts, eye stripe, and tail. If that wasn't showy enough, the male puts on a spectacular aerial display, climbing higher and higher in the sky, seemingly by steps, and then suddenly dive-bombing near the female in a "**TOP GUN**" salute to her. The female has no red at all and looks like the Galápagos flycatcher, but has a much brighter yellow belly.

Photo Opportunities: Usually they're on a fence post at a distance or on a plant right next to you, that is until you pick up the camera.

Once in a while, though, you can find a "Hollywood" flycatcher that just seems to pose for your pictures. If you get a reasonably good opportunity, try to position yourself where the red color really pops out. If the red looks washed out to your eyes, it will to the camera as well. Try to keep the background simple and out of focus (with a wide open aperture setting), so that the total emphasis will be on the bird (see Chapter VII, PHOTOGRAPHING THE GALAPAGOS ISLANDS). If you're shooting video, when the flycatcher flies off, resist your reflexes and leave the camera rolling, with the viewfinder fixed on the now-bare branch. Every so often, the bird will return to the same exact spot – seems that it's typical flycatcher behavior.

Where To See Them: In the Highlands of Santa Cruz, San Cristóbal, and (for those on 2 week trips) Isabela Island.

GALAPAGOS HAWKS – (*GAVILANES DE GALAPAGOS*)

While birds of prey (raptors), Galápagos hawks are mostly scavengers, feeding on carrion and playing a useful role in the ecosystem. It has exceptional vision, which refines its skill as a hunter. An endemic species, the Galápagos hawk has an interesting social mating and breeding system in which two or more males mate with a single female and help raise the young. The texts refer to this as cooperative polyandric behavior.

Photo Opportunities: Soaring in wide circles above the coastlines, the Galápagos hawk is easy to spot in the air. With a telephoto lens, you can get some great back-lit shots, lighting up their outstretched rounded wings and broad, fanned tail. Owing to curiosity, a hawk will occasionally perch near-by, and by approaching slowly and carefully, some excellent close-ups can be had. Before approaching, however, ask the Guide if it is safe, for if it is nesting (typically in the summer months), the protective instincts can result in aggressive behavior.

Where To See Them: In the outlying islands. You are most likely to encounter the Galápagos hawk on Española (Hood), Santa Fé, Isabela, Fernandina, and occasionally on James.

While the Galápagos hawk has no natural enemies, it has been hunted (as a varmint) by man to extinction on several islands, including Floreana, San Cristóbal, N. Seymour, Baltra, and Daphne Major. In all, there are just over 100 pairs remaining.

GALAPAGOS MARTINS – (*GOLONDRINAS*)

A large, dark swallow with swept-back wings, this endemic bird is designed for "fighter plane" service, using its swoop-flap-and-glide flight behavior to catch insects.

Photo Opportunities: They dart around at a distance and are not much of a photo object. Just watch and enjoy their flight patterns.

Where to See Them: Here and there, but always in the Highlands of Isabela Island near the Sierra Negra Volcano (for those on 2 week trips).

MOCKINGBIRDS – *(CUCUVES)*

The Galápagos mockingbirds are unusual in several respects. Belying their name (and differing from other mockingbird species), they do not mimic other birds. In many ways, they seem to fill the niche left vacant by the absence of small land mammals. The Galápagos mockingbirds feed on insects, small lizards, young finches, carrion, as well as unprotected food. They tend to get around more by running than by flying. Their breeding behavior is communal, with several generations staying with and defending the family territory as well as assisting in the care and feeding of the juveniles.

To classify this entire group as Galápagos mockingbirds is convenient, but at the same time a bit of a misnomer as there are actually several endemic species and subspecies. The endemic species include the Hood, Chatham, and Charles mockingbirds. The species actually called the Galápagos mockingbird is divided into several subspecies, each named for the island it inhabits. The island-to-island variations include overall size, length of leg, color, voice, and shape of bill. Collectively, they are another excellent example of adaptive radiation, and provided further evidence (in addition to the finches) to support Darwin's theory.

Photo Opportunities: The best opportunities are along the beaches. It might prove interesting to take a shot or two on several islands, making note of the frame numbers, and (with the aid of a field guide) compare the pictures to see if you can spot the variations between the species. The Hood mockingbird, a scavenger, has the longest bill, which you will probably see used to break open an abandoned booby egg; this is part of nature and makes for a good documentation shot and/or video sequence (see Photo #55).

Where To See Them: On most of the main islands. You will see the Hood mockingbird only on Española (Hood) and the Chatham mockingbird only on San Cristóbal (Chatham). The Charles mockingbird is extinct on Charles (Floreana) and is found only on the islets of Champion-near-Floreana and Gardner-near-Floreana, neither of which have Visitor Sites.

SHORT-EARED OWLS – *(LECHUZAS DE CAMPO)*

Not all owls are nocturnal. If there is a lack of competition in the hunting territory, these birds of prey can choose the day shift (diurnal) or even twilight time (crepuscular). Both of these options are selected by the resident short-eared owl, a medium-sized brownish bird. Ask your Guide about all the advanced hunting adaptations that owls are equipped with.

Photo Opportunities: They are difficult enough to find, let alone photograph. Every once in a while there is a short-eared owl eating a storm petrel within camera range on Prince Philip's Steps, Tower Island.

Where to See Them: Tower Island (see above) and the Highlands of Santa Cruz.

Note: There are also barn owls in the Galápagos, a nocturnal species not typically seen by tourists. They are not discussed in this section.

YELLOW WARBLERS – *(MARIAS or CANARIOS)*

The yellow warbler, true to its family name, is a brightly-colored songster, trilling a rapid series of clear, sweet notes. Its feeding habits are variable, including picking insects off trees, catching them in the air, and patrolling the intercoastal zone.

Photo Opportunities: The yellow warbler is one of the prettiest and the only bright yellow bird in the Galápagos. The male has a beautiful rusty-red cap and red stripes on the breast. The ideal pose is against a green foliage background. They tend not to sit still, so you have to be fast with the camera. A telephoto lens is recommended.

Where To See Them: On most of the main islands containing green vegetation, from the beaches to the highest hills. The yellow warbler is very common and abundant throughout the Galápagos. It is amazing that one species is adaptable enough to successfully inhabit all these different environments.

MAMMALS

As discussed in Chapter 11 (see the sections on The Arrival of Life and Reptiles), mammals were generally not suited to the rigors of the long ocean voyage to the archipelago. Although understandable, it is still amazing to note that there are but seven species of mammals that are indigenous to the Galápagos. It is even more amazing that, of these, there are only three land mammal species – all are rice rats! The balance of this under-represented Class were either carried through the air by storm-force winds (two bat species) or by long-distance swimming (the sea lions and fur seals).

While mammals were not readily able to make the journey to the Galápagos on their own, once transported there by man they survived all too well, usually at the expense of other wildlife members. Even the indigenous rats couldn't withstand the onslaught of the introduced black rat; of the seven species of native rice rats, all but three are now extinct, having been out-competed for the available food. Unfortunately, as we all know, the story doesn't end there. Introduced mammals are largely responsible for the long list of extinct and endangered Galápagos wildlife species. We are accountable and have the unpleasant, extremely difficult but necessary task of attempting to reset the balance of nature. Somehow, even though you know it's essential for the survival of the endangered species, it still sounds a bit incongruous to actively take steps to return things to their natural state. Especially when those steps are poisoning and hunting animals as well as stealing tortoise eggs for placement in incubators. I guess cleaning up a mess is a dirty job.

Note: While not considered indigenous to the Galápagos, bottle-nosed dolphins and whales are briefly discussed; the rice rats and bats are not.

GALAPAGOS SEA LIONS – *(LOBOS MARINOS)*

Entertainment will be provided on your Galápagos adventure, courtesy of the sea lions. These playful aquatic mammals will swim with you, serenade you in the morning (and the rest of the day for that matter), and play catch with a twig (or sometimes a marine iguana). As they lie on the beach, they will follow you with inquisitive eyes as you take your land tour of an island.

Sea lions, fur seals, true seals, and walruses are pinnipeds (meaning "finned feet"). They are all strong swimmers and divers. Unlike true seals, however, the sea lions and fur seals have external ears as well as highly-developed front flippers which enable them to be quite agile on land, even on very rocky terrain. The Galápagos sea lion is endemic to the islands and a subspecies of the larger California sea lion. Members of this extremely intelligent species are often trained as "performers," and after touring the Galápagos it's easy to see why.

The Galápagos sea lions may be smaller than their ancestors, but the bulls are pretty hefty and can weigh up to 600 pounds. Males are distinguished by a larger girth, thicker neck, and a noticeable bump on the forehead. Their large size is used to advantage in territorial defense.

A bull will actively protect a territory with boundary lines of up to 70 ft of shoreline. The territory extends into the shallow waters and encompasses all the beach-front real estate. All the females within the territory (numbering up to thirty) are claimed by the bull as mating partners, and along with the juveniles are diligently watched and protected (although females are free to leave one territory for another). The bull is constantly at work defending his territory, barking out his warning to would-be challengers as he swims from one end of the territory to the other. As there are many bulls and few herds, the dominance of the resident bull is often tested. Often, he can stare (and bark) down the challenger, but occasionally fierce, bloody battles erupt.

After no more than a few weeks of round-the-clock patrol duty, often going without food and sleep for extended periods, the beachmaster bull finally tires and is vanquished. There is a new champion, and the cycle repeats itself. Again and again. It's a curious process, and it's easy to think in terms of male vanity, chauvinism, etc. Perhaps, but I think it goes beyond that. The behavior is obviously useful or it would have evolved out. It doesn't seem related to family behavior, as there is no family unit per se. Could it be that, as with the terrestrial lion, territorial defense is an evolved mechanism to best defend and ensure the survival of the colony? Call it a designated guard, one that's always on the job.

The first order of protection is from the sharks that often lurk in the off-shore waters. This involves lifeguard duty as well, and the bull is very good about keeping the playful pups confined to the shark-free shallow pools. Killer whales (orcas) are another concern, as they prey on sea lions in the western portion of the archipelago.

The sea lion pups require quite a bit of attention, as they nurse for up to 3 years, depending on the availability of food. In good times, a pup will be weaned within a year. In the event of a food shortage, however, the pup is fed quite a bit longer, while any new pups are not nursed and basically left to die. This is an extremely sad sight to see, but is necessary for the survival of the colony, as the older pup will generally make it through the tough year. The amount of milk would have been insufficient to feed both pups, and most likely neither of them would have survived. This would have also physiologically stressed the mother, making her susceptible to life-threatening diseases (such as the recently-prevalent sea lion pox). In an interpretation of nature, this is yet another example of a natural insurance policy often seen at work in the Galápagos (see the section on Blue-Footed Boobies).

This grim picture became all too vivid during the 1982-83 *El Niño/Southern Oscillation* (ENSO) weather condition when the food supply of fish and squid was reduced, and successful hunting required a lot of work and deeper dives. Such food as was caught was not sufficient to feed the young pups, and most youngsters were lost that season. Stress-induced diseases took their toll as well.

These unfortunate facts of life fade from thought as you watch the sea lions frolic in the water. During adolescence, the playful aquabatics of the sea lion pups are excellent practice for the feeding skills required later in life. Owing to their large pressure-reinforced lungs and oxygen-rich blood, adult sea lions are capable of diving to depths of 500 feet and remaining under-water for up to a half hour.

The Galápagos sea lion has about a 20 year life span.

Photo Opportunities: Nursing, barking, playing, sleeping, and swimming, the sea lions will provide you with an endless supply of photographic opportunities. Every time you walk past them, you'll see a different expression or pose worth capturing on film.

Often they'll emerge from a quick cooling dip in the water, with the wet portion of their fur a shiny jet black and the dry portion a golden tan; the contrast is visually striking (see Photo #16). By the way, the use of a polarizing filter will take away the bright "hot spot" reflection on the wet fur of a sea lion. Galápagos sea lions will occasionally hop into and seemingly commandeer a *panga*, especially during the early morning hours. If you rise with the sun, bring your camera topside and you'll often be rewarded with great shots of sea lions or pelicans at the helm of the *panga*. I've seen as many as seven sea lions in a single *panga*; I wonder if there's a category in the **GUINNESS BOOK OF WORLD RECORDS**?

While photographing sea lions on a beach, try to get down on one knee and get a more dramatic perspective. Sea lions can not pant or sweat to control their temperature, so you will often see them with a flipper in the air, a cooling-off behavior that works in a similar fashion to a car's radiator. This "thermoregulation" makes for a great photo opportunity. So does the behavior of stretching their heads way back, almost onto their shoulders. This resting behavior is related to the fact that pinnipeds do not have clavicles, which in turn seems to be an adaptation that gives them more head flexibility for catching fish.

The Galápagos sea lions also make excellent subjects beneath the surface (see Photo #15). As the waters can be quite murky, depending on the amount of upwelling activity, you're going to have to shoot from a close distance. The problem is compounded as the sea lions tend to zoom past you, resulting in a situation not unlike trying to photograph a speeding race car at close distance. Panning the camera is the only way to get good results. You may want to take several shots, as getting the whole sea lion in the frame isn't easy.

Where To See Them: All along the sandy beaches and rocky shores, where many of the 50,000 Galápagos sea lions can be seen and heard.

Older bulls that have fought and been defeated in one battle too many live out their later years in exile, often in retirement communities. One such bachelor colony can be seen on the rocky cliffs of South Plaza Island. Here, several battle-scarred ex-champs lie around with a sad look in their eyes as they stare down at the shore.

Caution: Resident bulls will see you as invaders of their territory, and will occasionally charge right at you. Back away or move to the side at a steady pace. The basic rule is not to get between them and the beach they're defending. Do not taunt them; respect them and the situation. They can be on edge, guarding their territory day and night, often going without food to do so. The increase of tourism seems to have made them slightly more irritable, and occasionally people do get bit. When you sense an overly aggressive bull, take a safe detour; it's also best not to snorkel in this type of situation. In all cases, follow your Guide's instructions!

Females and juveniles are not dangerous; they are often on the trail and will usually move out of the way after a few moments. If in doubt about proceeding, the Guide will assist you.

GALAPAGOS FUR SEALS – *(LOBOS DE DOS PELOS or FOCAS PELETERAS)*

The fur seals seem as out of place on the equator as the penguin. Both originated in the cold waters off the southern coast of South America and made their way north along the Humboldt Current (probably during an Ice Age) to the Galápagos. Here they were isolated (after the waters warmed and the glaciers melted, according to the theory), and an endemic species developed.

Fur seals have a double coat for insulation (owing to their origin), which makes it more difficult for them to adapt to the warmer northern climates than the penguin or even the sea lion. Thus, when resting on land, they need more shade and must seek the shelter found only in the grottos formed on steep, rocky shores. The young pups have an even harder time of it as they cannot be cooled by the water; smaller than sea lions, they are in danger of being washed away by the powerful surf. Thus, until they are grown and their temperature-regulating mechanisms are developed, they have to be shuttled continuously between shade and sun.

The poor fur seal pups seem to have all sorts of survival problems, including each other. Fur seals nurse for 2-3 years (depending on the quantity of the food supply). The older pups fiercely compete for the highly nutritious milk (with four times the protein value of cow's milk), occasionally starving out the younger ones.

As the swallow-tailed gull, the Galápagos fur seal does its fishing at night, and quite possibly for the same reasons – to avoid predators and/or to take advantage of the greater number and variety of fish nearer the surface. In the case of the fur seal, the predators are sharks. Also, since fur seals cannot dive as deep as the sea lions, there is a greater dependence on fishing closer to the surface. The favored varieties of fish are more likely to surface-feed at night for the same reason as the fur seal – to avoid the majority of their predators.

The inability to dive as deep as the sea lion resulted in a much higher *El Niño*/Southern Oscillation (ENSO) mortality rate among the fur seals. None of the pups survived, and there is a large age gap in the population. In addition, the fur seals suffer from the same seal pox that has inflicted the Galápagos sea lions and reduced their numbers.

Photo Opportunities: It would be nice to get a few documentation shots, especially those that are useful for identification. Photographed head-on, the elongated flippers look like the prototype for the snorkeling variety that we use; a wide-angle lens will exaggerate this feature, making for a visually-interesting shot. The same picture will also show the pointed ears and rounded head, also helpful in distinguishing fur seals from sea lions. So too is their characteristic "sad" expression (see Photo #60).

Where To See Them: There are about 30,000-40,000 fur seals in the Galápagos, almost as many as sea lions but nowhere near as conspicuous to the visitor. We are fortunate to have the Galápagos fur seal still with us. It was thought that the sealers, seeking the valuable coat of the fur seal, had hunted the animal to extinction during the 1800s. A scientific expedition in 1906 reported finding only one fur seal during an extensive search throughout the Galápagos. It was their secluded locations that saved the fur seal.

The majority of Galápagos fur seals are found in the northern and western parts of the archipelago, where the waters are cooler and provide more upwelling activity. Thus, many fur seal colonies are established on Marchena and Pinta Islands (where there are presently no Visitor Sites), as well as on Fernandina and Isabela.

Such fur seals that are seen inhabit islands with sheltered caves. The best example is the Fur Seal Grotto on James Bay, James (Santiago) Island. The Galápagos fur seal can also be viewed on Tower (Genovesa) Island near the landing at Prince Philip's Steps.

DOLPHINS – *(DELFINES)*

"We've seen the dolphins," the passenger said, "now where are the whales?" Well, dolphins are whales – toothed whales. This sort of surprises some people, but the biological order called cetaceans (whales) are divided into the toothed whales and the baleen ("toothless," filter-feeding) whales. The toothed and baleen whales are in turn divided into several families. One of the toothed whale families is called *Delphinidae* – the dolphins. If you want to get more confused, one of the members of the dolphin family is the killer whale (orca). Okay, hang in there for one more. Not all orcas are killer whales. There are resident (fish-eating) orcas (such as the populations commonly seen in Puget Sound) and transient (marine-mammal-eating) orcas. These two different "types" of orcas may someday be called different species because they have been reproductively isolated for over 100,000 years; according to the definition of the term "species" (a reproductively-isolated population), there should be two species of orcas. We'll see what the scientists say in the coming years.

Now that you know about orcas, you want to see them in the Galápagos. Which you probably won't. They do show up now and then, typically in late summer and fall when the sea lions are pupping (yes, these are the transient orcas). What you will see are bottle-nosed dolphins, which will probably make more than one appearance during your trip. Other dolphins that you may see are pilot whales and common dolphins.

Photo Opportunities: Dolphins (usually the bottle-nosed species) are likely to appear any time the boat is under way. While on-deck, keep your camera loaded and by your side. If you're lounging near the bow, protect the camera from the ocean spray by covering it with a plastic bag. The distance will vary, as some dolphins will be leaping alongside (see Photo #6), while others will "pilot" the boat, riding the bow wave. A 70-210mm zoom lens is ideal for this porpoise (who said that?). You might try bracketing the exposure, using slow shutter speeds for the dolphins off to the side, thus capturing the motion of the water while freezing the animal. To achieve this effect, use a shutter speed a little less than the numerical value of the focal length of the lens. Thus, with a 200mm lens, the shutter speed should be about 1/125th of a second.

If you're shooting a video, try using manual focus on bow-riding dolphins, as the autofocus sometimes goes a little crazy, focusing on the wave crests instead of the dolphins.

#19

The word Galápagos is the Spanish name for the giant tortoise. With the facial features that were actually used to create the visage of E.T. (#19), these gentle giants are generally thought to live upwards of 125 years. While there is no precise method of determining the age of older tortoises, there are growth rings on the shells of younger animals, as seen in a 2 year old (#20) and 8 year old (#21).

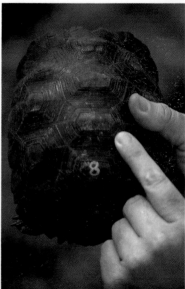

#21

#20

#22

You'll be able to observe the aggressive male "posturing" behavior, 2-3 tortoises stretching their necks skyward and at each other (#22), seeing who will back down or get a bloody nose (#23) and who will reign supreme and eat a victory dinner of straw pasta al dente (#24).

#23

#24

#25

With a visit to the lush Highlands of Santa Cruz Island, you may get the opportunity of photographing several tortoises in a colorful duckweed-covered pond (#25).

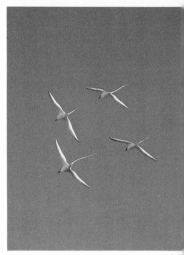

#26

#27

The red-billed tropicbird is the most beautiful and graceful bird in the Galápagos. Hearing their piercing cries as they fly back and forth near the steep cliffs, either solo (#26) or in squadrons (#27), your eyes are drawn upwards, riveted by the long, streaming tails. Occasionally, one can get a surreal in-motion shot as the tropicbird fights the off-shore wind to land safely in its cliffside nest (#28).

#28

#31

#29

Your tour of the islands will include views of the sometimes dried-and-cracked lagoon bottom on Floreana Island (#29) and Bartolomé Island (#30) — including Pinnacle Rock (#31).

#30

Whether singly (#32) or in groups (#33), close-ups (#34) or wide-angle shots (#35), the marine iguanas will provide you with endless colorful photo opportunities of Beauty on the Beast. While fewer and harder to find, the land iguana will show you its colors as well (#36).

#36

#37

#38

Frigatebirds are the pirate ships of the air, a name earned by reputation and habit. They are built for and look the part (#37). It takes the juveniles (#38) over a year to learn the flying skills required for survival. The bright red, inflated, balloon-like sac of the male is used for display purposes during courtship (#39).

#39

Where To See Them: In front of and around your boat. If you're the first to spot them, call out to your shipmates. The dolphins are actually putting on a show for you, and will do encores after the 5 minute performance if you cheer them on and applaud. Seriously! Some captains will toot the horn, which sort of does the same thing.

WHALES – *(BALLENAS)*

The larger whales that you are likely to see are two of the filter-feeding rorquals (a group of baleen whales with expandable, pleated throats) – the minke (about 25-30 ft) and Bryde's (pronounced "broodes" – about 50 ft). While there are resident sperm whales in the Galápagos, they are found in very deep water (feeding on squid at depths of 1000-2000 ft), deeper than the coastal waters you will be cruising. Thus, the chance for sperm whale sightings are very slim. There are also a few humpbacks that migrate through the Galápagos towards the end of summer, but once again, the odds for seeing one are not very high.

The key to whale-watching is to watch for whales. Which is what most supposed whale-watchers don't do. The more time you spend actively watching, the more you will see. Not only whales, but sharks, turtles, and manta rays as well. Those that are inside reading a book waiting for someone else to find the whales usually manage to get outside just after the whale has made its farewell dive.

Photo Opportunities: Not many; they just don't get that close. Not as close as you can get in Baja or Alaska. Usually, you just see their blows (spouts) and their dorsal fins.

Where To See Them: Typically in the more productive western waters, especially in the Bolivar Channel (between Isabela and Fernandina) and in the area of Punta Albemarle (northeastern Isabela). After a whale dives, its great size is enough to break the ripple of the water, forming a whale "footprint" on the surface. Also, a flock of sea birds on the ocean is more indicative of a productive ocean – in other words, an ample supply of whale food. So if you're cruising the western islands, look for the footprints, look for the birds, and look for the blows. And keep looking! It's all worth it when you're the first one on the boat to yell, "Thar she blows!"

MARINE LIFE

The subject of whale watching serves as an appropriate introduction to the underwater world of the Galápagos. Actually, many of the wildlife descriptions thus far would have served the same purpose. This shouldn't be very surprising given the pelagic setting, with the Galápagos surrounded by thousands of miles of open Pacific. For it is this very ocean that interconnects and affects all of the wildlife. Some in a direct basis, including the marine mammals, marine iguana, marine turtle, sea birds, and several shore birds. These animals depend on the ocean as a source of food. At this time, we will take a very brief look at the residents of the nutrient-rich waters of the Galápagos archipelago.

Note: Most visitors to the Galápagos spend very little time under the water, and at that, mostly to do some casual snorkeling. The vast majority of the marine life is therefore seen by very few tourists. Those species that are viewed will probably not be discussed at length with the Guide (with the notable exception of dive trips). The subject matter is somewhat specialized, and with this thought in mind, I have intended this section to be simply an overview. For those wanting more comprehensive information, several books are suggested including **A FIELD GUIDE TO THE FISHES OF GALAPAGOS** by Godfrey Merlin, **FISHES OF THE PACIFIC COAST** by Gar Goodson, **REEF FISH IDENTIFICATION: GALAPAGOS** by Paul Humann, and **GALAPAGOS FISHES: A COMPREHENSIVE GUIDE TO THEIR IDENTIFICATION** by Jack Grove & Robert Lavenberg (see the Literature section).

Marine plant life, corals, and mollusks will not be discussed.

THE FISHES

Included here are the cartilaginous fishes (sharks and rays) and bony fishes. Recent literature estimates that there are just over 400 species (including pelagic fishes) in the archipelago, with over 10 percent being endemic to the islands. These numbers are quite interesting and are worth analyzing.

The species count is very high when compared to other Pacific Islands; Easter Island, for example, has little more than 100 species. Also, just as the land animals, many shore fishes would have had difficulty making the 600 mile ocean crossing. The large number of Galápagos fish species is related to the wide variety of habitats that the islands provide, such as mangroves, sandy bottoms, and rocky shores. The numbers would no doubt be higher with a fully developed coral reef system, which the cool waters of the archipelago do not allow; such coral as does exist is sparse.

When reading these numbers, it is important to bear in mind that, as opposed to the study of land animals, the Galápagos marine life is still in the early stages of investigation; thus, the species count is ever on the increase. Also, the percentage of endemic species would be much higher (about 20 percent) if the pelagic fishes were excluded. This makes sense in that the open ocean fishes are not likely to become isolated and evolve unique characteristics.

BONY FISHES

These are vertebrates with a skeleton formed of true bone. Commonly seen bony fishes include the following:

King Angelfish – One of the prettiest of all the fishes in the Galápagos and commonly seen while snorkeling near rocks. The black coloring with white vertical stripe beautifully contrasts against the orange-yellow tail.

Creole Fish – These little (5-8 inch) grey fish form the largest schools to be found in the Galápagos and are commonly seen in reef areas, such as Devil's Crown. Locally, they are also called *gringo* fish, due to their red, sunburned-looking bellies.

Damselfish – These little beauties are very territorial. If you see a little fish on the bottom pushing a sea urchin around, it's a damselfish evicting another creature from its territory. You will see several species, including the yellow-tailed damselfish (yellow lips too), the sergeant major (with dark stripes on a yellow & silver body), and the giant damselfish (blue with large fins – the juveniles have bright, iridescent spots).

Flying Fish – You'll hear the splash more often than you'll see these "winged" fishes. The name "gliding fishes" is more accurate but has less PR image. What appear to be wings are actually greatly enlarged pectoral fins. They reach high speeds (about 30 mph) with the aid of the tail (which beats up to 50 times per second), enabling them to propel out of the water. Once air-borne, flying fishes extend their fins and may glide for several seconds and over a hundred yards (the length of the field, as they say)! They "fly" to escape predators in the sea, but often leap into the waiting mouths of frigatebirds, red-footed boobies, or red-billed tropicbirds.

Grouper – You're more likely to see them on the dinner table than in the water. The Ecuadorians call these fishes *bacalao,* and they are commercially caught and dried. Your cook will serve them as fillets. Many species are endemic to the Galápagos.

Yellow-Tailed Grunts – They are usually seen in schools close to the bottom while snorkeling at Devil's Crown, off Floreana Island. Their name is derived from the sounds that (if disturbed) are produced by grinding teeth located in the pharynx (throat).

Hieroglyphic Hawkfish – One of the strangest-looking fish you'll see when snorkeling the Galápagos. A small predator fish, dressed in complete camouflage garb of stripes and bands (which look like "hieroglyphics"). It hides among the rocks where it waits for its dinner (other fish and crustaceans) to come by.

Moorish Idols – Another beauty, with a very tropical appearance (vertical black, white, and yellow bands) and a long, streaming, white dorsal fin.

Moray Eels – The moray eel looks and acts more like a snake than a bony fish. They are fierce predators, waiting in caverns and crevices for their unwary prey (typically crabs) to come by. While morays are generally harmless to man unless provoked, caution must be taken while snorkeling, especially the urge to poke your face between rocks to see what fishes may be hiding on the other side. Their bites are not poisonous, but untreated wounds quickly become infected.

Parrotfish – These very colorful reef-dwelling fishes feed on algae and are named for their teeth which are fused into a "parrot-like" beak. The beak is used to bite off chunks of coral which are then broken down by grinder teeth in the throat, separated from the food (algae), and excreted as sand.

The species you are likely to see are the blue-chin parrotfish, the azure parrotfish, the bicolor parrotfish, and the bumphead parrotfish; they are well named.

Concentric Pufferfish – These shallow water fishes are the ones you will see from your yacht and *panga*. They are not as good as they look, as their skin is covered with a very poisonous substance – quite an excellent defense mechanism. Their name is derived from another method used to deter predators (their ability to "puff up" by sucking in water or air) as well as from their concentric markings.

Yellow-Tailed Surgeonfish – You will see these beautiful fishes traveling in schools quite often on your snorkeling adventures. With their grey body and brightly-colored tail, they are easy to identify. Found near reefs and rocks, yellow-tailed surgeonfish use their chisel-like teeth to scrape minute plant and animal food from the rocky substrate. Their name is derived from the scalpel-like spines located on both sides of the tail and used in defense (by waving the tail back and forth).

Yellow-Bellied Triggerfish – These reef and rock fishes have striking black and yellow coloring. They are named for their ability to escape predators by swimming into a crevice and then cocking their first dorsal spine (like a "trigger") against the second spine, thus wedging themselves in.

Wrasses – This is an amazing assortment of fishes. Equally amazing is their reproductive behavior. Almost all of them (as well as the parrotfish, their close relatives) are (in bio-vernacular) protogynous hermaphrodites – they are capable of actually changing sex during their development from female to male. Generally speaking, the larger females become what are called in the identification books as "supermales" or "secondary-phase males." Absolutely incredible.

You will see rainbow wrasses (with multicolor stripes), sunset wrasses (with orange-to-pink heads), and streamer hogfish (also wrasses, with bump-headed supermales).

CARTILAGINOUS FISHES

These are the sharks and rays, vertebrates with a skeleton formed of cartilage. Vertebrae are formed by layers of cartilage around a notochord. Commonly seen cartilaginous fishes include the following:

Cow-Nosed Rays – Also called golden rays, these mustard-colored beauties really do have cow-like noses. With any luck, you will see a school of them swimming along the surface at Black Turtle Cove. If you're taking a picture, make sure your polarizer is on to minimize glare.

Manta Rays – The word manta in Spanish means "blanket," an appropriate name for these giants that measure 10-20 ft in diameter and weigh over 1000 lbs. They filter-feed on zooplankton and are open-ocean fishes.

Spotted Eagle Rays – Their name is derived from their swimming motion, in which they gracefully flap their strong, wing-like pectoral fins. They are often seen swimming (occasionally leaping) on the surface at Black Turtle Cove. With a keen eye, you will usually see one or more during your snorkeling sessions. For underwater photos, dive down to an area alongside them. If you swim easily and under control (stay about 4-6 feet away), you can usually get a great shot. If you try to dive at them, they will be gone in a flash-beat of their "wings." This goes for underwater fish photography in general.

Sting Rays – While snorkeling, you will see them on the bottom, partially buried in sand (for camouflage). Sting rays are often sighted just offshore from the white, fine-sand area known as Flour Beach, Floreana Island, where they are feeding on mollusks and crustaceans. While they are not aggressive to humans, and will generally not "sting" unless stepped on, their tail spines are poisonous. Keep your distance!

Caution: The following listings briefly discuss some of the sharks found in the Galápagos. You may encounter sharks when snorkeling; you certainly will if diving. These sharks are not aggressive, as your Guide and captain will be quick to point out, and snorkeling activities will be encouraged in several areas where there are known to be sharks present. The only reported attack that I am aware of occurred during very poor visibility conditions (toward nightfall) while the swimmer was hunting lobster. So my advice is not to be afraid, but be cautious; if you have cut yourself while scraping against some rocks, get out of the water.

The Spanish word for shark is *tiburón*.

Galápagos Sharks – To me they look like white-tipped sharks without the "white tip." So, if I can't identify it as a white-tip, I call it a Galápagos shark. It may not be the scientific method, but it usually works.

Scalloped Hammerhead Sharks – They have a very distinctive appearance, with their eyes and nostrils located at the ends of the lateral hammer-like projection. Aside from any improvements to their field of vision, the enlarged snout amplifies the already astounding electro-sensitivity of the animal. Capable of sensing one-millionth of a volt, sharks can detect an animal's natural electrical output from a long distance.

White-Tipped Reef Sharks – You will see these harmless sharks on several of your snorkeling sessions. As they are nocturnal in their feeding habits, they will generally be found resting on the bottom during the day. For you non-snorkelers, they can also can be seen in several of the sheltered lagoons fringed with mangrove trees, such as Black Turtle Cove (Caleta Tortuga Negra) on Santa Cruz Island. Their white tips are easily recognizable, and a good photographic subject (see Photo #17).

CRUSTACEANS

These are the arthropods (jointed-limbed creatures) having a segmented body surrounded by a tough "crusty" shell. Commonly-seen crustaceans include the following (lobsters and shrimps will not be discussed):

Barnacles – These sedentary crustaceans look more like shelled mollusks than they do cousins of shrimp and crabs, but they actually have six pairs of thoracic legs. These feathery, filter-feeding appendages (called cirri) are usually hidden beneath two sliding plates which form the roof of the shell. At feeding time (when they are covered over with water) the roof opens, the feet are extended through the aperture, and sweep rhythmically through the water, trapping suspended food particles on feathery bristles called setae. A lot more complicated than they appear, grouped together, attached to the rocks along the shore line.

Fiddler Crabs – The males really have a giant claw which they carry around like a cello, waving it about during courtship to attract females and ward off other males. Don't worry about being pinched, as these crabs are no larger than an inch and will disappear into their wet sand burrows when they feel the vibration of your approaching footsteps. Fascinating to watch, you can find fiddler crab communities along the high tide line at Darwin Bay, Tower Island.

Ghost Crabs – You will see their burrows, tracks, and discarded sand balls ("leftovers," after filtering out food particles) more frequently than you'll see the ghosts themselves. Named for their elusive nature, speed, and nocturnal activity cycle, ghost crabs will sometimes peer out of their burrow, their eyes extended vertically at the end of movable stalks. Until you approach, that is, and then back down they go. If you're very patient, have a telephoto lens, and are willing to lie very still in the sand for a while, you may be rewarded with a reasonably good shot as they peek out to see if the coast is clear.

Hermit Crabs – Lacking the hard, external skeleton typically associated with crustaceans, these "hermits" live in discarded houses – the empty shells of snails. These beggars are choosy, and will select a shell of just the right size -- not too small as to be uncomfortable and not too large as to restrict mobility. They change shells continuously as they grow.

Sally Lightfoot Crabs – These beautiful bright-red crabs are everywhere to be seen on the black lava rocks, a scene offering striking contrast and great photographic opportunities (see Photo #47). They are named for their nimble, "light-footed" scurrying motion, sometimes up & down or upside-down, across the rocks and over the water. Incidentally, the little black crabs you see everywhere on the lava rocks are juvenile Sally Lightfeet. Being smaller and more vulnerable to predation by shore birds, they need more camouflage coloring.

ECHINODERMS

Echinoderms (spiny-skinned creatures) are typically built with five-sided or radial bodies. As adults, they live on the seabed. Commonly seen echinoderms include the following (sea cucumbers will not be discussed):

Green Sea Urchins – Endemic to the Galápagos, their round, sculptured skeletons (often seen on beaches – see Photo #48) are composed of a series of interlocking plates. Sea urchins are scavenging herbivores, typically grazing on algae (their preferred food), using a complex feeding/locomoting network of tube-feet to transfer particles to a relatively sophisticated chewing apparatus called Aristotle's lantern; ask your Guide to show you the five teeth of this fascinating structure.

Pencil Sea Urchins – Seen on the ocean bottom, they are not to be stepped on, as the sharp spines are poisonous. Their skeletons are often spotted washed up on beaches (see Photo #49). The spines are supposedly "pencil shaped," while some say the name is derived from the ability to use a spine as a writing instrument on rocks. Don't try it!

Sea Stars – These colorful bottom dwellers are commonly called starfish, but most sources will refer to sea stars, attempting to avoid the confusion with the other types of "stars," including brittle stars, basket stars, and feather stars. There are several beautiful species in the Galápagos. The beauty, however, does not extend to their eating habits, which largely consists of extruding the stomach, wrapping it around the food item, and externally digesting it.

PLANT LIFE

It comes as little surprise that there are only about 600 indigenous plant species in the Galápagos (compared to upwards of 20,000 on mainland Ecuador). The archipelago has a relatively small land area to begin with, about 3,000 square miles. Also, it is still in its early stages of formation, especially the western islands, where the flora are actually in the "primordial stage" of pioneering plants. These "pioneers" seem to grow out of the lava itself, while providing the humus for future generations of more advanced plant life. Helping keep the number of plant species down is the lack of pollinating insects (consisting of basically the carpenter bee and a few butterfly species). For this reason, then, large colorful flowers are less likely to survive, and therefore occur less frequently than non-pollinators. In general, we have a pretty harsh environment without a lot of very rich soil; for the most part, the Galápagos is not exactly your typical orchid jungle.

As you've gathered from our look at the animals of the Galápagos, the life forms are fairly basic. So it is with the plants, but for somewhat different reasons. With the animals it was related to arrival and survival factors. While any exotic plant seed could have arrived, perhaps stuck on the wings or feet of a bird, surviving once there was another matter. And once the formula for survival was achieved, it had to be modified from island to island. Thus, the process of adaptive radiation is as much a factor in the evolution of the prickly pear cactus and scalesia as it is the giant tortoises, mockingbirds, and Darwin's finches.

The result of adaptive radiation is endemism – new, unique species. Thus, the evolutionary process has resulted in one-third of the Galápagos plants being endemic to the islands. This is the same pattern we saw with the animals – species-poor and endemic-rich. I would suspect that this high rate of endemism will decrease in the future, as the islands are studied more thoroughly and new species discovered, especially in the relatively humid and soil-rich highland areas.

With this orientation, we will take a look at the different growing environments (typically referred to as Vegetation Zones) and get a feel for the plant communities in these areas.

Note: Once again, this section is intended to be an overview, an introduction to the plant life of the Galápagos. For a comprehensive treatment of this subject, you are referred to **FLORA OF THE GALÁPAGOS** by Wiggins and Porter; for a compact field guide, there is Eileen Schofield's **PLANTS OF THE GALAPAGOS ISLANDS** (see the Literature section).

COASTAL AREA PLANTS

The coastal plant community grows in what is frequently referred to in the texts as the Littoral (Latin for "shore") Zone. These plants can be described as having, of necessity, a high salt tolerance and form two distinct groups.

MANGROVES

These are the evergreen trees you will see along the shore throughout the islands, forming groves in and around sheltered lagoons. There are several species, including the black, button, red, and white mangrove, each readily identifiable by leaf structure. Also, aerial prop (support) roots are unique to the red mangrove. The red is the most common and arrived in the Galápagos on its own; the pod-shaped seedlings, typically dispersed by sea, were able to float across the ocean, root in the mud, take hold, and grow. If you are *panga*-riding through Black Turtle Cove (Caleta Tortuga Negra), Santa Cruz Island, take a look at the oysters fixed to the base of the red mangrove.

The black mangrove has the highest salt tolerance, as its leaves are equipped with special salt-excreting glands. Actually, several of the varieties have root systems that filter out salt, allowing the leaves to receive fresh water. Depending on the location, these same roots will anchor the tree to the rocks, gather material all around to help stabilize the beach or lagoon shore, and/or project into the air for breathing purposes.

SAND DUNES

The Galápagos beaches are kept intact by (and are a home for) several salt-tolerant herbs, shrubs, and vines found on these shores.

Beach Morning Glory – Sometimes called *Ipomoea*, this is a creeping vine that helps stabilize beaches. It is recognized by the purple, funnel-shaped, daylight-opening flower (characteristic of morning glories).

Salt Bush – A most prominent beach plant, the salt bush has heart-shaped, puckered leaves; they even look (and supposedly) taste salty. Some of the Guides will call it *Cryptocarpus*, part of its Latin (scientific) name.

Sesuvium – During the dry season, this ice plant turns red and is among the most colorful plants in the Galápagos, forming extensive mats (see Photo #8).

The small, star-shaped flowers are quite distinctive. It is seen near the shore of several islands, most notably on South Plaza.

DRY AREA PLANTS

Arid conditions prevail throughout most of the Galápagos. Thus, it is no surprise that drought-resistant, dry area flora dominates much of the harsh landscape. On several islands, you will only find a Dry Zone and a Shore (Littoral) Zone.

CACTI

Cacti are succulents, a classification of plants having thick, fleshy leaves or stems for the purpose of storing and conserving moisture. In the case of the cactus family, it is the leaf-like stems (called pads) that achieve this function. Aside from serving as water-storage vessels, the pads also replace leaves as the photosynthetic organs. In addition, spines have also evolved (as a means of protection).

Candelabra Cactus – "Super-endemic" to the Galápagos (unique at the genus as well as the species level), and named for its characteristic shape, the candelabra cactus can also be readily distinguished by its tube-like pad segments. It is readily observed (from your boat) on the cliffs at Academy Bay, outside the town of Puerto Ayora, Santa Cruz Island.

Lava Cactus – On islands that are still dominated by lava formations, such as James (at Sullivan Bay) and Fernandina (at Punta Espinosa) the also super-endemic lava cactus (see above) is one of the few visible plants; it is considered a "pioneer" or colonizer plant. With bright yellow-tipped coloring and microphone shapes, the clumped formations are visually appealing and dramatically stand out from the barren fields of lava (see Photo #52).

Prickly Pear Cactus – Also called *Opuntia,* the prickly pear is an outstanding example of adaptive radiation. In all, six endemic species and several endemic varieties (the plant world equivalent of subspecies or race) of *Opuntia* shrubs and trees have evolved. Some of the trees are impressively tall (see Photo #53), a survival necessity from the days that tortoises roamed the islands in great numbers, seeking food and water from the fleshy stems. The trunks are now well-protected with spines and a heavy bark. The flat pads of the *Opuntia* shrubs are also covered with clusters of spines; this armor notwithstanding, the prickly pear pads are a major food and water source of land iguanas as well as tortoises. While the land iguanas are known to roll the pads on the ground to break the sharp spines, they frequently are seen eating the pad as is, spines and all!

The hardened spines were not a necessary adaption on Tower Island, since no land reptiles colonized there. Some theorize that the lack of hard spines was an adaption in itself, to make for a more user-friendly nesting area for birds and thus increasing the chances of pollination. Either way, it's truly fascinating! So if you visit Tower, you can touch the hairy, flexible spines of the prickly pear cactus.

CUTLEAF DAISY

There's no mistaking that this beautiful plant is a daisy. A super-endemic daisy at that. That's a rather unscientific way of saying that the cutleaf daisy is endemic at the genus level. There are seven endemic plant genera in the Galápagos; this one is called *Lecocarpus*. Your only opportunity to see it will be at Punta Cormorán, Floreana Island.

LANTANA

This endemic shrub has beautiful little white flowers (usually five-lobed) with a yellow center and is readily observed on Tower (Genovesa) Island. The indigenous species was once prolific on Punta Cormorán, Floreana, but is now in some danger; an introduced *Lantana* species is winning the competition for the available water and taking over. Brought to the islands in 1938 as an ornamental for a family garden, the introduced *Lantana* is readily dispersed by the native birds and roots easily. It has spread to over 5000 acres, where the dense thickets have significantly limited the access of the endangered dark-rumped petrel to its nesting area.

LEATHER LEAF

Leather leaf grows in the Galápagos as either a large shrub or small tree; it is easily recognized by the vertical orientation of the flat, yellow-green leaves. The net effect here is energy conservation, minimizing the leaf surface area exposed to the heat of the sun, also reducing water loss. Your Guide may refer to this plant by its partial Latin name, *Maytenus* (pronounced, "my tennis").

MANZANILLO

This large fruit tree is the only indigenous toxic plant in the Galápagos and is called the "poison apple" tree. Touching the sap causes dermatitis, and eating the fruit can be lethal to humans (although it is a favored food of the tortoises, doing no harm to their primeval digestive systems). A *manzanillo* (Spanish for "little apple") tree, complete with warning label, adorns the grounds of the Hotel Galápagos, next to the Darwin Station in Puerto Ayora, Santa Cruz Island.

MOLLUGO

This endemic plant looks more like a weed and is the most widely-distributed colonizer (pioneering plant) in the Galápagos; it is seen growing on many of the lava fields, especially at Sullivan Bay, James Island.

MUYUYO

Easy to recognize by its large, brilliant yellow flowers, the large shrub is common throughout the dry regions of the Galápagos. The *muyuyo* is often referred to by its Latin (scientific) name, *Cordia lutea.*

PALO SANTO

In an effort to conserve moisture, these trees are leafless for much of the year. They have a lichen-covered bark which is silvery-grey in appearance and grow in forests which dot the rolling hills on several islands (see Photo #51). The view has a mystical quality to it, and the feeling is not lessened by the name *palo santo*, which is Spanish for "holy stick." This name actually has a couple of other derivations. First, the tree takes leaf and blooms around Christmas, which happens to correspond with the beginning of the rainy season. Second, the *palo santo* is related to frankincense, and the sap contains an aromatic resin. The branches are shipped to the mainland where they are burned as incense in churches. Supposedly the branches are also burned locally to repel insects. The Guide may also refer to the tree by its partial Latin name, *Bursera*.

PALO VERDE

These trees are characterized by long, green, leafless stalks, giving rise to its name, which is Spanish for "green stick." The Guide may also refer to it by its partial Latin name, *Parkinsonia*. The arched branches have several extremely sharp spines, which have impaled many a juvenile blue-footed booby during an attempted flight. *Palo verde* trees are seen near the blue-footed booby colony on N. Seymour Island and along the lagoon on Punta Cormorán, Floreana Island.

TIQUILIA

This endemic woody herb is recognized by the dull grey coloring and mat-like growth, usually standing out against the sandy areas that it pioneers. It is pronounced "ta-keel-ee-yah" and is not related to the stuff that margaritas are made from!

TRIBULUS

At one time this plant was better known by its common name, puncture vine. One look at the seed (which has two very sharp, hard spines that can penetrate into shoes and tires) and the origin of this name is apparent. The seed also looks like a goat's head (complete with horns), which is its name in Spanish *(cacho de chivo)*. Since the publication in 1995 of the Pulitzer Prize-winning book, **THE BEAK OF THE FINCH** by Jonathon Weiner, the genus name, *Tribulus,* is recognized by many Galápagos tourists. The seed of this plant is so hard that only medium ground finches with relatively large beaks could crack them open, and it provided them with about the only available food during a very dry year on Daphne Major Island. Thus, the larger-beaked medium ground finches survived in greater numbers and the species evolved. All this (including the evolution) was observed and documented by researchers Peter and Rosemary Grant (see the Literature section).

HUMID AREA PLANTS

Some of the islands have highlands, typically starting at about 900 ft, that receive an almost constant misty precipitation (called a *garúa*) for a good portion of the year (see the section on Climates in Chapter II). This lush, humid area is typically classified into several regions – the Scalesia, Miconia, and Fern-Sedge Zones. If you visit the Highlands of Santa Cruz Island, you will ascend into and through many of the Vegetation Zones; the differences in the plant communities will be most obvious and quite fascinating to behold.

BRACKEN FERNS

There are about l00 fern species in the Galápagos. Many of those seen near the road in the moist Highlands of Santa Cruz Island are bracken ferns, characterized by their large curving fronds.

MICONIA

Endemic to the Galápagos, the tall *Miconia* shrub is one of the only plants in the islands with red flowers. The grazing of cattle in the Highlands of Santa Cruz and San Cristóbal has taken its toll on the *Miconia,* which is now endangered. In fact, what was once called the *Miconia* Zone is now called the Agricultural Zone.

SCALESIA

Having evolved into 11-14 species (open to interpretation), ranging from shrubs to trees 65 ft in height, *Scalesia* is an excellent example of adaptive radiation. It is another of those "super-endemic" plants, unique to the Galápagos at the genus as well as the species level. Related to daisies, several species have beautiful yellow flowers, characteristic of the sunflower family to which they belong.

Note: When the topic of "conservation of the Galápagos wildlife" is raised, many of us think of endangered tortoises and land iguanas. This is certainly what I was thinking of when Dr. Daniel Evans, former Director of the *Charles Darwin Research Station,* (in an answer to my question concerning the progress made by the conservation programs), stated, "We're winning the battles and losing the war." I was very surprised when Dr. Evans went on to explain that the "war" referred to plants – introduced plants. Since 1985, over 100 new plants have been introduced by man on Santa Cruz Island alone. Not only do these introduced plants take over an area and threaten several species of indigenous (and sometimes endemic) plants, they also drastically upset the entire biological community by altering habitats and breaking several food chains. To date, there is no ready fix for this problem, although plans for quarantine and education/awareness programs are underway.

CHAPTER IV

CHOOSING A TOUR

It is the fate of most voyagers, no sooner to discover what is most interesting in any locality, than they are hurried from it....
                                                                Charles Darwin, 1845

There are many ways to tour the Galápagos and have an exciting 1-2 week experience. Depending on your interest, comfort level, pocketbook, and resourcefulness, you can cruise the islands at a cost ranging from $75-$400/day per person. In each case, all meals are included and the boat is fully-crewed, complete with a Guide trained at the *Charles Darwin Research Station* in the Galápagos. The cost depends on a number of factors that we will discuss and will require you to make a number of decisions. The first of your decisions, however, concerns the duration of your visit to the Galápagos.

DURATION OF YOUR TOUR

The great majority of Galápagos tours are 8 days, 7 nights. Actually, only 7 full days are spent touring the islands, because the first and last days are partials, with an early afternoon arrival and departure. Throughout this book, these are referred to as 1 week tours. The itineraries are, for the most part, well-planned, and a diversity of wildlife can be observed. I would classify this as the **minimum** recommended tour duration (to come away with a good feeling and a good feel for the Galápagos). While there are 3-4 day tours, you will spend so much of your time getting there, getting unpacked, repacked, and ready to leave that the irritations of travel, especially South American travel, will probably outweigh the brief experience itself.

A 2 week tour of the Galápagos Islands is recommended for maximum observation, photographic opportunities, and just plain enjoyment. Each island is different, with its own unique ecosystem and wildlife distribution. Not only are many species endemic to the Galápagos Islands, they are often endemic to a specific island. In other words, each island has plants and animals that you're not going to see on any other island. So, the more islands you visit, the more unique wildlife you're going to see. If you want to see the red-footed booby, you have to go to either Tower (Genovesa) Island or Punta Pitt on San Cristóbal Island. If you want to see the waved albatross, you have to go to Hood (Española) Island. If you want to see the flightless albatross, you have to go to Isabela or Fernandina Island. And the list goes on.

There are official touring areas, called Visitor Sites (established by the *Galápagos National Park Service*), on ten (out of thirteen) major islands as well as on several of the islets (including Rábida, N. Seymour, and Sombrero Chino). In many cases, there are two or more Visitor Sites per island, with a total of over forty Visitor Sites in the Galápagos. While several of the central islands can be viewed on a two-a-day basis, there are an equal number that will require a single day unto themselves. In addition, tours of the outer islands (such as Española, Tower, and Isabela) require significant inter-island travel time. A tour of Isabela itself can be a 3-5 day process to adequately see the resident wildlife, especially if a hike/ horseback ride up one of the volcanoes is included.

When I recommend a 2 week tour as being ideal, I am referring to 14 days actually spent in the islands. Many of the 1 week trips are advertised as 10-14 day tours, whereas 2-6 of those days are spent in mainland Ecuador. On a typical "12 day tour," Day 1 is "in-flight" to Ecuador (usually Quito), Day 2 is usually spent touring Quito, and it's not until Day 3 that you actually travel to the Galápagos. Your 1 week Galápagos Islands tour ends on Day 10 when you fly back to Quito; you then spend Day 11 touring Quito and depart for home on Day 12. I would do everything you could to swing an 18 day vacation. This allows for 2 days of travel to and from mainland Ecuador, 2 shopping/touring days in Quito, and a 14 day Galápagos Islands cruise. If you have a total of 2 weeks of vacation time, the best you can do is a 10 day Galápagos tour, of which there are only a few to choose from.

Many tours have optional "trip extensions" in the mountains and jungles of Ecuador as well as Peru. My feeling is that if you want to visit the Andes, the Amazon, the Inca ruins at Machu Picchu, etc., do it on another trip. It simply isn't feasible to take a comprehensive tour of the Galápagos and have time left over unless you have several weeks to spend. On this subject, there's some interesting feedback from the Tour Operators. Many of them say that the 1 week Galápagos tours with "trip extensions" are easier to sell (and generate more profit). They go on to say, however, that a lot of customers who bought these packages expressed regret for not spending more time in the Galápagos.

SELECTION OF A TOUR

Once you've selected the duration of your tour, you are faced with the decisions of what type of tour and boat you want to go on. Let's start by looking at what determines the cost of a Galápagos Islands vacation.

As pointed out above, tour prices can vary significantly. Some of the price differences are directly related to very tangible factors. A tour on a converted fishing vessel with bunk beds, shared toilet facilities, and a common shower (located on-deck) is going to cost less than one on a modern yacht that has features such as cabins with double beds and private bathrooms. If the Tour

Operator provides an expert-class Tour Leader (often a biologist), you would expect to pay a bit extra for this service. Also, some Tour Operators provide specialty tours, such as dive packages and photographic workshops; professional guidance and instruction are provided, and a premium price is justified.

But sometimes the cost differential is little more than a series of markups (through the tour network distribution system) of prices originally set by an Ecuadorian-based Tour or Boat Operator. There may or may not be sufficient value added (such as airport transfers, lodging, food, local tours of Quito, etc.) to justify the higher price. So it is possible to save a reasonable amount of money by booking a "Base Rate" tour. You can also deal directly with the Ecuadorian Tour and Boat Operators via FAX or E-mail; for your convenience, some of the larger Ecuadorian Operators have a U.S. representative with a TOLL FREE number.

You can possibly save even more by going to mainland Ecuador and arranging your tour once you arrive. A Boat Operator may have a couple spaces available on a yacht ready to leave the next day and might be willing to settle at a very reasonable price to fill the boat. On the other side of the coin, part of the price you pay for the possibility of saving money is time, as it may take up to a week to arrange a suitable tour. And at that, you may not save much (if at all). There is also a chance you may not get an English-speaking Guide. Is it worth it? That depends on the situation, which we will now try to define. Let's take it one step at a time.

CRUISE SHIPS VS. PRIVATE YACHTS

First off, would you prefer to tour the Galápagos Islands on a 90 passenger Cruise Ship or an 8-20 passenger yacht? The larger ships may appeal to you for reasons of comfort, convenience, security, social activities, etc. It will be the least difficult transition to make for those who do not enjoy the feeling of ocean travel. If you're thinking this would be the best choice for you, turn to the section on Cruise Ships in this chapter. If you're not sure what type vessel is best for you, read the section on Life At Sea in Chapter IX, which discusses a typical day in the Galápagos on both yachts and Cruise Ships.

The smaller yachts do provide for a more personal, relaxed, and thorough tour of the Galápagos Islands. Your island tour-walks will be in groups of about 10-15 people. Cruise Ships bring their passengers ashore in groups of 20, the maximum allowed by the National Park. With the larger groups, it's a little harder to take pictures, there's less of an opportunity to ask questions, and there's more time spent waiting – either for your opportunity to go ashore or for the last groups to return to the ship.

Another difference between a yacht and ship tour is that the Cruise Ships are only allowed access to certain islands, presumably the larger, safer anchorages. In addition, there are presently no Cruise Ships with itineraries longer than 1 week. If your choice is to see as much of the Galápagos wildlife (and thus as many of the islands) as possible, a tour on a small yacht is the way to go. It is my personal preference and recommendation as well.

GENERAL TOURS VS. SPECIALTY TOURS

If you have decided that touring the islands on a 8-20 passenger yacht is for you, look at the tour categories listed below and see where you fit.

Birding Tours – You're a serious birder and want to identify and observe the maximum number of Galápagos avifauna. Birding Tours are accompanied by an experienced leader in addition to the required Galápagos Guide.

Diving Tours – You're interested in exploring the underwater world of the Galápagos. Dive trips are available, but you must be a Certified Diver.

General Tours – You want to see and photograph the unique wildlife of the Galápagos archipelago. I put myself in this category.

Photography Tours – You want to concentrate on (forgive the pun) developing your photographic skills in this visual paradise. Tours are typically led by noted wildlife photographers, several with extensive Galápagos shooting experience. There are evening workshops, etc.

TOUR LEADER VS. NO TOUR LEADER

If you have opted for a General Tour, you now have to decide whether or not you want to select a tour that offers a Tour Leader (TL). Think of a TL as a natural history expert. This is much the same concept as a Specialty Tour emphasizing birding or photography and offering an expert leader.

The expertise of a Tour Leader will heighten your understanding of the many natural forces at work in the Galápagos. Several TLs have graduate degrees in the biological sciences; some are PhDs. Many have conducted research, written scientific papers, and authored books on the Galápagos Islands. I take several groups to the Galápagos each year and am impressed with the Tour Leaders I meet; they tend to be excellent teachers and raise the level of the tour experience quite a few notches.

The Licensed Guide Program – The Tour Leader is there in addition to the Licensed Guide, who will conduct your tour-walks and point out the wildlife along the way. While the Guides are all trained at the Darwin Station, some are more knowledgeable than others. Several Tour Operators will refer to "our Naturalist Guide." There are two misnomers here. First, the Guide is not "theirs," but rather a crew member required and trained by the *Galápagos National Park Service*. The Guide is also a representative of the Park Service and is there to explain and enforce the National Park Regulations. The Park rules state that one Guide per 16 passengers be on-board each touring vessel.

The second misnomer is the term "Naturalist Guide." Not all licensed Galápagos Guides are what many of us would call "naturalists," a title reserved mostly for those holding a Naturalist III license. These are bilingual college graduates in the biological sciences who have successfully completed an extensive course given by the *Galápagos National Park Service* and the *Charles Darwin Research Station*. Many of the Galápagos Guides have a Naturalist II license, indicating that their background and level of training are more limited than a Naturalist III. While there are several excellent Guides who are Naturalist IIs, there is generally a knowledge gap between the two classifications. And then there are the Naturalist I Guides, who usually lack training, knowledge, and English-speaking ability; their function is to guide South Americans tourists who visit the Galápagos. So, as you can see, the term "Naturalist Guide" is very generic. And as this chapter develops, you will also see that one of the variables in the tour you choose is the level of the Naturalist Guide.

In addition to the different Naturalist levels, there is also the distinction between a "contract Guide" and a "free-lance Guide." The contract Guides are basically under contract to a particular boat or Boat Operator. They are paid a fixed salary, whether or not the boat is operating. They are usually new Guides that need the security of a fixed salary as they develop their skills. The free-lance Guides are only paid when they work, but at a much higher rate. They are typically experienced Guides and have the confidence that they can work whenever they want. They will usually try to affiliate themselves with one or more U.S. Tour Operators.

The Tour Operators that provide a Tour Leader will almost always choose the top free-lance Naturalist Guides. The Guide and the TL will work as a team. This is an ideal situation; you'll have two sources of information and more of an opportunity for private discussions.

In addition to providing the services of an expert naturalist to you and your shipmates, the Tour Leader typically meets you at the airport, confirms your reservations, checks you in at the hotel, conducts excursions in and around Quito, and often accompanies you on your flights to and from the Galápagos. You're very well taken care of. By now you may be asking, "Why shouldn't I select a tour that has a Tour Leader?" It's a good question. To provide an answer, let's look at the alternatives.

1. A General Tour without a Tour Leader at "tour-led" premium prices (about $2000/week per person, excluding airfare). The U.S.-based Tour Operator will usually have an Ecuadorian affiliate meet you at the airport, provide transportation to the hotel, and take care of your flight arrangements. The price will usually include airport transfers, hotels, most meals in Quito or Guayaquil, and some local sightseeing. Your tour of the Galápagos, however, will be led only by the Licensed Guide, who will typically be one of the top free-lance Naturalists. There is no on-board Tour Leader; even though their brochure states "On Tuesday we do this," they really mean, "you do this" because "they" aren't there. Quite often, you're not getting the same value for your money (as with a tour providing a TL). These Tour Operators **have** chartered the boat, which is very significant. They probably have a say in the Guide selection, the boat maintenance, and the itinerary. They certainly have a say in one critical feature – the passengers, who have all booked their tour. There tends to be more of a cohesive spirit, a common interest – much more so than is typically found in the FIT Tour category (see below).

2. A General Tour without a Tour Leader for about half to two-thirds the price – about $1200-$1800/week (excluding airfare, although hotels, airport transfers, and meals in mainland Ecuador are sometimes included). We will call this the FIT Tour. FIT is a travel industry term which stands for Foreign Independent Travel. Basically, this refers to 1 or more passengers that a Tour Operator or travel agent has booked on someone else's trip (another Tour Operator or the Ecuadorian Boat Operator). The booking agent receives a commission. Often, the passengers do not know that the agent they booked with is not operating the trip. Brochures often have a way of being misleading. These FIT Tours, by definition, are more likely to mix passengers that have different

interests and trip expectations. Also, the itinerary may not be the best, and you may actually get stuck on what I call a "fake full week" tour (see the section on Boat Operators in Ecuador at the end of this chapter). In addition, the chances are greater that the boat will have a lower-level contract Guide. This could significantly affect what you learn as well the overall experience. Is it worth it? You have to make the determination, but the problem is that you may not have (or be able to obtain) all the necessary information to make an informed decision.

The challenge then is to determine if the Tour Operator has actually chartered the boat. Several Tour Operators, especially those with destinations to many countries, actually act as a travel agent for many of the destinations, booking passengers on trips run by Boat Operators and other Tour Operators. This isn't easy to determine from their brochures and catalogs, so you have to call and ask the right questions. All of the Tour Operators listed in this book run their own tours, but many of them may also act as agents for other Operators. So take your time, make your calls, gather the brochures, make lists, and use this chapter to sort out what you're getting for what you're paying.

3. A General Tour without a Tour Leader for as little as one-third the price. Sounds great, doesn't it? It can be done, but it's by no means a sure thing. It's also going to cost you some time, perhaps a lot of time. It will depend on a lot of factors, including the Boat Operator, the time of the year, the amount of the discount, your personality, and luck! It involves flying to Ecuador without a pre-arranged tour. Then, once in Quito or Guayaquil you will make the rounds of Boat Operators and negotiate the best deal you can. If you're the resourceful type, **and** if you have some time on your hands, this is a definite opportunity for you. This book will provide you with the necessary details (airline information, the Boat Operators, pricing structures, etc.), but ultimately it will be up to you to put things together and make it happen.

FAMILIES

Before we get into the Galápagos Tour Operations, let's discuss the subject of bringing the kids along. As wonderful and exciting as the Galápagos is, it is not the place for most children. There are several factors to consider:

Safety – There are slippery rocks and cliff edges to deal with on the island tours. While kids are more agile than many of us adults, they also tend to be less careful. Which makes falling overboard another point of concern.

Lack of Medical Facilities – If by chance an accident should occur that requires medical attention, you will have to interrupt your vacation and get the child to the mainland. There are emergency facilities in the Galápagos, but in general they are not recommended for anything more than immediate first aid. The Cruise Ships have either a doctor or nurse on-board, but the rule of getting to the mainland for medical attention still applies.

The Restrictive Environment – On the island tours, kids can not even wander 1-2 ft off the trail and must be quiet while the Guide is lecturing. Compared to most places, including your house, the yachts have cramped quarters. Everyone's "space" has to be respected, which is sometimes difficult enough for adults to achieve. If you have a problem with a child on-board the boat, everyone shares that problem with you. Also, there are no bathrooms on most islands, and it is illegal to "go behind a bush," because of the danger of introducing organisms to the island.

With the above in mind, many of the yachts and Cruise Ships do not allow children on-board under the age of 7; I would tend to raise that to 10-12. Even then, I would not take children to the Galápagos unless they were extremely well-behaved, tended to not be "accident-prone," and had a demonstrated interest in natural history and wildlife. For those children, the Galápagos will be very special indeed, and they will make the trip even more special for the adults on the trip.

For those who have decided to make the Galápagos a family adventure, there are several options:

Cruise Ships – They have less confined quarters, ample deck space, lounging areas, and on-board medical facilities.

Chartering a Small Yacht – There are a few small passenger yachts that would give a family (or perhaps a couple of families) the opportunity to be by themselves.

Day Trip Programs – Once you're on a week-long cruise, there's no turning back, with the exception of an emergency. So if you have a problem, you can't just get off. With a series of Day Trips, you always return to port in the evening. One or more members of the family can decide to skip a day or two, staying at the hotel and perhaps touring the surrounding area.

GALAPAGOS TOUR OPERATIONS

During the last few years, there have been some major changes in the dynamics of Galápagos tour operations – some for better and some for worse. On the "better" side, we have more boats to choose from. A lot of money has recently been invested in a number of very attractive yachts. The listing below is significantly different than the list in the first edition of this book. You will notice that many of these boats have only been in service for a short time. Also, the vessels are now generally a lot safer than they were just a few years back. The BARTOLOME disaster in 1990, where 5 passengers died in a fire that quickly sank the yacht, resulted in several safety measures; there are now strict regulations regarding equipment in addition to annual inspections and rescue courses for crew members. While there are still incidents (mostly on the lesser Economy Class and Day Trip Yachts), the safety situation has improved tremendously.

Now for the negative side. With all the investment in newer yachts, the "marketing plan" of the investors was evidently to promote the boats through the U.S. Travel Agent Network, more or less in the same way that the Galápagos Cruise Ships are sold. These newer boats have even gone so far as to mimic the 3-4 night itineraries of the Cruise Ships. This "fake full week" concept is discussed more fully in the Boat Operators in Ecuador section at the end of this chapter.

Unfortunately at this time, there's not a chance that (with very few exceptions) travel agents can help you, even if they wanted to, with your plans to visit the Galápagos – and most of them don't want to. Unless it's on their computer screen, they don't want to know about weirdo nature tours. Thus, they will sell only the Cruise Ships and the newer yachts with the "3 and 4 night programs." And up to now, most travel agents can't even decipher that there are 2 airports in Galápagos, not to mention which boats operate out of which airport harbor. Some day this will probably change, which is great. But it hasn't changed as of this writing, and for those still trying to work through travel agents to pick a Galápagos tour, it ain't so great.

The problems aren't limited to travel agents. At least they have an excuse – the lack of information. There are those that know better – alumni tours, museum groups, zoological associations, etc., that offer short trips on Cruise Ships – simply because they need that many passengers to amortize the national marketing and advertising costs. Which brings us face to face with the symbol of change in Galápagos tourism – the slick brochure. Not that fancy brochures necessarily reflect an undesirable tour of the Galápagos. It just means you have to concentrate harder to find out what you're really getting. And that's what the rest of this chapter is going to help you do.

BOATS OF THE GALAPAGOS

This section will list most of the boats that sail the Galápagos archipelago. The yacht listings are to be used in conjunction with the Tour Operator sections later on in this chapter. The section on Cruise Ships is more of a complete guide and contains pricing information as well as the primary sources to book your tour with.

First, a word on yacht classification. During the first printing of this book, I used the categories "Tourist Class Yachts" and "Luxury Class Yachts." In retrospect, the terms are somewhat inappropriate. Basically, I used the term "Luxury Class" to denote yachts that had air-conditioned cabins and hot water showers. In reality, the air conditioning is not reliable on many of these yachts, nor is it necessary for a good part of the year. Further, some of the "Tourist Class" Yachts are more spacious and offer a higher degree of overall service (including the food) than some of the "Luxury Class" boats. Finally, almost all the yachts now have satellite navigation (GPS), VCRs, stereo sound systems, and full bars onboard. So it comes down to evaluating each yacht on its own merits and overall reputation.

Another sort of misunderstanding involves the yacht designation "motor-sailer." Everyone loves a sailboat, or nearly everyone, but the "motor-sailers" in the Galápagos are almost "all motor" and "no sail." By necessity, the motors (diesel inboards) need to be running to get the vessel from island to island each night. You want to be at the next island by sunrise, wind or no wind. It's generally too much trouble for the crew to hoist the sails at 2:00 a.m. – the passengers aren't awake to appreciate it, so why bother. And during daylight hours, travel is at a minimum, typically from one side of the island to the other (usually less than an hour). So the sails are hoisted during the first day of the cruise (leaving the harbor), the last day (returning to the same harbor), and maybe a couple other times. And that's about it for most motor-sailers.

Now for the real bad news. By necessity, sailing vessels need to be sleek in design. That results in better performance under sail. It also results in a very crowded interior, with small cabins, and a minimum of deck space (with lots of cleats to trip on as well). The common area is often reduced to a multi-purpose dining room/lounge. My idea of a 1-2 week cruise is to have as much privacy as possible for those times you don't want to be with the other passengers. And that's just what you don't get with many of the motor-sailers in the Galápagos.

While there are notable exceptions to this negative-sounding description, it's true enough to encourage you to think twice after seeing the pretty photos of the motor-sailers in the brochure – these yachts are pretty (if and when the sails are up), but do look at the available space with regard to the number of passengers before you make a decision.

NOTE: Some yachts do advertise their "superior service," but it must be understood that a tour of the Galápagos Islands is more of an adventure than a luxury cruise. The islands are isolated and depend on air cargo service to bring in a lot of the food consumed on-board the boats. The fancier the menus, the greater the chance that a key ingredient will be missing. So if you can't do without your favorite mustard or brand of coffee, the Galápagos may not be the best destination for you. If you're on a particular diet, this should be discussed with the Tour Operator as early as possible.

Finally, as Galápagos tourism expands, yachts are constantly being upgraded and new yachts are added. Occasionally, and for various reasons, boats are also withdrawn from service on either a temporary or permanent basis.

Here then are the registered Galápagos yachts:

AGGRESSOR I (aka ALBATROS) – The AGGRESSOR I, a 90 ft steel-hulled, air-conditioned yacht, was built in Ecuador specifically for Galápagos service, which began in 1992. The air-conditioned, spacious yacht carries 14 passengers with a crew of 8 and is completely designed and built for diving. There are 7 double cabins, each with 2 lower beds and private bathroom with hot shower and electric toilet. The yacht has a beautiful teak interior and is equipped with a water maker and ice machine. For diving trips, she has a large custom dive platform, fitted with 35 tanks (80 cu. ft.), an electric compressor, gear lockers, camera table/ battery charging station, and 2 rinse tanks (one for photo equipment and another for scuba gear). E-6 film processing and camera rentals are available. The AGGRESSOR I is operated by GALAMAZONAS in Ecuador and represented by AGGRESSOR FLEET LIMITED in the U.S.

AGGRESSOR II (aka PODEROSO II and JESUS DEL GRAN PODER) – This is an excellent dive boat, a sister ship of the AGRESSOR I (see above). The AGGRESSOR II is operated by GALAMAZONAS in Ecuador and marketed through the prestigious AGGRESSOR FLEET (of excellent live-aboard dive boats) in the U.S.

AHMARA (Motor Sailer) – This 48 ft catamaran was built in 1989 by Philippe Jeantot (3-time around-the-world sailing champion) and began its Galápagos service in 1993. She carries 10 passengers and a crew of 5. The yacht is fitted with 5 double cabins, each with a double bed, private bathroom, and hot shower. The wood-paneled interior is beautifully finished. Other features include a desalination water-making system and ice machine. A gourmet-style menu is offered for each meal, served with complimentary beer and wine. The yacht is equipped with an electric compressor for diving; windsurfing is also available on request. The AHMARA is owned and operated by NIXE CRUISES.

ALTA (Motor Sailer) – A classic 3-masted schooner, the 140 ft air-conditioned ALTA began her Galápagos service in 1996. Elegant inside and out, she has several features not typically found on Galápagos yachts, including a bow thruster (for maneuverability), autopilot, and satellite telephone/FAX. The yacht carries a crew of 9 and 16 passengers; there are 8 double cabins (4 with double beds, 2 with a lower twin & an upper single, and 2 with L/L berths) each with a private bathroom and hot shower. There are 2 water makers and an ice maker on-board the spacious, finely-finished ALTA, which is owned and operated by QUASAR NAUTICA and representated in the U.S by TUMBACO, INC.

AMIGO I – The 62 ft AMIGO I carries 14 passengers with a crew of 7. The yacht has 6 double and 2 single cabins; there are 5 bathrooms, each with a shower. The singles on the upper decks have commanding views. A large lounging area is located on the upper deck. The AMIGO I is an older boat and a bit cramped, but it has a friendly feel to it and was refit in 1997. The yacht is represented by GALAHOST.

ANDANDO (Motor Sailer) – Completely refurbished in 1988 and in great demand, the 105 ft yacht is most spacious, both topside and below. She is a charming blend of a square-rigged brigantine equipped with modern conveniences (including air conditioning). The 22 ft beam allowed the vessel to be fitted with 6 comfortably-sized double cabins, each having an upper single & a double lower berth and a private bathroom with hot shower. This yacht carries 12 passengers with a crew of 6. An ice maker and a large supply of fresh water are carried on-board. Beverages are complimentary. The ANDANDO is owned and operated by Fiddi and Jane Angermeyer. Fiddi was born and raised in the islands and carries on the seafaring tradition of the well-known Angermeyer family. Charters are handled through ANDANDO TOURS.

ANGELIQUE (Motor Sailer) – The spacious 97 ft double-masted brigantine began its Galápagos cruising operations in March, 1990. She carries 12 passengers and a crew of 6; there are 6 double cabins, each with an upper double & single lower berth, private bathroom, and shower. There always seems to be festivities on-board, which can often be heard by adjacent vessels at anchor. The ANGELIQUE is owned and operated by Captain Franklin Angermeyer, a long-time Galápagos resident. The yacht is represented by ETNOTUR.

ANGELITO I – Built in 1992, this 70 ft air-conditioned yacht carries 16 passengers and a crew of 7. There are 8 double cabins (U/L berths), each with a private bathroom and hot shower. The ANGELITO I is represented by ANGERMEYER'S ENCHANTED EXPEDITIONS.

BEAGLE III – Formerly the research vessel used by the Charles Darwin Research Station and converted for passenger cruising in 1978, the BEAGLE III is 66 ft long and carries 10 passengers with a crew of 6. There are 5 double cabins on-board, each with U/L berths. The yacht has 2 large bathrooms and 1 hot shower. She is well suited for family charters. The BEAGLE III is owned and operated by Captain Agosto Cruz, a Galápagos native, and his wife Georgina. It can be booked with most of the Tour Operators in Ecuador.

BELUGA – Built in Germany in 1968, renovated in 1986, the 110 ft, twin-engine BELUGA began its Galápagos service in 1994. The modern-designed, air-conditioned yacht carries 16 passengers with a crew of 9. There are 8 comfortably-sized double cabins, 2 with U/L berths, 4 with L/L berths, and 2 suites with large beds; each cabin has ample storage space, a private bathroom, and hot shower. The steel-hulled BELUGA is attractively furnished and has a fully-equipped galley and a desalination water-making system. She is equipped for diving and has an electric compressor on-board. One of the owners, Martin Schreyer, an expert navigator and long time Galápagos resident, manages the BELUGA and CACHALOTE (see below) in the islands. The yacht is owned and operated by ANGERMEYER'S ENCHANTED EXPEDITIONS.

CACHALOTE (Motor Sailer) – This popular 70 ft vessel carries 10 passengers and a crew of 5. The CACHALOTE (Spanish for sperm whale) was built in 1971, was refit in 1997, and is equipped for diving. The stable motor sailer has 5 double cabins (U/L berths) and 3 bathrooms, each provided with a hot shower. The yacht is owned and operated by ANGERMEYER'S ENCHANTED EXPEDITIONS.

CORAL I – The 109 ft steel-hulled CORAL I has 10 double cabins located on 2 decks. She has a crew of 11 and carries 20 passengers. There are 6 standard cabins (with lower double and upper single beds), 2 superior cabins (Upper Deck – w/ double beds), and 2 smaller cabins (U/L berths), all with a private bathroom and hot shower. The air-conditioned yacht has beautiful teak paneling, 2 spacious Sun Decks, a terrace restaurant & interior buffet area, and is equipped with 2 large water makers and ice makers. The CORAL I is operated by KLEINTOURS, which has 2 offices in the U.S.

CORAL II – The younger sister of the CORAL I (see above), the 118 ft CORAL II has 13 crew members and carries 22 passengers in 11 air-conditioned double cabins on 3 decks, each with a private bathroom and hot shower; there are 4 standard cabins on the Main Deck (2 with U/L berths and 2 L/L), 6 standard cabins on the Sun Deck (with lower double and single upper beds), and 1 suite on the Upper Deck. The CORAL II is operated by KLEINTOURS.

CRUZ DEL SUR – This 75 ft yacht was built in 1991 and began its Galápagos touring operations in December of that year. She has a crew of 8 and carries 16 passengers in 8 double cabins (2 on the upper deck); all have a lower double/ single upper berth, private bathroom, and hot shower. The fully air-conditioned yacht is very spacious thoughout, has wide Sun Decks, and is elegantly furnished. The CRUZ DEL SUR is owned and operated by GALASAM.

DAPHNE – The 70 ft DAPHNE was built in the Galápagos in 1996-97 and was launched in 1998. She has a crew of 8 and carries 16 passengers in 8 double cabins, each with U/L berths, private bathroom, and hot shower. The DAPHNE is operated by SANDAES TURISMO.

DARWIN – The 60 ft DARWIN was built in 1996 and began its Galápagos operations in 1997. She has a crew of 6 and carries 16 passengers. There are 8 double cabins, each with U/L berths, a private bathroom, and hot shower. The yacht is operated by GALASAM.

DARWIN EXPLORER – Formerly the ISABELA I, this 108 ft yacht was totally refitted and modernized, returning to Galápagos service as the DARWIN EXPLORER in 1992. She carries 16 passengers and a crew of 8. There are 6 double cabins (5 with U/L berths and 1 suite), a triple cabin, and a single cabin on- board, each with a private bathroom and hot shower. The yacht is extremely spacious, both inside and out, including lots of outdoor lounging area. The interior has a polished wood finish and is decorated with brass and copper. The DARWIN EXPLORER is operated by SANGAY TOURING.

DIAMANTE (Motor Sailer) – The 112 ft, fiberglass brigantine schooner is a modern scaled-down version of the classic naval training ships. Built in 1987 and completely refit in 1992, she began her Galápagos service in 1993. The yacht has a crew of 6 and accomodates 12 passengers in 6 large air-conditioned cabins, each with a private bathroom and hot shower; 4 cabins have double lower/ single upper berths, and 2 cabins have double beds. The beamed main salon is tastefully decorated with beautiful mahogany and teak; there is a water maker on-board, and kayaks are available if requested in advance. The DIAMANTE is operated by QUASAR NAUTICA and represented in the U.S by TUMBACO, INC.

DORADO – This 75 ft yacht was built in 1988 and carries 16 passengers with a crew of 8; she is owned and operated by GALASAM. The air-conditioned DORADO is very spacious throughout, and the interior is very nicely laid out and furnished. It is a very reasonably-priced yacht for the features and high class of service offered. There are 8 cabins (all have lower twin and upper single berths), each with a private bathroom and hot shower; 2 of the cabins are on the Upper Deck and are considered suites. The dining room and lounge area are very large and comfortable; the full-service bar is beautifully designed.

ENCANTADA – This 70 ft staysail schooner has a red hull and is one of the most photogenic boats in the islands. Built in 1969 and fully renovated in 1998, it carries a crew of 6 and 12 passengers. There are 6 air-conditioned cabins, each with U/L berths, a private bathroom, and hot shower. Equipped for diving and ideal for family charters, the ENCANTADA is owned and operated by GALAPAGOS EXPEDITIONS (GALAPEX).

ERIC – Inaugurated in January, 1991, this beautiful, air-conditioned, 83 ft yacht carries 20 passengers and a crew of 10, including 2 Naturalist Guides. She has 10 double cabins located on 3 decks; each has lower twin beds (some have a larger double bed), a private bathroom, and hot shower. The ERIC is very spacious throughout and has a beautifully-polished wood interior; its large windows provide dramatic panoramic views. The ERIC and her 2 sister ships, FLAMINGO and LETTY, are operated by ECOVENTURA and represented in the U.S. by GALAPAGOS NETWORK.

ESCAPADA (Motor Sailer) – A sister ship of the AHMARA (see above) having identical specifications. The yacht is owned and operated by NIXE CRUISES and began its Galápagos service in 1998, replacing its predecessor (also named the ESCAPADA) which had an accident in 1997.

ESTRELLA DEL MAR – This 75 ft yacht joined the GALASAM fleet in 1990. The ESTRELLA DEL MAR is a sister ship of the CRUZ DEL SUR and DORADO (see above) and has identical specifications.

FLAMINGO – This beautiful 83 ft yacht began her Galápagos service in November, 1991. She has identical specifications as her 2 sister ships, ERIC and LETTY (see the description of ERIC above); the 3 sisters are operated by ECOVENTURA and represented in the U.S by GALAPAGOS NETWORK.

FRAGATA – Built in 1994, the 75 ft FRAGATA began its Galápagos service in 1996. She carries 16 passengers and a crew of 8; there are 8 double, air-conditioned cabins (2 on the Upper Deck), each with U/L berths, a private bathroom, and hot shower. She is a well-designed yacht and has a good use of space. There is a lecture room, library, and an upper Sun Deck on-board the FRAGATA, which is operated by GOLONDRINA TURISMO and represented in the U.S. by FORUM TRAVEL INTERNATIONAL.

FREE ENTERPRISE (Motor Sailer) – The FREE ENTERPRISE is a beautiful 102 ft catamaran which has a crew of 6. She carries 20 passengers and has 10 large double cabins on 2 decks (with either L/L berths or twin-size beds), each with a private bathroom and hot shower. The yacht is air-conditioned and has a desalination water-making system. The FREE ENTERPRISE is operated by GLOBAL ASSOCIATES NETWORK in the U.S.

FREEDOM (Motor Sailer) – The FREEDOM is a very nice 76 ft catamaran. She is air-conditioned, carries 12 passengers, and has a crew of 8. There are 4 standard cabins (U/L berths) and 2 suites (L/L berths), each with a private bathroom and hot shower. The interior is beautifully finished in oak and maple, including a spacious lounge and dining room. The yacht, which also has a Jacuzzi on the Sun Deck, is owned and operated by LATIN TOUR.

GABY – Built in the Galápagos and completed in 1989, the GABY is 71 ft long and carries 12 passengers with a crew of 6. There are 6 large double cabins, each with a lower twin & upper single bed, private bathroom, and shower. The yacht has ample deck space, including lounge chairs in both sun and shade locations. There is a full bar and spacious dining area on-board. GABY is equipped for diving and is available through most major Tour Operators in Ecuador.

GALAPAGOS ADVENTURE – Built in Ecuador specifically for Galápagos service, the 90 ft yacht was launched in 1991. She carries 20 passengers in 10 double cabins (2 with double beds, 2 with U/L berths, and 6 cabins with 2 lower beds), each with its own bathroom and hot shower. There are 8 crew members on-board. The air-conditioned GALAPAGOS ADVENTURE is very modern and spacious; it is operated by NUEVO MUNDO EXPEDITIONS.

ISLAS PLAZAS – This 70 ft yacht was built in Ecuador and began its Galápagos service in 1992. The ISLAS PLAZAS carries 16 passengers and a crew of 8. There are 8 double cabins, each with private bathroom and hot shower. The 6 lower cabins have L/L berths, and the 2 upper cabins feature panoramic windows and a lower double bed (along with an upper single). The air-conditioned yacht is quite modern in appearance and has a very comfortable outside lounge on the Upper Deck. The ISLAS PLAZAS is operated by GALASAM.

LAMMAR LAW (Motor Sailer) – Designated one of the largest trimarans in the world, the 93 ft LAMMAR LAW was designed by the well-known team of Duncan and Annie Muirhead; it joined the fleet of yachts operated by QUASAR NAUTICA in 1990. She is very spacious throughout, air-conditioned, and carries 18 passengers with a crew of 9. There are 9 double cabins, each with a private bathroom and hot shower. Many of the beds are queen-sized doubles that convert to 2 twin beds. The amount of deck space is vast as is the lounging room down below, fitted with soft comfortable chairs and sofas. There is a large capacity water maker and ice machine on-board. The yacht was designed and built for diving; tanks are conveniently located at the stern along with storage lockers for each diver. For underwater cameras, there is a work table and freshwater rinse tank. The LAMMAR LAW is represented in the U.S. by both TUMBACO, INC. and LANDFALL PRODUCTIONS.

LETTY – This beautiful 83 ft yacht began her Galápagos service in 1993. She has identical specifications as her 2 sister ships, ERIC and FLAMINGO (see the description of the ERIC above); the 3 sisters are operated by ECOVENTURA and their U.S. representative, GALAPAGOS NETWORK.

LOBO DE MAR III – The 84 ft yacht carries 18 passengers and a crew of 7; she began her Galápagos service in 1998. There are 9 double cabins (L/L), each with a private bathroom and hot shower; the yacht is air-conditioned and has a nice Sun Deck terrace. The LOBO DE MAR III is represented in Ecuador by NUEVO MUNDO EXPEDITIONS.

MARIGOLD – The 55 ft fiberglass-hulled yacht carries 8 passengers with a crew of 4. It is fitted with 2 double cabins (with double lower and single upper beds) and 1 quad cabin (with a pair of U/L berths), each with a bathroom and shower. The air-conditioned MARIGOLD, equipped for diving, is operated by GALAPACIFICO TOURS.

MISTRAL II – The 74 ft MISTRAL II carries 12 passengers and has a crew of 6. There are 6 double cabins (4 with a lower twin & an upper single, and 2 with a twin bed; there are 5 bathrooms with hot showers (cabins 5 & 5A share a bath/shower). Equipped for diving, the very attractive, air-conditioned yacht is fitted with an ice machine and 2 water makers. The MISTRAL II is owned and operated by QUASAR NAUTICA and represented in the U.S by TUMBACO, INC.

MOBY DICK – This new, 70 ft yacht began its Galápagos service in 1998. She has a crew of 8 and carries 16 passengers in 8 air-conditioned cabins, each with a private bath and hot shower; 5 of the cabins have L/L berths and 3 have U/L berths. There is a beautiful solarium on the MOBY DICK, which is operated by GALASAM.

NORTADA – Built in France in 1986, the 66 ft NORTADA carries 10 passengers with a crew of 5. The sleek, very attractive, air-conditioned yacht has 5 double cabins (2 with a lower twin and an upper single, 1 with L/L berths, and 2 with a twin bed), each with a private bathroom and hot shower. Owned and operated by QUASAR NAUTICA, she is equipped with a 2 water makers and an ice maker. The U.S. representative for QUASAR is TUMBACO, INC.

ORCA – The 54 ft ORCA carries 8 passengers with a crew of 4 and is represented by ETNOTUR. The yacht is fitted with 4 double cabins, each with a private bathroom and shower. This is an extremely stable vessel, providing a very smooth ride.

PARRANDA – One of the most elegant yachts in the islands, the 125 ft PARRANDA joined the QUASAR NAUTICA Galápagos fleet in 1996. Fitted with twin stabilizers, she rides comfortably in most any weather condition. The air-conditioned yacht carries a crew of 8 and accommodates 14 passengers in 7 double cabins (6 with L/L berths and 1 with a double bed), each with a private bathroom and hot shower. She is very spacious and has a nice partially-shaded upper Sun Deck, a water maker, and an ice maker. The PARRANDA is represented in the U.S. by TUMBACO, INC.

PELIKANO (formerly the SAMOA I) – Built in 1986 and refitted in 1989, this 72 ft yacht carries 16 passengers with a crew of 7. There are 8 double cabins (U/L berths), each with a private bathroom and shower. The PELIKANO has a natural history library and is owned and operated by LATIN TOUR.

PULSAR – This 50 ft fiberglass catamaran was constructed in 1981 and reconditioned for Galápagos service, which began in 1992. She has a capacity of 10 passengers in 5 double cabins (2 have queen-size beds and 3 have U/L berths); all cabins have wash basins), and there are 2 bathrooms and showers on-board. The overall space is on the cozy side, but the yacht is well-suited for family charters. The PULSAR carries a crew of 4 and is owned & operated by GALAPAGOS CRUISES 2000 (GALAPATUR).

REINA SILVIA – Named after the Queen of Sweden, the REINA SILVIA began its Galápagos Island service in December of 1989. This 90 ft vessel sails with 16 passengers and a crew of 9. The yacht is extremely spacious and impressively equipped. There are 6 double cabins (each with upper and lower full-size beds), 2 single cabins, and 1 luxury suite (with king-size bed and complete sound system). All cabins have a private bathroom with hot shower as well as a piped-in music system (on/off switch). The galley is restaurant-scale and includes a commercial-size freezer, ice machine, and water maker. The rates include pre-dinner cocktails. The REINA SILVIA is equipped for diving, including a large capacity electric compressor. The REINA SILVIA is operated by PLACES TRAVEL PRODUCTION in Sweden.

RESTING CLOUD (Motor Sailer) – Built in 1985, carrying 10 passengers with a crew of 6, this 84 ft air-conditioned ketch joined the fleet of yachts operated by QUASAR NAUTICA in 1989. There are 5 double cabins (3 with a lower twin & an upper single, and 2 with a twin bed), each with a private bathroom and hot shower. There is a large capacity water maker and ice machine on-board. The fiberglass-hulled, teak-paneled RESTING CLOUD is fitted with a large galley. The U.S. representative for QUASAR NAUTICA is TUMBACO, INC.

SAMBA (Motor Sailer) – This classic 78 ft steel-hulled trawler was built in 1966 and totally refitted and converted in 1994 into a Galápagos touring vessel. She carries 10 passengers and a crew of 5, and has 5 air-conditioned double cabins, each with private bathroom and hot shower. The SAMBA is owned and operated by Fiddi and Jane Angermeyer, who did an excellent job of reconditioning the ANDANDO (see above), making it one of the most popular boats in the islands. They continue to work towards a similar success with the SAMBA, which can be chartered through ANDANDO TOURS.

SAN JACINTO – The 80 ft. SAN JACINTO was built in in 1989 and began its Galápagos cruising operations in 1990. She carries 16 passengers and a crew of 9. The vessel has 8 double cabins (2 on the upper deck), each with 2 lower berths (in most cabins, they can slide together), ample storage space, private bathroom, and hot shower. The lower cabins are air-conditioned. The yacht is very spacious throughout; there are 3 decks, including a Sun Deck with lounge chairs. The interior has attractive, polished teak paneling, with a large lounge area, most suitable for evening workshop discussions. The dining room is also quite spacious as is the well-stocked bar area. The SAN JACINTO is represented by GALAPAGOS TRAVEL in the U.S.

SAN JOSE – Built in Ecuador in 1996 specifically for Galápagos service, the SAN JOSE is 92 ft long and carries 16 passengers with a crew of 9. There are 8 large double cabins (4 on the Bridge Deck and 4 on the Lower Deck), each with two lower berths (which slide together), ventilation controls (the 4 lower cabins are air-conditioned), ample storage space, and private bathroom with hot shower. The interior has beautiful teak paneling throughout, including a spacious dining room and lounge/ conference area. The yacht has 3 decks, including a large Sun Deck with lounge chairs. The SAN JOSE, which celebrated its maiden voyage in January 1997, is represented by GALAPAGOS TRAVEL in the U.S.

SEA CLOUD (aka PANCHITA) – Constructed in 1984, the SEA CLOUD was one of the well-known Cloud Series, of which 10 were built. The 85 ft fiberglass-hulled ketch began its Galápagos service in 1992. Carrying a crew of 7, she accommodates 8-12 passengers in 4 cabins, each with a double lower and single upper berth, private bathroom, and hot shower. This attractive, air-conditioned yacht, equipped for diving, has rich teak paneling throughout the interior. She is ideal for family and diving charters. The SEA CLOUD is operated by ECOVENTURA and their U.S. representative, GALAPAGOS NETWORK.

SEA MAN – Built in 1995, the 76 ft, steel-hauled yacht began her Galápagos service in 1997. She has a crew of 8 and carries 16 passengers in 8 air-conditioned cabins (U/L berths), each with a private bathroom and shower. The SEA MAN, equipped for diving, has a very nice teak interior and a comfortable Sun Deck for lounging/ reading/ viewing; the yacht is owned and operated by GALACRUISES EXPEDITIONS.

SULIDAE (Motor Sailer) – The 60 ft gaff-rigged ketch is a classic; built in 1907, it is kept in beautiful appearance and condition. She carries 12 passengers and a crew of 6 and is fitted with 6 double cabins (U/L berths), each with a private bathroom and shower. There is also a desalination water-making system, a deck shower, and an ice maker on-board. The SULIDAE (named for the family of boobies and gannets), is equipped for diving and is represented by ANGERMEYER'S ENCHANTED EXPEDITIONS.

SULLIVAN – Built in 1996 for Galápagos service, the SULLIVAN was launched in 1997. The 85 ft, steel-hulled, air-conditioned yacht carries 16 passengers and a crew of 7. There are 8 double cabins, 2 with queen-size beds and 4 with twin lower berths, each with private bath and hot shower. There is a very nice shaded lounge area on the Bridge Deck of the SULLIVAN, which is represented by EUROGALAPAGOS.

SYMBOL (Motor Sailer) – This 37 ft ketch carries 4 passengers with a crew of 3. It has an outside shower, connecting (semi-private) cabins and 1 bathroom. Equipped for diving, the SYMBOL is ideal for a small family or a group of 3 – 4; the yacht is available through most major Tour Operators in Ecuador.

TIP TOP II – The steel-hulled TIP TOP II was built in 1983, is 70 ft long, and holds 12 passengers with a crew of 6. Accommodations are 6 double cabins (U/L berths), each with a private bathroom and shower. Owner Rolf Wittmer knows the islands extremely well (see the TIP TOP III below), and the passengers are treated to a special experience – a family-style dinner at the Wittmer Pension on Floreana Island. The TIP TOP II, equipped for diving, is operated by ROLF WITTMER/ TURISMO GALAPAGOS.

TIP TOP III – A larger (118 ft), more modern younger sister of the TIP TOP II (see above), the steel-hulled, air-conditioned TIP TOP III was totally reconditioned in 1994 and began her Galápagos service in 1995. She has a crew of 8 and carries 18 passengers in 10 double cabins (6 with L/L berths and 4 cabins with double beds and a single upper), each with a private bathroom and shower. The yacht is equipped for diving, with an electric compressor and 50 tank capacity. She has a library and Sun Deck; there is a desalination water making system and an ice maker on-board. The captain is often Rolf Wittmer, the first natural resident of Floreana Island, born in 1933. As with the TIP TOP II, the passengers enjoy dinner at the Wittmer Pension on Floreana. The yacht is operated by ROLF WITTMER/ TURISMO GALAPAGOS.

ECONOMY CLASS YACHTS

The boats in this classification have both private (double) and shared (quad) cabins with bunks, as well as shared bathroom and shower facilities. Occasionally the cold water showers are located on-deck. While these vessels are typically recommended for budget travelers, I can not go along with the recommendation. As a classification, the Economy Class Yachts have a poor track record with regard to customer satisfaction. I have heard numerous complaints regarding overcrowding, not fulfilling tour obligations, the Guides, and just general hassles. For a few hundred dollars more per week, you can book a yacht on which the comfort and service levels are up at least a notch; more important, you're less likely to have unpleasant surprises. In all fairness, you'll probably do just fine with an Economy Class Yacht; I just can't recommend taking a reasonable chance on spoiling a once-in-a-lifetime adventure while saving a small percentage of the total cost of the vacation.

NOTE: Your chance of getting a Naturalist I Guide (who usually lacks training, knowledge, and English-speaking ability) is higher on an Economy Class Yacht (see the section on the Licensed Guide Program in this chapter). If it is important for you to have a university-level, licensed Naturalist Guide, communicate this to the Tour Operator and have it included in the contract. You may be told that a more expensive yacht will be required. Shop around!

DAY TRIP YACHTS

By definition, these boats cruise by day, and you sleep ashore (at one of several hotels). As a classification, it's really a mixed bag ranging from overcrowded, poorly conducted budget operations that are giving a black eye to Galápagos tourism to organized programs offering a series of 1 day mini-adventures.

We'll start from the bottom and work our way up, although there's not a single option I can recommend. Somehow, a lot of people show up in the Galápagos each year without a prearranged tour. Many of them fit the "backpacking through South America" category. There are a number of Boat Operators that cater to these budget travelers. While some of them do a reasonable job, others have blatantly violated the laws of the National Park. This includes overloading the boats, which is unsafe as well as illegal. Some have an insufficient number of Licensed Guides on-board (sometimes none). Another regulation that is sometimes violated is the one that calls for the captain to report the ship's itinerary to the Port Captain and receive clearance to sail to the requested island(s). This law is meant to reduce the impact of tourism by controlling the number of visitors per day to each island.

The end result is not good. The tourists are not controlled and are free to wander off the trails, thus damaging the fragile terrain and in many ways upsetting the ecology of the islands. The effects are amplified by the number and frequency of these tours, and also because many of the trips visit the same close-by islands, such as South Plaza, Bartolomé, and North Seymour. These islands are said to have already been impacted, as evidenced by a reduction in the numbers of animals seen as well as trail erosion. The information received from the Guides on these tours is often quite minimal.

Many well-intentioned travelers think that you can get a standard tour of the islands cheaper once you arrive there. At first glance, this isn't an unreasonable concept, especially considering the lack of objective information written about Galápagos touring. However, it turns out that almost all the Boat Operators have their reservation and office operations in mainland Ecuador. The better Boat Operators do keep an operations office in the Galápagos, mainly to handle day-to-day logistics such as maintenance and supplies. The bottom line is that you can't expect to show up in the Galápagos and put together a cruise on any of the better boats; this includes the vessels listed in this book, and the ones of like quality that I may have missed for one reason or another.

These visitors are then "stuck" on the islands without a tour, typically in the town of Puerto Ayora on Santa Cruz Island. They usually wind up staying in one of the hotels and taking a series of Day Trips to the islands close by. These boats, which are advertised on signs throughout town, provide a reasonable service and, by and large, conform to the National Park regulations. But they do add to the overload on the close-by islands. In addition, the experience is not one of the best. Often, you have to board a bus at 5:30 a.m. which bounces across Santa Cruz Island to the channel near Baltra Island, where the boat is anchored. This process is reversed in the evening, and you often arrive back at the hotel after dark. Then there's the 2-3 hour boat ride each way as well as the island tour itself, often conducted by a lower classification Guide with "limited English." It isn't very informative, and it isn't very relaxed or pleasant. And it also isn't necessary. You can avoid this type of experience by not going to the Galápagos until you have arranged a tour. If you want to put together your own tour on a direct basis and possibly save some money, do it in mainland Ecuador (see the section, Galápagos Tour Operations in Ecuador, towards the end of this chapter).

Finally, there are many people who simply do not enjoy the experience of sleeping on a boat, regardless of the comfort level. There are also families that don't find the arrangements to be practical or convenient. Still there's too much back-and-forth time, and the nearby islands are the ones most frequently visited.

The most organized program of the bunch is run by METROPOLITAN TOURING; their high speed yacht, the 36 passenger DELFIN II, is capable of single day round-trips to some of the central islands. Nights (including dinner and breakfast) are spent at the Hotel Delfin, one of the few First Class hotels in the Galápagos. The yacht anchors in Academy Bay, Puerto Ayora with transfers to/from the hotel via quick dinghy (*panga*) rides. Two university-level Naturalist Guides are on-board and also provide evening lectures and briefings at the hotel. The problem is the itinerary. They have a 4 day program (which visits 3 nearby islands) and a 5 day program (which does about the same, with the addition of a day in the Highlands of Santa Cruz Island); there is also a combined 1 week program.

While there are several other the Hotel/Day Trip Programs, I do not feel it appropriate to present this option (Day Trips) as a viable alternative to touring the Galápagos Islands.

GALAPAGOS CRUISE SHIPS

There are presently six Cruise Ships which tour the Galápagos Islands – the AMBASADOR I, CORINTHIAN, ECLIPSE, GALAPAGOS EXPLORER II, ISABELA II, and SANTA CRUZ. A seventh vessel is rumored to be "on the way." The AMBASADOR I and GALAPAGOS EXPLORER II carry 100 passengers, the SANTA CRUZ carries 90, the CORINTHIAN and ECLIPSE carry 48, and the ISABELA II carries 38. To conform with National Park regulations, each ship carries 1 Guide per 20 passengers (although the legal number seems to fluctuate between 16 and 20). Each passenger is thus assigned to a group (based primarily on language) of up to 20 people. Due to the relatively large numbers, the land tours tend to be more regimented.

Breakfast and lunch are typically served buffet style, while dinners are seated. These ships require a formal attire (no shorts) for the evening meal, which is a marked difference from the casual atmosphere of the smaller yachts. After dinner, the Guides conduct briefings on the islands to be toured the following day; in addition, there are Galápagos videos that are shown a few times per week. At some point in the evening, things get decidedly less formal, the music begins, and people stroll out to the center of the lecture room (which is now a disco) to do their best blue-footed booby imitations. For most of the vessels, the ship's clock is set on mainland Ecuador time (rather than on Galápagos time) which is convenient for the quick 3-4 day trips that most of the passengers take. There is an infirmary and a full-time doctor on-board.

The air-conditioned cabins are very spacious and comfortable, with ample storage space, private bathrooms with hot showers and flush toilets, as well as piped-in music (via on/off switch). There is a P.A. system that lets you know about upcoming activities well in advance. Satellite telecommunication is typically available, often from your cabin. Snorkel equipment is available on a rental basis; snorkeling activities are more restricted (in the time allotted and where they let you go) than on the smaller yacht tours.

Here then are the Galápagos Cruise Ships:

AMBASADOR I – Built in 1958 and totally refurbished in 1992, the 298 ft AMBASADOR I began its Galápagos service in September, 1993. She carries 100 passengers & crew of 66, including 4-6 Naturalist Guides. Ship features include a swimming pool, solarium, boutique, beauty salon, library, and grand lounge with nightly entertainment/ dancing. Electricity is 220 VAC (110 VAC adapters available upon request). Children under 7 not permitted.

CRUISES:

Itinerary "A" – Sunday to Wednesday (3 nights)

Itinerary "B" – Wednesday to Sunday (4 nights)

Combined Itinerary – "A"/ "B" or "B"/ "A" (7 nights)

CABINS: There are 53 cabins on 3 decks, (34 exterior and 19 interior), including singles (inside and outside), doubles (L/L), triples, quads, and Deluxe Suites.

RATES: Priced by cabin type and cruise selection: Double cabins are about $250-$350/night (per person, double occupancy); deluxe doubles are about $425-$475/night (per person, double occupancy); single cabins are about

$400-$425/night; triple cabins are about $225-$250 /night (per person, triple/quad occupancy).

RESERVATIONS: The AMBASADOR I is owned and operated by **ISLAS GALA-PAGOS TURISMO Y VAPORES C.A.,** Av. República del Salvador 935, (PO Box 135-A), Quito. PHONE: 011-593-2-451-522; FAX: 011-593-2-439-888; E-mail: ambasador@ecnet.ec

COMMENTS: The operations/ booking office in Quito is very well organized and efficient.

CORINTHIAN – A former research vessel operating in Alaska, the 195 ft CORINTHIAN was renovated in 1993 and began its Galápagos service in February, 1994. She carries 48 passengers and a crew of 31, including 3 Naturalist Guides. The spacious dining room (1500 sq. ft) has large picture windows. Other features include an observation lounge, solarium, a "bar & grill", Jacuzzi, boutique, and library.

CRUISES:

> Itinerary "A" – Monday to Thursday (3 nights)
>
> Itinerary "B" – Thursday to Monday (4 nights)
>
> Combined Itinerary – "A"/ "B" or "B"/ "A" (7 nights)

CABINS: There are 24 double cabins on 2 decks, most with either U/L or L/L berths, with a few triple cabins. There are also a few larger cabins, with double or queen-size beds. All cabins are exterior with windows (portholes in Category 1).

> Category 1 – Rabida (Lower) Deck – U/L berths.
>
> Category 2 – Daphne (Main) Deck – U/L berths.
>
> Category 3 – Daphne (Main) Deck – L/L berths.
>
> Category 4 – Daphne (Main) Deck – Larger cabins w/lower double bed and upper singles.
>
> Category 5 – Daphne (Main) Deck – A large suite w/queen-size bed.

RATES: Priced by cabin type and cruise selection, ranging from $225-$325/night (per person, double occupancy). Single occupancy is about $325-$475.

RESERVATIONS: The CORINTHIAN is owned and operated by **ECOVENTURA S.A.,** Av. C.J. Arosemena – km 2 1/2, Guayaquil. PHONE: 011-593-4-206-708; FAX: 011-593-4-202-990; E-mail: ecosales@ecoventura.com.ec. It may be more convenient for you (or your travel agent) to work through their U.S. representative, **GALAPAGOS NETWORK,** 7200 Corporate Center Drive, Suite 309, Miami FL 33126. PHONE: (305) 592-2294; TOLL FREE: (800) 633-7972; FAX: 305-592-6394; E-mail: gpsnet@aol.com.

COMMENTS: The CORINTHIAN has an ownership affiliation with SAETA & SAN AIRLINES, including complete travel packages marketed through travel agents.

ECLIPSE – The newest Cruise Ship in the islands, the 210 ft ECLIPSE was built in 1982, and refit for Galápagos service, which began mid-1998. She carries 48 passengers and 27 crew members, including 4 Naturalist Guides. She is very spacious throughout, has a reading room/ library, boutique, several social areas, and both inside and outside (poolside) dining areas.

CRUISES: The ECLIPSE has full-week itineraries, which is highly commendable; she departs Baltra on Sundays.

CABINS: There are 26 exterior cabins on 2 decks, each with L/L berths (some with double beds). There are Junior and Single Suites on the Lower Deck, while the larger Double Suites are on the Boat Deck.

RATES: Priced by cabin category. Junior Suites are about $2600/week (per person, double occupancy); Deluxe Suites are about $2900/week (per person, double occupancy). Single Suites are about $3400/ week.

RESERVATIONS: The ECLIPSE is owned and operated by **QUASAR NAUTICA, S.A.,** Av. Shyris 2447 and Gaspar de Villarroel (P.O. Box 17-17994), Quito. PHONE: 011-593-2-257-822 (or 441-550); FAX: 011-593-2-436-625; E-mail: qnautic1@ecnet.ec. Reservations can also be made through their U.S. representative, **TUMBACO, INC.**, Miami International Commerce Center, 7855 NW 12th St., Suite 221, Miami, FL 33126. PHONE: (305) 599-9008; TOLL FREE: (800) 247-2925; FAX: 305-592-7060; E-mail: tumbaco@gate.net.

COMMENTS: QUASAR NAUTICA is a very established company. Their boats are all attractive, modern, and very popular with many of the U.S. Tour Operators. They are attempting to operate the ECLIPSE in much the same manner as a yacht, with each Guide and group (of about 12-16) having their own meeting/ briefing room. The absence of a discotheque is unique.

GALAPAGOS EXPLORER II – Beginning its Galápagos service in January, 1998, the 294 ft. GALAPAGOS EXPLORER II was formerly the RENAISSANCE III (part of RENAISSANCE CRUISE LINES). She is a luxury ship designed for comfort, carrying 100 passengers and 65 crew members, including 6 Naturalist Guides. Amenities include a large swimming pool, an elegant restaurant, and a library. The GALAPAGOS EXPLORER II has a bow-thruster in addition to the main engines, which adds considerable maneuverability to the ship.

CRUISES:

> Itinerary "A" – Wednesday to Saturday (3 nights)
>
> Itinerary "B" – Saturday to Wednesday (4 nights)
>
> Combined Itinerary – "A"/ "B" or "B"/ "A" (7 nights)

CABINS: There are 50 double exterior Suites, each with 2 twin beds (or a queen bed), sitting area, panoramic windows, a marbled bathroom (w/hair dryer), VCR, refrigerator, and mini-bar.

> Top (Explorer) Deck – Renaissance Suites, which feature a picture window and sliding glass doors leading to a private balcony.

Third (Erickson) Deck – Renaissance & Premium Suites, which feature 3 picture windows and 2 full-length wardrobes.

Bridge (Marco Polo) Deck – Deluxe Suites, which feature 3 windows, 2 full-length wardrobes (or walk-in closet); Single Cabins.

Main (Columbus) Deck – Deluxe Suites.

Lower (Magellan) Deck – Deluxe & Classic Suites, which feature 3 windows, a walk-in closet, and a curtain separating the sleeping/ sitting areas.

RATES: Priced by Suite category and cruise selection.

Renaissance Suites are about $525-$575/night (per person, double occupancy); Deluxe Suites are about $475-$500/night (per person, double occupancy); Premium Suites are about $425-$450/night (per person, double occupancy); Classic Suites are about $375-$400/night (per person, double occupancy); single cabins are about $500-550/night.

Rates include soft drinks, beer, cocktails, and hard liquor (but not wine or consumption from the in-suite mini-bar).

RESERVATIONS: The GALAPAGOS EXPLORER II is owned and operated by **CANODROS S.A.,** Urdenata 1418 and Av. del Ejärcito (P.O. Box 8442), Guayaquil. PHONE: 011-593-4-285-711 (or 280-173); FAX: 011-593-4-287-651; E-mail: eco-tourism1@canodros.com.ec. Reservations can also be made through their U.S. representative: **GALAPAGOS, INC.,** 7800 Red Road, Suite 112, South Miami, FL 33143. PHONE: (305) 665-0841; TOLL FREE: (800) 327-9854; FAX: 305-661-1457; E-mail: wwhgps@icanect.net

COMMENTS: The GALAPAGOS EXPLORER II is truly a luxury Cruise Ship, the only one of its class in the islands. It replaces the GALAPAGOS EXPLORER, which ran aground in january, 1996. The management, which is very experienced in the Galápagos, remains the same. The ship operates out of San Cristóbal Island and has an affiliation with SAETA and SAN AIRLINES; convenient package plans are sometimes offered.

ISABELA II – The 166 ft. ISABELA II made its first Galapagos Islands voyage in December, 1988. She carries 40 passengers with a crew of 24 (including 3 Naturalist Guides). The ship has 3 decks, a large salon and bar, as well as a spacious dining area. For relaxation, there is a covered Sun Deck with comfortable lounge chairs, a Jacuzzi, sauna & exercise room, and a library/reading room. The dining and reading rooms are entirely non-smoking areas. In addition to the main engines, there is a bow-thruster which adds to the maneuverability of the vessel.

CRUISES:

Itinerary "A" – Tuesday to Friday (3 nights)

Itinerary "B" – Friday to Tuesday (4 nights)

Combined Itinerary – "A"/ "B" or "B"/ "A" (7 nights)

CABINS: There are 20 spacious, exterior cabins which open onto a promenade. Most of the cabins have L/L berths, while 4 rooms have double beds.

RATES: Priced by cruise selection. Full week tours are about $2900/person (double occupancy – singles are about $3500); the Friday/Tuesday (4-night) program is about $1700/person (double occupancy – singles are about $2000); the Tuesday/ Friday (3-night) program is about $1300/person (double occupancy – singles are about $1500).

RESERVATIONS: The ISABELA II is operated by METROPOLITAN TOURING, Av. República de El Salvador 970 (PO BOX 17-171649), Quito. PHONE: 011-593-2-464-780; FAX: 011-593-2-464-702. While reservations can be made directly with METROPOLITAN, they usually prefer that you (or your travel agent) work through their U.S. representative, ADVENTURE ASSOCIATES, 13150 Coit Rd., Suite 110, Dallas, TX 75240. PHONE: (972)907-0414; TOLL FREE: (800) 527-2500; FAX: (972) 783-1286.

COMMENTS: The ISABELA II has the comfort of a Cruise Ship with almost the same degree of privacy as the larger yachts. The ship is in great demand and is booked solidly by the Tour Operators.

POLARIS – Carrying 80 passengers, the 238 ft POLARIS has been used worldwide as an expedition ship since 1988 by SPECIAL EXPEDITONS. There are a number of inviting public areas, including a sunny, comfortable observation lounge on the Boat Deck (complete with piano bar), a library (with an outside, covered reading room), a great viewing area (called Lookout Point) on the Sky Deck, a boutique shop, a small gym, and a sauna. The spacious dining room on the Upper Deck has wraparound views through picture windows. A glass-bottomed boat is available to introduce the undersea world to the "non-snorkelers" on-board. In addition to the Naturalist Guides, there is an Expedition Leader on the POLARIS, which is standard practice for companies like SPECIAL EXPEDI-IIONS that provide natural history cruises throughout the world.

CRUISES: The POLARIS has full-week itineraries, which is highly commendable; she departs Baltra on Saturdays.

CABINS: There are 41 large, exterior twin cabins on 3 decks, each with 2 lower berths. All cabins are above the waterline with windows (portholes on A-deck only).

Category 1 – A (Lower) Deck

Category 2 – Main Deck

Category 3 – Upper Deck

Category 4 – Upper Deck (Larger cabins)

Category 5 – Upper Deck (Suites)

RATES: Priced by cabin selection, ranging from $3800 – $5500/ week (per person, double occupancy) including round-trip airfare – Miami/Ecuador/Galápagos, 2 nights at a first-class hotel in Ecuador, National Park Entrance Fee, and Departure Tax.

RESERVATIONS: The POLARIS is owned and operated by **SPECIAL EXPEDI-TIONS,** 720 Fifth Ave., New York, NY 10019. PHONE: (212) 765-7740; FAX: 212-265-3770; TOLL FREE: (800) 425-2724; E-mail: travel@specialexpeditions.com

COMMENTS: SPECIAL EXPEDITIONS was founded in 1979 by Sven-Olaf Lindblad, carrying on the adventure travel tradition of his well-known family. SPECIAL EXPEDITIONS began offering trips to the Galápagos in 1996, making a serious effort to put an educational focus on all their trips. In addition to the Naturalist Guides, there is an Expedition Leader on-board.

SANTA CRUZ – Built in 1980 specifically for Galápagos service, the 3-decked, 228 ft SANTA CRUZ sails with 90 passengers and a crew of 48, including 6 Naturalist Guides. She has a boutique, a spacious dining room, cocktail lounge, and social areas.

CRUISES:

Itinerary "A" – Monday to Thursday (3 nights)

Itinerary "B" – Thursday to Monday (4 nights)

Combined Itinerary – "A"/ "B" or "B"/ "A" (7 nights)

CABINS: There are 45 cabins on 3 decks – Boat Deck/ Upper Deck/ Main (Lower) Deck. The majority of the cabins are exterior twins (with L/L berths), although there are some inside triples and singles on the Upper and Main decks.

RATES: Priced by cabin and cruise selection. Twin cabins are about $350-$400/night (per person, double occupancy); triple cabins are about $300-$350/night (per person, triple occupancy); single cabins are about $450/night.

RESERVATIONS: The SANTA CRUZ is operated by **METROPOLITAN TOUR-ING;** tours are generally booked through their U.S. representative, **ADVEN-TURE ASSOCIATES.** For details, refer to the section above on the ISABELA II.

COMMENTS: The SANTA CRUZ (and the ISABELA II) are operated by MET-ROPOLITAN TOURING, the Ecuadorian company that carefully and profes-sionally introduced tourism to the Galápagos Islands. METROPOLITAN is very highly respected in the industry and is the largest Tour Operator in Ecuador.

TRIPS WITH TOUR LEADERS

The value of a Tour Leader has been discussed in detail earlier in this chapter (see the section "Tour Leader vs. No Tour Leader").

TOUR OPERATORS PROVIDING
TRIPS WITH TOUR LEADERS

NOTE: Prices do not include airfare, Galápagos National Park Entrance Fee, Ecuador Departure Taxes, or gratuities unless noted.

AMERICAN MUSEUM OF NATURAL HISTORY/DISCOVERY CRUISES, Central Park West at 79th St., New York, NY 10024-5192.
PHONE: (212) 769-5700   **FAX:** 212-769-5755
TOLL FREE: (800) 462-8687
BOATS: ISABELA II (Cruise Ship).
TOUR LEADER: 2 museum lecturers accompany the trip (see Comments).
PRICE RANGE: 1 week tour (+2 nights in Quito and a city tour of Quito, 2 nights in the Highlands and tours of the surrounding area, and 1 night in Guayaquil) for $5200 incl. airfare from Quito/Galápagos/Guayaquil.
COMMENTS: Two AMERICAN MUSEUM lecturers accompany each trip; each is truly an expert. Dr. Charles Cole, Curator, Department of Herpetology and Ichthyology, is a specialist in amphibian & reptile evolution and genetics; Dr. Cole has accompanied several AMERICAN MUSEUM trips. Carol Townsend is an Associate in the same department and has also lectured on several AMERICAN MUSEUM voyages to the Galápagos.

CHEESEMAN'S ECOLOGY SAFARIS, INC., 20800 Kittredge Road, Saratoga, CA, 95070-6322.
PHONE: (408) 741-5330   **FAX:** 408-741-0358
TOLL FREE: (800) 527-5330   **E-mail:** cheesemans@aol.com
BOATS: BELUGA
TOUR LEADER: Doug & Gail Cheeseman lead most of their own trips; Luis Tam also leads some of their Galápagos tours.
PRICE RANGE: 2 week tour (+2 nights in Quito) for $3900.
COMMENTS: The Cheesemans are very highly regarded, as is Tour Leader Luis Tam. Doug Cheeseman is a Professor of Zoology; his wife Gail is a birder. Their trips are birding oriented and are described as being ". . . for people who enjoy being in the field all day and are non- smokers. Our leader/ participant ratio is one of the highest in the business. We know our participants want information and leadership excellence."

GALAPAGOS TRAVEL, 783 Rio Del Mar Blvd., Suite #47, Aptos, CA 95003.
PHONE: (831) 689-9192   **FAX:** 831-689-9195
TOLL FREE: (800) 969-9014   **E-mail:** galapagostravel@compuserve.com
BOATS: SAN JACINTO, SAN JOSE.
TOUR LEADER: Various, including Barry Boyce, the author of this book.
PRICE RANGE: 11 day tour (+3 nights in Quito) for $2950 incl. most meals in Quito and all non-alcoholic beverages on the cruise;
        11 day Darwin tour (+3 nights in Quito) for $3150 incl. most meals in Quito and all non-alcoholic beverages on the cruise;
        2 week tour (+3 nights in Quito) for $3550 incl. most meals in Quito and all non-alcoholic beverages on the cruise. This tour emphasizes the western islands of Isabela and Fernandina and includes a hike/ horseback ride to and around the rim of the Sierra Negra Volcano.
COMMENTS: GALAPAGOS TRAVEL offers a series of workshop-oriented tours of the Galápagos. The 11 day format allows sufficient time to visit the outer islands and to see a significant representation of the plant and animal species; the 11 day Darwin tour attempts to retrace and focus on Darwin's Galápagos experience; the 2 week trips present a rare opportunity to explore the western

islands of Fernandina and Isabela in-depth. In addition to the daily guided island visits, evening workshop sessions focus on topics such as island formation and history, wildlife distribution, evolution, and conservation. These sessions always include a photography briefing for the following day. An emphasis is placed on providing optimum photographic opportunities and guidance to each passenger.

NATURAL HABITAT ADVENTURES, 2945 Center Green Court, Boulder, CO 80301.
PHONE: (303) 449-3711   **FAX:** 303-449-3712
TOLL FREE: (800) 543-8917   **E-mail:** nathab@worldnet.att.net
BOATS: ALTA, BELUGA, FREE ENTERPRISE, GALAPAGOS ADVENTURE, MISTRAL.
TOUR LEADER: Various, including Steve Morello and Ron LeValley (see Comments).
PRICE RANGE: 1 week tour (+3 nights in Quito) for $3500 incl. round-trip airfare from Quito to the Galápagos, and the National Park Entrance Fee.
    2 week tour (+3 nights in Quito) for $5700 incl. round-trip airfare from Quito to the Galápagos, and the National Park Entrance Fee.
COMMENTS: NATURAL HABITAT Co-Director Ron LeValley has been actively teaching bird watching classes for 15 years. He has a long involvement with the *Point Reyes Bird Observatory* and spent 2 years as a biologist at the *Farallon Islands Research Station.* Field Director Steve Morello is a professional photographer and has taught for several years at the *Audubon School* in Maine.

NATURE EXPEDITIONS INTERNATIONAL, 6400 E. El Dorado Circle, Suite 210, Tucson, AZ 85715
PHONE: (520) 721-6712   **FAX:** 520-721-6719
TOLL FREE: (800) 869-0639   **E-mail:** naturexp@aol.com
TOUR LEADER: Various scientists and teachers (see Comments).
BOATS: ERIC, FLAMINGO, LETTY, SEA CLOUD.
PRICE RANGE: 1 week tour (+3 nights in Quito) for $2600 incl. a Quito City Tour. Meals in Quito not included.
    1 week tour (+5 nights in Quito, 1 night in Otavalo, and 4 nights at Sacha Lodge in the Amazon) for $3600 incl. a 2-day Otavalo Tour and a 4-day Amazon Tour. Meals in Quito not included.
COMMENTS: NEI has offered wildlife and natural history expeditions since 1974. Company President Christopher Kyle states, "We take special pride in our Trip Leaders, who are specialists in anthropology, biology, or other applicable fields. Every NEI leader is required to have an M.A., Ph.D., or equivalent professional training, and teaching experience at the college level."

NEW YORK BOTANICAL GARDEN, ATTN: Carol Gracie, Bronx, NY 10458-5126.
PHONE: (718) 817-8647   **FAX:** 718-562-6780
E-mail: cgracie@nybg.org
TOUR LEADER: Carol Gracie and Scott Mori.   **BOATS:** Various.
PRICE RANGE: 1 week (+3 nights and most meals in Quito) for $3700 incl. round-trip airfare from Quito-Galápagos and a full day tour of the Cotopaxi Volcano.
COMMENTS: This is one of the few tours that emphasize the plants of the Galápagos Islands. Carol Gracie and Scott Mori are veteran Tour Leaders and have extensive research experience in the tropics. Comprehensive educational material is provided to each participant.

OCEANIC SOCIETY EXPEDITIONS, Fort Mason Center, Building E, San Francisco, CA 94123.
PHONE: (415) 441-1106   **FAX:** 415-474-3395
TOLL FREE: (800) 326-7491 **BOATS:** TIP TOP II.
TOUR LEADER: Various.
PRICE RANGE: 1 week tour (+2 nights in Quito/ 1 night in Guayaquil) for $3400 incl. round-trip airfare from Miami.
COMMENTS: In 1997, *OCEANIC SOCIETY EXPEDITIONS* celebrated its 25th anniversary of providing natural history educational and research experiences around the world. It is a non-profit corporation.

SIERRA CLUB, Outing Dept., 85 Second St., 2nd Floor, San Francisco, CA 94105.
PHONE: (415) 977-5588   **FAX:** 415-977-5795
BOATS: Various.
TOUR LEADER: Various, including Margie Tomenko.
PRICE RANGE: 1 week tour (+1 night in mainland Ecuador) for $3500.
COMMENTS: The *SIERRA CLUB* is a conservation-oriented organization. As stated in their OUTINGS brochure, "Unlike ordinary tour agencies, the *SIERRA CLUB* seeks to promote an understanding of environmental issues on all its outings.... Trips are led by experienced and competent leaders...." Participants must be members of the *SIERRA CLUB.*

ZEGRAHM EXPEDITIONS, 1414 Dexter Ave. N., Ste. 327, Seattle, WA 98109.
PHONE: (206) 285-4000   **FAX:** 206-285-5037
TOLL FREE: (800) 628-8747 **E-mail:** zoe@zeco.com
BOATS: ERIC, FLAMINGO, LETTY.
TOUR LEADER: Various, incl. Jack Grove and Peter Harrison (see Comments).
PRICE RANGE: 1 week tour (+2 nights in Quito) for $3500 incl. most meals in Quito and all non-alcoholic beverages on the cruise.
COMMENTS: Tour Leader Jack Grove is the author of **GALAPAGOS FISHES: A COMPREHENSIVE GUIDE TO THEIR IDENTIFICATION** (see the Literature section). Jack also worked as a Licensed Galápagos Guide for 7 years. Other credentials include being recognized as Underwater Photographer of the Year by the BBC. In his "spare time," he also serves as a Research Associate at Hubbs-Sea World Research Institute in San Diego. Tour Leader Peter Harrison is one of the world's leading authorities on sea birds. His **SEABIRDS: AN IDENTIFICATION GUIDE** is the definitive book on the identification of sea birds. Jack and Peter co-founded ZEGRAHM EXPEDITIONS in 1990. The other co-founders are equally impressive – and they each lead their own trips. By the way, their company name, "ZEGRAHM," is some sort of confluence of their names put together, and there's about 6 of them!

CANADIAN TOUR OPERATORS PROVIDING TRIPS WITH TOUR LEADERS

QUEST NATURE TOURS, c/o WORLDWIDE ADVENTURES, 36 Finch Avenue West, North York, Ontario, M2N 2G9.

PHONE: (416) 221-3000   **FAX:** 416-221-5730
TOLL FREE: (800) 387-1483 **E-mail:** travel@worldwidequest.com
BOATS: ANGELITO I, BELUGA, ERIC, FLAMINGO, LETTY.
TOUR LEADER: Biologists and graduate-level professionals (see Comments).
PRICE RANGE: 1 week tour (+3 nights in Quito) incl. all tips and a 1 day tour of
the Otavalo Market for U.S.$2800.
COMMENTS: Barry Griffiths, President of QUEST, states, that "the strong educational focus adds a very personal touch and distinctive dimension to our international nature tour program." Barry leads some of the tours. He is a
widely-published wildlife photographer, a former *President of the Federation
of Ontario Naturalists* and Director of the *Canadian Nature Federation.*

TRIPS WITHOUT TOUR LEADERS

Most Galápagos Island tours do not include the services of a Tour Leader.
However, the Tour Operators listed below have chartered the boat, which is very
significant in terms of overall trip quality (see the section Tour Leader vs. No Tour
Leader at the beginning of this chapter). Generally, the value of the trips in this
category is less than those with a Tour Leader and greater than those in which the
yacht is not chartered by the Operator selling the trip (on an FIT basis). These dis-
tinctions are very important and often are not easy to discern in the fancy
brochures.

TOUR OPERATORS PROVIDING
TRIPS WITHOUT TOUR LEADERS

NOTE: Prices do not include airfare, Galápagos National Park Entrance Fee,
Ecuador Departure Taxes, or gratuities unless noted.

ELDERHOSTEL, 75 Federal Street, Boston, MA 02110-1941.
PHONE: (617) 426-8056   **FAX:** 617-426-8351
BOATS: CRUZ DEL SUR, DORADO, ESTRELLA DEL MAR, ISLAS PLAZAS.
PRICE RANGE: 1 week tour (+3 nights and most meals in Quito, incl. a City
Tour, Equatorial Monument Tour, and a lecture on Ecuador) for $2700 incl.
round-trip airfare from Miami.
COMMENTS: *ELDERHOSTEL* is a non-profit, educational organization that provides programs to senior citizens (age 60 and older – spouses may be under
60); the programs are offered at educational and cultural institutions (including national parks) in the U.S., Canada, and in 43 countries overseas. Although
their Galápagos itinerary requires that "Elderhostelers be physically fit and vig-
orous, as it is a strenuous program," the groups tend to be mixed in physical
ability; possibly for this reason, it has been observed that their walks are somewhat limited on certain islands.

FORUM TRAVEL INTERNATIONAL, 91 Gregory Lane, #21, Pleasant Hill, CA
94523.
PHONE: (510) 671-2900   **FAX:** 510-946-1500

E-mail: info@forumtravel.com
BOATS: CRUZ DEL SUR, DARWIN, DORADO, ESTRELLA DEL MAR, FRAGA-TA, ISLAS PLAZAS, MOBY DICK, and several Economy Class Yachts.
PRICE RANGE: 1 week tour (+2 nights in Quito) for $2200 incl. round-trip airfare from Miami (Economy Class Yachts less expensive).
COMMENTS: FORUM has been putting together Galápagos trips since 1965, and according to Director Nicolas Hetzer, they were the first North American company to offer tours to the islands. His packages have excellent prices.

GEO EXPEDITIONS, P.O. Box 3656, Sonora, CA 95370.
PHONE: (209) 532-0152   **FAX:** 209-532-1979
TOLL FREE: (800) 351-5041 **E-mail:** info@geoexpeditions.com
BOATS: ALTA, CORAL I, ISABELA II (Cruise Ship), PARRANDA, REINA SILVIA.
PRICE RANGE: 1 week tour (+3 nights in Quito) incl. most meals in mainland Ecuador for $2900-$3900 (varies by boat).
        1 week tour (+4 day Amazon Tour, 3 nights and most meals in Quito) for $3800-$4300 (varies by boat).
COMMENTS: GEO has been offering tours to the Galápagos since 1982 and has a most knowledgeable staff.

HOLBROOK TRAVEL, INC., 3540 NW 13th St., Gainesville, FL 32609.
PHONE: (352) 377-7111   **FAX:** 352-371-3710
TOLL FREE: (800) 858-0999 **E-mail:** travel@holbrooktravel.com
BOATS: Several, including CRUZ DEL SUR, ESTRELLA DEL MAR, and ISLAS PLAZAS.
PRICE RANGE: 1 week tour (+2 nights and all meals in Quito) for $2000 incl. round-trip airfare from Quito to the Galápagos.
COMMENTS: HOLBROOK TRAVEL has over 20 years of experience in the Galápagos and knows the travel logistics in this part of the world very well.

INCA FLOATS, 1311 63rd St., Emeryville, CA 94608.
PHONE: (510) 420-1550   **FAX:** 510-420-0947
E-mail: incafloats@aol.com
BOATS: ANDANDO, CORINTHIAN (Cruise Ship), ERIC, FLAMINGO, LETTY, PARRANDA, REINA SILVIA.
PRICE RANGE: 1 week tour (+2 nights in Quito and 1 night at the Hotel Galápagos) for $3000-$3700 (varies by boat) incl. most meals in Quito;
        1 week tour (+3 nights in Quito and 3 nights at the Hotel Galápagos w/ day treks on Santa Cruz Island) for $3800-$4200 (varies by boat) incl. most meals and a City Tour in Quito;
        1 week tour (+3 nights and most meals in Quito, 1 night in Otavalo, and 1 night at the Hotel Galápagos) for $3400-$4000 (varies by boat) incl. a 2 day Imbabura Province (Otavalo) Tour;
        1 week tour (+2-3 nights and most meals in Quito, a 9 day Peru/ Machu Picchu Tour, and 1 night at the Hotel Galápagos) for $5800-$6600 (varies by boat and number of days);
        1 week tour (+4-5 day Amazon Tour, 3 nights and most meals in Quito, and 1 night at the Hotel Galápagos) for $3900-$4700 (varies by boat and number of days).

COMMENTS: INCA FLOATS (started in 1976) offers over 60 tours a year to the islands. Owner Bill Roberson was a Licensed Galápagos Guide, and his knowledge of the islands is extensive. They are one of the few U.S. Tour Operators that have a resident manager in the Galápagos to look after their passengers (before and after the boat tours).

INTERNATIONAL EXPEDITIONS, INC., One Environs Park, Helena, AL 35080.
PHONE: (205) 428-1700   **FAX:** 205-428-1714
TOLL FREE: (800) 633-4734 **E-mail:** intlexp@aol.com
BOATS: GALAPAGOS ADVENTURE, LOBO DE MAR III.
PRICE RANGE: 1 week tour (+3 nights in Quito) for $3400 incl. all meals and a City Tour in Quito, round-trip airfare from Miami, and the National Park Entrance Fee.
COMMENTS: INTERNATIONAL EXPEDITIONS is a very progressive company and has a very knowledgeable staff.

INTERNATIONAL WILDLIFE ADVENTURES., P.O. Box 1410, Vashon, WA 98070.
PHONE: (206) 463-1943   **FAX:** 206-463-4081
TOLL FREE: (800) 593-8881 **E-mail:** info@wildlifeadventures.com
BOATS: ALTA, LAMMAR LAW, MISTRAL II, NORTADA, RESTING CLOUD, PARRANDA.
PRICE RANGE: 1 week tour (+2 nights in Quito) for $2400-$2900 (varies by yacht). Occasionally, a 10 day tour is offered at no extra cost.

MOUNTAIN TRAVEL.SOBEK, 6420 Fairmount Ave., El Cerrito, CA 94530.
PHONE: (510) 527-8100   **FAX:** 510-525-7710
TOLL FREE: (888) 687-6235 **E-mail:** info@mt.sobek.com
BOATS: Various, including DIAMANTE, NORTADA, and RESTING CLOUD.
PRICE RANGE: 1 week tour (+3 nights in Quito) for $3000-$3300 (based on the number of passengers signed up).
   11 day tour (+3 nights in Quito) for $4000-$4700 (varies by yacht and the number of passengers signed up). This tour includes a hike/ horseback ride to and around the rim of the Sierra Negra Volcano.
COMMENTS: MOUNTAIN TRAVEL has been in the adventure travel business since 1968 and merged with SOBEK EXPEDITIONS in 1990. They have handled Galápagos excursions since 1972 and currently offer about 40 trips per year. Kayaking is offered on all their Galápagos tours, and their groups are limited to 12 passengers.

OVERSEAS ADVENTURE TRAVEL, 625 Mt. Auburn St. Cambridge, MA 02138.
PHONE: (617) 876-0533   **FAX:** 617-876-0455
TOLL FREE: (800) 221-0814 **BOATS:** ERIC, FLAMINGO, LETTY.
PRICE RANGE: 1 week tour (+1 night in Guayaquil, 3 nights in Lima, 3 nights in Cuzco and 1 night in Machu Picchu) for $4500, incl. tours in Lima, Cuzco, & Machu Picchu, most meals on the mainland, National Park Entrance Fee, and round-trip airfare from Miami.
COMMENTS: OVERSEAS ADVENTURE TRAVEL, in business since 1979, has a very impressive, professional operation.

VOYAGERS INTERNATIONAL, P.O. Box 915, Ithaca, NY 14851.
PHONE: (607) 273-4321   **FAX:** 607-273-3873
TOLL FREE: (800) 633-0299 **E-mail:** voyint@aol.com
BOATS: ERIC, FLAMINGO, LETTY.
PRICE RANGE: 1 week tour (+2 nights in Quito) for $2200.
COMMENTS: VOYAGERS does an excellent job of providing pre-trip briefing
    information.

WILDERNESS TRAVEL, 1102 Ninth St., Berkeley, CA 94710-1211.
PHONE: (510) 558-2488   **FAX:** 510-558-2489
TOLL FREE: (800) 368-2794 **E-mail:** info@wildernesstravel.com
BOATS: ANDANDO, SAMBA.
PRICE RANGE: 5 day tour (+3 nights and most meals in Quito) for $2100.
        6 day tour (+3 nights and most meals in Quito) for $2300.
        1 week tour (+3 nights & most meals in Quito and 1 night at the Hotel
    Galápagos on Santa Cruz Island) for $2900.
COMMENTS: WILDERNESS TRAVEL has, over the years, put together excellent
    Galápagos packages.

WILDLAND ADVENTURES, 3516 NE 155th St., Seattle, WA 98155.
PHONE: (206) 365-0686   **FAX:** 206-363-6615
TOLL FREE: (800) 345-4453 **E-mail:** info@wildland.com
BOATS: Various.
PRICE RANGE: 1 week tour (+3 nights in Quito, breakfasts in Quito, and a city
    tour) for $2000-$2700 (depending on the yacht).
COMMENTS: Formerly called JOURNEYS, the company has been in operation
    since 1986. Part of the proceeds go to the *Traveler's Conservation Trust,* a
    non-profit organization founded in conjunction with WILDLAND ADVEN-
    TURES, supporting conservation projects and community development in
    host countries.

CANADIAN TOUR OPERATORS PROVIDING
TRIPS WITHOUT TOUR LEADERS

GALAPAGOS HOLIDAYS, 745 Gerrard Street East, Toronto, Ontario M4M 1Y5.
PHONE: (416) 469-8211   **FAX:** 416-463-5131
TOLL FREE: (800) 661-2512 **E-mail:** galapagos.holidays@sympatico.ca
BOATS: Several, including everything from Economy Class Yachts to modern,
    air-conditioned boats.
PRICE RANGE: 1 week tour (+1 night in Guayaquil, 5 nights in Quito, and tours
    of the surrounding area) for U.S.$2700. incl. round-trip airfare from Miami.
COMMENTS: GALAPAGOS HOLIDAYS works exclusively on Galápagos
    Islands tours. The owner, Ingrid Versteeg, lived in Ecuador and owned a trav-
    el agency in Quito from 1969 to 1982. Their prices are very reasonable, con-
    sidering that airfare is included.

QUEST NATURE TOURS, c/o WORLDWIDE ADVENTURES, 36 Finch Avenue
    West, North York, Ontario, M2N 2G9.

PHONE: (416) 221-3000   **FAX:** 416-221-5730
TOLL FREE: (800) 387-1483 **E-mail:** travel@worldwidequest.com
BOATS: ANGELITO I, BELUGA, ERIC, FLAMINGO, LETTY.
PRICE RANGE: 1 week tour (+3 nights and all meals in Quito) incl. all tips and a 1 day tour of the Otavalo Market for U.S.$1800-$2600 (depending on yacht and cabin selection).
COMMENTS: QUEST, Canada's largest nature tour company, has been operating trips to the Galápagos for over 10 years.

GALÁPAGOS SPECIALTY TOURS

NOTE: Prices do not include airfare, Galápagos National Park Entrance Fee, Ecuador Departure Taxes, or gratuities unless noted.

BIRDING SPECIALTY TOURS

Of land-birds, I obtained twenty-six kinds, all peculiar to the group and found nowhere else, with the exception of one lark-like finch from North America.

Charles Darwin, 1845

Since the historic visit by that well-known Galápagos birder, we have determined that twenty-two of the twenty-six land bird species are endemic to the islands. Most of these resident land birds (and the sea birds) are quite approachable, and their locations more or less predictable, based on the island and Vegetation Zone. In this respect, you will get clear, up-close looks at the majority of these birds on a general tour of the Galápagos. The upper level of Galápagos Naturalist Guides (and/or of the Tour Leaders) are capable of identifying most of the birds you will see and interpreting the relevant natural history.

On the other hand, birders have specialized requirements and priorities, which would be more likely to be fulfilled on a specialized Birding Tour. Birders tend to be "list-oriented;" the distribution (and daily updating) of a bird list is a very important part of a birding trip. The pace of a birding tour is also different. The shore visits are apt to begin a bit earlier and end later on these tours, to match pace with the activity cycles of the birds. The meal-time conversations are even different, more "bird-oriented." Another difference is the quest for the "rare bird." In general, birders would trade an afternoon of whale-watching for a "hunt" to find the mangrove finch; many would also trade a snorkeling session for an opportunity to look for the Floreana mockingbird. Since most passengers on a general tour would opt in favor of the whale-watching or snorkeling, the birders would lose out on what they felt was a more important opportunity. Finally, it will take an experienced eye to identify a few of the Darwin's finches and the migrant (and vagrant) shore birds that can make their way to and through the Galápagos. An expert Birding Tour Leader can make these sorts of identifications and also describe the precise keys needed to make such identifications.

If you have decided that a Birding Tour of the Galápagos is for you, a problem you may face is the decided lack of Operators providing such tours (see below). Another option is to form a group and charter a yacht through a Tour Operator or Boat Operator. With enough advance notice (to get National Park approval), you can ask for a custom itinerary, request a Naturalist who is a good birder, and even invite a Birding Tour Leader of your choice.

As is often the case, it is up to the prospective traveler to decide if a special interest warrants a specialty tour. It is hoped that this section will provide enough information to facilitate an intelligent decision.

TOUR OPERATORS OFFERING BIRDING TRIPS

CHEESEMAN'S ECOLOGY SAFARIS, INC., 20800 Kittredge Road, Saratoga, CA, 95070-6322.

PHONE: (408) 741-5330   **FAX:** 408-741-0358
TOLL FREE: (800) 527-5330   **E-mail:** cheesemans@aol.com
BOATS: BELUGA.
TOUR LEADER: Doug & Gail Cheeseman lead most of their own trips; Luis Tam also leads some of their Galápagos tours.
PRICE RANGE: 2 week tour (+2 nights in Quito) for $3900.
COMMENTS: The Cheesemans are very highly regarded, as is Tour Leader Luis Tam. Doug Cheeseman is a Professor of Zoology; his wife Gail is a birder. Their trips are birding oriented and are described as being ". . . for people who enjoy being in the field all day and are non-smokers. Our leader/ participant ratio is one of the highest in the business. We know our participants want information and leadership excellence."

FIELD GUIDES, INC., P.O. Box 160723, Austin, TX 78716-0723.
PHONE: (512) 327-4953   **FAX:** 512-327-9231
TOLL FREE: (800) 728-4953   **E-mail:** fgileader@aol.com
BOAT: Various.
TOUR LEADER: Various professional birders, including Ron Naveen.
PRICE RANGE: 10 day tour (+2 nights and most meals in Guayaquil) for $3000 incl. National Park Entrance Fee.
COMMENTS: FIELD GUIDES is one of the leading Birding Tour Operators. Director Allan Griffith states, "All of our tours are birding tours. At FIELD GUIDES INCORPORATED we believe that experienced and personable leadership is the most important feature of a tour." Ron Naveen is indeed an expert birder and a very experienced Tour Leader as well as an author and professional photographer.

MASSACHUSETTS AUDUBON SOCIETY, Natural History Travel, South Great Road, Lincoln, MA 01773.
PHONE: (617) 259-9506 ext. 7411   **FAX:** 617-259-8899
TOLL FREE: (800) 289-9504   **E-mail:** nhtravel@massaudubon.org
BOATS: FLAMINGO, POLARIS (Cruise Ship).
TOUR LEADER: Various, including Robert Buchsbaum and Wayne Peterson, one of the country's best-known birders.

PRICE RANGE: 1 week birding tour on the FLAMINGO (+2 nights in Quito) for $4000 incl. round-trip airfare from Miami.

1 week birding tour on the POLARIS (+2 nights in Quito and 1 night in Guayaquil) for $3800-$5500 (depending on cabin selection) incl. round-trip airfare from Miami/ Galápagos, most meals in Ecuador, and National Park Entrance Fee.

COMMENTS: The Natural History Travel Program is part of the *MASSACHUSETTS AUDUBON SOCIETY's* Conservation Department; a diverse array of conservation-oriented travel is offered across the country and throughout the world.

DIVING SPECIALTY TOURS

In 1986, with the creation of the *Galápagos Marine Resources Reserve*, the Galápagos National Park was extended to the waters surrounding the islands (a 15 nautical mile boundary zone was established). This event received extensive media coverage, and the wonders of this underwater world came to the attention of many divers.

The waters of the Galápagos are nutrient-rich (a result of strong upwelling activity), attracting a multitude of unique wildlife. About 10 percent of the 400 or so Galápagos fish species are endemic to the islands; the figure would be around 20 percent if the pelagic species were excluded. As you explore and perhaps photograph the unique subtidal life, sea lions will be your constant dive companions, swimming alongside you and seemingly sharing your curiosity (see Photo #15). Other occasional native swimmers and divers include penguins, marine turtles, flightless cormorants, and marine iguanas. Several species of rays are commonly seen, as well as white-tipped reef sharks and hammerhead sharks. Then there's the yellow-tailed surgeonfish, parrotfish, pufferfish, creolefish, grouper, and king angelfish, not to mention the yellow-bellied triggerfish, moorish idol, and hieroglyphic hawkfish.

Caution: While an exciting experience, diving in the Galápagos is not easy and is definitely not recommended for the inexperienced. The seasonal upwelling activity (especially in the waters off the western and northern islands) that has resulted in the diversity and abundance of marine wildlife, is itself a result of mixing of strong ocean currents (up to 2-4 knots) that the diver must contend with. The upwelling also causes prolific plankton growth, and the waters tend to be murky for the first 40-50 feet; it is thus relatively easy to lose your points of reference. In addition, the waters are often cold (60-65 Deg. F) and quarter-inch wet suits must be worn. Finally, there is virtually no emergency medical help available in the islands, and the closest operational decompression chamber is in Guayaquil.

Added to the above cautions, it is my recommendation that you do not dive the Galápagos until your second trip there. Much of the fascination and beauty of Galápagos is on land, and mixing a land-dive tour simply doesn't work. It's like ordering "steak and lobster;" you get the worst of both. The majority of the great dive sites (e.g., Darwin & Wolf Islands, Roca Redonda) are not anywhere near a land Visitor Site. Even if you're a diver, I recommend that your first trip to the Galápagos be on a non-dive tour, but one that visits as many of the islands as possible (a 10 day or 2 week tour) and allows you to do quite a bit of snorkeling (free-diving there is most rewarding). Then, if you can, go back to the islands on a dive trip that emphasizes the best dive sites.

All divers must bring their Certification Cards and full scuba gear, including mask & snorkel, full wet suit (1/8" or 1/4", depending on the season and your cold sensitivity), gloves, hood, boots, fins, regulator, buoyancy compensator, gauges, compass, cyalume "glow" sticks, and a dive light. A dive computer, dive "sausage" ("scuba tuba"), and DIVE ALERT® horn are highly recommended. Tanks, weights, and weight belts are provided. For a discussion of photographic equipment, see the Underwater Photography section in Chapter VII.

For more comprehensive information about the underwater world of the Galápagos, there are some excellent books on the subject, including **REEF FISH IDENTIFICATION: GALAPAGOS,** by Paul Humann, and **GALAPAGOS FISHES: A COMPREHENSIVE GUIDE TO THEIR IDENTIFICATION,** by Jack Grove and Robert Lavenberg; see the Literature section at the end of this book.

Finally, while the Dive Master will be sure to caution you, caution yourself to observe the rule about waiting at least 24 hours after your last dive before getting on the airplane for the flight back to Ecuador.

TOUR OPERATORS OFFERING DIVE TRIPS

NOTE: Prices do not include airfare, Galápagos National Park Entrance Fee, Ecuador Departure Taxes, or gratuities unless noted.

AGGRESSOR FLEET LIMITED, P.O. Drawer K, Morgan City, LA 70381.
PHONE: (504) 385-2628   **FAX:** 504-384-0817
TOLL FREE: (800) 348-2628 **E-mail:** divboat@aol.com
BOATS: GALAPAGOS AGGRESSOR I (aka ALBATROS) and GALAPAGOS AGGRESSOR II (aka PODEROSO II).
DIVE GUIDE: Locally provided.
PRICE RANGE: 1 week dive tour for $2600.
COMMENTS: These are two of the best dive boats in the Galápagos. The AGGRESSOR I typically offers a southern island route, while the AGGRESSOR II usually offers the more exciting but decidedly more challenging northern islands (for advanced divers only). On-board film processing is offered on both yachts. AGGRESSOR FLEET LIMITED operates and represents high-quality dive live-aboards throughout the world; they are very well known in the diving community. This is a sales office for several dive destinations, however, and their knowledge of the Galápagos is limited.

AQUATIC ENCOUNTERS, INC., 1966 Hardscrabble Place, Boulder, CO 80303.
PHONE: (303) 494-8384   **FAX:** 303-494-1202
E-mail: Aquatenctr@aol.com   **BOATS:** REINA SILVIA.
DIVE GUIDE: Marc Bernardi, the owner of AQUATIC ENCOUNTERS.
PRICE RANGE: 1 week diving tour (2-3 dives per day) + 4 nights (and some meals) in Quito for $3200.
COMMENTS: AQUATIC ENCOUNTERS offers several Galápagos diving trips

each year, many of them led by owner Marc Bernardi. Marc, who has a lot of diving experience in the Galápagos, states that each trip "always includes the high voltage diving at the northern islands of Darwin and Wolf."

LANDFALL PRODUCTIONS, 39675 Cedar Blvd., Ste. 295B, Newark, CA 94560.

PHONE: (510) 794-1599   **FAX:** 510-794-1617
TOLL FREE: (800) 525-3833 outside CA   **E-mail:** lndfall@aol.com
BOATS: LAMMAR LAW.   **DIVE GUIDE:** Locally provided.
PRICE RANGE: 1 week diving tour (2-3 dives per day) for $2400 (hotel, meals, and transfers in Quito not included).
COMMENTS: LANDFALL PRODUCTIONS, a Dive Tour Operator, is the "stateside booking office" for the owners of the LAMMAR LAW, the largest trimaran in the world.

PHOTOGRAPHY SPECIALTY TOURS

These trips are accompanied by a professional photographer in addition to the licensed Naturalist Guide. During the daily tours, photographic opportunities will be suggested, and guidance will be offered as requested. Evening workshop sessions will be held, and a variety of topics will be discussed, based on the interest of the group and the Tour Leader. The photography experience level of the tour members will vary quite a bit, from beginner to professional, and is generally not a factor; the common denominator is that everyone enjoys photography and wants to learn more. Photographic information will typically be supplied with the pre-departure briefing packet.

These trips offer a real opportunity to improve your photographic technique and to develop your "eye." As a photographer, I have never failed to learn a great deal from the instructor and the fellow members of a photographic field trip. Also, on a trip that is oriented towards photography, you are in a better position to take advantage of lighting conditions. The equatorial sun produces harsh shadows and bleaches out a lot of the rich natural color; some of the best shooting times occur on overcast days and during twilight (which is extremely brief on the equator). A photography group will be more apt to get up extra early in order to get on the first Visitor Site right at dawn and take advantage of the morning twilight. In the evening, the group will usually prefer to stay on the island a bit later for some twilight shots rather than go swimming or back to the boat for a cold one.

Another advantage to a Galápagos photography tour is that if you're doing something wrong, there's a high probability that someone will notice and point it out; better to find out on the second day of your tour that your polarizer or sun shade wasn't on than after you get home and start looking at the results of the 40 rolls of film you shot.

The only real negative (did I say that?) to a photographic safari of the Galápagos Islands is that it might be an overload situation. The main emphasis in the Galápagos is the wildlife. Many visitors, myself included, spend the evenings and early morning hours reading up on (and discussing) the flora and fauna to be observed on the next couple of islands to be visited. If there's going to be an evening photography discussion, I would want it to be relevant to what we're going to be seeing tomorrow, as opposed to a discussion of advanced photofinishing techniques. While on tour, you are dividing precious time (you're only on an island for 1-3 hours and have to keep moving) between listening to the Guide/ Tour Leader, being awed by what you're seeing, and trying to take pictures. There's not a lot of extra time for discussion.

Before deciding on whether to take a photographic specialty tour of the Galápagos, you might think about taking a photography field trip at home. In any case I recommend that, whenever possible, you speak directly with the Photo Tour Leader (Tour Operators often provide their phone numbers), and get a feel for the orientation of the trip that they're coordinating. In addition, you might ask if they've been to the Galápagos Islands before. One thing to watch out for is a "big name" photography Tour Leader who doesn't understand that a Tour Leader's prime responsibility concerns logistical details – and lots of them. Also you don't want a laid-back, "do your own thing becuase all pictures are won-derful" type of instructor on your once-in-a-lifetime trip to the Galápagos Islands. What you do want is a photographer who will provide you with and alert you to the unique photographic opportunities on each island and how best to take advantage of them.

TOUR OPEARATORS OFFERING PHOTOGRAPHY TRIPS

NOTE: Prices do not include airfare, Galápagos National Park Entrance Fee, Ecuador Departure Taxes, or gratuities unless noted.

GALAPAGOS TRAVEL, 783 Rio Del Mar Blvd., Suite #47, Aptos, CA 95003.
PHONE: (831) 689-9192   **FAX:** 831-689-9195
TOLL FREE: (800) 969-9014 **E-mail:** galapagostravel@compuserve.com
BOATS: SAN JACINTO, SAN JOSE.
TOUR LEADER: Various, including Barry Boyce, the author of this book.
PRICE RANGE: 11 day tour (+3 nights in Quito) for $2950 incl. most meals in Quito and all non-alcoholic beverages on the cruise;
       2 week tour (+3 nights in Quito) for $3550 incl. most meals in Quito and all non-alcoholic beverages on the cruise. This tour emphasizes the western islands of Isabela and Fernandina and includes a hike/ horseback ride to and around the rim of the Sierra Negra Volcano.
COMMENTS: GALAPAGOS TRAVEL offers a series of workshop-oriented tours of the Galápagos. The 11 day format allows sufficient time to visit the outer islands and to see a significant representation of the plant and animal species; the 2 week trips present a rare opportunity to explore the western islands of Fernandina and Isabela in depth. In addition to the daily guided island visits, evening workshop sessions focus on topics such as island formation and history, wildlife distribution, evolution, and conservation. These sessions always include a photography briefing for the following day. An emphasis is placed on providing optimum photographic opportunities and guidance to each passenger.

INTERNATIONAL WILDLIFE ADVENTURES., P.O. Box 1410, Vashon, WA 98070
PHONE: (206) 463-1943   **FAX:** 206-463-4081
TOLL FREE: (800) 593-8881 **E-mail:** info@wildlifeadventures.com
BOATS: MISTRAL II.
TOUR LEADER: Various, including Darrell Gulin (see below).
PRICE RANGE: 1 week photo tour (+3 nights in Quito) for $3300 incl. a 1-day Otavalo Market Tour.
COMMENTS: Darrell Gulin is a professional photographer, and his photos have appeared in most major nature magazines.

JOSEPH VAN OS PHOTO SAFARIS, P.O. Box 655, Vashon Island, WA 98070.
PHONE: (206) 463-5383   **FAX:** 206-463-5484
E-mail: info@photosafaris.com
BOATS: MISTRAL II, LAMMAR LAW.
TOUR LEADER: Various photographers, including Wayne Lynch and Joe Van Os (see Comments).
PRICE RANGE: 1 week photo tour (+2 nights in Quito and 1 night in Guayaquil) for $3500 incl. round-trip airfare from Miami and all meals in Quito.
COMMENTS: JOSEPH VAN OS PHOTO SAFARIS has been offering quality photo tours and workshops since 1980. Some of the trips are led by Joe Van Os, the director of the company and professional wildlife photographer. Veteran Tour Leader Wayne Lynch is a science writer and Canada's best known and most widely published nature photographer.

VOYAGERS INTERNATIONAL, P.O. Box 915, Ithaca, NY 14851.
PHONE: (607) 273-4321   **FAX:** 607-273-3873
TOLL FREE: (800) 633-0299 **E-mail:** voyint@aol.com
BOATS: ERIC, FLAMINGO, LETTY.
TOUR LEADER: Several photographers throughout the year including John Gerlach, Ron Rosenstock, David Muench, David Middleton, and Cliff Zenor.
PRICE RANGE: 1 week photo tour (+2 nights in Quito) for $2900 – $3200.
COMMENTS: Owner David Blanton has worked as a professional photographer for several years and has authored a book on nature photography. VOYAGERS conducts a unique series of photographic workshops led by prominent nature and travel photographers throughout the year; brochures are offered describing the background and orientation of each of the photographic instructors. VOYAGERS does an excellent job of providing pre-trip briefing information.

GALAPAGOS TOUR OPERATIONS IN ECUADOR

The prices you will be quoted by the Ecuadorian Operators will be about the same as you have received from their U.S. Representatives and Tour Operators. These are reputable Ecuadorian Tour and Boat Operators, not discount houses! You may have some bargaining power, however, if you travel to Ecuador and personally visit their offices. Occasionally there are a few vacancies on a boat scheduled to sail in the next couple of days, and the Operator may decide to offer you a discounted price to fill the empty slot(s). I do want to make it clear that there's no telling how often, when, or even if this opportunity will present itself.

The amount of any discount is totally open to negotiation; depending on you and the situation, a $1000 1 week cruise could wind up costing anywhere from $600-$1000 and anywhere from 5 minutes to a week or more of your time. This kind of activity can only occur in Ecuador with the Boat Operator and only during the week before the boat is scheduled to sail. There will be those companies, however, that will not want, or need, to offer a discount for whatever reason. The Cruise Ship Operators, for example, are used to sailing with vacancies and rarely discount.

Before you visit a particular Ecuadorian Boat Operator, look at their listing in this chapter (see the section below) and make a note as to which boats they operate and/or directly represent. The point here is that while they will act as an indirect representative for just about anyone's boat, they are only in a position to lower the price to fill a vacancy, as they deem necessary, on the boats they are directly involved with. To determine which boats you're potentially interested in, turn to the section, Boats of the Galápagos, earlier in the chapter and note who the Boat Operator and/or direct representative is.

As you make the rounds of the Boat Operators in Quito and/or Guayaquil, ask the following series of questions:

1. "Do you have any available space on 1-2 week Galápagos tours in the next week or so?" If there isn't anything available, thank them for their time, and ask if they know of another company that has something available.

2. "What boats are they on?" (Refer to the listing as discussed above.) Let them know which airline (SAN or TAME) you have reservations on. As discussed in Chapter V (FLIGHT PLANS), SAN only flies to the island of San Cristóbal and TAME only to Baltra. A particular boat will be leaving from one or the other island, and this must be clearly understood. The section below on Ecuadorian Boat Operators states the island the boat typically sails from, but this is subject to change. This detail must be worked out with the Boat Operator.

3. "Who is the Naturalist Guide on this trip?" After they answer, you can ask the follow-up question, "Is this Guide a Naturalist 1, 2, or 3?" You may even ask for a copy of the Guide's License. (See the Tour Leader vs. No Tour Leader section at the beginning of this chapter.) At this point, they will begin to think you're smarter than you look.

4. "What is the price of the tour?" After this question is answered, you can decide if the tour sounds good and the price is acceptable. If you want a better price, proceed to the following questions.

5. "When is this tour scheduled to leave?"

6. "How many vacancies are there?" Go on to say that you would like to be on the tour, but you're looking for something less expensive. At this point, the Boat Operator will get the idea of what you're up to, and either they'll want to play or they won't. If they do, the rest is up to you; this is where your negotiating skills go to work.

If you don't come to an agreement, let the Boat Operator know which hotel you're staying at (just in case the situation changes). If you do agree to terms, you will be required to pay in advance for your tour. Once you agree on a tour, the Operator will also help you confirm your flight arrangements to the Galápagos. This is an important detail, as the TAME flights to Baltra, in particular, are often overbooked; those passengers that have a firm tour are given priority consideration. Also, the Boat Operator may be escorting some of their other passengers to the airport, in which case they can arrange for you to join them (usually for an "airport transfer" charge). Again, this is not a minor detail as you may need some "inside help" at the airport (read Chapter V for a blow-by-blow description). In addition, they will be happy to assist you with local tours and excursions to the surrounding areas before or after your Galápagos cruise.

If you're not immediately successful in putting together an acceptable tour, you're going to have to make some contingency plans. You can stay in Quito and/or Guayaquil for a few days and wait to be contacted by one of the Boat Operators you visited. While you're waiting, you can do some shopping (which you would have done at the end of your vacation), tour Quito, and/or take Day Trips to the outlying areas. The amount of time you spend in the mainland depends on how tight your schedule is; the more time you appear to have, the better your negotiating position. Also, most cruises are 1 week in duration, and a particular boat may be sold out this week and have several vacancies the next.

Caution: At some point you'll decide on a particular tour and you'll be off to the islands. Do not, however, under any circumstances, go to the Galápagos without having purchased a tour. People do this, thinking they can get a cheaper or better tour directly from a local agency, the boat owner, or captain. This situation is a disaster – for you and the Galápagos. As pointed out earlier in this chapter (in the section on Day Trip Yachts, which is worth rereading at this time), virtually all the Boat Operators have their reservation and office operations in mainland Ecuador, so you can't just show up in the Galápagos and put together a cruise on any of the better boats. You then get stuck with the Day Trip companies which, once again, won't do you or the islands much good. **Please heed this warning!**

BOAT OPERATORS IN ECUADOR

Note: All phone numbers are local. When calling from the U.S., you must first dial the international access code "011" followed by the country code for Ecuador "593" followed by the city code for Quito "2" or Guayaquil "4" and then the local number. When calling Guayaquil from Quito, dial "04" followed by the local number; when calling Quito from Guayaquil, dial "02" followed by the local number. If you place an international call, remember that mainland Ecuador is on Eastern Standard Time throughout the year.

The FAX numbers listed below include the international, country, and city codes. For some reason, it is a lot easier for Ecuador to receive than to send a FAX communication; don't be surprised if it takes several attempts to get a message to you. E-mail numbers are listed if available.

Caution: Unfortunately, in the name of "progress," many of the newer yachts (and there are many of them) are imitating the itineraries of the Cruise Ships by offering 3 and 4 night (4 and 5 day) programs. This means that, if you've purchased a full week cruise, you might really be getting 2 partial weeks put together – a "fake" full week. Thus, you're making an extra stop at an airport and losing some fellow passengers while picking up others. In my opinion, aside from losing time, it takes away from the overall feeling of the trip. The problem is that the Boat Operator probably won't tell you that your 1 week cruise is really Cruise A + Cruise B. Be careful in your selection! See the Comments sections below to get an idea which of the yachts may follow this practice. But you still need to be cautious; other boats may change their operations at any time. By the way, this type of situation is avoided by booking through a U.S. Tour Operator who has chartered the yacht for the entire length of the Cruise. **This Caution will be referred to several times in the section below.**

BOAT OPERATORS IN QUITO

ANDANDO TOURS, Av. Amazonas 629 and Carrión, 2nd floor (P.O. Box 17-21-0088).
LOCAL PHONE: 550-952 or 548-780   **FAX:** 011-593-2-228-519
E-mail: andando1@ecnet.ec   **CONTACT:** Paulina Salazar.
BOATS: ANDANDO and SAMBA, which operate out of Baltra Island on Wednesdays.
PRICE RANGE: Available both on a charter and per-passenger basis. Approximate charter prices are: ANDANDO = $23,000/ week; SAMBA = $20,000/ week. Approximate per-passenger prices are: ANDANDO = $2000/ week; SAMBA = $1700/ week.
COMMENTS: The ANDANDO is a very popular boat and is booked solid by U.S. Tour Operators. The SAMBA is also popular, but seems to have more availability. Reservations should be made well in advance.

ANGERMEYER'S ENCHANTED EXCURSIONS, Foch 726 (off Av. Amazonas).
LOCAL PHONE: 569-960 or 221-305   **FAX:** 011-593-2-569-956
E-mail: angerme1@ecnet.ec   **CONTACT:** Judy Carvalhal (General Manager); Consuelo Gabela (Galápagos Sales Manager).
BOATS: ANGELITO I, BELUGA, CACHALOTE and SULIDAE. ANGELITO I typically sails from Baltra on Sundays, the BELUGA from Baltra on Saturdays, the CACHALOTE from Baltra on Wednesdays, and the SULIDAE from Baltra on Saturdays.
PRICE RANGE: Available both on a charter and per-passenger basis. Approximate charter prices are: ANGELITO I = $21,000/ week; BELUGA = $27,000/ week; CACHALOTE = $12,000/ week; SULIDAE = $14,000/ week. Approximate per-passenger prices are: ANGELITO I = $1500/ week; BELUGA = $1800/ week; CACHALOTE = $1200/ week; SULIDAE = $1100/ week.
COMMENTS: Owner and General Manager Judy Carvalhal lived in the Galápagos for several years and knows the islands very well. In addition, the BELUGA and CACHALOTE are partially owned and fully managed in the Galápagos by excellent captains.

ECOVENTURA, Av. Colon and 6 de Diciembre.
LOCAL PHONE: 507-408   **FAX:** 011-593-2-507-409

E-mail: ecosales@ecoventura.com.ec   **CONTACT:** Lourdes Mena.
BOATS: ERIC, FLAMINGO, LETTY, SEA CLOUD, and the Cruise Ship
   CORINTHIAN, all of which sail from San Cristóbal Island – the ERIC and
   FLAMINGO on Tuesdays and Fridays, the LETTY and the Cruise Ship
   CORINTHIAN on Mondays and Thursdays, and the SEA CLOUD on Fridays.
COMMENTS: Their main office is in Guayaquil. See the section on Boat
   Operators in Guayaquil for complete details, including pricing information.

ETNOTUR, Luis Cordero 1313 and Juan León Mera (P.O. Box 4770).
LOCAL PHONE: 560-297 or 564-565 or 563-379   **FAX:** 011-593-2-502-682
E-mail: pat@etnot.ecx.ec   **CONTACT:** Patricia Bastidas (General Manager).
BOATS: ANGELIQUE and ORCA. The ANGELIQUE sails from Baltra Island on
   Wednesdays and/or Saturdays; the ORCA operates from San Cristóbal on
   Tuesdays and/or Fridays.
PRICE RANGE: Available both on a charter and per-passenger basis.
   Approximate charter prices are: ANGELIQUE = $14,000/ week; ORCA =
   $7,500/ week. Approximate per-passenger prices are: ANGELIQUE =
   $1100/week; ORCA = $900/ week.
COMMENTS: The ORCA is a very comfortably-riding boat, and the
   ANGELIQUE is a classic brigantine motor sailer.
U.S. REPRESENTATIVE: FORUM TRAVEL INTERNATIONAL, INC., 91 Gregory
   Lane, #21, Pleasant Hill, CA 94523. Phone: (510) 671-2900; FAX: 510-946-
   1500; E-mail: info@forumtravel.com

EUROGALAPAGOS, Av. Amazonas 330 and Washington.
LOCAL PHONE: 549-912 or 542-888 or 553-750   **FAX:** 011-593-2-500-075
CONTACT: Sandra Solis.
BOATS: SULLIVAN, which sails from Baltra on Mondays and/or Thursdays.
PRICE RANGE: Available both on a charter and per-passenger basis.
   Approximate charter price is $14,000/ week; per-passenger price is about
   $1000/ week.
COMMENTS: The SULLIVAN is a nice enough boat at a very good price.
   However, this is one of the boats offering full week and "fake full week" (3 +
   4 night) programs; insist on a full week – see the Caution above.

GALACRUISES EXPEDITIONS CIA LTDA, Jorge Washington 748.
LOCAL PHONE: 523-324 or 556-036   **FAX:** 011-593-2-224-893
E-Mail: seaman@uio.satnet.net
CONTACT: Lucero Cevallos, General Manager.
BOATS: SEA MAN, which operates from Baltra on Mondays and/ or Fridays.
PRICE RANGE: Available both on a charter and per-passenger basis. Charter
   price is about $13,000/ week. Approximate per-passenger price is $800/
   week.
COMMENTS: The boat is a bit cozy for 16, but otherwise it is very nice, as is the
   price. There is an ownership affiliation with the Hotel Mar Azul in San
   Cristóbal, and they offer attractively-priced packages for those wishing to
   spend extra time in the Galápagos before or after the cruise. This is, however,
   one of the boats offering full week and "fake full week" (4 + 4 night) programs; insist on a full week – see the Caution above.

GALAPACIFICO TOURS S.A., Juan Severino 181 and Almagro.
LOCAL PHONE: 525-764 and 520-709   **FAX:** 011-593-2-504-740
CONTACT: Jorge Valdivieso, President.
BOATS: MARIGOLD, which operates from Baltra.
PRICE RANGE: Available by charter only at approximately $800/ week.

GALAPAGOS CRUISES 2000 (GALAPATUR), Juan León Mera 358 and Robles.
LOCAL PHONE: 226-432   **FAX:** 011-593-2-567-622
E-mail: aaagalap@uio.satnet.net
CONTACT: Patrice Teyssedre, President; Lourdes Bastidas (Sales Manager).
BOATS: PULSAR, which operates from Baltra on Thursdays and/or Sundays.
PRICE RANGE: Available both on a charter and per-passenger basis. Charter
price is about $7,000/ week. Approximate per-passenger price is $800/ week.
COMMENTS: The boat is a nice-looking catamaran and caters mostly to young
European travelers. The overall space is on the cozy side, but the yacht is well-
suited for family charters. If you're not chartering the yacht, however, this is
one of the boats offering full and "fake full week" (3 + 4 night) programs; insist
on a full week – see the Caution above.

GALAPAGOS EXPEDITIONS (GALAPEX SA), E. Salgado 1347 and Santa Rosa
(P.O. Box 170379).
LOCAL PHONE: 525-964   **FAX:** 011-593-2-503-740
CONTACT: Carlos Pacheco (General Manager); Pamela Pacheco (Sales).
BOATS: ENCANTADA, which operates out of Baltra on Sundays and/ or
Wednesdays.
PRICE RANGE: Available both on a charter and per-passenger basis. Charter
price is about $15,000/ week. Approximate per-passenger price is $1400/
week.
COMMENTS: This is another yacht offering full week and "fake full week" (4 + 4
night) programs; insist on a full week – see the Caution above.

GOLONDRINA TURISMO, Juan León Mera 639 and Carrión.
LOCAL PHONE: 528-570 or 528-616   **FAX:** 011-593-2-528-570
CONTACT: Xavier Serrano.
BOATS: FRAGATA, which operates out of Baltra on Fridays and/or Mondays.
PRICE RANGE: Available both on a charter and per-passenger basis. Charter
price is about $15,000/ week. Approximate per-passenger price is $1000/
week.
COMMENTS: This is another yacht offering full week and "fake full week" (3 +
4 night) programs; insist on a full week – see the Caution above.
U.S. REPRESENTATIVE: FORUM TRAVEL INTERNATIONAL, INC., 91 Gregory
Lane, #21, Pleasant Hill, CA 94523. Phone: (510) 671-2900; FAX: 510-946-
1500; E-mail: info@forumtravel.com

ISLAS GALAPAGOS TURISMO Y VAPORES C.A., Av. República del Salvador
935, (PO Box 135-A).
LOCAL PHONE: 451-522   **FAX:** 011-593-2-439-888
E-mail: ambasador@ecnet.ec
CONTACT: Patricia Batallas; Fernando Rodriguez.

BOATS: Cruise Ship AMBASADOR I, which operates out of Baltra on Wednesdays and Sundays.

PRICE RANGE: See the section on Cruise Ships.

COMMENTS: The operations/booking office in Quito is very well organized and efficient.

KLEINTOURS, Av. Shyris 1000.

LOCAL PHONE: 430-345 or 267-000   **FAX:** 011-593-2-442-389

E-mail: kleintou@uio.satnet.net   **CONTACT:** María Klein, General Manager.

BOATS: CORAL I and CORAL II, which operate from Baltra Island on Wednesdays and/or Sundays.

PRICE RANGE: Available both on a charter and per-passenger basis. Charter price is about $37,000/ week for the CORAL I and about $41,000/week for the CORAL II. Approximate per-passenger price is $1900-$2400/week (based on cabin selection). Soft drinks and 2 tropical cocktails per day are included.

COMMENTS: KLEINTOURS began its operations in 1983, and it is now one of the largest Tour Operators in Ecuador. Both of their yachts are very comfortable. Once again, however, both boats offer full week and "fake full week" (3 + 4 night) programs; insist on a full week – see the Caution above.

U.S. REPRESENTATIVE: TOLL FREE: (888) 505-5346; E-mail: (Northern/Eastern U.S./ Canada) kleintoursne@jadeinc.com / (Southern/ Western U.S.) kleinsw@bellsouth.net

LATIN TOUR, Almagro 1219 and La Niña (Blanquius Building).

LOCAL PHONE: 508-811 or 238-909   **FAX:** 011-593-2-568-657

E-mail: latintur@uio.satnet.net   **CONTACT:** Maria Jijon.

BOATS: FREEDOM and PELIKANO which sail from Baltra on Sundays and/or Wednesdays.

PRICE RANGE: FREEDOM is available both on a charter (about $19,000/week) and per-passenger (about $1700/ week) basis. The PELIKANO is also available both on a charter (about $13,000/ week) and per-passenger (about $1000/ week) basis.

COMMENTS: The FREEDOM was formerly called the SAMOA I. Both yachts offer full week and "fake full week" (3 + 4 night) programs; insist on a full week – see the Caution above.

METROPOLITAN TOURING, Av. República de El Salvador 970 (P.O. Box 17-12-0310).

LOCAL PHONE: 464-780   **FAX:** 011-593-2-464-702

CONTACT: Marcela Romero.

BOATS: Cruise Ships ISABELA II and SANTA CRUZ. The ISABELA II sails from Baltra Island on Tuesdays and Fridays; the SANTA CRUZ sails from Baltra on Mondays and Thursdays. A combination hotel/ Day Cruise program is offered in affiliation with the yacht DELFIN II and the Hotel Delfin on Santa Cruz Island.

PRICE RANGE: For pricing information on the ISABELA II and SANTA CRUZ, see the section on Cruise Ships. The Hotel Delfin/ DELFIN II Day Cruise 1 week program (Wednesday/Wednesday or Sunday/Sunday) is about $1500/person (double occupancy – singles are $2000); the Wednesday/

Sunday (4-night) program is about $900/person (double occupancy – singles are $1200); the Sunday/ Wednesday (3-night) program is about $700/person (double occupancy – singles are $900).

COMMENTS: METROPOLITAN TOURING is the Ecuadorian company that carefully and professionally introduced tourism to the Galápagos Islands. METROPOLITAN is very highly respected in the industry and is the largest Tour Operator in Ecuador.

U.S. REPRESENTATIVE: ADVENTURE ASSOCIATES, 13150 Coit Rd., Suite 110, Dallas, TX 75240. PHONE: (972) 907-0414; TOLL FREE: (800) 527-2500; FAX: 972-783-1286.

NIXE CRUISES, S.A., La Tierra 392 and Shyris (P.O. Box 17-17-6646).
LOCAL PHONE: 448-985   **FAX:** 011-593-2-437-645
E-mail: nixecru1@ecnet.ec
CONTACT: Martha García (Sales Manager); Federico Dreyer (General Manager).
BOATS: AHMARA and ESCAPADA, which typically sail from Baltra on Saturdays.
PRICE RANGE: Available both on a charter and per-passenger basis. The approximate charter price is $15,000/ week; per-passenger price is about $1600/ week.
COMMENTS: NIXE CRUISES operates a pair of beautiful catamarans – a bit cozy, but well suited for family and dive charters.

NUEVO MUNDO EXPEDITIONS, Coruña 1349 and Orellana (P.O. Box 1703-402A).
LOCAL PHONE: 552-617 or 553-826   **FAX:** 011-593-2-565-261
E-Mail: nmundo@uio.telconet.net
CONTACT: Oswaldo Muñoz (President); Silvia Duarte (Tour Coordinator).
BOATS: GALAPAGOS ADVENTURE and LOBO DE MAR III, which sail from Baltra Island on Fridays.
PRICE RANGE: Available both on a charter and per-passenger basis. Approximate charter prices are: GALAPAGOS ADVENTURE = $29,000/ week; LOBO DE MAR III = $23,000/ week. Per passenger price is about $1500/week for the GALAPAGOS ADVENTURE and $1200 week for the LOBO DE MAR III.
COMMENTS: NUEVO MUNDO is a very professional, well respected Tour Operator; they are very active in many conservation programs.

QUASAR NAUTICA, S.A., Av. Shyris 2447 and Gaspar de Villarroel (P.O. Box 17-17994).
LOCAL PHONE: 257-822 or 441-550   **FAX:** 011-593-2-436-625
E-mail: qnautic1@ecnet.ec   **CONTACT:** Dolores de Diez.
BOATS: ALTA, DIAMANTE, LAMMAR LAW, MISTRAL II, NORTADA, PAR-RANDA, RESTING CLOUD, and the Cruise Ship ECLIPSE. The yachts sail from Baltra Island – the DIAMANTE on Fridays, the ALTA and MISTRAL II on Saturdays, and the LAMMAR LAW, NORTADA, PARRANDA, & RESTING CLOUD on Sundays. The Cruise Ship ECLIPSE sails from Baltra on Sundays.

PRICE RANGE: The yachts are available both on a charter and per-passenger basis. Approximate charter prices are: ALTA = $37,000/ week; DIAMANTE = $22,000/ week; LAMMAR LAW = $39,000/ week; MISTRAL II = $22,000/ week; NORTADA = $20,000/ week; PARRANDA = $35,000/ week; RESTING CLOUD = $18,000/ week. Per-passenger price for the yachts is about $1900-$2600/ week (depending on yacht, cabin selection, and season). For pricing information on the ECLIPSE, see the section on Cruise Ships.

COMMENTS: QUASAR NAUTICA is a very established company. Their boats are all attractive, modern, and very popular with many of the U.S. Tour Operators.

U.S. REPRESENTATIVE: TUMBACO, INC., Miami International Commerce Center, 7855 NW 12th St., Suite 221, Miami, FL 33126. PHONE: (305) 599-9008; TOLL FREE: (800) 247-2925; FAX: 305-592-7060; E-mail: tumbaco@gate.net

SANDAES TURISMO, Pinto 447 and Amazonas.
LOCAL PHONE: 565-385 or 508-353   **FAX:** 011-593-2-565-385
CONTACT: Alexandra, Sales Manager.
BOATS: DAPHNE, which operates out of Baltra on Wednesdays and/or Sundays.
PRICE RANGE: Available both on a charter and per-passenger basis. Charter price is about $15,000/ week. Approximate per-passenger price is $1000/ week.
COMMENTS: This is another yacht offering full week and "fake full week" (4+4 night) programs; insist on a full week – see the Caution above.

SANGAY TOURING, Amazonas 1188 and Cordero.
LOCAL PHONE: 550-180 or 550-176 or 524-878   **FAX:** 011-593-2-560-426
E-Mail: turgal@uio.satnet.net   **CONTACT:** Carlos Albuja.
BOATS: DARWIN EXPLORER, which sails from Baltra on Saturdays and/or Wednesdays.
PRICE RANGE: Available both on a charter and per-passenger basis. Approximate charter price is $15,000/ week; per passenger price is about $1000/ week.
COMMENTS: The DARWIN EXPLORER was formerly called the ISABELA I. This classic yacht offers full week and "fake full week" (3 + 4 night) programs; insist on a full week – see the Caution above.

ROLF WITTMER/ TURISMO GALAPAGOS CIA. LTDA., Av. Amazonas 621 and Carrión (P.O. Box 17-07-8989).
LOCAL PHONE: 553-460 or 526-938   **FAX:** 011-593-2-448-173
E-mail: rwittmer@tiptop.com.ec
CONTACT: Enrique Wittmer (GeneralManager).
BOATS: TIP TOP II and TIP TOP III; these yachts operate out of Baltra Island on Tuesdays and/or Fridays.
PRICE RANGE: TIP TOP II is available both on a charter (about $18,000/week) and per-passenger (about $1300/ week) basis. The TIP TOP III is also available both on a charter (about $26,000/week) and per-passenger (about $1600/ week) basis.

COMMENTS: TURISMO GALAPAGOS is owned by Captain Rolf Wittmer, the first natural resident of Floreana Island (born in 1933); he knows the islands extremely well. These boats both offer full week and "fake full week" (3 + 4 night) programs; insist on a full week – see the Caution above. Diving programs are offered on both yachts.

BOAT OPERATORS IN GUAYAQUIL

CANODROS, S.A., Urdenata 1418 and Av. del Ejército (P.O. Box 8442).
LOCAL PHONE: 285-711 or 280-173 or 280-143   **FAX:** 011-593-4-287-651
E-mail: eco-tourism1@canodros.com.ec
CONTACT: Lurdes Diaz-Granados, Marketing/Sales Supervisor.
BOATS: Cruise Ship GALAPAGOS EXPLORER II, which operates out of San Cristóbal on Wednesdays and Saturdays.
PRICE RANGE: See the Section on Cruise Ships for pricing information.
COMMENTS: The GALAPAGOS EXPLORER II is truly a luxury Cruise Ship. It replaces the GALAPAGOS EXPLORER, which ran aground in January, 1996. The management, which is very experienced in the Galápagos, remains the same.
U.S. REPRESENTATIVE: GALAPAGOS, INC., 7800 Red Road, Suite 112, South Miami, FL 33143. PHONE: (305) 665-0841; TOLL FREE: (800) 327-9854; FAX: 305-661-1457; E-mail: wwhgps@icanect.net

ECOVENTURA S.A., Av. C.J. Arosomena – Km 2^{1}/$_{2}$.
LOCAL PHONE: 206-708   **FAX:** 011-593-4-202-990
E-mail: ecosales@ecoventura.com.ec
CONTACT: Jose Miguel Urunuella, General Manager.
BOATS: ERIC, FLAMINGO, LETTY, SEA CLOUD, and the Cruise Ship CORINTHIAN, all of which sail from San Cristóbal Island – the ERIC and FLAMINGO on Tuesdays and Fridays, the LETTY and the Cruise Ship CORINTHIAN on Mondays and Thursdays, and the SEA CLOUD on Fridays.
PRICE RANGE: The ERIC, FLAMINGO, and LETTY are available both by charter (about $36,000/ week) and on a per-passenger basis (about $1800-$2100/ week, based on deck level). The SEA CLOUD is also available on a charter basis (about $12,000/week) as well as per-passenger (approximately $1700/ week). For the CORINTHIAN, see the section on Cruise Ships.
QUITO OFFICE: Av. Colon and 6 de Diciembre.
LOCAL PHONE: 507-408   **FAX:** 011-593-2-507-409.
COMMENTS: ECOVENTURA has an ownership affiliation with SAETA and SAN AIRLINES, and convenient, attractively-priced package plans are sometimes offered. It also means that these yachts are in the travel agent computer systems and can be readily booked by them. The ERIC and FLAMINGO now offer full week programs most of the time; the LETTY offers both full week and "fake full week" (3 + 4 night) programs; see the Caution above. The SEA CLOUD is ideal for family and diving charters.
U.S. REPRESENTATIVE: GALAPAGOS NETWORK, 7200 Corporate Center Drive, Suite 309, Miami FL 33126. PHONE: (305) 592-2294; TOLL FREE: (800) 633-7972; FAX: 305-592-6394; E-mail: gpsnet@aol.com

GALAHOST S.A., Junin 504 and Baquerizo Moreno.
LOCAL PHONE: 312-697   **FAX:** 011-593-4-566-575
E-mail: galahost@gye.satnet.net   **CONTACT:** Eric Galvez, Sales Manager.
BOATS: AMIGO I, which sails from San Cristóbal Island on Sundays.
PRICE RANGE: Available primarily on a charter basis for about $14,000/ week.
COMMENTS: The AMIGO I is an older boat and a bit cramped, but it has a
friendly feel to it and was refit in 1997.
   U.S. REPRESENTATIVE: GALAHOST, ATTN: Arnie Galvez, 11 Belmont Place,
   Staten Island, NY 10301. TOLL FREE: (888) 687-1349; FAX: 718-273-0777;
   E-mail: galvez@panix.com

GALAMAZONAS, J.T. Marengo, Km. 1.8, 5th Floor (P.O. Box 09-01-5600).
LOCAL PHONE: 299-950   **FAX:** 011-593-4-299-955
E-mail: galamazo@gye.satnet.net   **CONTACT:** Herbert Frei, President
BOATS: GALAPAGOS AGGRESSOR I (aka ALBATROS) and GALAPAGOS
   AGGRESSOR II (aka PODEROSO II).
PRICE RANGE: 1 week dive tour for about $2600.
COMMENTS: These are two of the best dive boats in the Galápagos. The
   AGGRESSOR I typically offers a southern island route, while the AGGRESSOR
   II usually visits the more exciting but decidly more challenging northern
   islands (for advanced divers only). On-board film processing is offered on both
   yachts.
U.S. REPRESENTATIVE: AGGRESSOR FLEET LIMITED, P.O. Drawer K, Morgan
City, LA 70381. PHONE: (504) 385-2628; FAX: 504-384-0817; TOLL FREE:
(800) 348-2628; E-mail: divboat@aol.com

GALASAM CIA. LTDA., Av. 9 de Octubre 424, Gran Pasaje Bldg., #1106.
LOCAL PHONE: 306-093   **FAX:** 011-593-4-313-351
E-mail; galapago@galasam.com.ec
CONTACT: Antonio Samán (General Manager), Gianna (Reservations).
BOATS: CRUZ DEL SUR and ESTRELLA DEL MAR, which sail from San Cristóbal
   Island on Mondays; DORADO and MOBY DICK, which sail from Baltra on
   Mondays; ISLAS PLAZAS, which sails from Baltra on Wednesdays and
   Saturdays; DARWIN, which sails from San Cristóbal on Wednesdays and
   from Baltra on Saturdays.
PRICE RANGE: Available both on a charter and per-passenger basis.
   Approximate charter prices are: MOBY DICK = $20,000/ week; CRUZ DEL
   SUR, DORADO, ESTRELLA DEL MAR, and ISLAS PLAZAS = $19,000/ week;
   DARWIN = $17,000/ week. Approximate per-passenger prices are: MOBY
   DICK = $1500/ week; CRUZ DEL SUR, DORADO, ESTRELLA DEL MAR and
   ISLAS PLAZAS = $1400/ week; DARWIN = $1200/ week.
COMMENTS: GALASAM is a large Boat Operator, whose fleet includes several
   Economy Class Yachts, which are run on a budget basis. Their trend over the
   last few years, however, is to concentrate more on the middle to upper end of
   the market. The yachts listed here are excellent throughout, a good value, and
   highly recommended. You should be aware, however, that the DARWIN,
   ISLAS PLAZAS, and MOBY DICK have full week and "fake full week" (3 + 4
   night) programs – see the Caution above.

U.S. REPRESENTATIVES:

FORUM TRAVEL INTERNATIONAL, INC., 91 Gregory Lane, #21, Pleasant Hill, CA 94523. Phone: (510) 671-2900; FAX: 510-946-1500; E-mail: info@forumtravel.com

GALAPAGOS, INC., 7800 Red Road, Suite 112, South Miami, FL 33143. PHONE: (305) 665-0841; TOLL FREE (800) 327-9854; FAX: 305-661-1457; E-mail: wwhgps@icanect.net

REPRESENTATIVES AND DISTRIBUTORS OF ECUADORIAN BOAT OWNERS/ OPERATORS

The companies in this list are direct U.S. (or worldwide) representatives for the leading Tour and Boat Operators in Ecuador; these representatives work with U.S. Tour Operators, travel agents and the general public. They typically will quote the same retail list prices to the public for a Galápagos tour as their affiliated Ecuadorian Tour/ Boat Operator. This arrangement makes it very convenient to book a Galápagos Tour in the U.S. Remember, though, that the per passenger list price (often called the FIT price) does not include airport transfers, hotels, local tours, and meals in mainland Ecuador (although all Tour Operators can put together a "package" for you). The greatest concern in booking direct is that you could be buying what is generally called in the travel industry an FIT (Foreign Independent Travel) Tour. As stated earlier in this chapter in some detail (see the section Tour Leader vs. No Tour Leader), FIT Tours, by definition, are more likely to mix passengers that have different interests and trip expectations. Also, the chances for a lower classification Guide and a "fake full week" tour are greater. Once again, make your calls, gather the brochures, make lists, and use this chapter to sort out what you're getting for what you're paying.

NOTE: The following companies are not necessarily exclusive representatives of the Boat Owner/Operator.

ADVENTURE ASSOCIATES, 13150 Coit Rd., Suite 110, Dallas, TX 75240.
PHONE: (972) 907-0414   **FAX:** 972-783-1286
TOLL FREE: (800) 527-2500
BOATS: Cruise Ships ISABELA II and SANTA CRUZ. A combination hotel/Day Cruise program is offered in affiliation with the Hotel Delfin (yacht DELFIN II) on Santa Cruz Island.
PRICE RANGE: For pricing information on the ISABELA II and SANTA CRUZ, see the section on Cruise Ships. For the Hotel Delfin/ DELFIN II Day Cruise programs, see the METROPOLITAN TOURING listing in the section on Boat Operators In Quito.
COMMENTS: ADVENTURE ASSOCIATES is the U.S. representative for METROPOLITAN TOURING, the Ecuadorian company that carefully and professionally introduced tourism to the Galápagos Islands. METROPOLITAN is very highly respected in the industry and is the largest Tour Operator in Ecuador.

AGGRESSOR FLEET LIMITED, P.O. Drawer K, Morgan City, LA 70381.
PHONE: (504) 385-2628   **FAX:** 504-384-0817
TOLL FREE: (800) 348-2628   **E-mail:** divboat@aol.com
BOATS: GALAPAGOS AGGRESSOR I (aka ALBATROS) and GALAPAGOS
   AGGRESSOR II (aka PODEROSO II).
PRICE RANGE: 1 week dive tour for about $2600.
COMMENTS: These are two of the best dive boats in the Galápagos. The
   AGGRESSOR I typically offers a southern island route, while the AGGRES-
   SOR II usually offers the more exciting but decidedly more challenging north-
   ern islands (for advanced divers only). On-board film processing is offered on
   both yachts. AGGRESSOR FLEET LIMITED operates and represents high-quality dive live-aboards throughout the world; they are very well known in the
   diving community. This is a sales office for several dive destinations, however, and their knowledge of the Galápagos is limited.

FORUM TRAVEL INTERNATIONAL, 91 Gregory Lane, #21, Pleasant Hill, CA
   94523.
PHONE: (510) 671-2900   **FAX:** 510-946-1500
E-mail: info@forumtravel.com
BOATS: ANGELIQUE, CRUZ DEL SUR, DARWIN, DORADO, ESTRELLA DEL
   MAR, FRAGATA, ISLAS PLAZAS, MOBY DICK, ORCA, and several Economy
   Class Yachts.
PRICE RANGE: See the ETNOTUR, GALASAM, and GOLONDRINA TURISMO
   listings in the section on Boat Operators In Ecuador.
COMMENTS: FORUM has been putting together Galápagos trips since 1965,
   and according to Director Nicolas Hetzer, they were the first North American
   company to offer tours to the islands.

GALAHOST, 11 Belmont Place, Staten Island, NY 10301.
TOLL FREE: (888) 687-1349   **FAX:** 718-273-0777
E-mail: galvez@panix.com   **CONTACT:** Arnie Galvez.
BOATS: AMIGO I.
PRICE RANGE: See the GALAHOST listing in the section on Boat Operators In
   Guayaquil.

GALAPAGOS, INC., 7800 Red Road, Suite 112, South Miami, FL 33143.
PHONE: (305) 665-0841   **FAX:** 305-661-1457
TOLL FREE: (800) 327-9854   **E-mail:** wwhgps@icanect.net
BOATS: CRUZ DEL SUR, DARWIN, DORADO, ESTRELLA DEL MAR, ISLAS
   PLAZAS, and MOBY DICK; Cruise Ship GALAPAGOS EXPLORER II.
PRICE RANGE: For the yachts, see the GALASAM listing in the section on Boat
   Operators In Guayaquil. For the GALAPAGOS EXPLORER II, see the section
   on Cruise Ships.

GALAPAGOS NETWORK, 7200 Corporate Center Dr., Ste. 309, Miami, FL
   33126.
PHONE: (305) 592-2294   **FAX:** 305-592-6394
TOLL FREE: (800) 633-7972   **E-mail:** gpsnet@aol.com.

BOATS: ERIC, FLAMINGO, LETTY, SEA CLOUD, and the Cruise Ship CORINTHIAN.

PRICE RANGE: For the yachts, see the ECOVENTURA listing in the section on Boat Operators In Guayaquil; for the CORINTHIAN, see the section on Cruise Ships.

COMMENTS: The operator of these yachts, ECOVENTURA, has an ownership affiliation with SAETA and SAN AIRLINES, and convenient, attractively-priced package plans are sometimes offered. It also means that these yachts are in the travel agent computer systems and can be readily booked by them. Finally, the staff at GALAPAGOS NETWORK are most knowledgeable about Galápagos operations – especially their manager, Doris Welsh.

GALAPAGOS TRAVEL, 783 Rio Del Mar Blvd., Suite #47, Aptos, CA 95003 .
PHONE: (831) 689-9192   **FAX:** 831-689-9195
TOLL FREE: (800) 969-9014   **E-mail:** galapagostravel@compuserve.com
BOATS: SAN JACINTO, SAN JOSE.

PRICE RANGE: The SAN JACINTO and SAN JOSE are available only on a charter basis for about $21,000/ week.

COMMENTS: GALAPAGOS TRAVEL, the publisher of this book, maintains an office in Quito. In addition to its Galápagos operations, a number of extension trips are offered in mainland Ecuador.

GLOBAL ASSOCIATES NETWORK, INC., P.O. Box 150514, Brooklyn, NY 11215
PHONE: (718) 788-4453   **FAX:** 718-788-4498
E-mail: ganeeuu@aol.com
Contact: Pablo Proaño.
BOATS: FREE ENTERPRISE, which sails from Baltra on Sundays.

PRICE RANGE: Available both on a charter and per-passenger basis. Charter price is about $26,000/ week. Approximate per-passenger price is $1300/ week.

COMMENTS: GLOBAL ASSOCIATES NETWORK operates the yacht; all bookings are through the U.S. office. The FREE ENTERPRISE is a beautiful 102 ft catamaran.

KLEINTOURS   **TOLL FREE:** (888) 505-5346
E-mail: (N & E U.S./ Canada) kleintoursne@jadeinc.com
           (S & W U.S.) kleinsw@bellsouth.net
BOATS: CORAL I and CORAL II.

PRICE RANGE: see the KLEINTOURS listing in the section on Boat Operators In Quito.

COMMENTS: KLEINTOURS began its operations in 1983, and it is now one of the largest Tour Operators in Ecuador. They maintain 2 sales offices in the U.S.

PLACES TRAVEL PRODUCTION AB, S-104 31 (P.O. Box 14450), Stockholm, Sweden
PHONE: 011-46-8-301-645   **FAX:** 011-46-8-301-135
BOATS: REINA SILVIA, which sails from Baltra Island on Saturdays.

PRICE RANGE: Available mostly on a charter and occasionally on a per-passenger basis. The approximate charter price is $27,000/ week; per-passenger price is about $2600-$2800/ week. The per-passenger price variation is based on cabin selection, with the top of the line being the Luxury Suite they refer to as the "Owner's Cabin."

COMMENTS: The REINA SILVIA is an excellent, well-managed yacht. PLACES TRAVEL, although in Sweden, seems to be on top of most logistical details.

SPECIAL EXPEDITIONS, 720 Fifth Ave., New York, NY 10019
PHONE: (212) 765-7740   **FAX:** 212-265-3770
TOLL FREE: (800) 425-2724   **E-mail:** travel@specialexpeditions.com
BOATS: Cruise Ship POLARIS, which sails from Baltra on Saturdays.
PRICE RANGE: See the section on Cruise Ships.
COMMENTS: SPECIAL EXPEDITIONS was founded in 1979 by Sven-Olaf Lindblad, carrying on the adventure travel tradition of his well-known family. SPECIAL EXPEDITIONS began offering trips to the Galápagos in 1996, making a serious effort to put an educational focus on all their trips. In addition to the Naturalist Guides, there is an Expedition Leader on-board.

TUMBACO, INC., Miami International Commerce Center, 7855 NW 12th St., Suite 221, Miami, FL 33126.
PHONE: (305) 599-9008   **FAX:** 305-592-7060
TOLL FREE: (800) 247-2925   **E-mail:** tumbaco@gate.net
BOATS: ALTA, DIAMANTE, LAMMAR LAW, MISTRAL II, NORTADA, PAR-RANDA, RESTING CLOUD, and the Cruise Ship ECLIPSE.
PRICE RANGE: For the yachts, see the QUASAR NAUTICA listing in the section on Boat Operators in Quito. For the ECLIPSE, see the section on Cruise Ships.

CHAPTER V

FLIGHT PLANS

The only flights to the Galápagos Islands are from mainland Ecuador. You have a choice of flying to either Quito or Guayaquil, with little difference in cost. If you're part of a tour group, the decision of whether to fly to Quito or Guayaquil will be made for you. More than likely you will fly to Quito with your group or meet your group in Quito.

If you're going over without having booked a Galápagos tour in advance, I would recommend getting round-trip air tickets to Quito; there are many more Ecuadorian-based tour operators in Quito than in Guayaquil (see Chapter IV, CHOOSING A TOUR).

Most Tour Operators function as travel agencies and will offer to make flight arrangements for you. Take them up on it; they will usually get you at least as good a fare as you can get on your own. Besides, it'll save you the time and effort which you can use to read up on the Galápagos. If you are waiting to book your Galápagos tour in Ecuador, read the following flight information and make your airline reservations directly with the airline or through your travel agent. If you opt for the latter, tell the agent the flights you want as well as the quoted fares. If you do it this way, there will be no price difference between what the airline and the travel agency quotes you. I don't mean to imply that travel agents mark-up the prices; the agencies make their money in the form of a discount off the list price. It's just that there are not many travel agencies that are familiar with flights and air fares to Ecuador, not to mention the Galápagos Islands. There are several nuances and special "tied-fares" that are not in the travel agent's computer. Let's discuss them.

GETTING TO ECUADOR

Tourism in Ecuador has increased rapidly over the last few years, and passengers now have several air carriers to choose from. There are currently four main air routes from the U.S. to Ecuador:

1. Flights from Miami – direct on AMERICAN, ECUATORIANA, and SAETA; indirect on LACSA (stopping in Costa Rica) and SERVIVENSA (stopping in Caracas, Venezuela).

2. Flights from the New York City area – direct from JFK on SAETA and ECUATORIANA; indirect on CONTINENTAL from Newark (stopping in Panama City or Bogota), LACSA from JFK (stopping in Costa Rica), and SER-VIVENSA from JFK (stopping in Caracas and Bogota).

3. Flights from Houston – indirect on CONTINENTAL, stopping in Panama City.

4. Flights from Los Angeles – indirect on LACSA (stopping in Mexico City and Costa Rica) and TAME/ EVA (stopping in Panama City).

The direct travel time is approximately 4 hours from Miami and 6 hours from New York City.

FLIGHT SCHEDULES TO ECUADOR

As with prices, the following schedules are subject to change; verify the current schedule before making your reservations. Remember that mainland Ecuador remains on Eastern Standard Time throughout the year.

To/From Miami:

AMERICAN AIRLINES – AMERICAN has daily direct late afternoon and evening flights to Quito. There are also daily direct flights from Quito to Miami with morning departures.

AMERICAN has a daily direct evening flight to Guayaquil. There is also a daily direct flight from Guayaquil to Miami with a morning departure.

Comments: The AMERICAN flights to Ecuador are quite convenient as they provide same-day connecting flights and through-fares from most U.S. cities; this service is especially attractive to those beginning their journey from the West Coast (where overnighting in Miami is currently required to make the international connections on some of the other carriers). AMERICAN also provides separate daily flights to both Quito and Guayaquil, which knocks about an hour off the arrival time to the second city on a combined Quito/ Guayaquil or Guayaquil/Quito flight. Finally, there are the frequent flyer miles you can earn (as well as using frequent flyer awards to fly to Ecuador). On the negative side, AMERICAN cannot ticket you to the Galápagos, making it slightly more difficult and possibly more expensive for you to fly to the islands (see the section below, From Ecuador to the Galápagos).

ECUATORIANA AIRLINES – ECUATORIANA has daily direct afternoon flights to Guayaquil (with continuing service to Quito). There are also daily direct morning flights from Guayaquil to Miami; these flights originate in Quito.

Comments: ECUATORIANA (Spanish for Ecuadorian) is in fact an Ecuadorian airline. It is relatively new and privately owned. Previously, there was a government-owned airline with the same name; it had financial problems and stopped operations in 1994. While it is hoped that they do well, people in the travel industry wonder if there is room in the market for two Ecuadorian airlines (ECUATORIANA and SAETA) with basically the same schedules (see below). There was talk of a merger some time ago, but it didn't happen. ECUA-TORIANA has an affiliation with U.S. AIR (through LATIN PASS) to earn and use frequent flyer miles.

SAETA AIRLINES – SAETA has daily direct afternoon flights to Guayaquil (with continuing service to Quito). There are also daily direct morning flights from Guayaquil to Miami; these flights originate in Quito.

    Comments: SAETA (*Sociedad Ecuatoriana de Transportes Aeros*) is a privately owned Ecuadorian airline. They are affiliated with SAN, an Ecuadorian airline that operates flights within Ecuador and from the mainland to the Galápagos. There is a "tied-fare" between the two (see the section below, From Ecuador to the Galápagos).

    SAETA operates on a very businesslike schedule and has very competitive prices. Their service is excellent; the times I've flown with them to Ecuador, every seat on the plane was treated as First Class, with complimentary champagne prior to takeoff, complimentary cocktails during the flight, tasty appetizers (including Ecuadorian specialties) and your choice of 3 entrees served with very fine wines. There are now through-fares from most major U.S. cities. Finally, SAETA has an affiliation with U.S. AIR (through LATIN PASS) to earn and use frequent flyer miles.

LACSA AIRLINES – LACSA has late morning indirect flights to both Quito and Guayaquil several days a week. The flights stop in Costa Rica, and passengers must change planes to Guayaquil, with continuing service to Quito. They also have early afternoon indirect flights to Miami from either Quito or Guayaquil (depending on the day of the week). The flights stop in Costa Rica, and passengers must change planes to an evening flight, arriving Miami late at night.

    Comments: LACSA is a Costa Rican airline. While their service to Ecuador is not as convenient as other carriers, they do offer flights from several U.S. cities at reasonably-good fares. Also, with the increasing popularity of natural history tourism in Costa Rica, there is a growing number of passengers that visit both Costa Rica and Ecuador on the same trip; if you're thinking of doing this marathon combination, LACSA may be your airline of choice. Finally, LACSA has an affiliation with U.S. AIR (through LATIN PASS) to earn and use frequent flyer miles.

SERVIVENSA AIRLINES – SERVIVENSA has daily morning indirect flights to Quito. The flights stop in Caracas, Venezuela, and passengers must change planes to Quito, arriving early in the evening. They also have daily indirect morning flights to Miami from Quito. The flights stop in Caracas, and passengers must change planes to a late afternoon flight, arriving Miami in the evening.

    Comments: SERVIVENSA (*Servicios Avensa*) is a Venezuelan airline. While their service to Ecuador is not direct, it is convenient, as they are the only airline offering morning departures from both Miami & JFK and evening arrivals in Quito. Other carriers arrive Quito late at night or early in the morning (after a red-eye flight). SERVIVENSA has an affiliation with U.S. AIR (through LATIN PASS) to earn and use frequent flyer miles.

To/From New York City:

ECUATORIANA AIRLINES – ECUATORIANA has daily direct red-eye flights from JFK to Guayaquil (with continuing service to Quito). There are also daily direct early afternoon flights from Guayaquil to JFK; these flights originate in Quito, leaving at noon.
    Comments: See above.

SAETA AIRLINES – SAETA has direct red-eye flights from JFK to Guayaquil 5-6 nights/ week (with continuing service to Quito). There are also direct late morning flights from Guayaquil to JFK 5-6 days/week: these flights originate in Quito.
    Comments: See above.

CONTINENTAL AIRLINES – CONTINENTAL has 2 daily afternoon departures from Newark to Quito, one stopping in Bogota and continuing on to Quito and the other stopping in Panama City, requiring a plane change to Quito (or Guayaquil). There are also 2 daily morning flights from Quito to Newark, one stopping in Bogota and continuing on to Newark, arriving late afternoon; the other flight (originating in Guayaquil), stops in Panama City, requiring a plane change to Newark, arriving late afternoon.
    Comments: CONTINENTAL offers through-fares from many U.S. cities. Then there are frequent flyer miles you can earn and the prospect of flying to Ecuador on frequent flyer awards. The disadvantages are indirect flights to Ecuador and the lack of through-fares to the Galápagos, making it somewhat more difficult and possibly more expensive for you to fly to the islands (see the section below, From Ecuador to the Galápagos).

To/ From Houston:

CONTINENTAL AIRLINES – CONTINENTAL has a daily afternoon departure to Quito, stopping in Panama City. Guayaquil passengers disembark in Panama City and change planes. There are also daily morning flights from Quito to Houston, stopping in Panama City, arriving Houston mid-afternoon. From Guayaquil to Houston, there are 2 flights per day; the first is a direct red-eye, arriving Houston early morning, and the second is an indirect morning flight, stopping in Panama City and requiring a plane change, arriving Houston mid-afternoon.
    Comments: See above.

To/ From Los Angeles:

LACSA AIRLINES - LACSA has indirect morning flights to Ecuador 5 days/ week, stopping in Mexico City and Costa Rica; a plane change is required in Costa Rica, arriving Guayaquil in the evening and Quito about 8:00 p.m. There are also indirect mid-afternoon flights from Quito (originating in Guayaquil) to Los Angeles, stopping in Costa Rica; passengers disembark in Costa Rica and change planes, arriving Los Angeles about 9:00 p.m.
    Comments: See above.

TAME/ EVA AIRLINES – EVA has direct morning flights to Panama City 2 days/ week. Passengers then disembark and board an evening TAME flight to

Guayaquil, with continuing service to Quito, arriving about 9:00 p.m. There is also service 2 days/ week to Los Angeles. A TAME afternoon flight originates in Quito, stops in Guayaquil, and arrives in Panama City early evening; passengers deplane and board an EVA flight to Los Angeles, arriving about 10:30 p.m.

Comments: The TAME/ EVA connecting flights are the result of a recent (1998) joint venture. EVA is a Taiwanese airline, and the flight to/from Los Angeles is on a 747. TAME is an Ecuadorian government-owned airline (operated by the military) that runs flights mostly within Ecuador and from the mainland to the Galápagos. There are special through-fares from Los Angeles to Ecuador and from Los Angeles through mainland Ecuador to the Galápagos (see the section below, From Ecuador to the Galápagos). As of this 3rd Edition revision, there were special promotional fares being offered, including inexpensive upgrades to First Class on the Los Angeles/ Panama City flights. Also, using TAME/EVA allows you to get from Los Angeles to Quito without having to overnight in Miami.

AIRFARE TO ECUADOR

Fares to Ecuador are quite reasonable, although, as with the rest of the airline pricing schedules, they are constantly being adjusted and should be verified before purchasing a ticket. At the time of this writing, you can buy a 30 day maximum Excursion Fare round-trip Miami/Quito ticket for about $425. These tickets are in coach class and must generally be purchased at least 2 weeks in advance. Some carriers vary the price based on high/low seasons. The fares from New York City are about $550-$650, and $800-$1000 from Houston and Los Angeles. There is an additional $50-$60 in taxes on all the above fares.

Warning: Quite often (usually as soon as people decide that they're going to the Galápagos) they rush out and buy a round-trip ticket to Ecuador. The fact is they didn't know they would have to pay $325-$375 more to get to the Galápagos. They also didn't know that there were special "tied-fares" to the Galápagos. Neither did the airline or travel agent who sold them the tickets. Nor do their computers show that there are 2 airports in the Galápagos. Carefully read the section, From Ecuador to the Galápagos.

DEPARTURE TAX

In addition the the above air fares, each person must pay a $25 departure tax, payable in U.S. dollars or sucres, at the airport in Ecuador on the day of international departure (for the flight back to the U.S.).

DISCOUNT TICKET HOUSES

There are airfare discount houses (known in the trade as "bucket shops"). You see their ads in the travel section of the Sunday newspaper, offering "the lowest prices to anywhere". If you were going to London or flying from New York to Los Angeles, they could probably save you some money. These are common routes, and they have legitimate access to a certain amount of heavily discounted tickets. However, they're not going to beat the Excursion Fares to an out-of-the-way destination such as Ecuador, and there's no way that they're going to have "tied-fare" tickets to the Galápagos Islands.

SEAT SELECTION

Flights to and from Quito pass over the Andes, and the views are spectacular. Window seats are recommended if you will be flying during daylight hours. See the section below, Airplane III, South American Rules.

FROM ECUADOR TO THE GALAPAGOS

The cost of most flights within Ecuador is about U.S.$50; the round-trip airfare from Quito to the Galápagos is about U.S.$325-$375 (based on high/low season and whether flying to/from Quito or Guayaquil), which is fairly expensive. Things actually reached the absurd level in December, 1989 when the Ecuadorian government increased the fare by 30 percent (to about U.S.$480); this impulsive fare hike came under a lot of pressure and was rescinded only a month later. Even the present $325-$375 round-trip fare is very "unfair" when you consider that it's for foreigners (*extranjeros*) only; Ecuadorians pay only about U.S.$150 for the same flight, and Galápagos residents pay even less. Not exactly fair, but that's the way it is. Tours and hotel prices vary as well, based on nationality.

TIED-FARES TO THE GALAPAGOS

While there are no discounted fares from Ecuador to the Galápagos, the "tiedfare" options mentioned above are as follows:

SAETA AIRLINES – If you fly SAETA AIRLINES from the U.S. to Ecuador, there is currently a "tied-fare" for the Ecuador-Galápagos flights. As described above, SAETA is affiliated with another Ecuadorian airline, SAN (*Servicios Aereos Nacionales*). SAN has a daily morning flight from Quito (stopping in Guayaquil) to the Galápagos (San Cristóbal Island Airport). At San Cristóbal, you will either meet your boat or take local transportation to the town of Puerto Baquerizo Moreno. Return flights to mainland Ecuador are also daily, with an early after-noon flight to Guayaquil and then on to Quito.

While the town of Puerto Ayora on Santa Cruz Island is the hub of social and commercial activity, Puerto Baquerizo Moreno is the political capital of the Galápagos. Recently, efforts have been made to develop Puerto Baquerizo Moreno from the fishing and farming community that it was to a second major tourist center, rivaling Puerto Ayora. In this regard, the San Cristóbal Island Airport was completed in 1986, and several boat tours now leave from the har-bor at Puerto Baquerizo Moreno. While the tourist-oriented facilities are still basic compared to Puerto Ayora, the development push of this area is under way.

As part of the effort to promote tourism in (and their flights to) San Cristóbal, SAETA AIRLINES (in conjunction with SAN) is currently offering a special "tied fare" price of about $750 (including $50 in taxes) from Miami to mainland Ecuador to San Cristóbal Island in the Galápagos (for stays of up to 30 days). Considering the price as well as the excellent international service of SAETA, you may well want to consider this attractive option.

TAME/ EVA AIRLINES – If you fly EVA AIRLINES from Los Angeles, there is currently a "tied-fare" for the Ecuador/Galápagos flights. The special LAX/ Ecuador/ Galápagos (Baltra) through-fare is about $1300 including taxes, which is a very good price. As stated above, EVA is affiliated with an Ecuadorian government-owned airline called TAME (pronounced "tah-may"). TAME (*Transportes Aereos Militares Ecuatorianos*) is operated by the military and has a daily morning flight from Quito (stopping in Guayaquil) to the Galápagos (Baltra Island Airport). At Baltra, you will either meet your boat or take local transportation to the town of Puerto Ayora on Santa Cruz Island. Return flights to mainland Ecuador are also daily, leaving Baltra early in the afternoon and flying to Guayaquil and then on to Quito. Some days there is more than one flight and/ or some flights are direct to/from Quito.

I would guess that TAME will enter into other joint ventures in the future and thus be able to offer through-fares from other U.S. cities.

Warning: As stated above, buying a Galápagos ticket from a travel agent can be a bit risky. Many airline computers show only one airport in the Galápagos; at present the Baltra Airport is coded "GPS", and the San Cristóbal Airport is coded "SCY". The two airports are on separate islands, and there is a lack of dependable inter-island ferry service (although there is sometimes space available on a small plane). Basically, you have a problem on your hands. This problem gets worse when you find out that the Galápagos ticket can not be exchanged (for tickets to the "correct" island).

It would be convenient for all the tour operations if SAN and TAME would accept each other's tickets, but they are fiercely competitive. Since TAME and the Baltra Airport are operated by the military, they are not going to make life easy for SAN. And of course SAN returns the favor. Once again, it's the tourist that pays the price, which in this case is both a lot of money, inconvenience, and possibly missing the boat. Don't buy your ticket until you know which boat you're on and which airport that boat sails from. See the section below.

FLIGHT RESERVATIONS

If you're part of a group tour, the flight reservations will be taken care of for you. It is somewhat surprising to note, however, that several of the Tour Operators that have been booking Galápagos trips for many years do not know about some of the through-fare options. By all means, let them handle your flight reservations, but do get them to quote you air fares before you agree to a ticket purchase. Compare the prices with those listed above, and if there's a significant difference, ask why. There very well could be a valid reason for the difference, such as a recent price hike, peak season rates, or the leg from Des Moines to Miami costing as much as from Miami to Quito.

If you're not part of a group tour, you may wish to book your own flight reservations; the Toll Free numbers for the airlines with service to Ecuador are as follows:

AMERICAN AIRLINES (AA):	(800) 433-7300
CONTINENTAL AIRLINES (CO)	
(International Reservations) :	(800) 231-0856

ECUATORIANA AIRLINES (EU) :	(800) 732-8277
LASCA AIRLINES (LR) :	(800) 225-2272
SAETA AIRLINES (EH) :	(800) 827-2382
SERVIVENSA (VC) :	(800) 428-3672
TAME (EQ) :	(800) 990-0600

You may also choose to have your travel agent make your flight reservations for you. If you opt to do this, inform them of the "through-fare" situation, and once again compare the prices they quote you to those listed above. Remember, they probably have booked very few flights to the Galápagos, if any, and you want to double-check all the details.

Note: Mainland Ecuador is on Eastern Standard Time, while the Galápagos Islands are on Central Standard Time (with a 1 hour time difference between the two locations) throughout the year.

CONFIRMING YOUR FLIGHTS

Once you arrive in Ecuador, it is extremely important for you to confirm your flights to and from the Galápagos with TAME or SAN (24-48 hours in advance). The flights are typically overbooked, and priority is given to those with firm tour reservations. If you have booked a tour with a U.S. Tour Operator, their Ecuadorian affiliate company will take care of this detail for you. If you book your tour in Ecuador, the Boat Operator there will be sure to help you; the last thing they want is for you to miss their boat! Always ask for your Record Locator Number, which is your computer reservation number, thus "confirming your confirmation".

Flight confirmation is not a detail to be passive about, as is evidenced by the following quote from a U.S. Tour Operator who has been offering trips to the Galápagos Islands since 1969:

> "It's essential to have an operating office in Quito. We send someone to the airport 3 times to personally check the manifest. They go 30 days before the flight; this is the first day that the airline [TAME or SAN] will print out the manifest for a particular flight. If someone's not on the manifest, they [our affiliate] show them the international coupon that says 'Galápagos'. Well, the week before the flight we do it again, to catch the people that were dropped off the original manifest so that someone's brother could get on the flight. The third time is the day before the flight. There's actually a fourth time, because the people from the local office actually accompany the people to the airport."

Finally, once you get back to Ecuador, confirm your flight home with the international carrier. Once again, the Tour/Boat Operator will typically handle this detail, but it's up to you to verify the situation; ask for the Record Locator Number.

BAGGAGE REGULATIONS

On the international flights to and from mainland Ecuador, each person is allowed 2 pieces of checked baggage. The actual allowed weight varies by airline; the best is to ask the carrier, your Tour Operator, or your travel agent. Two carryons are also allowed. The flights to and from the Galápagos, however, limit you to one checked bag and 2 carryons.

Note: When you travel as a group, all your checked bags may go on as "Group Luggage," which provides more margin for "overages" in the number of bags and for a particular bag that may be over the weight limit.

A suggestion for you to consider is to take 3 bags to Ecuador - 1 checked piece and 2 carryons. While in Quito or on a visit to one of the markets, you can purchase a leather travel bag and use it to store the souvenirs, gifts, and other items you purchase. This leather bag will then be the second piece of checked luggage on your flight home. For a complete discussion of this subject, see the section on Luggage in Chapter VI. Also, see the section on Film in Chapter VII for a discussion on getting your photographic equipment and film through airport X-ray security machines.

Warning: If you are changing airline carriers between your domestic and international flights (in Miami, New York, Los Angeles, or Houston), pick up your luggage at the baggage claim area and take it to the international ticket counter. Do not depend on the domestic carrier to make the transfer. If your bags don't make it to Ecuador with you, you probably won't get them in time for your flight to the Galápagos, and there's not an efficient way for the bags to catch up to you; remember, you're going to be on a boat, cruising from island to island. Don't get yourself in this situation!

Also, do not pack your film or alcoholic beverages in your checked luggage. Quality film is not an item you can easily replace, and glass bottles will break!

AIRPLANE III - SOUTH AMERICAN RULES

Airport conduct is somewhat less defined in South America than it is in the U.S. I'm not referring to flight safety or security, but rather some basic situations, such as standing in line. Let me cite a few examples.

1.   Many of the flights to and from the Galápagos are on an open-seating basis. The rule is – don't linger; get on the boarding line as soon as it "forms" (if that is the correct verb to describe the activity). Now mind you, my airport behavior back home is very low-key; I try to be patient and avoid the rush of humanity. In South America, however, the airport situation is less structured, and one has to be a bit more aggressive.

For the best views of the Andes (at least on the days when the clouds decide to part), sit on the left side of the aircraft when flying from Quito and on the right side when flying to Quito. It is hoped that not everyone on-board the plane has read this section and that there will be sufficient passengers seated on both sides to maintain a balanced aircraft.

2.   If you're not part of a group tour and are waiting in line at the Quito Airport for your Galápagos flight, you may find the check-in procedure to be interesting. You may be third or fourth in line, and after a wait of a half hour or so, you may still be third or fourth in line. What's happening is that the Ecuadorian agents for the various groups are checking-in all the passengers

(while the passengers themselves are comfortably seated in the terminal). As you will find, each group can take quite a while.

That's the way it's done. This is part of an optional service (called an "airport transfer") provided by the Ecuadorian affiliates of U.S. Tour Operators. If you booked your tour in Ecuador, discuss this option with the local company (see the section on Tour Operations in Ecuador in Chapter IV).

On the return flight from the Galápagos, things will be much easier, because your Guide and/or Tour Leader will assist you with this procedure. While you're at the airport waiting for the return flight from the Galápagos to mainland Ecuador, make sure you have your Guide or Tour Leader take your passport to the National Park official, who will stamp it with the official *Parque Nacional Galápagos* seal (actually it's a tortoise). Really, it's a nice souvenir to have, and the officials won't do it unless asked.

Warning: With all the potential sources of confusion in the airports, combined with a tight schedule, you may be wandering back and forth from your place in line to clarify and/or expedite the situation for you and your group. During these times especially, keep track of your camera bags; they have a way of disappearing. Which brings us to the following topic:

TRAVEL PROTECTION INSURANCE

A variety of comprehensive travel insurance packages are available through the Tour Operators, travel agencies, and the insurance carriers themselves. The Tour Operators all recommend these packages. They do so for several reasons:

1.   Without knowing the habits, history, and travel experience profile of every customer, from their point of view it's good advice. They have certain up front costs (such as chartering or reserving space on a yacht) which is justification for the non-refundable deposit they ask for. Thus, they tell the customer, "To protect yourself, we recommend Trip Cancellation Insurance".

2.   They earn a commission from the insurance carriers.

3.   It is in the best interest of the Tour Operator for you to be covered. If a situation does occur that possibly requires your being compensated, it's taken care of by the insurance company. No matter what waiver forms you sign, given certain bad situations, you can find an aggressive attorney who will suggest that you can and should go after the Tour Operator. With Travel Protection Insurance, you are less likely to need or seek legal aid (also typically an expensive ordeal in its own right).

THE COST

A standard Travel Protection Insurance package will cost about $75-$150 per person for a 1-3 week vacation; family rates for a 1-3 week vacation are $150-$250. Many Tour Operators carry Group Policies, and as a courtesy will pass the Group Rate on to you. There may be an additional cost for certain types of medical evacuation coverage.

Let's look at the various kinds of situations and coverages in a standard Travel Protection Insurance package.

TRIP CANCELLATION/INTERRUPTION INSURANCE

Standard Trip Cancellation Insurance is a one-time-only policy that reimburses you for non-refundable air and land costs (including all deposits) should you have to cancel the trip (or part thereof) due to personal or family illness and/or accident.

The Coverage – Usually the full amount you prepaid

What it Usually Covers – These policies typically cover cancellations (on your part) due to sickness, injury, or death of/to you, a traveling companion, or member of your immediate family.

What it May Cover – Some policies cover cancellations/interruptions due to jury duty, financial default of an airline, Tour or Boat Operator, terrorist incidents, and traffic accidents en route to a scheduled departure. There may be a separate section of the policy that covers certain costs related to Trip Delays (including hotel rooms, rebooking flights, meals, etc.) incurred for reasons beyond your control; such reasons include bad weather, carrier or Operator delays, and lost/ stolen passports or money.

What it Usually Doesn't Cover – Not covered are cancellations due to a change in your plans, business obligations, financial circumstances, inability to obtain required travel documents, or a pre-existing sickness or injury (unless this condition is controlled by prescription medication). There are also the usual exclusions, such as self-inflicted harm, etc.

Analysis – The insurance companies have covered the odds on their side of the table; it's up to you to do the same on your side. Look at what's covered and not covered.

It is very important to note that the Galápagos Islands have very basic medical facilities, equivalent to a first aid station; at that, it is not recommended. Some of the Cruise Ships have an on-board physician or nurse. Even so, just about any serious illness or injury requiring medical treatment will most probably result in the patient being flown to at least mainland Ecuador. From the standpoint of a medical situation interrupting your tour, Trip Cancellation/ Interruption Insurance begins to make sense, especially for families. Finally, if you do opt for this coverage, it is important to note that several carriers will waive the pre-existing condition clause if the insurance is purchased within a week of making the initial trip deposit.

BAGGAGE PROTECTION INSURANCE

This one-time-only policy covers the loss of or damage to your baggage.

The Coverage – Actual cash value at the time of loss (replacement cost less depreciation as defined by the insurance carrier) up to a limit, which is usually less than $1000 per traveler.

What it Usually Doesn't Cover – Items not covered include breakage to cameras or other "fragile" articles such as musical instruments and electronics, any loss or damage to eyeglasses, contact lenses, false teeth, animals, automobiles, boats, motorcycles, etc. The loss of money, securities, or documents is typically not covered.

Analysis – There is a section of your airline ticket called NOTICE OF BAGGAGE LIABILITY LIMITATIONS. It reads as follows:

> *For most international travel (including domestic portions of international journeys) the liability limit is approximately $9.07 per pound for checked baggage and $400 per passenger for unchecked baggage. For travel wholly between U.S. points, federal rules require any limit on airline's baggage liability to be at least $1250 per passenger. Excess valuation may be declared on certain types of articles. Some carriers assume no liability for fragile, valuable, or perishable articles. Further information may be obtained from the carrier.*

From the above, you've already got Baggage Protection Insurance each time your bags are checked in at an airport; in fact, some policies specifically state that their coverage is "secondary to any coverage provided by a common carrier". However, Baggage Protection is part of most Travel Insurance packages, and it doesn't pay to exclude it. At the same time, if you're not buying a Travel Insurance package, it may not make sense getting Baggage Protection by itself. Ecuador is a very safe country; the Galápagos Islands are even safer. The most common loss is a camera bag theft at the airport.

EMERGENCY EVACUATION INSURANCE

The Coverage – This policy covers expenses (up to a maximum) incurred if an injury or sickness commencing during the course of the scheduled trip results in a necessary emergency evacuation.

What it Usually Covers – Covered expenses include transportation costs as well as medical services and supplies.

What It May Cover – This is important. Some policies exclude the cost of medical evacuations resulting from injuries and medical emergencies related to certain activities, such as scuba diving or mountain climbing. Also, some policies require that the emergency evacuation must be ordered by a legally licensed physician, typically not available in the Galápagos in an emergency situation.

What it Usually Doesn't Cover – The cost of medical evacuations resulting from pre-existing illnesses or conditions are typically not covered.

Analysis – As discussed above, the Galápagos have very basic medical facilities, and a serious injury or illness will most probably result in the patient being flown to at least mainland Ecuador. Whether a commercial flight will suffice depends on the extent of the illness or injury. If you are on a diving trip to the Galápagos, the nearest decompression chamber is in Guayaquil, 600 miles away. If decompression treatment becomes necessary, time will be of the essence, and an expensive evacuation flight may be required.

TRAVEL ACCIDENT INSURANCE

The Coverage – This is generally a blanket policy covering the loss of life or limb and the cost of local medical treatment as a result of a travel accident.

What it Usually Doesn't Cover – Pre-existing medical conditions and injuries are typically not covered.

Analysis – Between your personal life insurance and major medical coverage, and the liability of the airlines and boat owners, this could be largely redundant coverage. On the other hand, if you're going to buy any part of the package, it's nice to have this as secondary protection.

Note: If you presently carry medical insurance, it would be a good idea to contact the carrier and verify the extent, if any, of your international coverage. While speaking with them, inquire as to the proper reporting procedure in the event that medical attention is necessary. Let them know that you will be in Ecuador. If you opt to get Travel Protection Insurance, make sure you understand the reporting procedures before you depart.

CHAPTER VI

PREPARE FOR DEPARTURE

The Galápagos Islands are a natural paradise and are anything but developed. From a social point of view, the bad news for some is that there are very few night clubs and discos; the real good news for most of us is that the dress code is very casual. Unless you plan to tour the islands on a 90 passenger Cruise Ship, there is no need to wear anything more formal than short pants and sleeves once you leave the Ecuadorian mainland.

The orientation of this book is to encourage you to visit the Galápagos Islands, to assist you in planning your trip, and to guide you in preparing for your tour. An important part of this orientation is to strongly suggest and recommend that, for the full appreciation of the islands and the diversity of wildlife that awaits you, this trip be an exclusive Galápagos odyssey (with the addition of a few days on the Ecuadorian mainland prior to and/or after your tour). Save the other "nearby" travel spots (the ones that the Tour Operators are pushing) for another trip. You'll silently thank me after your Galápagos tour is complete for harping on this subject every chapter.

While a relatively small blessing, the packing job for a Galápagos-only trip is a lot easier than for a whirlwind tour of South America. The game plan is simple – travel light and travel smart. We'll go through the items by category. A check list is provided at the end of this chapter; combine this list with the one found at the end of Chapter VII, PHOTOGRAPHING THE GALAPAGOS ISLANDS.

HOTEL RESERVATIONS

This is a category you don't have to think about if you are part of a group or package tour. If you have selected a Base Rate tour, the Tour Operator will usually offer to help you with these reservations. My advice is to take them up on the offer, assuming they quote you about the same room rates as you can get on your own (a list of the top hotels in Quito and Guayaquil appears in the Hotels sections of Chapter VIII, WELCOME TO ECUADOR). If you've decided to make your own hotel reservations, you can FAX or phone in your reservation. For most hotels, there's a more convenient alternative known as Overseas Reservation Services. These are authorized U.S. agents of selected hotels that take care of the reservation details for you. There is no extra charge for this service, and you do not have to pay in advance (as required with most Tour Operators); you settle your room bill on check-out. The Hotels sections in Chapter VIII include the phone and FAX numbers of any Overseas Reservation Service(s) for each hotel.

TRAVEL DOCUMENTATION

A valid passport is required for travel to mainland Ecuador and the Galápagos Islands. Tourists are allowed a stay of up to 90 days; visas are not necessary for U.S. or Canadian citizens travelling to Ecuador on a tourist basis. Locate your passport a month or so before your departure, and verify that it is current and will remain current for 6 months from your date of entry into Ecuador (check the expiration date). This will give you sufficient time to not only find out where your passport really is, but to get it renewed or replaced if necessary. When you find or get your passport, take two photocopies of the identification page along with any travel/tour vouchers, the I.D. numbers of your traveler's checks, an inventory of expensive personal items (including Model/Serial Numbers, when appropriate), and your airline itinerary. Keep one copy at home and take one with you. The purpose here is to have documentation in case of loss or theft (see the section on Safety and Security in Chapter VIII).

Carry your passport with you in Quito and Guayaquil. Actually, it's a legal requirement, and theoretically you could be asked for it by an official at any time. Besides, you will need it when exchanging money, buying airline tickets, paying with traveler's checks, and other situations requiring identification. Onboard your boat in the Galápagos, you may have to surrender your passport to the captain who is required to properly register and be accountable for all tourists on the vessel. This is part of the visitor control program of the *Galápagos National Park*. Your passport will be returned upon completion of the tour.

On your flight to Ecuador, you will be asked to fill out a T3 Tourist Information Card. On arrival, you will hand this card over to the Immigration Officer. Part of it will be returned to you. Do not throw it away; it will be requested by the Passport Control Officer when you leave the country.

CUSTOMS REGULATIONS IN ECUADOR

Each person is allowed to bring one bottle of liquor and 300 cigarettes into Ecuador duty-free as well as a "reasonable" quantity of perfume, gifts, and personal effects. There are the usual forbidden items – narcotics, firearms, and ammunition. In addition, fresh and dry meat as well as all plants and vegetables are illegal to bring into Ecuador.

MONEY

How much money should you bring? Well, you have already paid for the airfare. If you have selected a general or specialty tour, the cost of the hotel rooms and usually at least half of the meals in mainland Ecuador are included. If you have selected a Base Rate tour or are going to book your tour in Ecuador, you can put the hotel bill (at the better hotels) on a credit card. The same is true for meals at the finer restaurants in Quito and Guayaquil as well as local tours. Many Galápagos Packages include day and overnight tours of Quito and the surrounding area.

With this in mind, allowing for $50-$100 per day per person in mainland Ecuador for cash expenses is more than enough; cash here refers to currency and traveler's checks. Remember you're in a country where the dollar is very strong and goes a long way; a typical taxi fare is about $2. The per diem covers 1-2 small meals on your own, perhaps a bottle of wine for the room, incidental purchases & souvenirs (expensive gifts can typically be put on a credit card), a half-day city tour, cocktails in the evening, and gratuities. Save $25 per person (in currency, a combination of U.S. dollars and sucres is accepted) for the Exit Tax when leaving Ecuador.

For your Galápagos tour, allow about $350 per person in total cash expenses (currency and traveler's checks). This covers the $100 National Park Entrance Fee (traveler's checks usually not accepted), tips for the Guide and crew (about $100 per passenger per week in currency or traveler's checks), your beverage tab on the boat (settled in currency or traveler's checks on the last day of the cruise), as well as souvenirs and gifts purchased in Puerto Ayora or Puerto Baquerizo Moreno (the two principal towns in the islands).

TRAVELER'S CHECKS

You should be able to get traveler's checks without having to pay a service charge at the bank where you do the bulk of your checking. I say **should** because banks do vary in "service." Even with no service charge, the banks are still using your money interest-free. Yes, and they encourage you to get your traveler's checks early. Sure they do, so they can use your money longer. They also know that you'll probably hold on to the unused checks for a month or so after you return. Play it smart and get your traveler's checks as late as possible and exchange the unused ones as soon as you get home.

AMERICAN EXPRESS has a very organized service network. There is a variable service charge on their traveler's checks (about 1% if you buy direct from them and about 2% through a retail vendor), although their traveler's checks are free to AMEX Platinum and Gold Card members. If AMERICAN EXPRESS traveler's checks are lost or stolen, they have offices in Quito (on Av. Amazonas, across from the ALAMEDA REAL HOTEL) and Guayaquil (Av. 9 de Octubre, 1900). You should report any loss or theft to them immediately; call them collect from Ecuador at (801) 964-6665.

CREDIT CARDS

As stated above, major credit cards (including MASTERCARD, VISA, DINERS CLUB, and to a lesser extent, AMERICAN EXPRESS) are accepted at just about all the major hotels in Quito and Guayaquil. The same is true of most of the finer restaurants and gift shops. Having this option means that you can carry less cash and traveler's checks.

While there are a growing number of banks in Ecuador with ATMs, you can't use most of them to get cash with your North American credit cards. Currently, CIRRUS-type cards are accepted at the ATMs of BANCO DE PACIFICO and BANCO POPULAR, two of the largest banking institutions in Ecuador with many branch outlets. When your cards do work, please note that the cash you receive will be in sucres, not U.S. dollars.

In the past, I've seen a few cards get "eaten" by the machines, with the card owner forced to wait for the bank to open, then go inside and beg to get the card back. Having limited Spanish also limits your chances of succeeding in this kind of game. But times are changing, and there are more and more international banks (like CITIBANK) opening up branches in Ecuador, so I suspect that getting cash by this system will get easier. Just don't count on it! What you can count on, if you carry one of their cards, is the AMERICAN EXPRESS office in Quito or Guayaquil (see the Section above) to advance funds to you against a personal check.

Take your Telephone CALLING CARD with you (or at least have your number handy). Using your CALLING CARD will be less expensive than charging the call to your hotel room. Just dial "999 – 119" to access AT&T-DIRECT (alternatively 999-170 for MCI, 999-171 for SPRINT, or 999-175 for CANADA-TELEGLOBE). You can either call collect or charge it to your CALLING CARD. You may not be able to use your CALLING CARD if the call is placed at the telephone company (IETEL) office at the airport (see the Telephone section in Chapter VIII). Finally, you can not call a TOLL-FREE (800) number from Ecuador.

MONEY POUCH

While Ecuador is a relatively safe country, you may feel more secure with a money pouch, worn on the body (see the section on Safety and Security in Chapter VIII).

LUGGAGE

For luggage allowance, see the section on Baggage Regulations in Chapter V. My suggestion for the international flight to Ecuador is to take three bags – one checked piece, one major carryon, and a camera bag. For your check-on bags, I recommend "soft" luggage that stows easily. My personal choice is an internal frame backpack (see the section below).

Before or after your tour of the Galápagos, you'll probably want to do a little sightseeing and shopping in mainland Ecuador. Since one of the best (and most extensive) handicraft categories to choose from is leather goods, consider purchasing a leather travel bag. They have several styles that fold and zip-up into a small, convenient tote bag; when unzipped, it becomes a full size piece of luggage. Use it to store all of your gifts and bulky wool sweaters (another "best buy" category). The leather bag can then be your second checked bag on the return flight from Ecuador.

Note: It is necessary to lock all major compartments in your checked bags (see the section on Safety and Security in Chapter VIII).

THE SUITCASE BACKPACK

Instead of a rigid suitcase, I recommend a soft piece of luggage called an internal frame backpack. The frame is inside the lining and cannot be seen. The shoulder straps are contained within a zippered rear section and are not visible unless you decide to wear it as a backpack and open this section. There are many advantages:

1. It has a professional appearance; it doesn't look like you've been hitchhiking on the interstate when you arrive at the airport with these packs. I've used them for years while traveling on business.

2. On-board the boat, it's pliable and stores easily in the somewhat-tight storage areas of many cabins.

3. There are several compartments, so you can segment your stuff. This makes it real handy to find anything you need "on the fly." The large compartment can hold a pair of snorkel fins, and there are two vertical side compartments just right for stowing a water bottle and flashlight..

4. As a backpack, it's very efficient and comfortable. Put the pack on your shoulders, and adjust the straps so that the weight is on your hips. If you haven't worn one of these before, it will pleasantly surprise you. If the straps are adjusted right, you will hardly feel any weight or discomfort on your shoulders, even after an extended period of time. Believe me, our hips are normally very strong and can comfortably handle the load. Next chance you get, go into a mountaineering or camping store and try one of these packs on. Have one of the clerks show you how to adjust the straps for comfortable weight distribution.

5. Having the covered shoulder strap area will keep the straps from being eaten by airport baggage conveying equipment.

CLOTHING

As discussed at the beginning of this chapter, while on tour you'll be wearing either shorts or a bathing suit. Bring two or three of each. Pack your favorite bed clothes (pajamas, etc.), and bring about 1 week's worth of T-shirts, socks and underwear. All boats have a bucket (or stoppered sink), detergent, and a clothesline of some sort, so you can wear these clothes items twice during the cruise portion of your trip. Also, you'll probably supplement the supply by purchasing a few Galápagos T-shirts in the islands.

Pack a sweat shirt, jacket, or sweater for the evening (especially May – December). I don't recommend that you bring more than one sweater, because you will probably buy several beautiful wool sweaters in Quito or one of the markets. One pair of pants and 2-3 shirts (or a skirt and 2-3 blouses) will suffice for the few days you'll spend in Quito and the plane rides. If you plan on staying in mainland Ecuador for a longer period of time and/or will be touring the islands on-board a Cruise Ship (which has a somewhat more formal evening meal and social scene than the small yachts), you may need to add to this list, but not by much. I can't think of any reason to bring a suit, sport jacket, tie, or dress.

FOOTWEAR

The hiking isn't all that formidable, although much of the terrain can best be described as "uneven," so you do have to watch where you're walking. For the Galápagos itinerary, athletic shoes (sneakers) seem to be the best all-around answer. You'll be doing a lot of up and down hiking over smooth lava rock, so you want a pair that will give you excellent traction. For maximum ankle support, wear high-tops. These tennis shoes are going to get wet, salty, sandy, and scuffed up. Rather than buying a new pair and getting them old quickly, this may be a great farewell performance for an older, comfortable pair with some decent traction; put the white polish to them, and they'll look just as good as a new pair.

An alternative to athletic shoes is a light pair of hiking boots. You will get more traction and support; remember, you're also going to get them soaked with salt water and filled with sand. And from a cosmetic standpoint, you may not look that great in a bathing suit and hiking shoes.

The problem with tennis shoes and hiking boots is that they are a royal pain during wet landings; you have to go ashore barefoot (carrying your shoes), sit down on a rock, wipe the sand off your feet with a rag or washcloth, and finally put your socks and shoes on. At the end of the land visit, before boarding the *panga* you have to take off your shoes and socks and then dip the soles lightly in the water to remove the sand. A solution to this problem is to wear a pair of "4-wheel-drive" sport sandals (TEVA® is a popular brand). They have heavy tread, are built rugged, offer strong support, and you can get them wet. So you can wear them ashore during wet landings and keep them on as you traverse over lava or rocky terrain. You do have to keep putting sunscreen lotion on your feet to avoid getting broiled lobster claws. The last thing you want is to be hobbled by sunburned feet (see the section on Sunscreen Lotion).

My footwear habits have changed over the last few years. I bring both tennis shoes and sport sandals and mostly wear the TEVAs®. There are times when they feel abrasive and rub on my feet (which can be minimized by dipping them in the ocean now and then), and then I'll switch to tennis shoes for a day or so.

Note: To keep the boats from getting full of sand and grit, most of them do not allow you to wear your island shoes on-board (see the section on Life at Sea in Chapter IX). A dedicated pair of "deck shoes" is fine. Thongs or sandals are okay, as long a you apply adequate sunscreen to your feet before going on-deck. Socks and sandals are a good choice. I usually go barefoot, but I use a lot of sunscreen lotion.

Whatever your footwear, bring along a pair of laces as an all-purpose spare part.

HEAD WEAR

It is recommended that you wear a hat while you're on tour. You're going to be in and directly under the equatorial sun. Pack a couple of your favorites or buy a straw hat in Quito. You do want something that fits rather snug so it doesn't blow off while you're sailing the blue waters. You could also lose a hat to the wind on some of the islands; on South Plaza, for example, you'll be walking on trails near rocky cliffs where the gusts are fairly strong. If you are going to wear a wide-brimmed hat, make sure it has an adjustable chinstrap.

Most people realize that wearing a hat is good sun protection, but then they go snorkeling for an extended period of time without a hat. Wearing a hat in the water? Yes, a swim cap is highly recommended for sun as well as thermal protection (see the section below on Snorkeling Equipment).

For those who tend to perspire quite a bit, I suggest you pack a sweatband. It's no fun getting perspiration in your eyes (or on your camera lens as you're trying to take a picture).

TOILETRIES

Bring along a supply of your favorite brands, because you may not be able to find exactly what you're looking for once you arrive in Ecuador, and most probably not in the Galápagos. If you stay over in Miami prior to your international departure, take stock and make sure you didn't forget anything; if you did, there are excellent drugstores located in the Miami Airport.

You want as many of the toiletries as possible to be packed in small plastic bottles and containers. You may not have a private bathroom on-board the boat. Private or not, chances are the facilities will be a bit more compact than what you're used to. You will no doubt be packing and unpacking your toiletry kit and trying to balance all those neat little bottles on a small, narrow ledge while the boat is chopping through the waves. If you've got the picture, you can see that you don't want to bring glass jars with you. It's also better to bring three small containers of shampoo with you rather than a single large one. If your favorite brand only comes in large sizes or in glass containers, you can buy small plastic transfer bottles with flip-up spouts.

A check list of toiletries is found at the end of this chapter.

RECOMMENDED UTILITY ITEMS

Binoculars – This an essential item. You want a small rubber or plastic-coated pair that you can wear around your neck along with a camera. On your daily island tours, you will be transported ashore in the dinghy (*panga*). As you ride along the rocky shores, you will have unique glimpses of several animals you may not see very often during your visit – the Galápagos penguin being a good example. You'll be scanning with the binoculars and then possibly wanting to take a couple of quick photos. Thus, you want both the binoculars and camera handy. You can't dig into your pack very easily in the crowded little *panga.* Also, if your camera and binoculars were not secured around your neck, you could lose your grip and drop one of them if you get jostled about by a wave or another person.

For those of you who wear eyeglasses, as I do, it is very inconvenient (once an animal is spotted with the eye) to take off your glasses, raise, aim, and look through the binoculars. Often, the animal has moved, or you've looked in the "wrong tree;" you've then got to repeat the process, sometimes more than once. To even attempt this, you have to either be wearing CROAKIES® (see below) or to raise the glasses to a precarious position on your forehead. The answer to this problem is actually quite simple, assuming your binoculars have little suction cups on each eyepiece. Just bend the little rubber cups back, and you now see through the binoculars with your eyeglasses on. I can't believe all the years I didn't know you could do that!

Here's another little hint about the wonders of the binocular device. If you look through the "wrong end" of the binoculars and focus on an object held just a few inches away, your binoculars become a magnifying glass. This works great for the little stuff you see while tide-pooling.

Regarding specifications for binoculars, a 7 x 25 pair, for example, has a magnification power of 7 and a 25mm object lens (the one furthest from your eye) diameter. If you divide the lens diameter by the magnification, you get the brightness factor, which in this case is 3.57. The higher the brightness factor, the more light will hit your eyes, making it "easier" and more comfortable for you to see the subject. This is especially true when viewing in a low-light situation (such as trying to see a penguin against dark, shadowy rocks). Thus, if I had a choice between a 7 x 25 and a 8 x 22 pair of binoculars I would opt for the 7 x 25.

Another specification number is the field of view. Thus, a particular model may have a "376 ft field at 1000 yards," meaning that at 1000 yards the field of view is 376 feet wide. All things being equal or near-equal (including price), I would select the pair with the widest field of view. Try them out in the store before purchasing, using fixed boundaries to determine the "effective" field of view; also, look into a corner that isn't well lit.

Business Cards – You will meet a lot of interesting people and want to stay in touch with them. Instead of scribbling your name on a corner of a well-worn hotel brochure, hand them one of your cards. To save time, put your home address and phone number on the blank side of a number of cards before you leave.

Croakies® – This is a little band that either clips on or slips over your eyeglasses and keeps them from falling off. These prove very useful in all outdoor and water-related activities. For those near-sighted individuals, this allows you to take off your glasses while reading (supported, they rest on your chest), without having to set them down (and possibly break or lose them).

Daypack – You'll use a daypack on your daily tours to the islands; commonly-stowed items will include a water bottle, bandages, first aid cream, guide book, film, and camera equipment. You'll have to decide whether you want to carry the photographic accessories in your camera bag or daypack; you don't want the burden of carrying both. If there are two of you, a good compromise would be for one to carry the pack and the other the camera bag.

Another option, one that I use, is a fanny pack. The advantage here is that it puts the weight where you can best support it (on your hips) and still leaves your hands free. You can even wear these things sideways, so you can get at your field guide or sunscreen lotion without having to take the pack off. The model I have can even hold my camera and extra lenses. The better ones (available through mountaineering stores and their mail order catalogs) have adjustment/support straps to insure a snug, comfortable fit.

Whatever type of pack you opt for, I recommend treating it with two coats of water-repellent spray (such as SCOTCH-GARD®) about a week or so before you leave. The same holds true for your camera bag.

Earplugs – The cabin on board your boat is a lot smaller than your bedroom. Some of us have a tendency to snore, and a pair of earplugs will go far in insuring a good night's sleep.

Extra Pair of Eyeglasses (or Contact Lenses) – You don't want to be in a situation where you break or lose your glasses and can't see what you came all this way to look at. An old pair will do just fine as a backup; now's the time to start looking for them. Also, ask your eye doctor to write out and give you your correction lens prescription. This is a handy piece of paper to carry with you. While there are not too many eye doctors in the Galápagos, you could get a pair made in Ecuador if necessary, depending on the timing and the circumstances.

First Aid Kit – This is yet another reminder that you will be isolated once you reach the Galápagos, and someone in your group will probably have occasion to use most of the following recommended items to pack in your first aid kit: aspirin, bandages, first aid cream, foot powder, insect repellant, IMODIUM®, skin cream, topical anesthetic skin spray (for sunburn, insect bites, cuts, and scratches), and throat lozenges.

Flashlight/Book Light – You'll find these to be a couple of useful items to have along. The flashlight is especially important; a small plastic one will do just fine. You're likely to spend at least one night in Puerto Ayora on Santa Cruz Island, where the town's electricity is turned off at midnight; carry your flashlight if you're out and about. Your flashlight will also come in handy on-board the boat for finding your way after hours. If you're a stargazer, as I am, you may want to bring a small piece of red cellophane that you can put over the lens (using tape or a rubber band). Turning on the red light will enable you to occasionally refer to a star chart and then look back at the real stars with a minimal dark-adapt time. Bring extra batteries.

If you like to read in bed, your cabin may not be equipped with a reading lamp (or the generator could be off). You might want to consider packing one of those handy little book lights and a supply of batteries. You can also use it as a flashlight.

Plastic Bags – Oh so many uses! So many, in fact, that this item appears in two check lists (this chapter and the one on photography). The various applications include stowing dirty clothes, wet bathing suits (on your flight back to mainland Ecuador after swimming in the morning), shaving cream, shampoo, tooth brushes, snacks, disposables, etc. The most important application is to protect your camera gear (from splash and spray) when you're in the *panga*. Put your whole camera bag inside a large plastic bag. While any plastic bags will work, the sturdier the better. Bring various sizes and as many as you can. Remember to bring the twist ties!

Rain Gear/Poncho – Actually a windbreaker will do just fine. Something lightweight that doesn't take up much room and easily stuffs into your daypack. During the first half of the year, there can be an hour or so of rain per day. The second half of the year brings a mist (called a *garúa* – see the section on Climate in Chapter II) to the higher-altitude islands. Many tours take a trip to the Highlands of Santa Cruz Island, where it is often quite misty. You may also need the rain gear in Quito, which can get some rain (usually afternoons and/or evening) from October to May.

Sunglasses – What's a vacation without sunglasses? You might want to consider prescription sunglasses. I wear "photo grey" glasses, the ones that are photosensitive and darken in the sunlight. I never enjoyed the continual changing of glasses as I went from indoors out into the sunlight and then back again. I was always forgetting to take a pair from home or leaving my sunglasses in some dimly-lit restaurant!

Sunscreen Lotion – An absolutely essential item. Brings lots; the selection is very limited in the Galápagos, and the heaviest screen value available is a 15. Start off with a full screen block and gradually (after a couple of days, depending on your complexion) lighten up. Keep a second tube on-deck in your snorkel bag (see the Snorkeling Equipment section below). When the Guide announces that it's time to get ready for the next island tour, start applying the lotion. Don't forget the feet! After lunch, when you're taking a *siesta* on-deck, or if you're doing some whale-watching (sitting or standing in one place for an extended period of time), put on lots of sunscreen; that's when you really get zapped! Even the waterproof stuff fades in strength after you've been snorkeling. And don't forget to wear a hat!

    Caution: Do not put too much sunscreen on your forehead before snorkeling, as the lotion can get into your eyes and, besides stinging like hell, possibly cause some damage.

Swiss Army Knife – Always handy, this multi-purpose tool is especially useful in an isolated environment such as the Galápagos. You will no doubt have several interesting applications. If you are going to purchase one of these little gems, you probably already know that there are a million-and-one options, with some of the cases being as wide as they are long. Aside from the knife portion, the options that seem to get frequent use are the cork screw, screw drivers, and scissors. Actually the latest item on the market is not even the traditional red-coated knife; it's all-stainless steel and called a LEATHERMAN®. The feature I like the best is the extremely useful pliers/wire cutter that appears when you fold open both halves of this well-designed product (although it does tend to rust in a damp environment). Remember that a knife is considered to be a weapon, and you are not allowed to have it in your possession on-board an aircraft; pack it with your check-on luggage.

Tape Player – There are many occasions where the sound of your favorite music forms a perfect background for the activities going on around you. I can think of several such times for me – lying on-deck after lunch while sailing towards the next island (or at night, while stargazing or just watching the waves), "escaping" from the noisy kids across the aisle on the airplane, and beating the boredom of the 2 hour bus and ferry excursion from Baltra Airport to the town of Puerto Ayora on Santa Cruz Island. Many of the yachts have cassette players, so you can entertain your shipmates and the crew during meals and the evening "bull" sessions. Portable CD players are also highly recommended. If you are going to buy one, an "anti-shock" feature will dampen out the slight knocks and vibrations endemic to shipboard travel. Be sure to bring spare batteries.

Vitamins – Don't forget them! International travel has a way of fatiguing and stressing the body. You are also in contact with people carrying and spreading all sorts of little germs. Taking your vitamins could make the difference and keep you healthy.

Washcloth – Some boats have them and some don't. If you feel you need one, bring it. I actually bring two or three, but I call them "rags". I guess it's how I use them, which is to wipe sand off my feet (before putting on tennis shoes) and also to wipe sand off my hands (before touching my binoculars or camera equipment). I keep one my in back pocket (instead of a hankerchief).

Watch, Water-Resistant – Be the last one on your block to get one of these inexpensive wonders. You never have to think about where you left it because you're always wearing it, even while snorkeling and in the shower. Almost all of them have built-in alarm clocks, so you don't have to figure out how to arrange a wake-up call.

Water Bottle, Plastic – It can get fairly hot in the Galápagos, and some island tours (Punta Suárez, Española and Bartolomé Is. are good examples) require a bit of an uphill trek, so you could get thirsty. There is bottled water on-board the boat to fill your container with. Make sure the bottle you choose will fit into one of the side pouches on your backpack.

SNORKELING EQUIPMENT

"I expected the Galápagos to be very special, and it was, but I didn't expect the snorkeling to be one of the highlights of the tour." This is a comment I've heard at the end of almost every trip. You will have the opportunity to snorkel almost every day, and it is an experience that you want to take maximum advantage of. Even if you've never snorkeled before. Even if you have to go out and buy all this equipment that you'll never use again. It's worth it!

The star of the show will be the sea lions, which will swim up to you, and suddenly veer around you in a woosh of bubbles. The first time this happens, your composure will probably go south. For some reason, we tend to have a negative mindset regarding large, sleek, finned creatures brushing past us in the water. It takes a while to get used to it, but when you do, you'll treasure the experience and will welcome your further "encounters," which will be numerous.

Aside from the sea lion show, you will probably have the chance of snorkeling with penguins. The trick here is to stay still and let their natural curiosity take over, and it often does. People have actually had penguins pecking at their snorkel masks. Just don't try to follow or chase them – they will take off (penguins technically can fly through the water).

What else? There are sea turtles, rays, flightless cormorants, and sharks (don't worry, see the information below). And fish are everywhere. Lots of them. Beautiful angelfish, colorful parrotfish, elegant moorish idols, schools of yellow-tailed surgeonfish, and several other lovelies. Hopefully, you're now at least thinking about snorkeling in the Galápagos. So before we get into the equipment department, let me give you a few tips on how to maximize your snorkeling experience:

1. There's the old joke that starts, "How do I get to Carnegie Hall?" The quick retort is "Practice, practice!" It certainly works for snorkeling. Your Guide will offer instruction, but the most difficult part you have to do for yourself. And that is to get used to the sensation of having your face in the water and breathing through a tube. The first thought is that you're going to swallow water, which then becomes a self-fulfilled prophecy. You just have to get used to breathing through the tube in the water. Do this in a pool before you leave for your trip. You can even stand up. If you can achieve this much, the game is won.

2. Next, while floating, try to move through the water without using your hands. Kick or move your legs like you're riding a bicycle in the water. Keep your arms at your sides or clasped together behind your back. This may go against everything you've learned, but it's important. Using your arms while snorkeling has two really bad effects. First, it chases the fish away; second, it blocks your own vision. Give it a try.

3. Everyone hyperventilates when they enter the water, especially on the first snorkel. Don't try to continue snorkeling while you're breathing like crazy and/or you just got a glug of water in your mouth. Just roll over on your back, take the tube out of your mouth, relax, and get your breathing back under control. Then you can continue on.

4. If you feel really uncomfortable in the water, wear a life jacket. Almost all the boats will let you do this. Make sure it is cinched up good and tight, or it will ride up above your head. See the section below on Buoyancy Vests.

5. Try looking from side to side. Beginners have a tendency to look straight ahead and miss the side shows. Also, take your time and look into the crevices between the rocks; you'll be surprised at how much more you see this way.

6. Don't worry about sharks. The ones you'll see in the Galápagos are mostly white-tipped reef sharks and are quite harmless. There are virtually no incidents of shark bites in the islands, although several people do get bit by sea lion bulls each year, mostly by either antagonizing the bulls or by snorkeling off beaches where there are several territories.

7. Finally, don't be scared off by the equipment section below. While dive shops have a wide selection of items to choose from, they can be pricey. If you're not going to use the stuff very often, you can get by with basic gear. Discount department stores, sporting good chains, and even some oversized pharmacies often have snorkel kits (masks, tube, and fins) at bargain prices. There are also dive-oriented mail order catalogs that offer good equipment at inexpensive prices. You may not get the service, but if you can figure out which items to order, you can save a lot of money.

Mask & Tube – You don't want to be without snorkel equipment. Forget what the Tour Operator's brochure says or what they told you on the phone about the equipment being provided; bring your snorkel gear with you! The boats may or may not carry snorkel equipment, and if they do, it will have to be shared. And when it's your turn, you may find out that the mask leaks! The same is true of the large selection of masks available (for rent) on the Cruise Ships; I've seen Cruise Ship passengers basically waste an entire snorkeling session fooling with a mask that leaked. Maximize your opportunity of viewing the 400 or so species of fish that swim the waters of the Galápagos (over 10 percent of which are endemic to the islands). Bring at least a mask and snorkel tube (along with a spare tube strap that attaches the tube to your mask).

Incidentally, if you wear glasses or contacts and are nearsighted, most major brands of face masks offer lens inserts to match your correction. While these lens inserts are not precise corrections (being available in increments of 0.5 diopters), they are more than good enough for the intended purpose and will truly increase your appreciation of the underwater world. These lenses do take into account the natural correction that the water provides, which is about -1.3 diopters. The dive shop where you buy the mask will install the lenses for you, which will cost about $75 for the pair. Call your eye doctor and have the office send you the correction prescription for each eye; they will not read you the prescription over the phone.

If you already have a mask, go to the shop where you bought it or a local dive shop and see if custom lens inserts are offered for that particular mask. If not, you might decide it's time for a new mask, or you could take your old mask to the eye doctor who will have totally custom lenses ground (to match your prescription) and inserted into the mask. if you have some unique visual anomalies (such as astigmatism), you may wish for the eye doctor to do this for you anyway. Going this route will take a bit longer (allow 4-6 weeks) and will cost you a lot more (my guess is about $150).

Fins – I recommend that you bring fins as well. It may be quite a distance from the place where you enter the water to where the majority of the fish are (over by the rocks – it's not deep, just far). Without fins, unless you're a good swimmer, you'll probably give up trying to reach the area where the other snorkelers are, being content to stay in one general location, hoping that "a bunch of fish will decide to come by." So, without fins you'll most likely miss out on seeing the best fish, but I won't press the point. Packing space is at a premium, and fins are bulky; so are all those clothes that I'm trying to convince you not to take! As discussed earlier, the fins will fit in the large compartment of and internal frame backpack.

There is a chance that there will be a pair of fins on-board the boat, but only a small chance. Most of the Cruise Ships do not have an adequate selection that they rent out. By the way, if you're borrowing the fins from a friend, make sure they fit!

Gear Bag – While you're at the dive shop, buy a mesh diving gear bag. They cost about $10-$20 depending on the size and whether the bag has handles or a drawstring. These gear bags will easily hold 3-4 sets of masks and fins as well as any underwater camera equipment you may have. Once you get to the boat, you can put all your snorkel stuff inside the bag and keep it there; leave the gear bag on the aft deck. They usually have a few plastic equipment containers back by the *panga,* and you can store the bag in there. After the last snorkel of the trip, take the gear bag in the shower with you and give the snorkeling equipment an instant fresh water rinse job.

Buoyancy Vest – For those who do not feel comfortable snorkeling in the ocean, there's no reason for you to miss out on all the fun and fascination. Get a buoyancy vest at the dive shop, and you'll be right in there with the others. You manually inflate them just a little bit, and wear it as a vest. You'll feel like you can't sink, because you can't.

Wet Suit – The water temperature in the Galápagos is generally on the cool side. Which surprises many people, because the islands straddle the equator. But as we've pointed out several times (see the section on Climate in Chapter II), the rich food chain here is dependent on the productivity of the ocean, which is in turn dependent on upwelled cool water. There is more upwelling from May – November, with average water temperatures about 70-75 Deg F. The waters are warmer (and less productive) from December – April, with surface temperatures about 75-80 Deg F. There are variations between years and between islands, with the western islands usually a couple degrees cooler.

   Based on the feedback and the comfort level of many passengers, a wet suit is recommended for most times of the year. There were several years that I didn't wear a wet suit in the Galápagos, but I do now. Maybe it's my age. But regardless of **your** age, I must say that you will feel more comfortable with a wet suit on. Again, based on feedback, most people are comfortable wearing a 3 mil shorty wet suit (one-piece, short sleeves, short pantlegs, and a thickness of 3mm or 1/8 in). You should be able to get one of these on-sale for under $80. For those of you with very low body fat or with super-sensitivity to cold, there are thicker wet suits (7 mil or 1/4 in) and there are full-length wet suits.

   Note: A wet suit offers insulation which in part is due to the air spaces within the fabric. This trapped air also keeps you buoyant, which is great as long as you don't want to free-dive down to have a look below. For free-diving with a wet suit on, most people need a weight belt and about 4 pounds of weight. If you're good, you can get down without the weight, but it will cost you in bottom time. It's tough to justify packing 4 pounds of weight, but if you're thinking of free-diving, at least bring a weight belt and hope you can find some weights on the boat.

Swim Cap – In my opinion, a swim cap is a necessary item for sun protection, especially for those of us with thinning hair. It is also effective in preventing heat loss in cool water, as over 50% of our body heat escapes through the "attic." Also, a swim cap helps keep the hair out of your mask, thus preventing water from leaking in. And with a bright colored one, everyone will know where you are in the water!

Accessories to Consider – Snorkel masks tend to fog up. To prevent this, you can rub some spit (ugh) on the lens (which really works, sort of), or you can be more suave and use a tube of "instant spit," an isotonically-correct defogging solution sold under various brand names (which really works).

   If you wear glasses, you will want to wear them in the *panga* en route to/from the snorkeling site. The question is, where do you put your glasses when you're ready to go in the water? The answer is to get a sealed, plastic dry box (sold in dive shops), which can hold several eyeglasses, jewelry items, etc; there are also mini versions of the dry box, designed to hold a single pair of glasses.

Facial hair (even a mustache) has a way of breaking the seal of a snorkel mask. Applying a light coat of VASELINE® to the sealing surface of the mask will usually stop it from leaking. People with thin, angular facial features also tend to have leaky masks. While VASELINE® can also help here, it is very important for these people to carefully "face-fit" a mask at a dive shop before making a purchase. Essentially, this involves holding a mask in place on your face without the strap on, breathing in through your nose, letting go with your hands, and seeing if the mask sucks tightly to your face.

MEDICAL CONSIDERATIONS

A vacation in the Galápagos Islands can be put into the classification of adventure travel. While you will not be partaking in activity as strenuous as mountain climbing, there will be a reasonable amount of daily physical activity. This includes hiking (sometimes up steep hills and over rocky terrain), swimming, and snorkeling. The conditions will often be full sun/tropical heat. You will most likely experience the altitude (9300 ft) of Quito where you may be under some pressure to get a lot of shopping (and therefore walking) done during a brief stay.

Needless to say, it is preferable that you be in reasonable physical condition. The elderly and those with heart conditions or high blood pressure are advised to check with their physicians considering the advisability of the trip. Remember there are virtually no medical facilities in the Galápagos. Perhaps one of the larger Cruise Ships that carry a doctor or nurse on-board may be somewhat more practical for some travelers.

If you're not accustomed to working out on a regular basis, but in otherwise good health, you might want to consider starting on an exercise program a couple of months prior to your departure. As always, consult your physician whenever appropriate.

Altitude Sickness – A more serious version of the symptoms described in the section below on Motion Sickness occurs on the last day of the tour when you spend the morning on the boat (cruising to the airport), the afternoon on the airplane, and the evening in Quito (at 9300 ft). Some people just feel the shortness of breath and the fatigue associated with a sudden change to a high altitude. Other people get fairly sick, and are out of commission for a day or two.

Alcohol seems to be a predisposing factor relative to altitude sickness (as does smoking and eating heavily). If you're flying from the States directly to Quito, bear this in mind on your flight over. Also, you might want to take it easy the last night on-board your boat; have your "farewell party" the night before last. If you're taking any medication, including preventatives for motion sickness and/or altitude sickness, the use of alcohol is typically contraindicated; be very cautious.

There is a preventative medication for altitude sickness; it is an acetazoleamide diuretic marketed under the brand name DIAMOX®. This drug is used, among other things, to treat glaucoma, as it relieves sinus and cranial pres-

sure; thus, it can prevent some of the symptoms, including headaches, associated with altitude sickness. There are some side effects, and it seems to me that the
high altitude dries you out enough as it is. Consult your physician regarding this
medication. Good old aspirin does quite a bit of good for me, relieving the
headache and malaise associated with the first day of life at 9300 ft. I still feel a
decided loss of energy, which fades after 24-36 hours.

The air **is** drier at high altitudes, which, for one, causes the skin to crack.
This is where the skin cream and lip balm come in very handy. The dry air also
causes the eyes to be irritable; those that wear contacts might consider leaving
their lenses out whenever possible in Quito.

Dental – If you have any nagging dental problems or concerns, get them taken
care of before you leave. You don't want to be thinking about a dentist while
you're anchored off Española Island.

Don't forget to pack your dental floss. You'll probably find some unique
uses for it. I've seen some people use floss instead of CROAKIES® to tie between
the ear holders of their glasses. Also, if you have any caps on your teeth, take
some POLI-GRIP® along in case one comes loose.

Food – In Quito and Guayaquil, the rule is don't eat uncooked food, including
peeled fruits and vegetables (due to the water used in washing them). Salads
seem to be one of the main culprits. In the better restaurants (including the major
hotels), you probably won't have any problems; use your judgement. In other
establishments, it's best to be careful!

Speaking of being careful, I am extra-cautious during my stay in Quito (or
Guayaquil) before the Galápagos, not wanting to risk an intestinal problem prior
to the cruise; I'm slightly bolder after Galápagos, with the thought that I'll soon
be home. By the way, one of the first phrases to learn in Spanish is *"sin hielo"*
(without ice), a must expression in bars and restaurants as well as on the flights
to and from the Galápagos.

On your boat, there shouldn't be any problem. The cooks do a good job,
and the food is well prepared. Still, if you have a sensitive tummy, it's best not
to take any chances and minimize the possibility of discomfort. You're not going
to starve in any case, and the daily experience of sitting around the dining room
on the boat and being served good food while watching the Galápagos show
going on around you generally raises the meal rating from "very good" to "mem-
orable feast."

As a precaution, it is highly recommended that you take along some
IMODIUM®, an excellent over-the-counter medication that will usually plug
you up pretty quick.

Medication – If applicable, make sure you have an ample supply, and (solely as
a back-up) take your prescription(s) with you as well. Have your physician give
you the generic name(s) of the medication(s) as a specific brand name may not
be available in Ecuador. There are several pharmacies in Quito and Guayaquil
(even a few in the Galápagos) that dispense most major medications. Consult
your physician regarding any potential pharmaceutical side effects (as well as
the overall effects) of high altitude (Quito), sunlight, and being at sea for an
extended period of time.

Ibuprofen ("Vitamin I" as it is called by some) is a must, especially for those of us over 40 who are quite familiar with arthritic symptoms. I take 2 in the morning on the physically more demanding days of the trip, and it seems to keep me from getting sore in the evening. Cortisone skin cream is also recommended, as quite a few people tend to develop rashes, even though they are using ample amounts of sunscreen. Also worthy of attention is a natural product called echinacea that has grown in popularity over the last few years. Echinacea, said to stimulate the immune system, seems to be quite effective if taken when a cold is just beginning (you know, the "lump" in the throat when swallowing). I was skeptical at first, but it has worked for me several times. I also use it in high body stress situations, such as all-day air travel (which brings on resistance-lowering fatigue and lots of recirculated germs in the cabin). Echinacea (now sold in some pharmacies as well as health food stores) is available in tablet and liquid form.

Caution: It is vitally important for those of you with an extreme allergy response (possibly leading to anaphylactic shock) to identify this condition in advance to the Tour Operator, Tour Leader, and Guide. Let them know specfically what you are allergic to. In particular, there are a growing number of introduced wasps on Floreana Island; these wasps are being carried (mostly by the tour boats) to several other islands. Typical allergy medication (including BENADRYL®) is not strong enough for an anaphylactic reaction. Bring 1-2 norepinephrine jabber sticks with you (it's like a needle but simple to use – consult your physician), and make sure you have them with you at all times; also instruct the Tour Leader and Guide as to the location of this medication.

Motion (Sea) Sickness – While the seas are relatively calm in the Galápagos, it can get a bit rough from May – November, especially if you are traveling south, into the prevailing current. Tidal effects, especially during a new or full moon, can accentuate the motion of the ocean. And some people are just plain more sensitive. Generally, if you don't take anything for motion sickness, there's no reason to do so in the Galápagos. If you're accustomed to taking something, or you haven't spent a lot of time at sea, pack whatever brand or type works best and/or is recommended to you (two of the more popular brands are BONINE® and DRAMAMINE®). If nothing else, you'll feel more secure having the stuff with you.

Many of the pills are antihistamines and have undesirable side effects, such as drowsiness and disorientation. In fact, one of the popular preventatives, TRANSDERM SCOPE®, has been taken off the market for "remanufacture". According to the rumor mill, which seems to be the only information source, there were some "side effect problems" with this skin patch worn behind the ear. The active drug in the product, scopolamine (a nervous system depressant), is slowly released through the skin. Also, bear in mind that all the various forms of medication are preventative in nature. It will do little good to start taking them once the effects of motion sickness have begun. Follow the instructions; they typically recommend that you begin using the product several hours prior to the boat's departure (or entry) into potentially-choppy waters.

There are now alternate forms of motion sickness prevention. One item growing in popularity is ginger tablets (available in health food stores). Another new approach is SEA BANDS®, worn on both wrists. There is no medication involved, and they are said to operate by the exertion of pressure (by a button imbedded in the band) on the acupressure point on the wrist that (according to Chinese medicine) controls nausea.

Note: After touring the Galápagos by boat for several days, you may have a tough time getting your "land legs" back. This will be noticeable if you stop at Santa Cruz Island after a few days at sea. What seems to be happening is that the equilibrium center of the inner ear is still rocking back and forth while the rest of you is staying in one place. The brain doesn't particularly care for the contradictory signals, and the result is a feeling of dizziness. The effect is intensified inside a building (due to the fixed rectangular visual cues); going outside will make you feel better. The symptoms typically go away after a few hours.

Vaccinations – No inoculations are required in mainland Ecuador or the Galápagos Islands. However, if you plan to visit the Amazon region of Ecuador, a yellow fever shot (good for 10 years) and malaria tablets are typically recommended. You are urged to consult with your physician on this matter.

Water – As the saying goes, don't drink the water (unless it's bottled). You will typically find 1-2 bottles in your hotel room. Use this water for drinking as well as for brushing your teeth. There is always bottled water on-board the boat in the Galápagos.

Note: There is now both mineral water *(agua mineral)* and pure bottled water *(agua pura* or *agua sin gas)* available in mainland Ecuador and the Galápagos, although in the islands there can occasionally be shortages of one or the other. Also, most restaurants will charge you for water, and some of the boats may charge you for mineral water.

PACKING CHECK LIST

Use this list in conjunction with the Photography Check List at the end of Chapter VII, PHOTOGRAPHING THE GALAPAGOS ISLANDS.

CLOTHING

☐ Bathing Suits	☐ Pajamas, etc.	☐ Blouses
☐ Dress Shirts	☐ Hats	☐ Jacket
☐ Pants	☐ Shoelaces (spare)	☐ Foot Wear
☐ Shorts	☐ Skirts	☐ Socks
☐ Sweatband	☐ Sweat Shirt	☐ T-shirts
☐ Underwear	☐ Rain Gear/Poncho	

Notes _____

FIRST AID KIT

☐ Aspirin/Ibuprofen	☐ Bandages	☐ First Aid Cream
☐ Foot Powder	☐ Insect Repellent	☐ IMODIUM®
☐ POLI-GRIP®	☐ Throat Lozenges	☐ Sunburn Treatment
☐ Cortisone Cream (Heat Rash)		☐ Elastic Wraps

Notes _____

SNORKELING EQUIPMENT

☐ Defogging Solution	☐ Buoyancy Vest	☐ Fins
☐ Gear Bag, Mesh	☐ Mask	☐ Snorkel Tube
☐ Wet Suit	☐ Swim Cap	☐ Dry Box

Notes _____

TOILETRIES

☐ Contact Lens Solutions	☐ Contraceptive Materials	
☐ Combs & Brushes	☐ Cosmetics	☐ Dental Floss
☐ Deodorant	☐ Hair Spray	☐ Lip Balm
☐ Nail Clippers	☐ Plastic Bottles	☐ Razors
☐ Shampoos	☐ Shave Cream	☐ Skin Care Lotion
☐ Wash Cloth	☐ Tampons	☐ Toothbrush/Paste

Notes _____

ITEM	NOTES
☐ Backpack, Internal Frame	_____
☐ Binoculars	_____
☐ Book Light/Batteries	_____
☐ Books	_____
	_____
☐ Business Cards	_____
☐ Contact Lenses (extra pair)	_____
☐ Credit Card	_____
(MC, VISA, AM EXPRESS)	_____
☐ CROAKIES®	_____
☐ Daypack	_____
☐ Earplugs	_____
☐ Eyeglasses (extra pair)	_____
☐ Flashlight/Batteries	_____
☐ Hotel Reservations	_____
	_____
☐ Medication	_____
☐ Money/Traveler's Checks	_____
☐ Money Pouch	_____
☐ Motion Sickness Treatment	_____
☐ Passport	_____
☐ Photocopies of all	_____
Documentation/Tickets	
☐ Plastic Bags/Twists	_____
☐ Sunglasses	_____
☐ Sunscreen Lotion	_____
☐ Swiss Army Knife	_____
☐ Tape or CD Player/Batteries	_____
☐ Telephone Calling Card	_____
☐ Vitamins	_____
☐ Watch/Water-resistant	_____
☐ Water Bottle	_____
☐ Misc. Items	_____

CHAPTER VII

PHOTOGRAPHING
THE GALAPAGOS ISLANDS

*As a general rule don't take anything from the islands that belongs
there. Take only photographs, and leave only your footprints.*
                              General Rule, from the LIST OF RULES,
                              Galápagos National Park, Ecuador

The subject of preparing for your trip to the Galápagos Islands is incomplete without a discussion of photography and the photographic equipment that you take along. The advice that will be offered in this chapter can be briefly summarized (in the same fashion as the General Rule stated above) – brings lots of film and extra batteries, get a zoom lens, consider buying an underwater camera, think seriously about video, test all your equipment before you leave, always be ready, and leave your tripod home.

FILM

You cannot bring too much film to the Galápagos Islands! There are so many opportunities for spectacular shots the rolls will appear to sprout wings, flying out of your bag and into the camera, soon followed by a fast return flight. Shooting three or four rolls per day is not unusual. Just the thought of running low on film is enough to drive me to distraction. While there are a growing number of stores offering a reasonable selection of film in the Galápagos (in the towns of Puerto Ayora on Santa Cruz Island and Puerto Baquerizo Moreno on San Cristóbal Island), somehow I still believe that a roll in the bag (my bag) is worth at least two rolls of somewhat questionable quality film (storage and temperature – not brand name – considerations) in a shop that might be open on an island that we might visit. So, please, bring lots of film. Even if you have several rolls left over, you will have absolutely no problem selling them at cost to a very grateful tourist who didn't get this friendly advice.

Film selection is always a personal choice. I shoot both prints and slides. Prints are great for photo albums, and the chemistry of print film allows for greater tolerance in exposure value. When shooting prints, you can be off the perfect exposure by +/- 2 stops and still get a print that looks reasonably good, while slide film only has a +/- 1 stop tolerance before the transparency looks washed out or too dark. That's why the disposable cameras are always loaded with print film. On the other hand, shooting slides keeps the processing cost down. Also, with today's processing technology, you can get professional quality prints made from your best slides. This includes processing techniques that bypass the costly internegative phase altogether. I am able to get very reasonably-priced, good quality 11″ x 14″ prints from my slides.

It's your choice, but do bring an assortment of film speeds. I find that a mixture of 33% ASA (ISO) 50-100 and 66% ASA (ISO) 200-400 is reasonable. You'll be doing a lot of medium telephoto work and will want to be able to shoot at 1/125th to 1/250th of a second to avoid blurring the action. More on this later.

Note: Regarding the different systems used to rate film speed, ASA (American Standards Association) and ISO (International Standards Organization) numbers are the same. Thus, ASA 400 is equal to ISO 400. There is a numerical difference, however, when ISO or ASA sensitivity values are compared to European system DIN *(Deutche Industrie Norm)* values.

Plan on using 1-2 rolls per day of 400 ASA film. If you intend to do any underwater photography, increase the allowance by half a roll per day. Since I use mostly ASA 400, I buy rolls of 36 exposures, and am interrupted by having to reload film one-third less often; for 72 shots, that's one reload instead of two. In the Galápagos there are times when that's important as well as convenient, especially when it lets you continue shooting a key sequence. For the slower films, which I use less often, I buy rolls of 24 exposures; this makes a necessary change to ASA 400 that much easier.

Unless your camera performs the function automatically, remember to change the ASA dial on your camera when you change film speeds. If you're partially into a roll and decide to change film speeds, there is a way to deal with this situation and not waste film. Note the exposure you're on, and write it in your notebook (also write it on the film leader after rewinding). Rewind the roll, taking care not to rewind the film leader into the film canister. If you goof, there's always the film extractor (see the section on Accessories to Consider). When you want to use this roll again, make sure the lens cap is securely on before loading. Then, in a fairly dark location, advance the film to about two shots past the number you left off at (for a margin of safety).

Speaking of changing film, when you finish a roll, **do** wind the film leader into the canister. This will avoid that sinking, confused thought, "Is this a new roll of film, or did I already shoot it today?"

FILM PROCESSING

Don't have your film developed in Ecuador; the word is that the processing is not the best. On the other hand, it is not recommended that you keep undeveloped film for an extended period of time, especially in a warm climate. If you're planning a trip of longer than 2 months, try to bribe a departing friend into having your film processed and then keeping the prints or slides for you. This will give you both a good reason to get together after your return. To facilitate the accounting process, you could buy pre-paid processing film packs, and then your friend simply has to put them in the mail. While we're on the subject, don't post any photographic material from Ecuador; you're taking too much of a chance, and you'll always be wondering if the package arrived home safely, or if at all.

FILM STORAGE

Film emulsion chemistry is fairly sophisticated, designed to remain stable for a long time. But not forever! Check the expiration date before purchasing or packing film for your trip. Film chemistry is also affected by heat. Thus, you want to store unused film in a cool location, such as a refrigerator, taking care to pack the film in a plastic bag or moisture-proof container. Please note, however, that if the film is suddenly transferred from cold storage to a warm environment and then opened, moisture may condense on it. Let the film warm gradually before opening the container and loading the film.

THE CAMERA

As discussed throughout this book, taking pictures in the Galápagos is a continual sequence of opportunities, ones that lend themselves very nicely, and in many cases uniquely, to a hand-held 35mm camera. Many of these situations happen quickly and change from minute to minute as you're splashing through the waves in a dinghy shoulder-to-shoulder with eight other passengers. There's no time or room (or even a foundation) for a tripod set-up.

If you read this chapter and still have the motivation to drag a 4 x 5 view camera out to the Galápagos – then go for it! Your patience will be well-rewarded with the quality, detail, and extreme resolution of your final product. Remember, though, you're going to have to take your equipment ashore in the dinghy *(panga),* you can't walk off the trails to get a better angle, and you must stay with the Guide (and therefore with the rest of the group). The same flexibility limitations are true (although to a lesser degree) for those who use medium format cameras. To all of you that are dedicated to the "bigger piece of film," I can only say, "Bring a 35mm camera in addition to your larger format camera so you won't miss out on a lot of 'right now' opportunities."

Now I turn to all of you that haven't used and/or are afraid to use a 35mm camera. There are several 35mm automatic ("point-and-shoot") cameras on the market today that are perfectly acceptable and will allow you to take great shots of the Galápagos wildlife. These cameras are self-loading, they recognize and adapt to what film you're using, will automatically rewind and advance the film to the next shot, have built-in flash, and set the exposure to get consistently good results. And they're reasonably priced – starting at about $100. You do have to spend about $250 to get two of the best features – autofocus and dual-lenses. With the second feature, you can change from a wide-angle to a telephoto lens with the push of a button. While this suggestion may offend the serious photographers in the audience, you may want to consider purchasing a couple of the panoramic disposable cameras on the market. Priced at less than $15, they give you reasonably good 3" x 10" wide angle vista prints. They also offer disposable cameras that you can take with you in the water while snorkeling (see the section on Underwater Photography).

Note: If you're going to buy a point-and-shoot camera for the trip, select a model in which you can over-ride the automatic flash, as the use of flash will probably soon be prohibited for animal photography in the Galápagos; we get very close to the animals, and the flash can certainly affect them. Also, all things being equal, select a camera that has a minimum of noise pollution (beeping when you're in focus, etc.).

LENS SELECTION

Choosing the right lens for the situation is another highly personal decision, being a function of what you're trying to accomplish. There are times when just about any wide-angle, telephoto, or standard lens would be ideally suited (based on the given situation). A fixed wide-angle lens (28mm or 35mm) is certainly recommended. For the most part, however, the everyday reality of touring the Galápagos Islands strongly indicates the extreme suitability of a 70-210mm zoom lens (for a 35mm SLR camera). Here's why:

1.   Opportunities occur suddenly and often unpredictably. You're panning the sky trying to get the perfect spread-wing hawk shot when your companion tells you to look down; much to your surprise, a land iguana has stopped in his tracks, his lunch of "cactus pad salad" in mouth, about 5 ft from you. The telephoto is too much lens, and if you tried to move back or change lenses, the little creature would probably scurry off. With the zoom, you can go from 210mm, where you have been scanning the skies, to 70mm or whatever it takes to perfectly frame the iguana.

2.   The scene described above is very common. So is the reverse situation. You're honed in on two blue-footed boobies, waiting for their "dance" to begin when, suddenly, you hear the war cry of the photographer, "Wow, look at that!" You spin around and your companions' heads are all tilted skyward. There, lazily circling above you, is a male frigatebird, perfectly posed (see Photo #37). There's no time to change lenses, but you don't have to; just zoom in!

3.   Similar situations occur on the daily *panga* rides. You may not realize it at first, but these little boats present you with many unique photo opportunities, so once you get seated, have your camera out, ready, and protected (see the section on A Day at Sea in Chapter IX). This is the closest you're going to get (on the water) to the cliffs, which serve as home for many Galápagos sea birds and shore birds. The *panga* rides may also provide the best (sometimes the only) chances of observing and photographing penguins, white-tipped reef sharks, and possibly "rafts" of mating sea turtles.

Opportune situations are not without their challenges. Aside from the varying distances of the subjects, your little *panga* is bouncing up and down, you're occasionally getting splashed, and the quarters are very tight. The end result is that you don't have the time or the opportunity to change lenses, which is exactly what you need to do. Unless you have a zoom lens.

4. Once ashore and touring a Visitor Site, you must stay on the narrow trail, due to the fragile environment. Thus, if the picture composition isn't right, you don't usually have the luxury of backing up or moving forward. This problem can be solved by letting the zoom lens do the moving for you. The alternative is to change lenses and hope that you're exactly the right distance away to get the composition you want.

5. Speaking of composition (an art for some and an acquired skill for the rest of us), the zoom lens is an excellent instructional tool. As you zoom in, aside from getting a close-up view of the subject, the background changes dramatically, sometimes for better or worse. When time allows, it's fascinating to slowly zoom in and out, observing the continual change in composition. At some point, you stop and say, "Perfect, that's it!" Most of us can recognize excellent composition better than we can achieve it, and what the zoom lens is actually doing is showing us hundreds of shots, allowing us to pick the one with the best composition. As we analyze it further, we can see that the composition was right because the amount of sky was reduced or a certain rock was added to the foreground, etc.

The use of composing the shot "on-the-fly" is somewhat more important when shooting slide film, because you don't have the option of cropping as you do with prints.

6. The zoom lens is more than the compromise that it used to be. With today's lens-making technology, end-product results from a zoom lens are, for most purposes, of the same quality level as those from a fixed focal length lens.

A 70-210mm zoom allows you to focus to about 5 ft (depending on the lens), and even closer with macro zoom lenses. Read the following section, Exposure, for a discussion of correct aperture and shutter-speed determination with a telephoto (zoom) lens.

EXPOSURE

If you're taking a photo of a person with a blue-sky background, what are the key variables to pay attention to before clicking the magic button? "Making sure the person is in focus," says a voice in the corner of the room. This is obviously true, and in fact with most cameras today having auto-focus features, this is easy enough to achieve. "A good composition," is another good answer. We will address this variable in just a bit. For now, the response I'm looking for is "make sure the face isn't too dark." A "dark face" is the result of the averaging circuitry of the camera's built-in light meter. The camera calculated what it thought was the right exposure by "averaging" the different elements in the shot (sky, person, etc). For wide angle vista shots, this process works great. But in this example, the bright sky resulted in a "bad average." Of course, you could use flash, but we'll ignore this possibility, because we don't want you to use flash in the Galápagos (at least not for animal shots).

The answer to the right exposure is something called spot metering. Go up to the person and take a meter reading of the face. That's the right exposure. With many of today's cameras, you can take this kind of reading, push a button, and store this exposure value. You then go back and take the shot, with the camera basing the exposure value of the scene on the locked-in light reading. The sky may go a little white, but who cares? The face looks great, and the picture is a keeper! This isn't that hard, especially with the spot metering capability of many of today's cameras. When this function is selected, the camera "spots" or bases most of the exposure value on the center circle in the view finder. You've got the idea. It works for iguana faces too! Just decide what your subject is and spot-meter it. For more information, see the Spot Meter section below (under Accessories To Consider).

TELEPHOTO (ZOOM) LENS EXPOSURES

When using a telephoto or telephoto zoom lens, special consideration must be given to the exposure values. Your first concern is shutter speed. To avoid motion blur, you want a shutter speed with about the same numerical value as the focal length of the lens. Thus, with a 200mm lens, the shutter speed should be set to at least 1/125th of a second. With a 70-210mm zoom lens, the shutter speed should be set to at least 1/125th to 1/250th of a second, depending on the amount your zooming.

If you're shooting from an airplane (and the peaks of the Andes above the clouds **are** beautiful), use shutter speeds of 1/500th to 1/1000th of a second and keep the focus set at infinity. Also, in aerial photography make sure you have the skylight filter on the lens. A polarizing filter, on the other hand, may produce unwanted rainbows, as you're shooting through a plastic window.

Some cameras let you choose between aperture-priority and shutter-priority. This may sound complicated, but let's simplify it. Shutter-priority means that the shutter speed is more important than the lens opening value (or aperture). We've already determined that this is indeed the case when using a telephoto lens. Thus, select shutter-priority, and then select the appropriate aperture value to provide the right exposure. It really isn't that difficult!

COMPOSITION

The subject of picture composition combines technical and aesthetic qualities. If you examine what you feel are excellent natural history photographs, the description "magic moment" will often apply. It is very difficult to get a "magic moment" shot, especially if you're only going to be on a particular island once in your life and you don't know what to expect. You may get one or more of these truly special shots, but it will largely be a matter of luck. But what you can get are warm and wonderful portrait photos of just about all the animals you will see in the Galápagos. Here's how:

1. Focus on the eye of the animal. The eye is the key to the soul of the photo. You may have to select manual focus for this, especially if it's a small bird in a tree. The reason is that the autofocus will not "know" what the subject is, and will hunt for it, alternately focusing on a branch and the bird. You've heard that "hunting" sound, and so have the animals. So in addition to an out-of-focus bird, you also have a bird that has stopped doing what you wanted to take a picture of.

2. Select an angle where you can see a gleam of light reflected in the eye. Illuminate that soul! This is easier to do than it sounds.

3. Take the background out of focus. If there's a great secret to getting excellent portrait shots, this is it. As beautiful as the trees, sky, and water are,

they compete for attention in the photo; in other words, with everything in focus, the shot is "noisy." An out-of-focus background becomes an accent color and highlights the animal.

LIGHTING

As stated in other sections, the equatorial sun of the Galápagos tends to be harsh, often washing out the beautiful colors. Overcast days will produce more dramatic photographs (the lighting is softer and more diffuse) and should be taken advantage of. You can warm up the bleached midday colors by photographing subjects that are in the shade or by using a polarizing filter (see the section, Recommended Accessories).

Twilight also produces very warm colors. Unfortunately, with the Galápagos being on the equator, "twilight time" is very short; it gets light fast, and it gets dark fast! Still, your best lighting on most days will be early morning and late afternoon, and this is the time when you want to be "on the trail." The problem is that most of your other shipmates may want to be having a second cup of coffee or getting back to the boat for "a cold one." Unless you and your photography-oriented group are chartering the entire boat, your options are limited in this regard. You can select a Photography Tour (see the section on Specialty Tours in Chapter IV). If you're on a General Tour, while the captain and Guide do have a daily schedule to adhere to, there is a degree of flexibility based on the makeup and wants of the passengers. Thus, you can use your negotiating and teaching skills to advantage by suggesting to the other passengers that they can get better pictures by starting out earlier, taking a longer *siesta* in the afternoon, and staying on the island later, towards the evening.

Sunset light is shifted to the orange-red part of the spectrum, often producing dramatic results. Aside from the "obligatory" sunset shots, it's a good time to take some pictures of your fellow passengers, as the coloring adds a warm, flattering glow to skin tones.

TRIPODS

The tripod is a wonderful piece of equipment that I recommend for most situations due to the excellent stability it provides. Even at shutter speeds as fast as 1/1000th of a second, highly magnified prints of shots taken with and without a tripod show a significantly sharper image when a tripod was used. Another good feature of the tripod is that it helps your eye relax and takes in the total composition, thus facilitating the necessary adjustments. With hand-held shots, we often tend to see what's in our mind rather than what's in the view finder. The tripod also allows us the time to take detailed light readings and analyze them, enabling us to get the perfect exposure for the situation.

As useful a tool as it is, the tripod is usually (and unfortunately) large, heavy, awkward, and time-consuming to set up. It is my opinion, therefore, that in most cases the tripod is not suitable for use on the Galápagos Islands. Mind you, I said, "in most cases." I can think of beautiful shots (lava texture, the spatter cones on Bartolomé, the geological formations on Sombrero Chino Island) that would be greatly enhanced by the use of a tripod. There are even some animal shots (the marine iguana warming up on his favorite rock or a blue-footed booby with a recently-hatched chick) where the tripod would be most beneficial. The problems, as documented earlier, are those of logistics and practicality. It's difficult getting the tripod on-shore, you must set up on the trail, and you have to stay with the Guide and group.

There are small tripods on the market that would be more practical as far as transportation goes. There are other accessories available, such as "chestpods" and "bean bag" camera supports. But, in general, with these devices you're giving up the most important reason for having a tripod – stability. While not an easy decision, and a question that I've given a lot of thought to, my conclusion is to leave the tripod home. Again, this is a personal decision. There are those who thought I was somewhat impractical for toting a pair of swim fins half way out to nowhere. I decided I needed them, and I brought them.

RECOMMENDED ACCESSORIES

Batteries, Spare – Bring spare batteries for your camera(s). Make sure you get the right type, quantity, and voltage. Several models will take either two 1.55V silver-oxide batteries or a single 3V lithium battery. Consult your camera instruction manual.

Once you have gone to the trouble of bringing 2-3 spare batteries to the Galápagos, by all means carry them in your camera bag. Having the spares on the boat when your batteries die in the middle of a courting albatross sequence will not do wonders for your outlook on the universe.

Don't forget the spare batteries for your other photographic equipment, such as a spot meter or data back.

Instruction Manual(s) – There's a story about Albert Einstein at a party, where he is found looking over an instruction manual for a piece of equipment. Asked what he was doing, Albert merely replied, "You know how it is; you forget the stuff!" You do, and stuff happens too! So if you do or when it does, you'll need the instruction manual to figure it out. It might be a relatively simple "how-to" situation, such as using the self-timer, or taking multiple exposures. A good idea is to make a photocopy of the manual to take with you, keeping the original safe at home.

Lead Foil Film Bags – If you don't already use them, I recommend that you get a couple of lead foil film bags to protect your film from airport X-ray systems. These film shields typically have a layer of lead foil laminated (or sandwiched) between an outside layer of strong, puncture-resistant polyester and a black, barium-impregnated interior layer. Lead foil bags cost about $20 and are sold at most camera and travel stores.

Even with this level of protection, there is a disclaimer printed on the bag stating that it can keep only so much of the radiation out. Some airports are known to use "super-zapper" equipment, and there's no sure film protection available. The problem is intensified if you are shooting sensitive high-speed film (over ASA 400) and also by (repeated) multiple doses. The best way to deal with this situation is to hand the film (in the lead foil bag) to the Security Inspector as you walk through. Hand the Inspector the camera also, if it is loaded. Within the U.S., the FAA mandates that passengers have the right to hand their film to the Security Inspectors; on the other hand, most of the known "super-zappers" are outside the U.S. Aside from being a minor inconvenience, the procedure works quite well. There are times, though, when I've forgotten to do this (or quite frankly, have been too lazy), and that's when I'm grateful that I had the lead foil bags.

Lens Tissues, Cleaner, & Dust Brush – Camera care is a very important detail, very often neglected. It's a matter of consistency and discipline. Your camera is a precision piece of mechanical equipment and a carefully engineered optical system. You will visit a beach every day, and an accumulation of sand will stall that precise machine. Your daily supply of fingerprints on the lens will produce smeared photos despite your superior optics. The first step is to bring lots of lens cleaning tissue, a dust brush, and a plastic bottle of lens cleaning solution.

I usually choose the morning, when I feel fresh, to methodically clean the lenses. I also use this time to pack away the film shot the previous day as well as to sort through the remaining film, transferring a sufficient supply into my camera bag for the day's shooting.

Lens Hood – Lens hoods, as they are called, are perhaps better described as lens shades, as these round extensions (made of metal, plastic, or rubber) shade the lens from stray light, thus helping to prevent lens flare. Without a lens hood attached, the stray light can easily hit the front glass surface, bounce around inside the lens, and then strike the film, showing up as a flare.

Each lens should have its own hood, based on the characteristics of the lens (primarily the focal length). If you try putting a long telephoto lens hood over a wide-angle lens, you may cut off the corners in the final product, giving a spyglass effect called vignetting.

Even with the lens hood in place, you still have to guard against lens flare. If your eye can see it, your lens can. Occasionally, you can use your hand to shade the sun from the lens.

Neck Strap – You'll be in a lot of precarious, unstable situations where people are apt to bump into you or a sudden wave could cause you to lose your balance. The last thing in the world you want to do is drop your camera or get it wet. If you don't already have one, you are strongly advised to buy a neck strap and get in the habit of wearing it.

Note Pad – Keep a little note pad and a pencil in your camera bag. You think you can remember that the "X" on the film cartridge means to push the development one stop, but you may inadvertently make a similar mark on another cartridge with a completely different meaning. Write it down!

Taking another example, you may decide to experiment with different exposure settings and bracket a series of shots. While it's fresh in your mind, take the time to write down what you're doing. You'll learn from the situation and will be able to make better exposure decisions. Then, when you try to figure out how you got that great shot, you just might be able to. And that, my friends, is a real practical way to acquire a skill.

Plastic Bags – I've advised you to wear the camera around your neck and have it ready to fire when you're riding in the *panga*. But do take every precaution to keep the camera dry. Keep it covered as best you can in a plastic bag. Do this also when you're on-deck. Take a supply of plastic bags with you. They can be used to store film and will come in handy for general purpose use as well (see Chapter VI). In addition, I recommend treating your camera bag with two coats of a water-repellent spray (such as SCOTCH-GARD®) about a week or so before you leave. The same holds true for your daypack.

    Caution: If your camera does get wet, turn the power off immediately. Do not turn it on to "see if it's ok," as this may short the circuit. Take the batteries out, dry off the camera, and store it for a few hours in a warm environment (such as the engine room on the boat).

Polarizing Filter(s) – A polarizing filter is used to selectively reduce or eliminate reflected (polarized) light, often from glass or water, thus allowing one to photograph what is inside a window or under the water (instead of photographing a reflection). In the Galápagos, you will want to use a polarizer when photographing dolphins, marine turtles, white-tipped sharks, rays, and other seafaring subjects from the surface.

    Also, the lighting is often harsh in the islands. Since the light reflected off a subject is less saturated, the use of a polarizer will result in richer, more intense colors. A polarizing filter will also deepen a blue sky (by decreasing reflections from very small particles in the atmosphere). This also adds contrast between clouds and sky, thus "bringing out" the clouds. You are cautioned, however, about using a polarizer when photographing from an airplane; you may get an unwanted rainbow effect as you shoot through the plastic window.

    Polarized light, which causes reflections and glare, vibrates in only one plane (unlike ordinary light waves). A polarizer is a two-piece filter, each with a grid of fine lines, and the external filter can be manually rotated. When both filters have their grids aligned, the polarized light passes through. Then, as the external filter is rotated, the polarized light is increasingly blocked. The maximum blockage occurs when the grids are at right angles to each other. Functionally, with an SLR camera, you don't look at the front of the camera and rotate the external filter 90°; instead, you study the subject through the view finder and rotate the filter until the right amount of glare is removed, the animal can be seen underwater, the color of the sky is darkened, or the color tone of the subject is sufficiently enriched.

    When the two filter pieces are aligned, no light is absorbed. Thus, you can use the polarizer as a lens protector, instead of a skylight filter. When the external element is rotated, polarized light is absorbed, thus decreasing the total light that hits the film. You effectively lose about 1-2 *f*/stops (i.e., the filter factor is 1-2), and with a telephoto lens, you will probably need 400 ASA film (to allow you to shoot at 1/125th to 1/250th of a second).

    You will need a polarizer for each lens diameter. If your lenses are of the same diameter, you may choose to interchange the polarizing filter between lenses.

Note: If you have a camera with autofocus features, you will need to use a circular polarizing filter, due to the characteristics of the infrared beam that travels from the camera to the subject and "sets" the focus.

Scissors – Occasionally a roll of film doesn't have a straight edge (on the leader) and may be thus troublesome to load. A pair of scissors, kept at the ready in the camera bag, will quickly solve this problem. You will surely find some other applications for this useful tool.

Skylight Filter(s) – A skylight filter is primarily used as a lens protector and is typically left on the lens at all times. Thus, you should have one for each lens. A skylight filter also cuts out haze (to reveal more detail) and removes the bluish cast of color shots taken at a great distance (from an airplane, for example).

Unlike most filters, a skylight filter does not reduce the amount of light entering the camera; it therefore does not affect the exposure value.

ACCESSORIES TO CONSIDER

Data Back – An accessory that I have found very functional is the data back, an optional feature (sometimes sold as an add-on, replacing the standard "back") available for many quality cameras. Basically, the data back imprints user-selectable information onto the film. The data can be the date, time of day, shot number, etc. The imprinting is typically done by an LED, the intensity of which is automatically adjusted, based on the film speed. Here's how I use this feature:

At the beginning of each roll, before I release the shutter 2-3 times (to advance the film to the zero point), I turn the print button to the "ON" position, allowing the data to appear on the film. I make sure that the lens cap is securely on before pressing the shutter. The result is a black background with the data neatly imprinted in the lower right hand corner. The data that I typically choose to imprint in the Galápagos, where I'm shooting several rolls per day, is Year/Month/Day on the first shot followed by Day/Hour/Minute on the second shot. I then turn the print button to the "OFF" position, so that the data doesn't appear on the "real shots."

Bring along spare batteries for the data back.

Film Extractor – This inexpensive gadget that looks like a pair of tweezers will reclaim a roll of film (by extracting the film leader) that has accidentally been rewound back into the cartridge.

Masking Tape – I find masking tape useful to label film canisters, plastic bags, and camera equipment. It's very easy to write on and can be easily removed if necessary (unless it has seen a lot of sunlight).

Lately I have seen a lot of passengers using the same brand of disposable underwater camera. A lot of these cameras are usually thrown into the same area of the *panga* after a snorkel session, and then the trick is to figure out who belongs to which camera. The trick is easily accomplished with a piece of masking tape and initials applied with a waterproof marker.

Neutral Density Filter(s) – There may be times when you actually have too much light coming into the camera. This may happen on Bartolomé Island; after your climb to the top, you may want to put a wide-angle lens on the camera to get a great panoramic view of the islands (see Photo #30). The problem is that you're still shooting ASA 400 film, and even with the wide-angle lens closed down and set at maximum speed, the light meter reads "overexposed." A neutral density filter, which basically cuts down the amount of light entering the camera, can solve this problem. These filters are not color-selective and can be used in series to achieve the desired results.

Spot Meter – The camera's built-in light meter works on a weighted average system. It takes an overall reading of the ambient light, and it also takes a reading of the central zone (usually a circled area located at the center of the view finder). It then calculates the exposure, giving importance (or weight) to the central area. This helps to somewhat negate the bright background when you're trying to get detailed definition in your subject. To cite an example, a center-weighted system, when used properly, will let the sky "go white" and fill in facial detail in the subject (rather than getting a blue sky at the expense of an underexposed face). See the Exposure section above.

The center-weighted system can only do so much, however. Your subject may not be in the center of the picture, or the contrast may be so great that the weighted-average is still not correct in terms of the detail you want. This is where a spot meter can help.

A spot meter is just that; it's a hand-held light meter that selectively meters a very small angle of view (or spot). In the PENTAX® model that I use, the angle of view is 1° (with a total view angle of 26°) which provides accuracy even from a distance. If you want facial detail, you aim the little spot meter (about the size of a water pistol) at the subject's face. The reading you get will orient (or center) the exposure around the facial features. You can then take a couple of other spot readings (of other areas of the picture) to determine how much variation there is. You then weigh these numbers and make a decision regarding the exposure value. If the overall contrast is too high, you either don't take the shot, fill with flash, or decide where to give up the detail.

Typically, the alternative to a spot meter is to walk up to the subject, aim the camera at the face, and take a reading. Based on this reading, you manually adjust the exposure or, if available, use the camera's exposure memory system to enter the reading. You then go back to the original location and take the shot. Again, the potential problem is that you're not allowed off the trail; you could use a zoom lens to do the "walking," however, zooming in and then back.

Reinforcing some of my earlier statements, you don't have time to be taking detailed readings and calculating average exposures on every shot. You do have a couple of minutes on each island to get an overall feel for the situation. What I usually do is compare the spot meter readings with those of the camera. If I think there's a bias in the camera's readings, I'll change the exposure settings if I'm in Manual, or adjust the Exposure Compensation Dial if I'm in Automatic.

As usual, bring spare batteries.

VIDEO

There is a dynamic element to the behavior of the Galápagos wildlife that lends itself wonderfully to video. I can think of so many emotional "video scenes" that are seen most every trip – sky-pointing blue-footed boobies, bill-fencing albatrosses, sea lion pups playing in tide pools, interacting giant tortoises, even interacting passengers. I have been photography-oriented for many years and avoided video – that is until a couple of years ago. Then I got bitten by the video bug. Bad! Now I shoot about 4 hours of video per trip and have gotten into underwater video and video editing. If you're thinking of bringing a video camera to the Galápagos, by all means, go for it. If you're thinking of buying a video camera to take with you, here are some recommendations:

1. Get a video camera with Hi-8 format. This is basically a high resolution form of the standard 8mm. You will find the overall picture quality to be clearer and sharper. This is critically important when you make copies, because you lose a significant amount of the picture quality with each copy generation. In other words, a copy of a copy is generally pretty grainy quality, and it is very important to have the highest definition master tape possible. So get Hi-8 format; it doesn't cost much more.

2. Get a video camera with a color view finder. It makes a tremendous difference. You can imagine how difficult it is to find a finch in a tree in a 1" black-and-white view finder. Also, the view finder is actually a little television set, allowing you to preview the scene and judge the quality before pressing the little red button. It's like looking at the finished picture before you take it. Finally, look for a color view finder with exposure control, which will allow you to vary the emotional tones of the color. I use this feature quite a bit. Once again, the cost difference between a black & white and color view finder isn't that much.

Caution: You do have to be careful with a color view finder. People generally carry a video camera slung over their shoulder, with the camera supported by the shoulder strap. Often, the view finder is pointed straight up. The problem here is that the sun's rays enter the view finder, are concentrated (as with a magnifying glass), and can burn out the little picture elements in the view finder. The end result is a series of "flare" lines in the view finder, which seriously impede viewing the image. This seems to be a recent problem, so recent that the instruction manuals haven't caught up with it. Sometimes there is a little warning sticker on the view finder. Basically, make sure the view finder is pointed away from the sun.

3. Image stabilization is a "must" feature. This wonderful bit of technology actually takes a lot of shake out of the camera. This is extremely important for hand-held video (which most of you will be doing), even more so on video taken from the boat or the *panga,* which adds its own "shake." This is a feature that you can turn on and off, but I leave it on all the time. The only negative is that it uses about twice the power, thereby draining the battery a lot faster. My "super 3 hour" batteries last about 1 hour with the "steady cam" feature on. Because of this, I carry 3 batteries on shore and have a fourth charging on the boat. This may be a bit extreme, but it's better than the extreme behavior I've seen when a passenger's last battery dies on the trail.

4. If you're thinking about editing, look at video cameras with time code. This will seriously limit the choices (SONY® currently has the most models with this feature), and the price will probably increase by a few hundred dollars. What time code does is allow the editing to be more precise. Instead of accuracy to plus/minus 1-3 seconds, you can achieve accuracy to plus/minus 1-3 frames (there are 30 frames per second). This difference won't seem significant until you really get into editing.

Misc: If you're bringing a video camera to the Galápagos, a minimum of three batteries is recommended. Batteries can be charged on the boat. A circular polarizing filter is also strongly recommended (see the Recommended Accessories section above). A few drops of clear nail polish on the little screws will keep them from oxidizing in the salty environment. You may also want to put little pieces of electrical tape over uncovered connectors, again reducing the chances of oxidation. As with still cameras, try using manual focus when shooting small birds in a tree (see the Composition section above).

UNDERWATER PHOTOGRAPHY

You will get many underwater photo opportunities in the Galápagos, and the investment in an underwater camera is highly recommended. Believe me, the first time you spot a sea lion through your snorkel mask about 3 ft in front of you, you will appreciate the true value of an underwater camera. Regarding the selection of an underwater camera, I have mixed feelings (as described in the following section).

DISPOSABLE UNDERWATER CAMERAS

This is the most popular choice. They are inexpensive (less than $15) and widely available. Both KODAK® and FUJI® make them. These cameras are preloaded with a 24 exposure roll of ASA 400 print film, have plastic housings, and are rated for underwater water use to a depth of about 12 ft. They are not going to get you award-winning shots, but they do a surprisingly good job. It is definitely much better than not having an underwater camera at all, certainly the case when you are able to document a sea lion coming straight at you. The trick is to only take pictures in bright sunlit water and be within 3 ft of the subject. Hold the camera at arm's length away from you instead of trying to hold it up to your mask and look through the view finder. This will put the camera closer to the subject without affecting the natural behavior, and don't worry, it is a wide angle lens, so everything you want (often more) will be in the picture.

Bring at least 2-3 disposables; they are cheap enough.

LITTLE YELLOW CAMERAS

There are several brands of underwater automatic cameras in the $200-$300 range that are good pieces of equipment. They are sealed against sand and dust so you can use them on the beach. You can also take them skiing, down the rapids, and into the pool. Typically, they can be used down to a depth of 15 ft, which is about all you need for snorkeling. They generally have all the automatic camera features, including autofocus, motor-driven film advance, autorewind, automatic exposure, built-in flash, etc.

You can use these cameras on land as well as in and under the water. In fact, the autofocus feature typically only works above water; underwater, they are fixed focus cameras. The MINOLTA® model that I have used has an underwater focus range of 4-12 ft, with a close-up button that sets the focus from 1.4-4.3 ft. This camera is also a dual-lens type; pressing a button will switch between a standard underwater (35mm) and a mild telephoto (50mm) lens. As you can tell by these numbers, underwater optics are different.

The problem with these cameras, at least underwater, is that you don't have the same control over the light (or the quality of the end product) as you do on land with a full-function 35mm SLR. Thus, what you wind up with are underwater snapshots. Pretty much the same as with the disposables, but for a lot more money. Is it worth it? I would say that the answer depends on whether you will use the camera for other applications as well – skiing, kayaking, etc. I finally made the decision to upgrade to the professional camera described below.

PROFESSIONAL UNDERWATER CAMERAS

For top quality underwater shots, we are left with the option of going all the way with a complete underwater photographic system, starting with a NIKONOS V® camera. It has through-the-lens metering capability with aperture-priority Automatic and Manual operation, interchangeable lenses, full focusing control, and is rated to a depth of 160 ft. The NIKONOS V® does have its limitations in that it is a bit inconvenient to use. The viewfinder does not see through the camera's lens, and a potential parallax problem is created; you have no way of "seeing" if you are in focus. There is a focus range indicator on the front of the lens along with the f/stop indicator (not exactly a convenient location). The biggest limitation, though, is that it has a NIKON® price – about $500 with the standard 35mm lens. Eventually you will want to upgrade to wide-angle underwater lenses (20mm and 15mm) which will allow you to get much closer to the subject. They will also allow you to get closer to poverty as they cost about $500 (20mm) to $1000 (15mm). Then there's the cost of the strobe system, but you can defer this, as you can get by without underwater flash at least as far as snorkeling is concerned (although you definitely need a strobe for underwater photography while scuba diving).

PHOTOGRAPHY CHECK LIST

Use this list in conjunction with the Packing Check List at the end of Chapter VI,
PREPARE FOR DEPARTURE.

ITEM	NOTES
☐ Camera Batteries, spare	_____
☐ Film	_____
☐ Film Extractor	_____
☐ Instructional Manual(s)	_____
☐ Lead Foil Film Bag(s)	_____
☐ Lens Cleaner/Tissue/ Dust Brush	_____
☐ Lenses/Caps/Hoods	_____ _____
☐ Light Meter/Spot Meter/ Batteries	_____
☐ Masking Tape	_____
☐ Neck Strap	_____
☐ Neutral Density Filter(s)	_____
☐ Note Pad	_____
☐ Plastic Bags	_____
☐ Polarizing Filter(s)	_____
☐ Scissors	_____
☐ Skylight Filter(s)	_____
☐ Underwater Camera/ Equipment	_____ _____
☐ Video Equipment/ Batteries	_____ _____
☐ Disposable Cameras	_____

CHAPTER VIII

WELCOME TO ECUADOR

From the standpoint of this book, mainland Ecuador is a base camp, a point of departure to (and return from) the Galápagos Islands. In addition, some of you will use the stay in Quito or Guayaquil to put together your tour of the islands. On the return trip, Quito becomes a city of shopping opportunity, a source of gifts for your friends and family as well as for yourself. While this may sound a bit cold and calculated, it's meant to be. The purposes of this book are to get you to go to the Galápagos Islands, to make you aware of all the touring possibilities, to get you there in an efficient manner, and to keep you there for as long as your vacation time allows. Being a travel guide to Ecuador is not one of these purposes. There are other books that do an excellent job of this (see the Literature section).

As the saying goes, something's got to give. And what's giving, if you accept the guidance offered here, is an extensive tour of Ecuador. For now anyway. If you like, consider this brief encounter to be a scouting mission for your next visit to Ecuador. I suspect that once you see the snow-capped peaks of the Andes and the beautiful city of Quito, you may well want to return for an extensive stay. At that time you can tour the Amazon jungles and visit the Andean Highlands, traveling the length of the "Valley of the Volcanoes." But for now you're passing through. Maybe with enough time to catch a peak or two (as the saying sort of goes), especially in and around the Quito area. Many of you on a Galápagos group tour may be provided with the opportunity of several Day Trips. With this orientation, then, let's take a brief look at Ecuador.

ABOUT ECUADOR

Ecuador is located on the west coast of South America and, as its name suggests, on the equator. Its neighbors are Columbia to the north and Peru to the east & south. The country has a population of about 10 million people and is a constitutional republic with an elected President and a House of Representatives. Ecuador consists of 21 provinces, including the Galápagos Islands, and is the second smallest Latin American country in South America (Uruguay is the smallest); the Guianas (Guyana, Suriname, and French Guyana), while smaller, are not considered to be part of Latin America.

Ecuador is divided into three geographic regions, more like three different worlds. First there is *La Sierra,* framed by the majestic Andes, with volcanic peaks as high as 20,000 ft. Running the length of Ecuador from Columbia to Peru, two Andean ranges are separated by the 25-40 mile wide Central Valley (termed the "Avenue of the Volcanoes") in which Quito is situated. To the west of the Andes is *La Costa* or coastal region, where Guayaquil is located; this is mostly lowland and Ecuador's main agricultural export area. To the east is *El Oriente,* the upper Amazon region with its tropical rain forests.

Until substantial oil discoveries were made in the 1970s (in the northern *Oriente* region, close to the Columbian border), Ecuador was a typical "banana republic." In fact, Ecuador is still the world's largest exporter of bananas. Coffee, though low yielding, is the most extensive of Ecuador's cash crops, accounting for about 20 percent of the total agricultural land. Other agricultural exports include sugar, cocoa, rice, cattle, and (yes) shrimp farming. Ecuador is also the world's leading producer of balsa wood. While employing about a third of the labor force, agriculture foreign exchange earnings fell to about 15 percent of Ecuador's total as petroleum exports rose to first place. By the 1980s, oil accounted for about half of the country's export earnings. Fishing and tourism are also growing industries.

With all that, Ecuador remains a Third World country with serious economic problems. With the big drop in oil prices in the mid-1980s, Ecuador's national income was greatly reduced (by about 50 percent). To make matters worse, in 1983 an extreme *El Niño* (a weather phenomenon associated with warming of the normally cool ocean waters) caused severe flooding of agricultural lands and completely disrupted the fishing industry. And then in 1987 a major earthquake hit Ecuador, causing great damage and loss of life. Over 30 miles of the nation's Trans-Andean oil pipeline were destroyed, and oil exports came to a standstill for almost 6 months. As a result, the economy is in a weakened condition, with considerable debt and a currency that has seen significant devaluation.

In terms of politics, Ecuador is relatively stable despite occasional shows of force by the opposing conservative and liberal factions as well as by the military. The tranquil setting seems to dominate the spirit of the people and in turn has kept Ecuador from the turmoil of other South American countries.

It wasn't always that way. As part of the Inca empire, Ecuador was not spared by the Spanish conquistadors, and fell in 1535 to the armored, cannon-firing forces of Francisco Pizarro. Ecuador then became a Spanish colony, and remained so until 1820 when the great liberator, Simón Bolivar, led the successful battle for independence which was fully achieved in 1830. Ecuador went to war with Peru in 1941, the result of which was a new border line between the neighboring countries, a boundary still in dispute (they fought again in 1996).

Through it all, an air of dignity has prevailed, a characteristic that best describes the Ecuadorians themselves, proud descendants of Indian and Spanish cultures. About 40 percent of the population are native Indians, progeny of the Inca empire, living mostly in the Highlands of the *Sierra.* An equal number are *mestizo* (mixed Indian and Spanish); about 10 percent are European with the balance of the population made up of Africans and Asians. The *Sierra* and *Costa* regions each have about half of Ecuador's total population, with the sparse remainder (less than 500,000) living in the rain forests of *El Oriente,* where development is slowly beginning.

The blend of Indian and Spanish cultures is also evident in the tradition of artistic achievement and expert craftsmanship. Made with skills handed down from Inca forefathers, today's Indian art ranges from intricately-woven tapestries, leatherwork, and hat-making to handsome wood carvings, ceramics, and finely-detailed jewelry. The dress of the Indians is an art form in itself, with the women wearing beautifully embroidered blouses and ornately-colored head cloths.

When the Spaniards departed, they left behind a vast collection of colonial art (mostly sculptures and paintings) and a legacy of religious architecture – superb churches and cathedrals with their golden altars, colored columns, gilded balconies, and richly sculptured facades.

And that is a very brief look at Ecuador. Fasten your seat belts and get ready for a real look, with your own eyes.

ARRIVAL IN ECUADOR

Whether you arrive in Quito or Guayaquil, your first goal is to get out of the airport, into a taxi or tour van, and be on the way towards your hotel. First, however, you will have to go through the Passport Control area, where, in addition to your passport, you must present the T3 Tourist Information Card that you filled out on the airplane. You may also be asked how long you intend to stay in Ecuador. Respond with the actual length of your stay. U.S. and Canadian citizens touring Ecuador are allowed a visit for up to 90 days without a visa. A part of the T3 card will be returned to you. Do not throw this portion of the card away; it states the legal duration of your visit (they usually write in 30 days), and will be required by any Ecuadorian official checking your passport as well as by the Passport Control Officer when you leave the country.

Note: If it turns out that you will be spending more time in Ecuador than allotted by the Immigration Officer, you will have to visit the Immigration Department in either Quito or Guayaquil and get an extension stamped on your passport and T3 card. The process is easy, but the wait is not very pleasant. You are advised to let the Tour Operator you are working with take care of this detail on your behalf. They do this kind of thing all the time and know their way around Immigrations pretty well.

During your visit, when asked where you are from, always respond, "The United States," or "The U.S." It's better than saying you're from "America" because South Americans are "Americans" too! By the way, it just about goes without saying that you don't want to bring any illegal substances (to be clear – drugs) into Ecuador. We all know about the reputation of South American prisons. End of subject.

After Passport Control, you'll go to the Baggage Claim area to gather up your checked baggage and then proceed to Customs. Remember, each person is allowed to bring in, duty-free, one bottle of liquor, 300 cigarettes, as well as a "reasonable" quantity of perfume and gifts. Typically, tourists do not have to go through the inspection procedure. But you will have to give the authorities your baggage claim ticket(s) (usually stapled to your boarding pass or airline ticket envelope) before you leave the airport. Waiting in line, you will see some of the largest suitcases ever made.

As you leave the Customs area, you will sometimes be met by a virtual wave of humanity – a greeting committee waiting for their friends, family, and loved ones to exit the hallowed gates of Customs. They all look happy, very excited, with lots of waving and yelling. The first time I went through this, I didn't exactly know what was going on. Images came to mind of visiting team outfielders staring up at the bleachers of Fenway Park or Wrigley Field.

If you're part of a group tour, look at the fringes of this congregation, and you will find a person holding a sign with your name on it (or the name of your group); you will be given written instructions about this from your Tour Operator. This person (who works for the local affiliate company of your Tour Operator) will tip the porter who carried your bag(s), and will transport you to your hotel. If you're not part of a group tour, see the section on Taxis below.

TAXIS

Next come the porters and taxis, both official and unofficial. The official porters wear uniforms; the unofficial ones are mostly kids. It doesn't really matter, they'll all do a good job carrying your bags to a taxi. The job is worth about 2000 sucres per full-size bag. If you haven't changed money, you can leave 50 cents per bag. U.S. currency is always welcome and actually preferred in Ecuador where the sucre is constantly being devalued.

Make sure you get a yellow taxi. They are official; the black ones are not. A cab ride from the Quito or Guayaquil airport to your downtown hotel will cost about 15,000 to 20,000 sucres with the meter off (about U.S. $4.00-$5.00), and a bit less with the meter on. No tips. The unofficial cabs can cost twice as much.

Agree on the fare in advance. If you're not up to trying this in Spanish, just say, "Hotel Colón (or the name of your hotel), *por favor* (please)." Keep a firm grip on your bags, because the driver will begin to put them into the taxi. Before the bags go in, agree on the price. Ask him how much, *"¿cuántos es?"* Chances are he will answer in English, and the price will be within the above-specified limits. He may point to the meter in which case everything is fine. If the driver answers in Spanish and you're not sure what he said, hand him a pen and piece of paper and once again say, *"por favor."* He'll understand. If the amount he writes is too much, write the amount you want to pay. You shouldn't have any problem.

You will find taxis to be a convenient, inexpensive way to travel in Quito and Guayaquil. Many of the hotels have a list of estimated fares to various locations. Negotiate the fare in advance if you don't see a meter with the fare numbers lit up.

CAR RENTALS

Renting a car in Ecuador is generally not necessary, nor is it recommended. The condition of many of the cars is suspect, and traffic can be congested in the business districts. Outside the cities, the roads are often unpaved, there is a lack of road signs, and trucks & buses are wild and loose. There are several reports of blown tires in remote locations, not a very comforting thought. Besides, taxis are cheap enough, and there are many organized tours of Quito and Guayaquil as well as excursions to the outlying areas.

If you insist on renting a car, do so at the airport where HERTZ®, INTER-NATIONAL®, AVIS®, BUDGET®, DOLLAR®, and others have cars for about U.S. $50 (including mandatory insurance and tax) per day with unlimited mileage. The steering wheel is on the left (just like home).

CURRENCY

The monetary unit of Ecuador is the sucre. While money may be sweet, that's not the origin of the sucre. During the battle for Ecuadorian independence from Spain, it was General Antonio José de Sucre who defeated the Spanish at the decisive Battle of Pichincha (the mountain that dominates the view from Quito) and became a national hero.

The sucre (often written as S/) has undergone a severe devaluation in recent years, due to the downturn in Ecuador's economy (primarily related to the drop in oil prices). For you, that's good news, in that your dollars are strong – very strong in fact. This will be evident to you in restaurants, hotels, clothing stores, and gift shops. The exchange rate in 1998 was about 4200 sucres per dollar (compared to about 650 sucres early in 1990, and 1800 sucres in 1993), with a 10 sucre daily variation. There are bills of 50,000, 20,000, 10,000, and 5,000 sucres. There are also 1,000, 500, and 100 sucre coins. When you consider that a sucre is currently worth a fraction of a penny, and that the sucre itself, until just recently, was divided into 100 centavos (with 50, 20, 10 and 5 centavo coins), you have an insight into the extent of the Ecuadorian currency devaluation.

There are several money exchange houses (*casas de cambio*) in Quito and Guayaquil. You will find them more accessible and convenient to use than banks in that there is rarely a line. The banks, on the other hand, are usually crowded; look for the "foreign currency" line. *Cambios* and banks are open 9:00 a.m. to 1:30 p.m., and from 2:30 – 6:00 p.m., Monday through Friday. Your passport will be required as proof of identification if exchanging traveler's checks.

Most banks and *cambios* will offer about the same exchange rates. So will the *cambio* in your hotel. A difference of 5 sucres in the exchange rate is a difference of only about a penny; on an exchange transaction of $500, this adds up to about $5.00. While we all want the best exchange rate, I don't recommend giving up valuable vacation time to get a little better exchange rate, especially if your time in mainland Ecuador is short, and there's shopping to be done and sights to be seen. Also, you'll get about the same exchange rate for cash dollars and traveler's checks. Finally, the exchange rates in mainland Ecuador are much better than you will get at the U.S. departure airport.

Try to estimate out-of-pocket expenses on the last couple of days in Ecuador so you can use up most of your sucres and won't have to exchange them back to U.S. dollars. One idea is to pay the required $25 exit tax with your remaining sucres. If you're a little short, they will let you pay the balance in U.S. dollars.

Note: Almost all of your transactions can be in U.S. dollars. For reasons stated above, U.S. dollars are actually preferred, and you'll get a pretty reasonable exchange rate in most places. Thus, you don't need to change a lot of currency. If you are going to spend some time in the market areas of mainland Ecuador and you have mostly traveler's checks, then you may want to exchange $100-$300 for sucres (depending on how serious a shopper you are).

LOCAL TIME

Mainland Ecuador is on Eastern Standard Time. The flight from Miami is almost due south. Since Ecuador is, logically enough, on the equator, there is an equal amount of night and day throughout the year. There is no need for, and therefore, no Daylight Saving Time. The Galápagos Islands, 600 miles west of the Ecuadorian mainland, are on Central (Chicago) Standard Time, year-round.

BUSINESS HOURS

Stores are generally open Monday through Saturday from 9:00 a.m. to 1:00 p.m. and from 3:00 p.m. to 7:00 p.m., with a mid-day *siesta* in between. Some of the tourist-oriented gift shops do not close for *siesta*. This is also true of the growing number of shopping centers. Some stores may only be open Monday through Friday, and others remain open for half a day on Saturday. If you find a shop that you like and plan on going back to buy more items or to "finalize" an expensive purchase, verify their business hours.

LANGUAGE

One way or another, you'll have to come to terms with Spanish. To be honest, in the tourist-oriented circle in which you will travel, you can get by completely without a single word of Spanish. It would be somewhat rude, though, not to make an attempt to learn at least the basic greetings. Besides, it's fun and part of the total travel experience. It can also be very practical! Being able to read a menu, even with a dictionary at the table, certainly has its advantages. So does asking the maid for an extra pillow (without having to phone the main desk) and finding out if a store has a larger sweater of the same color, etc. It's also nice to be able to ask directions (and find out how to get to the store in the first place).

Take a phrase book and dictionary with you; I recommend Barron's **SPANISH AT A GLANCE: PHRASE BOOK & DICTIONARY FOR TRAVELERS** (see the Literature section). There are enough word similarities between English and Spanish that you'll soon be putting sentences together. Do the best you can; the Ecuadorians will know you're trying and appreciate the effort.

In the Galápagos, many of you will find that learning the names of the animals in Spanish to be as interesting as learning about the animals themselves. Some of my favorites are sea lions (*lobos marinos,* or sea wolves), the dove (*paloma*), heron (*garza*), turtle (*tortuga*), penguin (*pingüino*), and blue footed booby (*piquero patas azules*). The word *Galápagos* itself is the Spanish name for the giant tortoise.

Incidentally, Ecuador has two official languages – Spanish and Quechua (spoken by the majority of the native Indians). Several other indigenous languages are also spoken, although not to a great extent.

TIPPING

A 20 percent surcharge is added to your hotel bill to cover tax (10 percent) and gratuities (10 percent). This includes meals at the hotel restaurant. Restaurants outside the hotel add a 10 percent service charge. Thus, leaving an additional 5 percent tip at a restaurant is customary. For a porter at the airport, a 50 cent (2000 sucre) tip per full-size piece of luggage is adequate. While you're not required to tip the porters at the hotel, you'll probably feel better by handing the porter about $1 (4000 sucre) per bag.

ELECTRICITY

The electric power in mainland Ecuador and the Galápagos Islands is 110 VAC, 60 cycles (the same as in the U.S. and Canada).

TELEPHONE

Ecuador has upgraded its local and international telephone service over the last few years. Calling and sending a FAX to and from Ecuador is a lot smoother than it was 3 years ago. Keep in mind, though, that it does cost about 4 times more to place a call or send a FAX from Ecuador to the U.S. than it does for us to call or FAX Ecuador from the U.S.; the differential is even more, of course, if your call or FAX is charged to your hotel room.

When calling or sending a FAX to Ecuador from the U.S., you must first dial the international access code "011" followed by the country code for Ecuador ("593"), the city code for Quito ("2") or Guayaquil ("4"), and then the local number. To place a call or send a FAX from Ecuador to the U.S., dial the international access code to the U.S. ("001") followed by the area code and local number. You can also charge calls (or place a collect call) by using your telephone CALLING CARD. This will be less expensive than charging the call to your hotel room. Just dial "999 -119" to access AT&T-DIRECT (alternatively 999-170 for MCI, 999-171 for SPRINT, or 999-175 for CANADA-TELEGLOBE). You may not be able to use your CALLING CARD if the call is placed at the telephone company (IETEL) office at the airport. Finally, you can not call a TOLL-FREE (800) number from Ecuador.

If you place an international call, remember that mainland Ecuador is on Eastern Standard Time throughout the year.

When calling Guayaquil from Quito, dial "04" followed by the local number. When calling Quito from Guayaquil, dial "02" followed by the local number.

TOURIST INFORMATION

Once you arrive in Ecuador, there is an excellent guidebook available called **THIS IS ECUADOR.** This booklet is published monthly and is available at all the major hotels and travel agencies. It contains handy maps, a calendar of events, useful sightseeing information, and advertisements of interest for restaurants, gift shops, Tour Operators, etc. There is also a listing of many useful phone numbers that is more current than those found in the telephone directories.

The Ecuadorian government operates a National Tourist Board called *CETUR (Corporación Ecuatoriana de Turismo).* There is at least one *CETUR* office in all the major cities and towns (including one in Puerto Ayora on Santa Cruz Island in the Galápagos). They have several brochures and maps and can help you find a specific location, store, etc. *CETUR* will also tell you where the important museums and key points of interest are located. They generally have an English-speaking person working at each office.

While *CETUR* is a good source of general information, don't depend on them to help you put together a tour of the Galápagos.That is not their function. The best they can do is tell you where the Tour Operators are located. If you run into a problem regarding a price negotiation, the quality of a product or service, or a refund not received, it would be worth going there in a peaceful attempt to settle the matter. I've heard the *CETUR* will occasionally intervene in this type of situation. Also, if they receive a number of complaints about a particular company or organization, they may take action.

Also, the Department of Ecuador Tourism has a U.S. office, and you may want to send away for some literature. Their address is 3785 NW 82nd Ave, Suite 317, Miami, FL 33166. PHONE: (305) 716-5252; FAX: 305-577-0531.

QUITO

Quito, the capital of Ecuador, is a quiet, beautiful city (see Photo #1). Flanked by the tall, snow-capped peaks of the Andes, Quito itself is at 9300 ft, yet located almost directly on the equator. On a clear day, as they say, you can see the snow cones of the volcanic peaks, giving the city an air of a mountain retreat. Based on your expectations of a bustling South American city, the serenity and the dramatic setting take you by pleasant surprise. While the population of Quito is over 1.5 million people, making it the second largest city in Ecuador (Guayaquil is the largest), it has a tranquil small town feel to it (the rush hour and center-city traffic notwithstanding). The people, the city, and the setting seem to blend together, all part of the rich artistic and cultural heritage.

Here at the foot of 15,700 Mt. Pichincha, an active volcano, you are in the Andean Highlands in what was once an Inca city. When the approaching conquistadors finally fought their way here in 1534, they found Quito in ruins. The Incas chose to destroy their city rather than surrender it. So the city was rebuilt in the grand colonial style architecture described at the beginning of this chapter. This legacy was formally recognized by *UNESCO* in 1978, proclaiming Quito a "Cultural Patrimony of Mankind," and sanctions were passed to preserve the character and architectural integrity of what is called Old Town.

Old Town is located in the central section of Quito, called *el centro* (I told you Spanish was easy). The modern business and main shopping district is in the north. This is also where the finer hotels are located.

THE AIRPORT

Mariscal Sucre International Airport is located at the end of Av. Amazonas, 6 miles north of the business, shopping, and major hotel district. This is an older airport (compared to the modern facility in Guayaquil) that tends to be somewhat crowded, especially the section for domestic flights; the international terminal is relatively tranquil.

Note: There is a $25 Departure Tax on international flights, payable in sucres or U.S. dollars (or a combination of both); they do not accept traveler's checks or credit cards.

TOURIST INFORMATION

There are three *CETUR* offices in Quito at the following locations:

Main Office: Av. Eloy Alfaro 1214 and Carlos Tobar in the Ministry of Tourism building. **Local Phone:** 553-995

Municipal Palace (*Palacio Municipal*) Office: In the Old Town district, located in the Municipal Palace (City Hall) on the southeast side of *Plaza de La Independencia.* **Local Phone:** 514-044

Airport Office: Mariscal Sucre Airport, in the arrival hall of the international terminal. They don't seem to be open all that often. **Local Phone:** 246-232

CLIMATE

The combination of the equatorial and mountain setting gives Quito an ideal climate of pleasant, warm days (in the 70s Deg F) and brisk, cool evenings, with temperatures in the 50s Deg F. The rainy season is from October to May, with frequent afternoon and/or evening showers. The heaviest rainfall is typically in April.

HOTELS

There are several First Class hotels in Quito at reasonable rates. Those that are not "reasonable" are the new, luxury hotels (and there are quite a few of them) that cater to business clientele. While Quito does have a complete selection of accommodations, including $10 hostels, pensions, and clean, budget-style hotels, my recommendation is to stay with the best. And why not? For about $90, you can have a spacious, elegantly-furnished double room at some of the finer hotels in Quito. Generally, they have excellent restaurants serving international cuisine as well as Ecuadorian specialties. There are also shopping arcades, lounges, and meeting rooms; some have casinos. These hotels are all centrally located, close to the finer gift shops, restaurants, *cambios,* and museums. From a security standpoint, they are your best choices. Finally, the staff speaks excellent English and will be able to help you with directions, confirming flights, etc.

By the way, the casinos are an experience. The slot machines take 5000 sucre tokens (about $1.25) and they seem to be programmed to pay off more often than the ones in the U.S. You don't really win much, but you don't seem to lose money either. You just keep playing... and playing. Finally, you're at the point where you want to lose, so you can go upstairs and get some sleep! There's also blackjack, *chemin de fer,* and roulette for the serious gambling types. I would suspect that playing these games of chance, you can get to go upstairs a lot faster.

Now, some special advice for those who are arriving in Quito without having booked a tour to the Galápagos. Make reservations at one of the finer hotels for 2 nights. By the second day, you'll have a good idea on the progress you're making with the Ecuadorian Tour Operators. If you think that you'll be staying on in Quito for a few days more, you may choose to switch to a lower price hotel. The following list contains some of the best hotels in the Tourist Class category. They all have clean, well-furnished rooms with a private bath, and they're in the same modern section of town as the premium hotels. Laundry service is provided, and the rooms have a telephone, refrigerator, and color TV with cable broadcasts from the U.S. These Tourist Class choices are also for those on a budget and for the traveler that doesn't especially care for fancy hotels with casinos and all the other glitz.

Note: The sink and shower faucets at some of the hotels are marked differently than you're used to, which could be cause for confusion as well as a potential problem. The left (hot) faucet is marked "C" for *Caliente;* the right (cold) faucet is marked "F" for *Frío.*

Many of the hotels provide bottles of mineral water and/or purified water in each room for drinking and rinsing when brushing your teeth.

All phone numbers are local. The FAX numbers listed below include the international, country, and city codes. E-mail numbers are listed if available.

Here then are the recommended hotels of Quito and their affiliated U.S. Reservation Service(s). Add 20% to all prices for tax and service. Prices listed are as of 1998.

First Class Hotels:

AKROS HOTEL – Av. 6 de Diciembre 3986 (P.O. Box 17-21-1544).
Local Phone: 430-600 or 430-610   **FAX:** 011-593-2-431-727
Rooms: Modern and comfortable.
Price Range: Single – U.S.$120; Double – U.S.$140; Triple – U.S.$200.
Comments: The Akros is a beautiful European-style luxury hotel. Their primary market appears to be the business traveler.
U.S. Reservation Services: Utell International (UI), TOLL FREE: (800) 448-8355, Nationwide.

HOTEL ALAMEDA REAL – Roca 653 and Av. Amazonas (P.O. Box 358-A).
Local Phone: 562-345   **FAX:** 011-593-2-565-759
E-mail: apartec@uio.satnet.net
Rooms: Rooms are very nicely furnished; all have refrigerators. For $5-$15 extra, you can get suites with living rooms, kitchenettes, etc. Room service is available 24 hours a day.
Price Range: Single – U.S.$90; Double – U.S.$100; Triple – U.S.$110.
Comments: I recommend the Alameda Real very highly. It is said that, of the finer hotels, they have the most personal service. The comments I hear time and again are, "I have stayed at all of the best hotels in Quito, and the staff at the Alameda Real get to know you real fast. You're treated more as an individual than as a number." My experiences strongly support this impression.
U.S. Reservation Services: Steigenberger Reservation Service (SRS), TOLL FREE (800) 223-5652 U.S. & Canada; FAX: 407-679-3361.

HOTEL HILTON COLON – Av. Amazonas and Patria (P.O. Box 17-01-3107).
Local Phone: 560-666 or 561-333 or 562-888   **FAX:** 011-593-2-563-903
E-mail: hcolon@uio.satnet.net
Rooms: All 415 rooms are finely furnished; the higher-priced suites are exceptional.

Price Range: Single – U.S.$150; Double – U.S.$170; Triple – U.S.$190.

Comments: The Colón has long been one of the best hotels in town and has recently become part of the Hilton Hotels chain. It has very good restaurants, an excellent mall consisting of several very fine stores, 14 convention and meeting rooms, an exercise facility with sauna & Jacuzzi, and a large casino.

U.S. Reservation Services: Hilton Reservations Worldwide, TOLL FREE: (800) 445-8667, U.S. & Canada.

CROWNE PLAZA – Av. de Los Shyris 1757 and Naciones Unidas.

Local Phone: 445-305 or 251-666   **FAX:** 011-593-2-251-958

Rooms: All 100 rooms are suites.

Price Range: Single – U.S.$200;   Double – U.S.$220.

Comments: Located near the airport and Quito's financial district, the Crowne Plaza is a luxury hotel for the traveling businessman. The Crowne Plaza hotels are owned by Holiday Inn.

U.S. Reservation Services: Crowne Plaza (CP), TOLL FREE: (800) 227- 6963, U.S. & Canada.

QUITO MARRIOTT HOTEL – Av. Orellana and Amazonas.

Comments: This business-traveler-oriented hotel is due to open in 1999.

U.S. Reservation Services: Marriott Hotels

HOTEL ORO VERDE – Av. 12 de Octubre 1820 and Luís Cordero (P.O. Box 17-21-565).

Local Phone: 566-497 or 567-128   **FAX:** 011-593-2-569-189

E-mail: ecovq@uio.satnet.net

Rooms: All 241 rooms in the 14 story complex have a safety deposit box and mini-bar. Suites have a separate reception area and valet service.

Price Range: Single – U.S.$240;   Double – U.S.$260.

Comments: Located within 15 minutes of the airport, the Oro Verde is the ultimate luxury hotel, catering to the traveling business clientele. They even have a Japanese restaurant w/sushi bar.

U.S. Reservation Services: The Leading Hotels of the World (LHW), TOLL FREE: (800) 223-6800, U.S. & Canada.

HOTEL QUITO – González Súarez 2500 at Av. 12 de Octubre (P.O. Box 17–01-2201).

Local Phone: 544-600 or 234-110   **FAX:** 011-593-2-567-284

E-mail: hoquito@ibm.net

Rooms: Mostly refurbished – great views.

Price Range: Single – U.S. $120; Double – U.S.$140; Triple –U.S.$160.

Comments: If you want a room with a view, this is the place. However, despite recent renovations, it still presents itself as somewhat "worn and faded." The Hotel Quito is located on a hilltop, near several of the embassies, and the central business and shopping district. The top floor restaurant and lounge, El Techo del Mundo (Roof of the World), provides a truly special panoramic vista of the city and surrounding peaks. It has beautiful gardens, a full-size outdoor pool, and a casino.

U.S. Reservation Services: Best Western Hotels (BW), TOLL FREE: (800) 528-1234, Nationwide, ask for the international desk.

RADISSON ROYAL QUITO HOTEL – Av. 12 de Octubre and Cordero 444 (World Trade Center).
Local Phone: 548-355   **FAX:** 011-593-2-543-200
E-mail: quito@uio.radisson.com.ec
Rooms: There are 98 luxury rooms and 14 royal suites.
Price Range: Single/Double – U.S.$195; Triple – U.S.$205.
Comments: Another luxury hotel oriented to the business person.
U.S. Reservation Services: Carlson Hospitality Worldwide (RD), TOLL FREE: (800) 333-3333, U.S. & Canada.

Tourist Class Hotels:

HOSTAL LOS ALPES – José Luís Tamayo 233 and Jorge Washington.
Local Phone: 561-110 or 561-128   **FAX:** N/A
Price Range: Single – U.S.$45; Double – U.S.$65.
Comments: Charming throughout and nicely decorated. The name is appropriate, because it does have a rustic Swiss Inn feel to it. The restaurant is also very good. Centrally located and highly recommended.

HOTEL ALSTON INN – Juan León Mera 741 and Baquedano.
Local Phone: 508-956 or 229-955 or 222-721 **FAX:** 011-593-2-508-956
E-mail: alston@uio.satnet.net
Price Range: Single – U.S.$17; Double – U.S.$23; Triple – U.S.$27
Comments: Very much on the spartan side of tourist class, but for those on a budget, the rooms are most acceptable. Located right in the "tourist district", next to the Libri Mundi bookstore.

HOTEL AMARANTA INTERNACIONAL – Leonidas Plaza 194 and Jorge Washington.
Local Phone: 560-585 or 543-619 or 238-385 **FAX:** 011-593-2-560-586
Price Range: Single/Double – U.S.$55; Triple – U.S.$65; Apartments (for 5-7) – U.S.$100-$160.
Comments: All rooms are suites with kitchenettes. The penthouse apartments have 3-4 bedrooms, each with a private bath. Good central location.

HOTEL AMBASSADOR – Av. 9 de Octubre 1052 and Colón (P.O. Box 17-07-8757).
Local Phone: 562-049 or 561-777   **FAX:** 011-593-2-503-711
Price Range: Single – U.S.$20; Double – U.S.$25; Triple – U.S.$30.
Comments: They have 60 nicely refurnished rooms in a good location at a great price.   .

HOTEL BARNARD – Queseras del Medio 598 and Av. Columbia (Across from the Military Hospital).
Local Phone: 543-864 or 540-629 or 569-277 **FAX:** 011-593-2-220-415
E-mail: hbarnar1@hbarnard.com.ec
Price Range: Single – U.S.$45; Double – U.S.$60; Triple – U.S.$70.
Comments: Prices include the 10% local tax as well as an American (or buffet) breakfast.

HOTEL CHALET SUISSE – Reina Victoria and José Calama (P.O. Box 17-07-87-03).
Local Phone: 562-700   **FAX:** 011-593-2-563-966
Price Range: Single – U.S.$50; Double – U.S.$60; Triple – U.S.$75.
Comments: Spoken of highly by several guests; they have a fine Swiss restaurant, gym, sauna, steam bath, and a casino. Good central location.

HOTEL EMBASSY – Av. Presidente Wilson 441 and 6 de Diciembre (P.O. Box 17-01-1314).
Local Phone: 561-990 or 563-103 or 563-243   **FAX:** 011-593-2-563-192
E-mail: hembassy@uio.satnet.net
Price Range: Single – U.S.$42; Double – U.S.$47; Triple – U.S.$52.
Comments: Prices include the 10% local tax and 10% service charge.

HOTEL REINA ISABEL – Av. Amazonas 842 and Veintimilla.
Local Phone: 554-454 or 554-941 or 554-604   **FAX:** 011-593-2-221-337
Price Range: Single – U.S.$60; Double – U.S.$70; Triple – U.S.$80.
Comments: Modern and comfortable rooms at a good price in an excellent location. When the Hotel Alameda Real is full, they will usually book the overflow guests into the Reina Isabel. Recommended.

HOTEL SEBASTIAN – Av. Diego de Almagro 822 and Luís Cordero (P.O. Box 17-07-9377).
Local Phone: 222-400 or 222-300   **FAX:** 011-593-2-222-500
E-mail: hsebast1@hsebastian.com.ec
Price Range: Single – U.S.$45; Double – U.S.$60; Triple – U.S.$70.
Comments: A very tastefully-designed, comfortable hotel, and it is highly recommended. A few blocks out of the way, but the location is still very good. The Sebastian is owned and operated by one of the major Ecuadorian Tour Operators, NUEVO MUNDO EXPEDITIONS (see Chapter IV, CHOOSING A TOUR), so the orientation of the hotel is ecotourism.

HOTEL TAMBO REAL – Av. 12 de Octubre and Patria (P.O. Box 17-01-2143).
Local Phone: 563-820   **FAX:** 011-593-2-554-964
Price Range: Single – U.S.$80; Double – U.S.$100; Triple – U.S.$120.
Comments: They have significantly raised their image, level of service, and their prices as well. Most of the 90 rooms have king-size beds and there is a casino on the premises.
U.S. Reservation Services: Utell International (UI), TOLL FREE: (800) 448-8355, Nationwide.

MEDICAL

Quito is at an altitude of 9300 ft. Be sensitive to the symptoms of altitude sickness (see the section, Medical Considerations, in Chapter VI). If medical attention is required, the First Class Hotels typically have a house doctor on call. For medical emergencies, contact Hospital Metropolitano (Av. Mariana de Jesús and Occidental). **Local Phone:** 431-520 or 439-030 (Emergency – 465-020).

Another recommendation is the Hospital Voz Andes (Vilalengua 267 and Av. 10 de Agosto, next to Voz Andes, the "Voice of the Andes" radio station). **Local Phone:** 252-142 or 449-374.

If your medical insurance has international coverage or you have Travel Protection Insurance, you may have to report the situation to the attention of the carrier ASAP (see the Travel Protection Insurance section of Chapter V).

RESTAURANTS

The eating schedule is a bit different in South America. If you enter a restaurant at 6:00-7:00 p.m., it will probably be almost empty. You may think that you've chosen the wrong place to eat. Along about 8:00, people will begin to arrive, and at 9:00 the place will be full. This is related to the 2 hour afternoon *siesta* and the subsequent work schedule, often til 7:00 p.m.

The list that follows is a brief one and does not include the hotel restaurants, which are of a much higher class of food and overall quality than American hotel restaurants. By the way, the *ceviches* (marinated seafood served with popcorn and toasted corn on the side) are wonderful appetizers everywhere in Ecuador.

BARLOVENTO – (Av. 12 de Octubre 2511 and Orellana) Good seafood restaurant.

BENTLEYS – (Juan León Mera 404 and Robles) Americanized throughout; highly recommended (closed Saturday and Sunday).

LA CASA DE AL LADO – (Valladolid and Luís Cordero) An excellent, highly-recommended restaurant serving a combination of typical Ecuadorian and international food. The name of the restaurant is as homey as the atmosphere – "the house next door."

LA CHOZA – (Av. 12 de Octubre and Cordero) Excellent local atmosphere. A spacious, open setting; the 2-story white walls are tastefully decorated with Andean *artesanías*. Even the chandeliers are beautifully crafted out of gourds. I recommend the *locro de queso* (a potato and cheese soup served with avocados) and the *llapingachos mondados* (mashed potato pancakes filled with cheese and served with peanut sauce on the side). A good lunch stop after shopping at the famous FOLKLORE gift store owned by the family of the late designer, Olga Fisch, just a couple of blocks away.

DELMONICOS – (Mariano Aguilera 331 and La Pradera) An excellent restaurant. The *origia de mariscos* is delicious and just what it sounds like – an orgy of shellfish.

EL ESPANOL DELI – (Juan León Mera, next to the Libri Mundi bookstore) A great take-out deli, featuring wonderful cheeses, good sandwiches, and excellent wines. The perfect spot when you're tired of shopping and would rather eat in the hotel room after taking a rest. Try to avoid the noon business rush.

EXCALIBUR – (Calama 380 and Juan León Mera) Cozy romantic atmosphere with a good selection of recorded music; a nice quiet spot to enjoy a well prepared lunch. The mushroom or cheese *tortillas* are not what we're used to; they're actually very delicious omelettes, a meal in itself for under $2.

THE MAGIC BEAN – (Foch 681 and Juan León Mera) A great combination of a good breakfast spot, an in-house bakery, and excellent coffee. Near all the major hotels.

MARE NOSTRUM – (José Luís Tamayo 172 and Foch) Excellent seafood in the atmosphere of what was once a colonial-style church. Highly recommended.

PIMS – (Calama 413 and Juan León Mera; they have grown and recently opened at a second location – Mariano Aguilera 326) A lively, cheerful eating and drinking spot for the young Ecuadorian working set, many of whom appear to have a college background. Open from 4:00 – 11:00 p.m., Pims is a great place to go with friends and share the day's adventures while Piaf-genre music plays in the background. I recommend the sea bass with mushrooms (*corvina con champignones*).

LA QUERENCIA – (Eloy Alfaro 2530 and Catalina de Aldaz) Frequented by many tour groups and featuring typical Ecuadorian cuisine.

LAS REDES – (Av. Amazonas 845) A highly-recommended seafood lunch spot; excellent *ceviche* and shrimp dishes to choose from.

LA REINA VICTORIA – (Reina Victoria 530 and Roca) Their business card states that they are "a cross between an English Pub and American Bar;" the description is apt. La Reina Victoria is the only "sports bar" in town with enhanced Cable TV, pulling in the major U.S. networks (ABC, CBS, and NBC). I watched the World Series from there. While you're viewing the game, you can feast on very appropriate sports food, including pizza, tacos, subs, Reuben sandwiches, and whatever else owner Dorothy Albright feels like cooking. Dorothy, who's from Chicago, is thus far resisting customer pressure for her to work on weekends, and the place is closed on Saturday and Sunday.

RINCON DE FRANCIA – (Roca 779 and 9 de Octubre) Ecuadorian and French selections. A favorite spot for entertaining; very elegant.

RINCON LA RONDA – (Bello Horizonte 400 and Almagro) Elegant dining complete with strolling musicians.

SPAGUETTI – (Av. Portugal and Eloy Alfaro) In case you couldn't tell, an Italian restaurant. A good one, too!

LA TERRAZA DEL TARTARO – (Av. Amazonas and Veintimilla) Take the rear elevator to the top floor of the Amazonas Building (*Edificio Amazonas*). Excellent food (my favorites are the filet mignon and the langostinos) with a great panoramic view of the city and surrounding mountains.

SHOPPING

At the focus of the modern business and shopping district is the main thorough-fare, Avenida Río Amazonas (Amazon River Avenue). Amazonas, as it is called, starts at the Hotel Colón at Parque El Ejido, the largest park in Quito, and heads north all the way to Plaza Olmedo by the airport. For the best shopping, stay between Av. Amazonas and Juan León Mera (which is to the east of, and paral-lel to, Amazonas – to your right as you're walking away from the Hotel Colón). Between these two avenues, and on the side streets between them, you will find many excellent shops selling arts & crafts, jewelry, books, clothes and leather goods. If you get hungry, you will probably take more than a passing look at some of the best restaurants in Quito, sidewalk cafes, and pastry shops. And for taking care of business, this is where you will find the airline ticket offices, Tour Operators, and *cambios* – exchange houses, remember?

If you have a limited time in Quito, you will want to set aside at least one afternoon for shopping. You'll have several categories of souvenir and gift items to choose from, including clothing and jewelry. Some of the better and well known stores are listed below, but you'll no doubt find several others to your personal liking as well. There is very little bargaining, unless you're buying from one of the outdoor stalls or actually travel to one of the Indian markets (see the section on Touring below).

Indian handicrafts (*artesanías*) will stare at you from many of the shop win-dows. You'll see a lot of wood carvings; some you'll like, and some you won't. Included in this category are figures made of balsa wood, carved in the Amazon rain forests of *El Oriente*. Ecuador is famous for its leatherwork, and the prices are quite reasonable. You will walk past a lot of shop windows displaying sev-eral styles of good looking wallets, handbags, jackets, and luggage. Also high on the shopping list are the rugged, coarse-woven wool sweaters and vests. Many beautiful colors and attractive patterns are available for about U.S.$20-$30. The sweaters made of alpaca wool are very high quality, extremely fine to the touch (with fibers only 25 microns thick), and naturally command a higher price, often a lot higher. The alpaca, by the way, is related to the llama, and both are raised, as they have been for centuries, by native Indians in the Andean Highlands.

The jewelry is of very high quality. Also relatively expensive. The precious stones are more reasonable, but not cheap. Oh well, you can always buy a Panama hat, for sale everywhere! It'll make a good sun shade for the Galápagos too, if it doesn't blow off.

Note: Keep the receipts from your purchases so that, if necessary, you can convince U.S. Customs Officials that you really bought all that stuff so cheap! Each person (children included) is allowed to bring back U.S.$400 worth of merchandise.

Be aware that black coral is an endangered species. You will see stores with signs advertising that they sell gift items made of black coral. Often the products are quite beautiful and usually quite expensive as well. Less often, but frequently, the items are fake. While at present there are no laws prohibiting these stores from selling goods made of black coral, from the standpoint of con-servation it is strongly suggested that you refrain from purchasing such items. At the same time, the store owners are often not to be blamed, as they themselves may not understand the significance of the issue. Thus, it is not suggested that you refrain from shopping at their stores; just don't purchase their black coral products.

A small selection of some of the better known gift shops in Quito include:

ARTE FOLKLORE DALMAU – (Bello Horizante 123 and Manuel Iturrey) Exclusive handicraft and jewelry designs.

ARTICULOS DE CUERO – (In the arcade mall of the Hotel Colón, the airport, and several other business district locations) Leather goods.

LA BODEGA – (Juan León Mera 614) Opposite the Libri Mundi bookstore.

LOS COLORES DE LA TIERRA – (Juan León Mera 838 and Wilson) – Fine traditional handicrafts and decorative items.

THE ETHNIC COLLECTION – (Amazonas 1029 and Pinta) Weavings, tapestries, jewelry, and balsa wood items.

EXEDRA – (Carrion 243 and Leonidas Plaza) Well known for their paintings and tapestries.

FOLKLORE OLGA FISCH – (Av. Colón 260) Probably the best known gift store in Quito, owned and operated by the family of the late Olga Fisch, internationally-acclaimed designer. There are also branches in the Hotel Colón and Hotel Oro Verde, Quito.

GALERIA LATINA – (Juan León Mera 823) Next to Libri Mundi. For my taste, the best overall selection of quality products that I have found.

LA GUARAGUA – (Jorge Washington 614) Good selection of *artesanías* and antiques.

HAMILTON – (Av. Amazonas 171) Ecuadorian gold and silver handicrafts. In front of the Hotel Colón.

ISCAIO – (Juan León Mera 1313 and Cordero) Sweaters with good designs, including pure alpaca.

LIBRI MUNDI – (Juan León Mera 851) Without a doubt the best bookstore in Ecuador. They have a comprehensive selection of Galápagos literature. The one stop to definitely make before you leave for the islands. While there is a smaller branch in the arcade mall of the Hotel Colón, the main store is just a few blocks away.

LA LLAMA – (Av. Amazonas 149) Ecuadorian handicrafts available for export.

MATICES YAPACUNCHI – (Av. 12 de Octubre and Garcia) Fine ceramic pieces.

PETER MUSSFELDT – (Juan León Mera 838) The main factory outlet for designer Peter Mussfeldt's colorful motifs – bags, clothes, tapestries. Across from the Libri Mundi bookstore.

OCEPA – (Calle Carrion 1236 and Versalles) Government *artesanía* store; also located near the Hotel Colón at Jorge Washington 718 and Av. Amazonas.

PRODUCTOS ANDINOS – (Urbina 111 and Cordero) An artesian co-operative with reasonably priced goods.

H. STERN JEWELERS – In the arcade mall of the Hotel Colón.

TOURING

On your return from the Galápagos, you may have some time for sightseeing in and around Quito. If you're on a group tour, the arrangements have most likely already been made. If you're on your own, there are several options; in each case the Tour Operator you worked with on your Galápagos excursion can handle all the arrangements for you. In fact, the following list is but a small representation of the vast number of half-day and full-day mainland tours that are standardly offered. The more time you have, the greater the number of possibilities. I won't elaborate, because as you well know by now, the orientation of this book is to get you to spend the maximum amount of time in the Galápagos.

THE AMAZON – Located in the eastern portion of Ecuador (or *El Oriente,* as the area is called) is the rich neotropical rain forest of the upper Amazon region. The area is also rich in other natural resources, namely oil, which is now Ecuador's leading source of export revenue.

While the Ecuadorian Amazon would be a great natural history destination all by itself (in much the same way that Costa Rica is), it is with mixed feelings that I recommend this area for an extension trip before or after the Galápagos Islands. Actually, except for hardcore naturalists (especially birders), I strongly recommend it as a pre-extension only – that is, to visit the Ecuadorian Amazon before the Galápagos. What happens is that, simply put, the Galápagos spoils you. You get used to seeing and photographing the animals within 4-6 ft; these animals have few natural predators and have not learned fear. This is not the case in the Amazon, where the animals need (and expertly use) the jungle as camouflage. The result is that "you can hear them, and you can see one way up there (between the fourth and fifth branches of the third tree to the right of that patch of red soil) but you don't usually get a close look." At least not for any length of time. Which reduces photography to the lush scenery. And since you can't observe the animals as closely as in the Galápagos, you have to bring more knowledge with you. This need is amplified because, while the Guides here are good and very knowledgeable, they are not trained to interpret nature as thoroughly as they are in the Galápagos. However, the Ecuadorian Amazon will get you warmed up and ready for the islands.

The other problems with the Amazon are logistical. It takes a minimum of 5 days to get any feel for this special place; the Amazon is the largest neotropical rain forest in the world. Of the 5 days, 2 of them will be spent getting in and out. Since the 1987 earthquake, the road system (such as it was) was reduced to the level of "undependable." Most Ecuadorian Amazon programs now include a flight from Quito to the town of Coca, located on the Napo River (a major tributary of the Amazon River). Even so, transportation each way will take up the greater portion of a day.

There are many Amazon tours to consider, including several newer lodges that have yet to distinguish themselves. Logistics and comprehensive interpretive programs are essentials; don't sign up unless you're convinced! The largest Tour Operator in Ecuador, Metropolitan Touring, runs a popular floating hotel in the Amazon, called, oddly enough, the Flotel Orellana. This tripledecker sleeps 48 passengers and has 4 & 5 day programs. It's not my idea of adventure travel but neither is touring the Galápagos on a Cruise Ship.

La Selva Lodge – In 1992, La Selva Lodge in the Ecuadorian Amazon was named and awarded the "Best Ecotourism Destination" by the World Congress on Tourism and the Environment. La Selva ("the jungle" in Spanish) overlooks a beautiful lake, consists of 16 double cabins, and features an exceptional restaurant. More important, they have excellent itineraries that blend guided dugout canoe rides and trail walks. If you're a birder, they have specialized programs (a full week is recommended) and excellent birding Guides; bring your birding scope and a copy of **BIRDS OF COLOMBIA** – both are essential.

Their general programs are not as individualized as the brochures indicate ("tailor-make your own jungle adventure"). In fact, their brochures and advertising do much to hurt their programs, in my opinion, by calling attention to "our exotic, gourmet cuisine." What happens is that they get some "Cruise Ship" passengers (sorry for the generalization, but it's mostly deserved) who aren't much interested in an educationally-oriented program. The problem is that these passengers can be put in the same group as some serious natural history types, and the Guides take the easy way out – "here's the stuff the natives dye their faces with, folks." If you have your own group, this problem is avoided.

Note: Full rain gear is essential for touring the Amazon. In addition, yellow fever shots and malaria pills are recommended for this area in some of the literature; consult your physician.

COTOPAXI NATIONAL PARK – Cotopaxi, at 19,700 ft, is the world's highest active volcano. If you have the time, it's definitely worth a look. There are organized full-day tours. The driver will take the Pan American Highway south for about 35 miles along the Central Valley, flanked by two parallel ranges of high mountain volcanoes (most are still active). This is the famous "Avenue of the Volcanoes," aptly named by the German explorer, Alexander von Humboldt.

Cotopaxi National Park, established in 1975, offers spectacular views of lava fields, colorful highland flora, llamas, deer, wild horses, and mountain birds, including an occasional glimpse of an Andean condor. When the clouds decide to part, you will be treated to a beautiful sight – the higher slopes of glaciatic blue ice and the snow-covered peak, a perfect cone if ever there was one.

Lunch is included on the full-day tour. Many trips take lunch at Hacienda La Cienega, a beautiful 300 year old estate now functioning as a country inn. If you have the time, you can overnight (advanced reservations required) at this romantic hacienda (many of the rooms have 20 ft ceilings) and make this a 2-day tour, taking in a traditional market on the return to Quito (the Saturday Zumbahua Market/Quilotoa Crater Lake or the Thursday Saquisilí Market is highly recommended).

CUENCA – Cuenca is considered by many to be the most beautiful city in Ecuador. Not as crowded as Quito, without the extensive high-rise business district, Cuenca offers the rich flavor of colonial history and traditional architecture. In all, Cuenca is a recommended visiting area for those that have 3-4 days to spend and have a cultural orientation – especially those who were interested in seeing Machu Picchu in Peru. Outside of Cuenca (2 hours north), one can visit the most significant Inca ruins in Ecuador – the Ingapirca Fortress. No, it's not Machu Picchu, but it's safer than Peru, more logistically feasible (for starters, you don't have to overnight in Lima), and a lot less expensive. A 3-day visit would start with a morning flight from Quito and include a half-day City Tour of Cuenca. In addition to viewing cathedrals, museums, and pre-Columbian ruins, you will have the opportunity to visit one or more of the factories where "Panama" hats are made. On the second day, you will visit the beautiful area west of Cuenca – the *Las Cajas National Recreational Area*. This is a day of hiking and enjoying the scenic and varied landscape as well as the natural history of the lake country. The third day is spent at Ingapirca, the Inca fortress complex, where each wing (built around a central structure called an *usnu*) was designed to offer the inhabitants a direct visual and religious orientation to the sun at a particular time of the day. After visiting the Ingapirca ruins, you fly back to Quito.

Optionally, you can take a 4-day Cuenca tour that combines the best of several trips. The first day you travel south by car (with a driver & Guide), visiting a local market (depending on the day) or *Cotopaxi National Park*. Following lunch at a local hacienda, you continue to the town of Riobamba for a brief afternoon tour. After an overnight in Riobamba, you get a very early morning start the following day on the train ride along a sheer mountainside, the famous *El Nariz del Diablo* (the Devil's nose). At the end of the excursion (mid-morning), you will again be met by a car (driver and Guide) and continue on to Ingapirca, which you will tour in the afternoon. The next day you visit *Las Cajas,* and the last day you take a City Tour of Cuenca, followed by a return flight to Quito. This option will give you more time, will be more adventurous, probably more fun, and will certainly cost more money. Highly recommended.

EQUATORIAL MONUMENT – If you always wanted to be right on the equator, here's your chance. There are tours to *La Mitad del Mundo* (Center of the World) located 15 miles north of Quito at latitude 0°00'00". In addition to the monument, there is a museum describing the 18th century expedition that established the exact location of the equator; there is also an interesting display of local Indian cultures. It's customary to have your picture taken straddling the northern and southern hemispheres; with the drifting clouds and the beautiful mountain scenery, some of the shots can be quite dramatic (see Photo #2).

OLD TOWN – In 1978, *UNESCO* declared Quito as one of the world's cultural heritage sites, and the Old Town section is now controlled so far as development is concerned. Thus, entering Old Town and walking down the narrow, winding cobblestone streets, one is immediately immersed in 16th century colonial architecture, by whitewashed walls, red-tiled roofs, heavy wooden doors, and fountained courtyards.

Starting at the *Plaza de Independencia,* your tour of Old Town takes in the *Palacio Municipal* (City Hall), *Palacio de Gobierno* (the Presidential offices), *La Catedral* (the site of the first church in Quito), and *Palacio Arzobispal* (the Archbishop's Palace), now a series of shops. Nearby is the most impressive architectural treasure Quito has to offer, *La Compañia* Church, whose interior is a virtual blaze of gold. It is decorated in renaissance style, and almost entirely in gold leaf; I've never seen anything quite like it.

Other attractions include the Church of *San Francisco* (the largest of Quito's 86 churches) and *La Merced,* housing Quito's oldest clock. As you wander through Old Town, you will notice scaffolding almost everywhere; in 1987, a severe earthquake damaged several of these structures, which were subsequently closed. Repair work is proceeding slowly, paced by available funds and the required expertise. Optionally, you can also tour some of the fine museums, including the *Archaeological Museum of the Central Bank;* here you will find the most complete collection of pieces from Ecuadorian prehistory, dating back to 10,000 B.C. This option is highly recommended.

Caution: While you could visit Old Town on your own, it is strongly suggested and recommended that you take one of the City Tours offered by virtually all the Tour Operators. The main concern is safety. While Ecuador is a very safe country, there have been incidents in Old Town, everything from bags being slashed to armed robbery. Panecillo Hill (see Photo #1) is a particular "place to avoid." With or without a Guide, do not carry any bags or wear any packs in Old Town.

In addition to the safety aspect, the Guides are well-versed in the architectural and general history of Quito. Finally, almost as important as the Guides' knowledge of the subject matter is their familiarity with the "unusual" visiting hours of the various churches and museums, which are sometimes only a couple of hours at a time.

OTAVALO MARKET – Ecuador is noted for its native markets, a tradition that predates even the Incas, to a time when agricultural products were first carried down from the Andean Highlands (on the backs of llamas) and traded for goods from the Amazon region, which were also transported to the "marketplace." The animals themselves (including pigs and goats) were traded for. Of these markets, none is more famous than the one at Otavalo, a few hours drive to the north of Quito, where one can experience the sights and sounds of the Saturday Market (if you have a free Saturday, that is).

Today's market is now more oriented to selling handicrafts to the tourist audience than it is to "local" trading. The market opens early every Saturday, the outdoor stalls displaying the most popular items – ponchos, blankets, scarves, sweaters, belts, tapestries, and rugs. The Otavalo region is known for its skilled weavers, but there may be as many (or more) mass-produced, synthetic items as hand-woven woolen products. Bargaining is the rule, and transactions are in sucres.

Note: While the "traditional" Otavalo Market is on Saturday, there is an "open" market at Otavalo every day of the week. In fact, tours to the Otavalo area (the Imbabura Province) are offered daily. For the same price as the Otavalo Market trip, you can visit several towns (including Otavalo) and quietly shop for quality handmade products, leather goods, wooden crafts, sweaters, tapestries, and bread dough figurines. For you non-shoppers, the Imbabura Province trip also offers excellent views of the Andes.

If you have but one day to spend in the mainland, this trip is very highly recommended. For those with a bit more time, a 2-day (more relaxing) version of the trip is offered by all the Tour Operators.

GUAYAQUIL

With a population approaching 3 million people, Guayaquil (pronounced gwah-yah-keel) is the largest city in Ecuador as well as the economic and industrial center of the country. Guayaquil has a coastal location on an unusually long 30 mile inward reach of the Gulf of Guayaquil, and is the major port (called *Puerto Nuevo* or New Port) of Ecuador. The city also has inland water access, being situated on the Guayas River, which winds down from the north. Almost all of Ecuador's imports (and about half of its exports) are handled here. Guayaquil is also surrounded by the major export farming areas of Ecuador and is the agricultural center of the country.

The potential economic importance of Guayaquil as a major trading center was recognized by the Spanish conquistadors, who founded the city in 1537 and developed it to its present status as an international port. Due to its business orientation, Guayaquil politics tends to favor government nonintervention with free trade. It is therefore labeled as "conservative," in contrast to the more "liberal" Quito, where, due to a greater incidence of poverty, government-sponsored social programs are favored.

While recognized as the business center of Ecuador, Guayaquil does not rank very high as a tourist attraction. It doesn't really try to be. There is a serious work orientation, and aside from the hotels and some Tour Operators, the tourist is not really catered to – almost ignored. I like Guayaquil. In many ways it reminds me of New York City; it has its own special personality which you can decide to become part of. Unfortunately, I feel that most tourists would decide not to become part of Guayaquil. There is simply too much street noise and congestion. It is not until one spends some time there that this perception begins to change. Considering the short 1 night pre-Galápagos stay here (at the most), there will be no attempt to introduce the reader to the restaurants, shops, and touring possibilities of Guayaquil.

THE AIRPORT

The Simón Bólivar Airport is very modern, located 3 miles north of the business district, shopping sector, and major hotels.

Note: There is a $25 Departure Tax on international flights, payable in sucres or U.S. dollars (or a combination of both); they do not accept traveler's checks or credit cards.

TOURIST INFORMATION

There are two *CETUR* offices in Guayaquil at the following locations:

Business District Office: Aguirre 104 and the Malecón
Local Phone: 328-312 or 325-607   **FAX:** 011-593-4-328-312

Airport Office: Simón Bólivar Airport

CLIMATE

During the warm rainy season from December-May, the average temperature is 80-85 Deg F. The heat and humidity tend to be on the uncomfortable side from January through April. Guayaquil is dry during the rest of the year, although the skies are frequently overcast and the evenings cool. The driest months are July-October when temperatures reach the 70s (Deg F) during the day and drop to the 50s (Deg F) at night.

HOTELS

As in Quito, there are many First Class hotels in Guayaquil. The prices are still reasonable but tend to be somewhat higher (than those in Quito).

Note: The sink and shower faucets at some of the hotels are marked differently than you're used to, which could be cause for confusion as well as a potential problem. The left (hot) faucet is marked "C" for *Caliente;* the right (cold) faucet is marked "F" for *Frío.*

Many of the hotels provide bottles of mineral water and/or purified water in each room for drinking and rinsing when brushing your teeth.

All phone numbers are local. The FAX numbers listed below include the international, country, and city codes. E-mail numbers are listed if available.

Here then are the recommended hotels of Guayaquil and their affiliated U.S. Reservation Service(s). Add 20% to all prices for tax and service. Prices listed are as of 1998.

First Class Hotels:

HOTEL HILTON COLON – Av. Francisco de Orellana, Ciudadela Kennedy Norte (P.O. Box 0904662).
Local Phone: 689-022   **FAX:** 011-593-4-689-728
Rooms: All 294 rooms are finely furnished and have satellite TV.
Price Range: Single – U.S.$230;   Double – U.S.$250.
Comments: The Colón has long been one of the best hotels in Quito (see above), and the Guayaquil facility recently opened (1997). It is located in the Ciudadela Kennedy Norte, a growing financial area located 5 minutes from the airport. They have an Italian restaurant, sushi bar, and casino. Amenities also include a complete workout facility, squash courts, indoor pool, sauna, and steam room.
U.S. Reservation Services: Hilton Reservations Worldwide, TOLL FREE: (800) 445-8667, U.S. & Canada.

HOTEL CONTINENTAL – Corner of Chile and 10 de Agosto.
Local Phone: 329-270 or 322-812   **FAX:** 011-593-4-325-454
Rooms: There is an AM/FM/tape player in all 160 rooms in addition to color TV.
Price Range: Single – U.S.$100;   Double – U.S.$125;   Jr. Suite – U.S.$160.
Comments: One of the more reasonably-priced hotels in Guayaquil. It is centrally located (facing the Bolívar Park). Recommended.
U.S. Reservation Services: Utell International (UI), TOLL FREE: (800) 448-8355 Nationwide.

GRAND HOTEL GUAYAQUIL – Boyacá and 10 de Agosto (P.O. Box 9282).
Local Phone: 329-690   **FAX:** 011-593-4-327-251
E-mail: grandhot@gye.satnet.net

Rooms: Courtesy coffee makers in all 180 rooms. There is an outdoor, pool-side barbeque restaurant (complete with the ambiance of a tropical waterfall), shopping mall, a fully-equipped gym, squash courts, sauna, steam bath, and massage room.

Price Range: Single – U.S.$85;   Double – U.S.$115;   Triple – U.S.$140.

Comments: Their brochure describes the Grand Hotel as "the only hotel in the world to share a whole city block with a cathedral." It must be true! It's actually a very nice facility.

U.S. Reservation Services: Utell International (UI), TOLL FREE: (800) 448-8355 U.S. & Canada.

HOTEL ORO VERDE – Av. 9 de Octubre and García Moreno (P.O. Box 09-01-9636).

Local Phone: 327-999   **FAX:** 011-593-4-329-350

E-mail: ecovq@telconet.net

Rooms: There are 213 finely-appointed rooms with mini-bars and video rentals.

Price Range: Single – U.S.$250;   Double – U.S.$270.

Comments: Generally rated as the finest hotel in Guayaquil, the Oro Verde has 4 restaurants, including Le Gourmet, offering award-winning French cuisine. There is also a restaurant by the pool. Other amenities include a casino, sauna, and gymnasium.

U.S. Reservation Services: The Leading Hotels of the World (LHW), TOLL FREE: (800) 223-6800, U.S. & Canada.

UNIPARK HOTEL – Ballén 406 and Chile (P.O. Box 09-01-563).

Local Phone: 327-100   **FAX:** 011-593-4-328-352

E-mail: ecuni@gye.satnet.net

Rooms: Very comfortable, with 150 rooms in two towers. The trick is to know which tower your room is in, and there is a long walk between towers. Get a park view if you can.

Price Range: Single – U.S.$120;   Double – U.S.$150.

Comments: Features include a sauna, whirlpool, gymnasium, and casino. The hotel complex contains an eighty store shopping mall.

U.S. Reservation Services: Prima Hotels (PW), TOLL FREE: (800) 447-7462 Nationwide.

Tourist Class Hotels:

HAMPTON INN CASINO BOULEVARD – Av. 9 de Octubre 432 and Baquerizo Moreno (P.O. Box 7524).

Local Phone: 562-888 or 566-700 or 560-076   **FAX:** 011-593-4-565-482

Rooms: Recently reconstructed (due to a fire in 1997).

Price Range: Pending

Comments: The reconstruction and Hampton Inn management (effective 1998) will hopefully help the image of the facility, which was run down. There is a large casino next door.

HOTEL PALACE – Chile 214 and Luque (P.O. Box 09-01-4642).

Local Phone: 321-080   **FAX:** 011-593-4-322-887

Price Range: Single – U.S.$50;   Double – U.S.$70;   Triple – U.S.$85.
Comments: Recently remodeled, the Palace is nice enough with a nice price too.

HOTEL RAMADA – Malecón and Orellana (P.O. Box 09-01-10964)
Local Phone: 565-555   **FAX:** 011-593-4-563-036
Price Range: Single/Double – U.S.$95;   Triple – U.S.$105.
Comments: The Ramada is located on the waterfront with a view of the Guayas River, but it is somewhat out of the way and approaching an area a bit unsafe to walk after dark.
U.S. Reservation Services: VIP International, TOLL FREE: (800) 858-8471, Nationwide.

RIZZO HOTEL – Ballén 319 and Chile (P.O. Box 7647).
Local Phone: 325-210 or 328-367 or 326-212   **FAX:** 011-593-4-326-209
Price Range: Single/Double – U.S.$45;   Triple – U.S.$55.
Comments: The excellent prices also include a continental breakfast and the 10% room tax.

HOTEL SOL DE ORIENTE – Aguirre 603 and Escobedo (P.O. Box 5875).
Local Phone: 325-500 or 325-601   **FAX:** 011-593-4-329-352
Price Range: Single – U.S.$45;   Double – U.S.$55;   Triple – U.S.$65.
Comments: Quite reasonably priced. They have a good Chinese restaurant as well as an exercise facility and sauna.

MEDICAL

If medical attention is required, the First Class Hotels typically have a house doctor on call. For medical emergencies, contact the Clínica Guayaquil (P. Aguirre and General Córdova). **Local Phone:** 563-555. Another recommendation is the Clínica Kennedy (Av. San Jorge and Kennedy). **Local Phone:** 286-963. See the section on Medical Considerations in Chapter VI.

If your medical insurance has international coverage or you have Travel Protection Insurance, you may have to report the situation to the attention of the carrier ASAP (see the Travel Protection Insurance section of Chapter V).

SAFETY & SECURITY

South America does not have the best reputation as far as theft is concerned. Some of the countries, notably Peru and Columbia, have unfortunately earned this reputation. Not so with Ecuador. I would say that Quito is safer than most U.S. cities, especially in the downtown hotel and business districts; the Old Town district is an exception (see above in the Quito section). The Galápagos and Guayaquil are also safe, but I would be more cautious about walking the streets alone at night.

No matter how safe Ecuador may be, never forget that you easily stand out as a "rich gringo tourist." Thus, you want to take reasonable precautions:

1. Crowded airports are a prime location for rip-offs, and camera bags are the number one casualty. I've even seen people "lose" their cameras at Baltra Island Airport in the Galápagos. Keep track of your carryon bags at all times.

2. The major portion of your money should be in traveler's checks. You may also choose to wear a money pouch.

3. Don't leave valuables in your hotel room any more than absolutely necessary. The major hotels have security boxes (*cajas de seguridad*) for money and jewelry. There are also safe storage areas for larger items. You are advised to take advantage of this service. In recent years, there have been occasional rashes of break-ins by professionals said to be from Peru or Columbia.

4. Do the bulk of your shopping on your return from the Galápagos. You'll have fewer valuables to keep track of and worry about. Besides, it's not real practical to be carting a lot of stuff out to the islands. There are also airline baggage and shipboard space limits to contend with. If you do purchase some items prior to your tour, you can store them at most of the major hotels.

5. Always carry your passport and T3 Tourist Information Card with you. Aside from the value of these documents as identification when you want to cash a traveler's check, it is a legal requirement that you have them in your possession. While an unlikely scenario, if you fail to present a passport when requested to do so by an official, you could be detained. And you don't want to be detained, so carry your passport!

6. Report a theft to the police ASAP. If items are missing from your hotel room, notify the management immediately and before contacting the police.

7. If you are on a group tour, report any loss to your Tour Leader (or Ecuadorian group contact person) immediately. Part of their job is to provide assistance in this type of a situation. They will advise you on contacting the police.

8. Report a loss or theft of traveler's checks ASAP as follows:

AMERICAN EXPRESS has a number that you can call collect 24 hours a day, (801) 964-6665, to report lost or stolen AMERICAN EXPRESS traveler's checks. For lost or stolen AMERICAN EXPRESS CARDS, call collect (919) 333-3211.

9. Report a loss or theft of your airline ticket(s) to the airline ticket or branch office ASAP. The way it usually works is that you purchase a replacement ticket and then fill out a lost ticket application form. You will get a refund from the carrier after 120 days if the original ticket was not used, thus making it urgent that you make this report as soon as possible.

10. Report a loss or theft of your passport to the U.S. consulate at the U.S. Embassy in Quito or Guayaquil. Have your passport number handy when you contact them (see Item 12 below). If you haven't made a copy of your passport identification page, your hotel has your passport number on the registration sheet that you filled out.

The U.S. EMBASSY locations are as follows:

Quito – Av. Patria 120 and 12 de Octubre.
   Local Phone: 562-890
Guayaquil – Av. 9 de Octubre and Garcia Moreno.
   Local Phone: 323-570

The U.S. Consulate will usually issue a new passport within 24 hours.

11. If you have Travel Protection Insurance, report a loss or theft of any personal items to the carrier (see the Travel Protection Insurance section of Chapter V).

12. For purposes of reporting lost or stolen items, it will be helpful to have some backup documentation. Remember, before you leave home, take two photocopies of the identification page of your passport, any Travel Vouchers, the I.D. numbers of your traveler's checks, an inventory of expensive personal items (including Model/Serial Numbers, when appropriate), and your airline itinerary. Leave a copy at home and take the second copy with you, keeping it in a secure location (such as the hotel security box).

CHAPTER IX

TOURING
THE GALÁPAGOS ISLANDS

This chapter will serve as an orientation to the Galápagos Islands, to most of the Visitor Sites, as well as to the on-board and daily activities that will make up your exciting adventure.

WELCOME TO THE ENCHANTED ISLES

The entrance point to the Galápagos is the airport at either Baltra or San Cristóbal Island. As you step down off the airplane and look around, perhaps trying to catch sight of a giant tortoise, you will most likely be underwhelmed; the view will be noticeably disappointing. Baltra, in particular, is pretty desolate, and you'll be looking at dry area vegetation. You will have to wait until you get on-board your yacht and are under way to the first Visitor Site (in about an hour or two) before you can begin to see and enjoy the Galápagos wildlife. For now, proceed to the terminal and prepare to line up one more time.

ENTRANCE FEE

While the line you wait on is "immigration-oriented" (you are entering a regulated National Park), and your passport will be examined, the main purpose here is to collect your $100 *Galápagos National Park* Entrance Fee. This fee is payable in U.S. dollars or sucres and is rarely included in the tour price. In return for your $100, you will receive an official Entrance Permit which you should keep with your passport. It is now possible to pay the Entrance Fees in the airports at Quito and Guayaquil, but you will still have to wait in line in the Galápagos and show the officials your Entrance Permit. Once on-board, the Guide will collect the permits; in turn they will be handed over to the *Galápagos National Park Service*. In addition, you will be asked to give your passport number (on some boats, the actual passport) to the captain, who in turn is required to report your name and passport number to the Galápagos port officials. This is all part of the tourism control system.

NATIONAL PARK REGULATIONS

The Entrance Officer will also give you a list of *Galápagos National Park* Rules, which ask you not to disturb or remove ánything (not even a rock or shell), not to touch or feed the animals, and to stay on the marked trails. With an increasing number of tourists visiting the Galápagos Islands each year, it becomes a matter of extreme importance that you not only follow these rules, but that you set an example for others, showing that tourists can be conservation-minded. There are those that look at the expansion of tourism as a double-edged sword, feeling that the delicate natural order of the archipelago will be adversely affected by the very visitors who want to experience this special place on earth. Man does not have a very good track record in the Galápagos; it won't take much in the way of insensitive behavior on the part of a few to result in the outraged cries of "enough."

My views on this subject are quite specific and have been stated in the section on Growth, Tourism, and Conservation in Chapter II. Once again, I am a strong believer in responsible and controlled tourism, with an emphasis on the need for tighter (translate that as "enforced") controls. With the revenue that Galápagos tourism is generating, the enforcement responsibility is Ecuador's.

GETTING TO YOUR BOAT

For most of you, the majority of the work is over, and your Galápagos vacation has really begun. Your Guide (perhaps the captain as well) will be waiting for you just past the "immigration" line. On passenger pick-up day, the crew all wear cute little white or tan shorts and matching shirts (typically bearing the name of the boat). A few of them also hold up signs announcing the boat. Some of you will be wearing a sign as well, a tag put on by the Tour Operator in the mainland. Once you and your Guide find each other, you will be warmly greeted and led to the waiting bus that will take you on a short journey to the harbor and, finally, to the boat. Your baggage will follow in about an hour. Skip to the section, "Life at Sea."

Alas, some of you will have to wait a bit more for the fun to begin. For those that have flown TAME to Baltra and have to meet their boat in Academy Bay on Santa Cruz Island, read the section below, Getting to Puerto Ayora. For those that have flown SAN to San Cristóbal and have to spend the night before boarding the boat, read the section below, "Getting to Puerto Baquerizo Moreno."

Finally, there is a slight chance that your boat hasn't arrived yet at the harbor (and therefore your Guide is a "no show" at the airport). In this case, the boat would have radio-contacted Baltra (or San Cristóbal) with a message to wait at the airport, proceed to the harbor, or at the worst, proceed to a hotel.

GETTING TO PUERTO AYORA

As of this writing, there are signs by each of the departing zones at Baltra Airport; one reads "Santa Cruz" and the other "Puerto Ayora." Since Puerto Ayora is on Santa Cruz Island, and with crowds of people filing onto buses by the "Santa Cruz" sign, those going to Puerto Ayora may start to get a bit anxious. Not to worry; the "Santa Cruz" sign refers to the Cruise Ship SANTA CRUZ.

The procedure is that the buses first transport those that are meeting their boats in Baltra Harbor, about a 10 minute drive. These same buses will then return and pick up those going to Puerto Ayora. Be prepared for a slow journey; all together it will take about 3 hours. First, from the airport you take a half hour bus ride to the southern tip of Baltra Island. The fare is $2. During the ride, you will get more of a feeling for the arid, desolate environment of Baltra island. When the bus reaches the narrow Itabaca Channel which separates the islands of Baltra and Santa Cruz, you cross via passenger ferry (about a 10 minute ride after a 20 minute wait) where another bus is waiting to take you to Puerto Ayora. The ferry costs about 10,000 sucres (just over $2). Pay on-board. The fare for the Puerto Ayora bus is 7000 sucres (a little less than $2). All bus tickets can be either purchased on-board or at a ticket counter at the airport.

Surprisingly, your tickets for the ferry and the Santa Cruz bus have numerical seat assignments on them. Also, the ticket is for a specific bus. Match the number on the ticket with the number displayed on the bus. The buses are numbered because there are several Day Tours that depart from Puerto Ayora (via bus). The passengers are dropped off at, you guessed it, the same place where the ferry drops you off. These buses are waiting for the Day Tour boats to return, and you don't want to get on them.

The bus ride (about 1 hour – a good deal less once the paved road is completed) to Puerto Ayora will be an interesting introduction to the climate of the Galápagos islands. You start and finish at sea level, traversing the typically moist central Highlands (see the section on Climate in Chapter II).

Once you arrive in Puerto Ayora, your boat will probably be anchored in Academy Bay; the dock is just a block or so from where you get off the bus. If all else fails, and no one seems to know anything about the boat, ask the bus driver to take you to the Hotel Galápagos. You can spend the night there, and they can radio-contact the boat and sort everything out for you.

GETTING TO PUERTO BAQUERIZO MORENO

The San Cristóbal airport is actually on the outskirts of Puerto Baquerizo Moreno. If you're not going to the boat, there are taxis (white pick-up trucks) that will take you to the town for 3000 sucres, where there are a number of hotels.

LIFE AT SEA

Once on-board the boat, your vacation shifts into a higher gear. First off, you will be assigned your quarters. If for some reason you arrive before some of the other passengers, you may have your choice of cabins. Don't make an obsession of going from cabin to cabin, and certainly don't get into a quarrel over the selection, but if you have the opportunity, look the cabins over. Some may have a private bathroom (possibly with shower), somewhat better sleeping arrange-

#40

#41

The waved albatross is a strikingly beautiful bird (#40). The overgrown, down-covered juveniles are the ultimate Baby Huey look-alikes (#41), adding a touch of humor to the feeding scene (#42).

#42

#43

#44

#45

The boobies are well-represented in the islands, with 3 resident species — blue-footed (#43), red-footed (#44), and masked boobies. In Photo #45, the somewhat vestigial nesting behavior of the photogenic masked booby is seen, whereby twigs and other materials are offered to the mate. Aside from the color of their feet, it is their courtship dance for which blue-footed boobies are so well known, part of which involves lifting the feet in sequence (#46).

#46

E. Heron

#47

The Galápagos Islands are home to Creatures great and small. Included in the latter category are the Sally Lightfoot crab (#47), green sea urchin (#48), pencil sea urchin (#49), and the leopard ray (#50).

#48

#49

#50

#51

#52

#53

The diverse Galápagos plants are well represented by drought-tolerant species, such as palo santo trees (#51), lava cactus (#52), and prickly pear cactus (#53).

#54

#55

Sea birds, shore birds, land birds; all are fascinating to observe and photograph. Seen here are the yellow-crowned night heron (the dark plumage resembling judicial robes — #54), the scavenging Hood mockingbird (breaking open an abandoned booby egg — #55), and the graceful common stilt (#56).

#56

#57

The classic shot of the flightless cormorant exiting the water and spreading its atrophied wings to dry the feathers (#57). During courtship, pelicans often intertwine their necks and bills in an amusing fashion (#58).

#58

The sun is setting over Kicker Rock (#59) and your Galápagos adventure as a fur seal sadly notes your departure time is approaching (#60).

ments and/or storage facilities, etc. A few boats have cabins on the upper deck, which have a nicer view. Ask the Guide for a recommendation.

Unpacking – Once you've been assigned (or chosen) your cabin, get unpacked. The cabins are much smaller than even the smallest hotel room (including those in Tokyo), so you have to really organize your stuff. Stow things away in a compartmental fashion, so you can easily find them. If there's not a lot of storage room, you may want to leave some clothes in the pack or suitcase (which usually goes under the bottom bed or bunk). Keep your snorkel gear and sunscreen lotion topside (in your mesh gear bag; see Chapter VI), near the aft deck. Have your photographic equipment together and ready to go. Keep a plastic bag handy for dirty clothes. Don't leave your things lying about, thinking that you'll tidy up after a bit. "After a bit" may be after dark; some boats have no cabin lights, and besides, your cabin "mate" might be asleep. You might want to be asleep too, only to be stymied by a bunk full of junk. Also, the boat may be under way, and trying to unpack on a moving boat is not my idea of fun. Keep a flashlight where you can easily find it.

Chow Time – Lunch is the next order of business. There are few things in life as enjoyable as your first meal on-board a yacht that will soon be departing on an adventure-filled journey. Savor the moment and everything that comes with it!

The Beverage Tab – While the policy varies from boat to boat, passengers are usually required to pay for what they drink. An "honor system" tab is set up on a clipboard that's usually kept by the refrigerator or cold box; on Cruise Ships and most yachts, a barman keeps a formal tab. Each person is listed on the tab sheet, followed by columns designating the various beverage categories, such as bottled water (the only "safe" water on-board), cola, and beer. Often that's all the choices there are, although most boats offer wine and cocktails. You settle the bar bill at the end of your tour.

The Head – The marine toilet is another minor inconvenience, although most of the yachts and all the Cruise Ships have flush toilets. There are still some yachts that have the old pump handle flushers. Regardless of the boat, no toilet paper down the toilet; separate waste baskets are provided, even on the Cruise Ships.

Electricity – If you have any appliances that need recharging (such as a video power pack), you may have to get tuned in to the boat's generator cycle. Different boats have different power generating systems. On several of the yachts, they run the diesel-driven electrical generators from dawn to about midnight; during this time, 110VAC power is available. If the boat has air-conditioning, the generators are on 24 hours per day. In addition, most boats have an alternate (back-up) 12VDC power system, also available 24 hrs. There are usually two sets of lights, one operating on 110VAC and the other on 12VDC. Do be careful, however, as a few boats (including some of the Cruise Ships) operate on 220VAC, and you have to use an adapter (sometimes available to rent on the Cruise Ships).

What To Wear – On the small yachts, most people wear their bathing suits or shorts all day, including at meals. The Cruise Ships are more formal, and they ask that short pants not be worn during dinner; the crew all wear their dress whites during and after dinner, and several "cruise-oriented" passengers wear jackets and ties. That's not my image of the Galápagos, but there you have it. Regardless of the boat, you will need to wear a sweatshirt or light jacket in the evenings, when it gets a little chilly (especially during the dry season, from about June-December).

Most of the boats do have a dress rule – you can't wear your "on the islands" footwear on-board. Designated deck shoes or sandals are fine. The idea here is that they don't want you leaving little sand deposits all over their boat.

Orientation – Getting to know the Rules is facilitated by the Guide; on Day 1, an orientation session is held. At this time the Guide will go through the various procedures on-board the particular boat. The Rules of the *Galápagos National Park* will also be explained to you. Remember, the Guide is a representative of the Park and is required to tell you the Rules and to enforce them. Most of them take this function quite seriously, which is commendable.

On a Cruise Ship, you will be assigned to a group at this time (based primarily on language). Each group will have its own Licensed Guide to conduct the island tours. Maximum group size is 20 passengers, per the National Park regulations. Your group will have a name, usually that of one of the animal species, such as "Boobies" or "Cormorants." When announcements are made, they may say, "Boobies will depart at 10:00 and Cormorants at 10:30." Just remember if you're a Booby or a Cormorant.

During or after the orientation, the boat will be under way. You will soon be arriving at (and visiting) your first Galápagos Island.

A DAY AT SEA
The Morning Schedule
Your day at sea begins at sunrise (about 6 a.m. throughout the year). Actually, I'm usually out of bed and on-board, camera in hand, by 5:30. I like to catch the first light whenever I can. While waiting for the sun to do its thing and for the coffee water to boil (there are no espresso machines or good coffee beans onboard any boat), I go through the ritual of cleaning lenses and sorting film. I also try to take some time and read up on the island to be visited, getting an idea of the wildlife to be seen, their characteristics, and the kinds of shots I may want to take. For study purposes, I would suggest using this book and/or the Jackson **GUIDE.**

You'll notice that the boat isn't where it was yesterday evening. In order to maximize your touring possibilities, the vast majority of the boats travel between islands at night. So you'll be gently woken from your sleep almost every night by the sound of the engine(s) starting up. For me, it's quite comforting to hear the engines in the background as I drift back to sleep. The actual sailing time varies quite a bit and depends on the speed capacity of the boat as well as the inter-island distance. The central islands are fairly close together, so the boat will usually depart about 4 a.m. to arrive before sunrise. The outer islands are further apart (sometimes 30-40 miles), and the departure time might be as early as midnight.

Soon after the sun rises, most of the passengers do the same. If you're a photographer, you'll want to take advantage of the early light and get on the island as soon as possible. You will also get more wildlife activity early in the morning. Legally, you can go ashore after 6:00 a.m., although 6:30-7:00 is usually good enough. However, unless you are on a dedicated natural history charter, photography trip, or birding tour, this may not happen. Most groups do not go ashore until 8:30-9:00, as many people like to sleep in, and the crew doesn't really push things. What you can do is make the other passengers aware that the lighting and animal activity are better earlier in the day. Also, if there is a Cruise Ship anchored nearby, you definitely want to get ashore and on the trail before they disembark their large contingent of passengers. If most of your group wants to go ashore early, you can probably convince the Guide and crew to get started earlier. The trick is to arrange it the night before, so the cook knows to get breakfast ready earlier.

On a Cruise Ship, these subtle flexibilities do not exist. By necessity (for handling up to 90 passengers), there are fixed times for all activities. These times are posted and announced each evening prior to the social functions. A public address system (heard everywhere on-board and even piped into your cabin) is used to announce pending activities.

Breakfast typically consists of eggs (prepared various ways on various days) or pancakes, fruit, juice, toast, and instant coffee or tea. The Cruise Ships have a buffet-style breakfast with several selections, much in the style of many hotels.

Once breakfast is over, the Guide will announce that "we're leaving in 10 minutes." On the Cruise Ships, the departure times will be announced over the P.A. system. Put on your sunscreen lotion (don't forget your feet and behind the ears), and gather up your gear. I usually just take my camera equipment (with first aid cream and a few bandages in the camera bag) and binoculars. I put my camera bag inside a plastic bag to protect it from splash and spray during the *panga* ride ashore. Many people take drinking water; this decision is up to the individual, as some of us get more thirsty than others, although the Guide will advise you during the briefing how rugged the trail will be.

Note: You may not take any food or drink (except for water) on shore. The fear is that of introduced organisms. Exceptions are made for diabetics. For the same reason, you may not use the island as a bathroom.

Wet Landings vs. Dry Landings – From the previous evening's briefing, you will know whether there's going to be a "wet landing" or "dry landing." The term "wet landing" seems to cause a degree of apprehension in some visitors prior to their tour. In my opinion, a dry landing is actually more cause for concern than a wet landing; a brief explanation is in order.

A wet landing is actually a beach landing. The *panga* cannot make it all the way to shore without damaging the propeller and fouling the engine. So you will have to step out into a foot or so of water. Actually, you swing your feet out over the side and then step into the water. Reverse the procedure when you get back in; sit down facing outwards and swing your feet in. Understandably, you don't wear your shoes during a wet landing. You're told to carry them, but I tie the laces together (with a bow or slipknot) and toss them onto my shoulder, thus freeing my hands for steadying myself if need be. You can avoid this situation altogether by wearing sport sandals for visits that have a wet landing (see section on Footwear in Chapter VI).

A dry landing is made up against a natural dock of lava rocks, and you wear your shoes. These landings are a bit tricky because the *panga* is moving with the wave action, and the rock you step onto often is slippery and has a small flat portion. It's important that you watch what you're doing and listen to the Guide, who will offer you a hand as you disembark. When accepting the Guide's hand, grasp the wrist and the Guide will grasp yours. This "wristlock" is much stronger than a handshake grip. Once on shore, continue to place your feet carefully along the first few feet of rocks, which are often quite slippery (depending on the tide level).

While the *pangas* are quite sturdy, they do have a balance point. Once again, listen to the Guide and when disembarking, don't stand up until the passenger in front of you is about to step out. Passenger loading and unloading should be done on an alternate side basis – first the left and then the right.

You want your hands free when getting in and out of the *panga,* so your bags should either be daypacks or fanny packs. Camera gear should be in a water-resistant case or bag. If you have your camera out, like I always do, keep it covered with a plastic bag. Those of you seated towards the bow will get a lot of spray action. You'll actually get more than that, probably a good splash or two, if the *panga* is going against the current. It's also important that you wear your camera (and/or binoculars), with the neckstrap around you; waves and other passengers have a way of knocking you off-balance.

Note: Your landing craft may be met by a reception committee of sea lions. All this presents no problem and actually adds to the entertainment value of the tour, with one notable exception – a bull sea lion. Sometimes the bulls are not real happy about letting tourists into their territory, and they'll stand there barking at the *panga*. There is some chance that the landing will have to be aborted in favor of an alternate landing area. Listen to your Guide.

The Morning Tour – Once you land, your island tour will take about 1-3 hours. Put your shoes on if you had a wet landing (unless you are wearing sport sandals). I wear socks as well; they prevent blisters and sunburn. If you brought your snorkel gear, set it down on a rock, well above the high tide line. Check with your Guide, and make sure the location is okay. Remember that you must stay on the trail. Don't get too far ahead if the Guide is looking after some stragglers. On several of the islands, you will be walking over lava rocks for a good portion of the tour. Some of them are not well-anchored, and will give way under you. Get the balance point of your feet figured out, and you'll be fine, literally skipping over the rocks.

Keep your eyes moving. Look up, and check-out the bird activity. Have your camera around your neck, the battery "On," the shutter advanced, and the exposure set. Your Guide knows where the wildlife is, so stay close. When you get a photographic opportunity, be courteous to, and mindful of, the others in your group. Be careful not to step in front of someone about to take a picture. Sometimes if the best photo angles are occupied, you'll just have to wait your turn. You actually help everyone, and get some excellent photos, by stooping down to take your shots. The perspective and composition are usually improved from this low vantage point.

If you are boarding the *panga* wet-landing-style, take off your shoes and rinse them in the water. If you are boarding dry-landing-style, you will be reminded to take off your shoes once you're on the yacht. Aside from keeping the yacht and *panga* clean, rinsing your shoes helps to prevent the accidental transmission of indigenous and (even worse) introduced plant seeds to another island.

After your tour, there may be swimming and snorkeling time (usually about an hour – the Guide will tell you). It helps if you wear an underwater watch. Don't wander off by yourself. If you're snorkeling, the best views are close to the rocks. You'll return to the boat about noon, and lunch will soon be ready, allowing you a little time to get cleaned up. You'll also be ready for lunch. The main course will consist of anything from fresh fish to meat. There is usually a hot soup, which is most welcome after the snorkel session, especially when the water is cool. There will be lots of vegetables with fresh fruit for dessert. If you're on a Cruise Ship, lunch will be buffet-style, and you can either eat in the dining room or outside on the sun deck.

The Afternoon Schedule – After lunch, the Guide will announce the next departure time – usually around 2:00-2:30. By now, many of the passengers are ready for a *siesta*. As you visit your cabin, you'll be pleasantly surprised to find your bed made and the waste buckets emptied. Incidentally, if you have any clothes to be dried, this is an ideal time. There are several clotheslines on the yachts, usually up by the radar and radio antennae.

I like to rest topside, maybe catching some rays and sleep at the same time. Also some good photos. The boat will be under way shortly, heading to the next island or to another Visitor Site on the same island you visited in the morning. Every once in a while, I open my eyes and look around – for dolphins! You never know when they're going to show up, riding the bow wave for a few miles before going back to their other business matters. I've been the first to spot them on several occasions, something I'm rather proud of. And, you bet, I have my camera on-deck with me.

I also use this time to read up on the next Visitor Site. If you're on a Cruise Ship, there may be a Galápagos video being shown; in due time a Guide or Big Brother (or Sister) on the P.A. system will announce that the departure time is nearing. Once again, get yourself and your stuff ready.

The Afternoon Tour – In some ways this will be a repeat performance of the morning show. In other ways, it will be a whole new show, with different plants, different animals, different landscape, and maybe a different landing. Different lighting too. I don't mind a late afternoon departure, because it means I can stay on the island later. The Guides must have you off the island by 6:00 p.m., but some passengers like to get back early to have a "cold one." If you're a photographer, try to convince the others of the great shots that can be taken by one and all as the sun gets lower in the sky. Afternoons are also great for sea birds, because there's more of them around, having returned or returning from their off-shore fishing activities.

Eventually it will be back to the boat time. Guess what's waiting for you? You got it – dinner! It's a rough life at sea, and it gets rougher as the days go by.

The Evening Schedule – Dinner is a little heavier version of lunch. On a Cruise Ship, it's a sit down, formal affair, with a Captain's Table, waiters, and wine lists. After the evening meal, there is a debriefing session during which the following day's schedule is announced and explained. Some of the Guides do a good job of sketching out the Visitor Sites and a list of the important features (see Photo #7). Take this time to ask any questions you may have.

After the debriefing session, the social functions usually begin. If you're on a yacht, this will include cards, music, swapping lies, and downing a few. On the Cruise Ships, there is live entertainment and a dance floor. On some tours with Tour Leaders (remember them?), there are evening workshops, and this is when you can really learn about the Galápagos. It adds another dimension to the trip.

After 9:30, people will begin to drift off – literally. It's been a long day, and the ocean sun has a way of getting to you. Tomorrow is another big one, and it's time to hit the sack. You'll soon wake up to that comforting sound of the engines starting. I'm a pretty light sleeper, and there are nights when, after the boat is under way, I'll go up on-deck. It's a beautiful sight to watch the bioluminescent particles drifting by; it seems like the whole ocean is lit up. There are times when I'll visit the bridge, stand next to the captain, and watch the radar equipment continuously form outlines of the surrounding islands. After a while, I'll go back to my cabin and will soon be back asleep.

TIPPING THE CREW

Before the islands are introduced, let's skip ahead to the end of the cruise, when it is customary to tip the crew for a job well-done. It may be customary, but there's no set procedure for it. There are, however, some basic ways of going about this awkward business; you can tip each crew member or give an overall "crew tip" to either the captain or Guide for distribution. You also have the choice of giving your own tip directly to the crew or putting the gratuity in a tip box. A lot depends on the situation, which we'll try to sort out.

First off, the total crew tip ranges from $75-$100 per passenger per week. This range is a 1998 estimate and is subject to the service you feel that you received. This is exactly the same concept as a restaurant, except the time span is a lot longer and the service is more extensive. Out of this estimated total, a little less than half (depending on the total number of crew members) goes to the Guide. This, after all, is the person you have had the most contact with. The remainder of the tip is split among the rest of the crew. On a yacht, this includes the sailor(s), cook, waiter, and possibly an engineer (who maintains the engine and equipment). On some yachts, the captain is an employee and shares in the gratuities; on other yachts, the captain is an owner. It's up to you to determine the situation. .

Having taken it this far, it sort of makes sense to tip the Guide personally. From there, it depends on the boat, how well you know the crew, and how much small change you have ($5 bills or lots of I0,000 and 20,000 sucre notes). Traveler's checks are welcome and accepted. Simply sign the bottom and print your passport number on the back. Do not write in the date or the name of the recipient; this will facilitate cashing the traveler's check by the "end user." You will be given instructions to put the money in an envelope or tip box. In addition, you may want to tip certain individuals a little extra, such as a particular waiter, etc.

INTRODUCING THE GALAPAGOS ISLANDS

... By far the most remarkable feature in the natural history of this archipelago ... is, that the different islands to a considerable extent are inhabited by a different set of beings. I never dreamed that islands, about fifty or sixty miles apart, and most of them in sight of each other, formed of precisely the same rocks, placed under a quite similar climate, rising to a nearly equal height, would have been differently tenanted....

Charles Darwin, 1845

The islands **are** different, each with its own population of wildlife. And the population on a given island will vary with the seasons as well as from year to year, depending on climatic conditions. These are natural cycles, an important part of the Galápagos learning experience. Keep this in mind as you visit each island. It may be very disappointing to find that most of the blue-footed boobies have abandoned their nesting site on a particular island 3 months earlier than usual. While this may have deprived you of an opportunity to observe and photograph them, their early departure is a vital part of natural history. You may witness sea lion pups that have been orphaned by their families and left to die; it's an extremely sad sight to behold, but this too is part of nature. You'll get lots of great photos and will see wildlife found nowhere else in the world. But most of all, you'll experience the living laboratory of evolution at work – the Galápagos Islands.
   Note: Most of the Galápagos (about 97 percent), including a few islands entirely, is "off-limits" to the public. The *Galápagos National Park Service,* in conjunction with the *Charles Darwin Research Station,* has established over forty official Visitor Sites. These are areas where, accompanied by a Licensed Guide, tourists may enter. The Visitor Sites are typically delimited by a series of trail markers. The following sections will introduce the reader to most of the Visitor Sites. It should be noted that from time to time, owing to necessity, certain areas are closed off and new Sites are opened. I see this happening with greater frequency in the future, in part because of the ecological impact of tourism on some of the central islands. At the same time, with more frequent flights to San Cristóbal Island, there will be pressure to open up more Visitor Sites in the southern islands.
   During the following sections, frequent references are made to the Map of the Visitor Sites; you will find the map at the end of this book.

THE CENTRAL ISLANDS

Many of these islands are commonly visited during a 1 week Galápagos tour. The island of Pinzon and the islets of North Plaza and Daphne Minor are off-limits to visitors.

BARTOLOME (BARTHOLOMEW)

The small island of Bartolomé is located off the eastern shore of James Island, across what is called Sullivan Bay (see the Map). Actually, Sullivan Bay is a Visitor Site on James Island (see below) as well as a body of water. Your two-part (sometimes three-part) excursion begins with a dry landing, followed by a strenuous 30-40 minute hike to the summit of a once-active volcano. I classify this as strenuous only because it is a steep climb; the footing is fairly easy, however (although loose and sandy), with a wooden stairway covering most of the distance. Also, there are no tricky rocks to traverse. The stairs are for your convenience as well as to prevent erosion; do not walk to the side of them. This is one of the most popular visits in all the Galápagos because of the beautiful panoramic views offered at the top (see Photo #30).

The view is educational as well as inspiring. The volcanic features include lava formations as well as spatter cones and cinder cones (see the section on Formation in Chapter II). Your Guide may refer to them as pyroclastic cones, which is a general term used to describe formations of solid material (as opposed to liquid lava) ejected from the volcano.

Speaking of cones, you will see Pinnacle Rock, a most striking example of a tuff cone (a vertical rock formation of hardened ash). There are also good examples of pioneering plants, including some beautiful stands of lava cactus.

After your descent to sea level, you will get back in the *panga* and perhaps take a short ride over to the "trail of two beaches" (on the left side of Photo #30). This will be a wet landing. Leave your snorkel gear at the north beach before taking the trail through the mangroves to the south beach. Here, one often sees mating sea turtles and white-tipped sharks close to shore. After retracing your steps back north, you will be rewarded with some excellent swimming and snorkeling. Occasionally, penguins are spotted in this area.

Unique Photo Opportunities: Pinnacle Rock is quite striking and the most photographed landmark in the islands (see Photo #31). You'll have all kinds of angles and distances to choose from, including close-ups from the *panga*. The view from the summit offers the best panoramic view of the islands; this is the best opportunity to take a shot of each other (and perhaps have a fellow passenger take a shot of both or all of you), posing in the foreground.

The volcanic features are also fascinating subjects. With several spatter cones grouped together, Bartolomé is your basic moonscape and offers excellent photographic opportunities of the unique geological formations. Finally, unless you visit the western islands, this may be your best opportunity for a penguin photo. Even if it's not the best composition, you might want to take a couple of shots just for documentation.

DAPHNE MAJOR

The Daphne twins, Major and Minor, are islets located north of Santa Cruz and west of Baltra. Daphne Minor is closed to the public. Erosion problems and other ecological considerations (as well as related research) have kept Daphne Major closed as well. Recently, the *Galápagos National Park Service* has reopened Daphne Major, but only to small yachts (with a rating of 12 passengers or less), and even they are limited to one visit per month. Daphne Major has of late become one of the best known islands in the Galápagos. This is where researchers Peter & Rosemary Grant actually have seen and documented evo-

lution in Darwin's finches. A captivating account of their observations is presented in the Pulitzer Prize-winning book, **THE BEAK OF THE FINCH** by
Jonathon Weiner (see the Literature section). While many passengers want to see
the island "where all this happened," most boats carry too many passengers to
legally visit this Site. Also, the landing is very tricky, and can only be safely managed in calm seas during high tides. The best is to see if the Guide and captain
can be persuaded to do a circumnavigation of Daphne Major during your trip,
during which time the Guide can give an on-deck summary of the Grants' fascinating research.

Unique Photo Opportunities: A circumnavigation of Daphne Major offers
good views and shooting opportunities of partially-eroded tuff formations as well
as red-billed tropicbirds, doing flybys over the boat. If you are fortunate enough
to land, you can get excellent shots of blue-footed boobies, which seasonally
nest in the interior craters.

JAMES (SANTIAGO)

James is a large, somewhat barren island northwest of Santa Cruz with a mostly
volcanic landscape. The once well-represented vegetation has been severely
altered by the feral goat population, at one time estimated at upwards of 100,000
(started by only four introduced animals in the early 1800s). Due to an extensive,
joint effort by the *Galápagos National Park Service* and the *Charles Darwin
Research Station,* the goat population has been significantly reduced in recent
years to around 60,000. Several of the visiting yachts have been known to sail
away with "a side of goat," and it is common to (somewhat in jest) refer to all
good on-board meat dishes as "*chivo de Santiago*" – goat from James Island.
      The Visitor Sites on James are as follows:

Buccaneer Cove – Located on the northwest corner of the island, this area was
a haven for pirates during the 1600s and 1700s. This is typically a cruise-by point
due to the sometimes unsafe (wet) landing conditions (when the sea is active)
and the lack of unique wildlife. Also, the large fenced-in vegetation
area (used as protection from the goats) doesn't make it the most popular of
Visitor Sites.

James Bay – Located on the west side of James Island, the wet landing on the dark
sands of Puerto Egas, James Bay leads to one of the more rewarding visits in the
Galápagos. First, a trail leads inland to the remains of a salt mining operation, one
of several largely unsuccessful attempts to commercialize the Galápagos. Some
groups will make the 1 hour round trip to the Sugarloaf Volcano (about 1000 ft
elevation). But it is the Fur Seal Grotto that produces the most pleasure for visitors.
Here one can get very close views of both fur seals and sea lions in a series of
rocky pools. For many, this is the only opportunity to see the Galápagos fur seal,
once thought to be on the verge of extinction (see Photo #60).
      In addition to the fur seals, James Bay offers the best opportunity for tide-
pooling in the Galápagos. Your Guide will point out sponges, nudibranchs & tiny
(nodilittorinoid) snails, barnacles, hermit crabs, and several fish species (including the endemic four-eyed blenny). Be careful in this area, though, as the wet
rocks are usually covered with very slippery algae.

Espumilla Beach – After a wet landing on a large beach, a walk through a mangrove forest leads to a lagoon usually inhabited by a group of flamingos as well as pintail ducks and common stilts. This is a nesting site as well as a feeding area for the flamingos. Sea turtles dig their nests at the edge of the mangroves, and care must be taken not to walk on these large depressed areas in the dark-hued sand. There is often time for swimming and snorkeling at the end of the tour.

Sullivan Bay – Located on the eastern coast of James Island, across from Bartolomé, Sullivan Bay offers a rare look at a recently-formed lava field. The eruptions are thought to have taken place around 1890, which is recent enough in geological terms. A dry landing is usually made, but if the seas aren't calm, a wet landing at the beach area may be necessary.

Unique Photo Opportunities: The clear, often sunlit water of the Fur Seal Grotto provides the best opportunity to get some great aquabatic shots and video sequences of both fur seals and sea lions; a polarizer is highly recommended. In addition, James Bay usually provides the visitor with a chance to photograph the Galápagos hawk and the yellow-crowned night heron, often at close range. There are also excellent wide-angle opportunities of naturally-sculpted tuff formations. At Sullivan Bay, it's all wide-angle photography, with great opportunities for texture shots of the smooth, rope-like *pahoehoe* lava flows.

MOSQUERA

Mosquera is a tiny islet located between Baltra and N. Seymour Islands (see the Map). It is basically a long, narrow beach with a large population of sea lions. Due to its proximity to the Baltra Airport, Mosquera is a favored Visitor Site for many of the yachts on the first or last day of the tour. Needless to say, this is a wet landing site; swimming and snorkeling are part of the activities.

You will note that Mosquera is flat, seemingly not related to the other volcanically-formed islands. Actually, as with several of the islands in the Galápagos (including Baltra, the Plazas, N. Seymour and Santa Fé), this area has been geologically uplifted. An uplift is a land mass formed by lava flowing through a subsurface geological fissure (a fault), gradually lifting the mass through and above the ocean surface. In the Galápagos, the uplifted islands have been over a million years in the making; marine fossils are still evident in many of these locations (see the section on Urvina Bay, Isabela Island in this chapter).

Unique Photo Opportunities: This is one of the best locations for sea lion shots.

SOUTH PLAZA

The Plazas are a pair of islets situated just off the east coast of Santa Cruz. Only South Plaza is a Visitor Site and is another example of a geological uplift. In this case, the southern portion of this narrow islet (only a couple hundred yards wide) has considerably more uplift to it, forming cliffs with spectacular views.

The tour begins with a dry landing. There is often a sea lion guarding the natural dock; let the Guide take care of the situation (which is often achieved with little more than a clapping of the hands). The trail leading to the cliffs goes through a combined Coastal and Dry Vegetation Zone with prickly pear cactus and extensive patches of salt-tolerant *Sesuvium*. The *Sesuvium* is usually seen as distinctive red mats, although it turns green when rainfall is abundant.

One of the first stops is in a small "forest" of prickly pear *(Opuntia)* cactus, which provides ample food to a population of land iguanas, also found in this area. For most visitors, it will be the only opportunity to see land iguanas. Over the last few years, the generally large population of land iguanas on South Plaza has been depleted by the 1982-83 ENSO *(El Niño/Southern Oscillation)* weather phenomenon, during which a high percentage of the cacti were destroyed by root rot (caused by the excessive rainfall). The cacti were never able to recover, due to a long-term drought, and in turn many of the land iguanas were starved off and their numbers reduced. The effects are still seen, with fewer and skinnier land iguanas in the area, but according to the Darwin Station, it is only expected to stabilize the population, not to threaten it.

The walk along the sea cliffs is a wonderful experience, with Audubon's shearwaters and red-billed tropicbirds whistling and shrieking overhead as they make seemingly endless back and forth flights; they are actually trying to locate and then land in their "homes," which are crevices found along the overhanging ledges. Swallow-tailed gulls are gliding by, occasionally landing on the cliff edge. For most of the year, you can see them courting and mating in this area. As you look down into the water, there is often a school of yellow-tailed mullet feeding on the surface. With the wind on your face, the entire walk is pure sensory overload.

Towards the end of the cliffside walk, you will encounter a bachelor sea lion colony, a battle-scarred collection of bulls (young and old) in various stages of recuperation or in total retirement. You can usually see one or more bulls actually climbing up the cliff to get to this haven, which is quite an amazing sight.

Owing to its proximity to Puerto Ayora, South Plaza is a very popular Visitor Site, and many of the Day Trip boats come here on a frequent basis. I would go so far as to say that this is an over-visited area, with already-noticeable effects, such as a decrease in the wildlife population densities as well as trail erosion.

Caution: Swimming and snorkeling opportunities are sometimes offered here. While some Guides would view this statement as over-cautious at best, the sea lion bulls here can be very aggressive, and I know of several incidents where tourists have been bitten. Be very careful!

Unique Photo Opportunities: South Plaza Island offers endless photo and video opportunities; for many of you, it will be the only opportunity for land iguanas. Standing near the cliffs and panning your camera across the skies, you should be able to get some spectacular gliding shots of red-billed tropicbirds and swallow-tailed gulls as they fight the offshore winds to land safely in their nesting areas. Don't stand too near the edge, though, for there is potential danger here; the records show that there have been a couple of tragic falls. The swirling winds increase the danger potential. Actually there are a few recessed areas where the drop-off is very gradual, and I find them to be safe and convenient shooting locations. It's where I took one of my favorite in-motion shots of a tropicbird (see Photo #28). This is one of the best opportunities for close-ups of the swallow-tailed gull; focus on the beautiful red-ringed eye, choosing an angle that shows a gleam of light reflected in the eye (see the section on Composition in Chapter VII). Just make sure your hat is on good and tight, so the wind doesn't get it.

This is the only bachelor sea lion colony you will see, and these veterans, complete with their battle scars, are worthy subjects. There are also good wide-angle lens opportunities with the red *Sesuvium* in the foreground and your anchored boat in the background (see Photo #8).

RABIDA (JERVIS)

Often termed the geographic center of the Galápagos, the islet of Rábida is located just south of James Island (see the Map). The tour begins with a wet landing on a dark red beach, the coloring of which is volcanic in origin. A short walk leads to a saltwater lagoon, where flamingos are sometimes seen; this is a feeding area for them, and not a nesting site, thus accounting for their only occasional presence. The salt bush just behind the beach **is** a nesting area for the brown pelican, providing a rare look at pelican family life, including incredible chick-feeding behavior. Try to imagine the chick's head completely inside the bill of the parent!

Rábida is said to have the most diversified volcanic rocks of all the islands The interior of the islet is a sloping hillside covered with *palo santo* trees.

The tour often ends with a swimming and snorkeling opportunity; actually, this is my favorite snorkeling site in the islands, offering a tremendous diversity of near-shore and pelagic fishes.

Unique Photo Opportunities: The dark red coloring of the beach is most picturesque and makes a great background for sea lion shots (see Photo #12). The flamingo lagoon may offer another opportunity for some beautiful pictures. For some reason, the flamingos here seem less skittish than other locations in the Galápagos, often approaching close enough to more than fill the frame. Video sequences can also be quite dramatic. This will probably be the only pelican nesting area you will see, and these always-interesting birds may oblige you with some unique poses (see Photo #58). If you have an underwater camera, definitely bring it with you for the snorkeling session.

Note: The colors are very pronounced late in the afternoon. If your tour includes an afternoon visit to Rábida, see if you can convince your group and Guide to do the snorkel first and the land visit after 4:00.

SANTA CRUZ (INDEFATIGABLE)

Centrally located, the island of Santa Cruz is also the center of Galápagos tourism. About half of the island's 16,000 residents live in or around the town of Puerto Ayora, many of them part of the infrastructure required to support the tourist trade. Puerto Ayora is also the home of the *Charles Darwin Research Station,* an important Visitor Site as well as the operations center for Galápagos wildlife conservation and preservation programs. These programs are carried out by the *Galápagos National Park Service,* also located in Puerto Ayora.

There are several Visitor Sites on Santa Cruz besides the Darwin Station, including Las Bachas Beach, Black Turtle Cove, Conway Bay, Dragon Hill, the Highlands, Tortuga Bay, and Whale Bay. The Highlands itself offers a number of tours, including *Los Gemelos* (the twin pit craters) and the Tortoise Reserve.

Puerto Ayora – As pointed out, Puerto Ayora (population approx. 8000) is the economic center of the Galápagos Islands. All the tour boats visit Puerto Ayora, anchoring in Academy Bay (named after the famous scientific expedition of 1905-06 by the *California Academy of Sciences* and their boat, the ACADEMY). After a visit to the Darwin Station (see below), tourists are allowed some free time in town to do some shopping as well as restaurant-and-bar-hopping. Occasionally, trips are made to the Highlands, making stops at some of the Visitor Sites located in this lush, fertile area (see below).

There are several gift and souvenir shops in Puerto Ayora, with the T-shirt being the prime commodity. There are several generic designs, with the best prices (about $8) coming from the low profile shops on the fringes of town. The fancier stores in town command some high prices, but keep in mind that you will have a hard time finding good Galápagos T-shirts on the mainland.

This is also a good opportunity to purchase any toiletry items you may have run out of. Don't forget those snacks you've been thinking about – a box of cookies, some candy, etc. Or maybe a bottle of rum. You can take care of most of your list at any of the general stores in town. There is even a supermarket near the dock, called Proinsular. They have a pretty reasonable wine selection.

Puerto Ayora has grown considerably over the last few years, and there are a lot more services available, including film stores, pharmacies, restaurants, hotels, a couple of dive shops, and a well-operated international telephone office (inside the modern Banco de Pacifico building). Most of the tourist-oriented services are along the main street (Charles Darwin Avenue, which parallels the ocean). Most all the shops will accept U.S. dollars at a fairly decent exchange rate (perhaps a little less than the mainland), and several stores will accept traveler's checks (you will have to put your passport number on them). For some reason, stores are paranoid about U.S. currency that has the slightest tear; they will usually refuse to accept any bill that doesn't pass inspection.

There are several good (but not great) eating spots in Puerto Ayora. Aside from the hotels (see below), for European-style dinners, there is the Four Lanterns (Quatro Linternas) and Trattoria de Pipó. For lunch, there is Media Luna Pizza and Cafe y Limón. Near the dock, there is Salvavidas (very good Ecuadorian seafood) and the recently-opened La Tolda Azul (The Blue Awning), which is a very classy (and somewhat expensive) *ceviche,* sandwich, and coffee spot. Even if you're not very hungry, several of these restaurants have outside tables and make good beer stops before heading back to the boat.

Speaking of beer, if you're out and about after dark in Puerto Ayora, you may consider heading over to Frank's Bar (next to the Four Lanterns restaurant) or La Garrapata, an outdoor pub and cafe. And if your feet get twitchy and demand to dance, next door to La Garrapata is one of the town's hot discos, La Panga, where the landings are said to always be wet. Another disco (just recently opened) is the Galapason.

Note: For those that wish to extend their stay in the Galápagos, Santa Cruz is the island to visit and Puerto Ayora is the place to stay. Activities include trips to the Highlands, kayaking, diving, and horseback riding. You can revisit the *Charles Darwin Research Station,* taking as much time as you like. I spent a few extra days in Puerto Ayora on my first visit to the Galápagos and thoroughly enjoyed it. The logistics for this "extension" are fairly easy to work out; your Tour Operator can help you with the details.

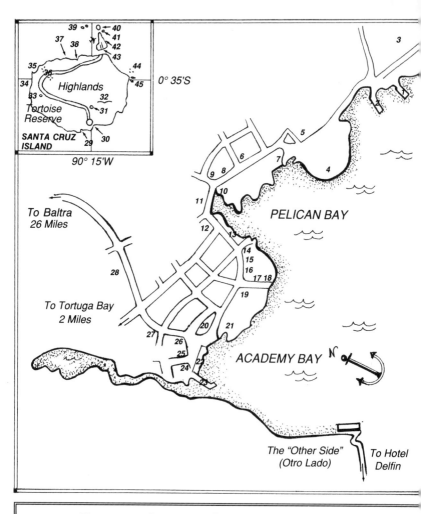

Puerto Ayora, Santa Cruz Island

1. Natl. Park Information Center
2. Natl. Park Dock
3. Darwin Research Station
4. Hotel Galápagos
5. Cemetary
6. Hotel Angermeyer
7. Red Mangrove Inn
8. Media Luna Pizza
9. Frank's Bar
10. Boat Works
11. Four Lanterns Restaurant
12. SAN Airlines
13. Banco del Pacífico
14. La Garrapata Restaurant
15. La Panga Disco Bar

16. Church
17. Hotel Lobo Del Mar
18. Police
19. TAME Airlines
20. La Tolda Azul Restaurant
21. Naval Base
22. Waterfront Park
23. Main Dock
24. Proinsular Super Market
25. Post Office
26. Salvavidas Restaurant
27. Pharmacies
28. IETEL (Telephone Office)
29. Tortuga Bay
30. Puerto Ayora

31. Bella Vista
32. Los Túneles
33. Santa Rosa
34. Whale Bay/Dragon Hill
35. Conway Bay
36. Los Gemelos
37. Las Baches
38. Caleta Tortuga Negra
39. Daphnes Islets
40. Seymour Is.
41. Mosquera Is.
42. Baltra Is.
43. Itabaca Channel
44. Gordon Rocks
45. Plaza Islets

While there are several accommodations, ranging from $10/night pensions, I heartily recommend the Hotel Galápagos. This is the kind of rustic hotel you envision when you visit an out of the way location. A double room, located in a separate cabin, goes for about $100. The ocean views are wonderful. HOGAL, as it is sometimes called, is owned and operated by Jack Nelson; Jack can help you put together several days worth of extension trips, including scuba diving. The hotel also has an excellent restaurant (advanced reservations required) and a well-stocked bar with a beautiful sitting room. The Hotel Delfin has a similar rate, and a nice location as well (on the other side of the bay, or "*otro lado*" as the locals say); rooms are subject to availability, and first priority is given to their Day Cruise Program (see the section on Day Trip Yachts in Chapter IV). The Red Mangrove Inn features rooms in a spacious, custom-built house (also right on the water) and offers kayaking as well as other activities. The new Hotel Angermeyer is also in the same category of first-rate hotels. The Hotel Fernandina, off the main street, is also very nice. For extended stays at a pleasant location (also at a pleasant price – double rooms for about $30-$40/night), consider the Lobo Del Mar or the Sol Y Mar; both are comfortable, ocean-view hotels.

Unique Photo Opportunities: If you visit the Hotel Galápagos, a walk around the grounds will provide some great opportunities to photograph the large marine iguanas that patrol this area. If your Guide takes you to the "other side," a tidal lagoon has a few resident stilts, lava gulls, and herons; this may be your best chance at getting some close-ups of these beautiful birds. While your boat is anchored in Academy Bay, you might find the uniquely-shaped houses up on the cliffside *(El Barranco)* to be interesting subjects. Many of the residents are interesting as well; ask your Guide to tell you who lives where and some of the local history.

Charles Darwin Research Station – Every Galápagos tour visits the *Charles Darwin Research Station*, which was established in 1961 to solve the problems of wildlife conservation in the archipelago. Aside from the development of operations to ensure the survival of endangered plant and animal species, the Darwin Station has coordinated several conservation-oriented educational programs for Ecuadorian students. In addition, a Visitor Center is actively managed. For many tourists, this is the only opportunity to see giant tortoises – certainly the closest-range opportunity. There are three tortoise pens housing animals of uncertain island ancestry; since their race hasn't been genetically determined (although the research is being conducted), they are not useful for breeding purposes.

The Tortoise Rearing Center is also visited. National Park Wardens have collected tortoise eggs from various islands where they have been preyed on and threatened to the point of extinction by several species of introduced mammals. The eggs are then incubated, and the hatchlings are raised for several years, until they are able to withstand the predatory efforts of the mammals that man has introduced to the Galápagos. Since 1970, several thousand tortoises have been repatriated to their native islands. The Hood (Española) Island subspecies is the most notable success. In the early 1960s, this race had been reduced to just three males and eleven females. As a result of the coordinated efforts of the Darwin

Station and the *Galápagos National Park Service,* over 1000 Hood Island tortoises have been repatriated.

Other parts of this unique tour include a Nature Trail, which winds through the Darwin Station and Park Service grounds. Along this trail are numbered posts alongside typical examples of the vegetation. The numbers correspond to a special brochure available at the Information Center. Your Guide will also take you to the Van Straelen Exhibit Hall, where the Galápagos natural history story is told in pictures and words. After the tour, there are occasional lectures on island conservation. As the speaker will point out, the Darwin Station has no fixed income and depends on contributions to carry out its conservation and education programs. Your donation would be well received at this time. See the section on Growth, Tourism, and Conservation in Chapter II for complete information on contributing to this worthy cause.

Groups can now be taken to the once "off-limits" pen of Lonesome George, the last-surviving member of the Pinta Island subspecies.The origin of his name is sadly evident. There is an excellent chance, however, that George, estimated to be about 50-60 years old (still young by tortoise standards) may not be lonesome forever. The Darwin Station has paired George with a couple of females from a different, but closely-related (Wolf Volcano, Isabela Island) subspecies, and he is said to be showing an "active interest." For all the gossip and complete details regarding the love life of Lonesome George, ask your Guide!

After your tour, you may want to stop at the two souvenir kiosks (one is operated by the Darwin Station and the other by the Park service – proceeds go directly to (and help support) these organizations). Several items are for sale, including books, T-shirts, etc.

Unique Photo Opportunities: For most visitors, this is the only opportunity for pictures of the giant tortoises. Take advantage of it! On sunny days, there is usually a bit of glare coming off the carapace (shell), and the use of a polarizing filter may be necessary.

The Highlands – Several tours visit the Highlands of Santa Cruz. As your bus or van leaves Puerto Ayora, the scenery will continuously change as you ascend through all seven Vegetation Zones of the Galápagos. If your journey is during the garúa season (approximately June-December), whatever sunlight there was down below has long since disappeared by the time you reach the top. Often, the "mist" feels more like rainfall, and a jacket is advised (as well as protective bags for your photographic equipment). See the section on Climate in Chapter II.

A favorite stop is *Los Gemelos* (The Twins), a pair of large pit craters (or sinkholes) formed by a collapse of the ground located over a subsurface fissure (fault). Another point of attraction is a trail leading to an area where there are usually several vermillion flycatchers.

Speaking of birds, the Highlands offer several unique habitats (due to the change in altitude and the consequent change in vegetation) to land birds, including tree finches, warbler finches, vegetarian finches, woodpecker finches, dark-billed cuckoos, yellow warblers, short-eared owls, and Galápagos flycatchers. The large black birds you see on the side of the road are the introduced smooth-billed anis (introduced to rid cattle of ticks, which turned out to be a bit of a fiasco, as they seem to be outcompeting the endemic Darwin's finches for food). The white birds often seen perching on the cattle are, logically enough, cattle egrets.

Visits are often made to *Los Túneles,* where you can descend into and walk through the largest known lava tunnels in the Galápagos.

The **Tortoise Reserve** provides those with a sense of adventure an all-day Highlands tour of giant tortoises in the wild. Since most groups only have a few hours to spend in the Highlands, giant tortoises are generally viewed in the wild on private farms. Here, during the later half of the year, (the *garúa* season), the tortoises roam freely through these cattle ranches. The best of these opportunities adjoins the Tortoise Reserve and is called *Rancho Mariposa.* Here you can some-times see a small herd of tortoises. Have your Guide arrange the tour in advance. Perhaps you can convince your Guide that this would be a good lunch stop as well, for owners Steve Divine and Jenny Montenegro operate a by-appointment-only restaurant, serving a lunch with selections of chicken, fish, and home-grown beef and vegetables.

Another family-owned eating spot in the Highlands is the Restaurant Narwhal. This is another "by-appointment-only" restaurant (for groups – not indi-viduals), and reservations have to be made at least a day in advance (by radio transmitter – ask your Guide). Owners Eduardo and Evelina Donoso will greet you with a "welcome drink" followed by a complete dinner. Your hosts, who have spent several years living in the U.S., will tell you all about the people of Galápagos (the *"Galápagueños"* as they call themselves). A third restaurant called the Altair, owned by Anita Salcedo, is also recommended.

By now you're wondering how all these cattle ranches, as well as the other farms, can legally exist in a National Park. Remember that when the Galápagos National Park was formed in 1959, it excluded about 3 percent of the land area, basically those zones that were already inhabited. This includes eight towns (on four islands) and their surrounding agricultural areas, with a total population of around 16,000 residents (1998).

Unique Photo Opportunities: The lush Highlands are a fully-saturated green during the garúa season. With a rising fog, a surreal background presents several interesting photographic possibilities. This may be your only chance to get a shot of the bright red male vermillion flycatcher, and at *Rancho Mariposa,* you may get the opportunity of photographing several tortoises, possibly in a colorful duckweed-covered pond (see Photo #25).

Las Baches – Located on the north shore of Santa Cruz, close to the Baltra Airport, Las Baches is a swimming beach that serves as a Visitor Site on your first or last touring day. There's not much to see while snorkeling. One of the few remnants of the U.S. World War II presence in the Galápagos, a floating pier, can be seen here.

Caleta Tortuga Negra (Black Turtle Cove) – This wonderful Visitor Site is locat-ed on the northern portion of Santa Cruz Island near Las Baches (see the Map). The tour consists of a *panga* ride through a series of mangrove-surrounded coves and inlets. Here one often views several pairs of mating marine turtles (especial-ly between September-February), white-tipped reef sharks, spotted eagle rays, and beautiful, yellow cow-nosed rays. In order to avoid disturbing the wildlife, the outboard motor on the panga is turned off and passengers are urged to be very quiet. This visit is frequently at the beginning or towards the end of tours originating at Baltra Airport.

Note: The National Park has deemed this site to be sensitive to the impact of tourism and (as of this writing) allows only boats with a capacity of 16 (or less) passengers to visit.

Unique Photo Opportunities: This will be your best opportunity for photos of marine turtles and white-tipped reef sharks; make sure your polarizer is on the camera (see Chapter VII).

Conway Bay – Situated on the northwestern shore of Santa Cruz close to the islet of Eden (see the Map), Conway Bay is an excellent location for viewing sea lions. The visit will most likely be a private one for your group, as most boats do not include this Visitor Site in their tour of the islands.

Dragon Hill (Cerro Dragón) – This beautiful Visitor Site has recently been opened by the National Park and a growing number of boats include Dragon Hill in their itineraries. After a dry landing at a dock, the walk takes you to a hypersalinic (saltier than the ocean) lagoon behind the beach, often frequented by flamingos. The trail then leads up a winding trail to Dragon Hill, which offers a great view of the bay. This area serves as a nesting site to a growing number of land iguanas. So far, most of the growth is not exactly natural, as many of these iguanas were repatriated from the *Charles Darwin Research Station.* This population will hopefully increase naturally, as the feral dogs that once preyed on them have been erradicated.

Tortuga Bay – Considered by many to be the most beautiful beach in the Galápagos, Tortuga Bay is a half hour walk from Puerto Ayora and is a favorite weekend spot of the locals.

Whale Bay (Bahia Ballena) – Located on the western coast of Santa Cruz (see the Map), Whale Bay is not landed on as much as it is pointed out from the boat as a navigational and historical landmark (going back to the days of the pirates and whalers).

SEYMOUR

This islet is located just north of Baltra and is also called North Seymour (with Baltra occasionally, but rarely, referred to as South Seymour). This is another geological uplift (see the section above on the islet of Mosquera). After a some-times-tricky dry landing, your 1 hour land tour will begin by negotiating a few feet of slippery rocks, past an area where you are likely to encounter some swallow-tailed gulls and, of course, a few sea lions. Soon you'll arrive at one of the major nesting areas of the blue-footed booby. The "nests" include the trail itself; watch where you step. Their breeding cycle does vary, however, and is influenced by several factors, including the overall feeding conditions. You may catch them at any phase of this cycle, and they may in fact have already departed (leaving a few juveniles behind to fend for themselves.

During the first quarter of the year, there is usually a strong northern swell, resulting in good-sized breakers off N. Seymour. As you walk along the beach, there is a good chance of spotting "body-surfing" sea lions. If they're out there riding the waves, this is a great spot to hang out for a few minutes and cheer them on.

Regardless of the time of year, the star attractions of the tour will be the largest colony of magnificent frigatebirds in the Galápagos. Remember, the word "magnificent" here is a noun, not an adjective, and is part of the species name (distinguishing these birds from the other species in the archipelago, the great frigatebird).

A fascinating part of the visit is a close look at a colony of unusual marine iguanas. What is fascinating and unusual is that these iguanas do not eat the algae that makes up the diet of "normal" marine iguanas. Instead, their diet has recently changed – to a succulent plant called *Batis maritima*. Is this an evolved adaptation to a food shortage, and if so, how did it take place? Current research is attempting to answer these questions.

In addition to marine iguanas, it is possible to occasionally spot a land iguana on N. Seymour. Oddly enough, these land iguanas, while endemic to the Galápagos, are an introduced species to N. Seymour. They were brought here from Baltra Island in the 1930s as part of an experiment. While introductions are not an accepted part of science, this one turned out to be fortunate, as the population on Baltra went extinct in the 1940s (after World War II). These animals are slowly being repatriated to Baltra. Your Guide will fill you in on the details.

N. Seymour is another popular destination for the Day Trip boats, and I would say that there is the same potential problem of over-visitation here as there is on South Plaza (see above).

Unique Photo Opportunities: Aside from Española (Hood) Island, this may be your best opportunity for blue-footed booby photos. If the birds have mostly vacated the nesting area, save your "blue foot" film for Española. Also, unless you visit Tower (Genovesa), this may be your only chance of getting some shots of the inflated pouch of the male frigatebird. If the sea lions are body-surfing, it's definitely worth a few shots (although, due to the distance, this is one of the rare times that you need the power of a 300mm telephoto lens to do justice to the subject matter). If you've got a video camera with you, this is an ideal scene to capture.

SOMBRERO CHINO (CHINESE HAT)

Located just off the southeast tip of James Island, Sombrero Chino owes its name to its shape. Perhaps more than any Visitor Site, this islet conveys the volcanic origin of the Galápagos. After a wet landing, the beach soon gives way to an almost primeval landscape of volcanic rubble, including sharp outcroppings, cracked lava formations, and lava tubes. The lava fields encountered here are very fragile and will break beneath your feet; one must be very careful to stay on the trail.

Through it all, Sombrero Chino conveys a strong feeling that you've come to a very special place in the world. The title of Tui de Roy's book, **GALAPAGOS:**

ISLANDS LOST IN TIME, takes on its full meaning here (see the Literature section).

After your land visit, there is usually a snorkeling session across the way, off James Island. This is another of my favorite snorkeling areas; if you have the opportunity, get in the water here!

Note: The National Park has deemed this Site to be sensitive to the impact of tourism and (as of this writing) allows only boats with a capacity of 16 (or less) passengers to visit.

Unique Photo Opportunities: There are several excellent wide-angle opportunities for both landscape and seascape photos, especially late in the afternoon. These shots can be quite dramatic, showing the lava formations in the foreground, with the Chinese hat itself in the distance. While attempting such a shot, I was fortunate enough to catch some sea lions at rest in a lava tube (see Photo #14). This is also one of the few places where you can usually manage to see a pair of oystercatchers if the tide is right.

For those snorkeling here, this is one of the best areas for excellent underwater photos. Under the category of "absurd, silly shots," as you sail away from Sombrero Chino, you can wait for just the right moment to frame the Chinese hat perfectly on the head of your cabin mate. As you sail further away, the boat may (depending on the seas and boat size) approach one of the many surrounding islets (actually and collectively called the Bainbridge Rocks). The particular islet referred to here has a lagoon in its crater, and several flamingos can usually be seen. For this view, you will have to get to the highest point on the boat that is permitted (the Guide will direct you). Both wide-angle and telephoto shots are recommended.

SOUTHERN ISLANDS

Most 1 week Galápagos tours visit all of the southern islands, which are significantly further apart than the central islands. Thus, unless you're on a Cruise Ship or an extremely fast yacht, almost all inter-island travel in these waters is done at night.

ESPANOLA (HOOD) – The southernmost island in the archipelago, Española is the gateway into and out of the Galápagos for some of the sea birds (which will leave the islands either after the breeding season and/or often in times of food shortage). Thus, you will find blue-footed boobies here while their nests further north (on N. Seymour Island, for example) have been abandoned. The remote location relative to the other islands has resulted in a high degree of species differentiation, such as the brightly colored marine iguanas; some species are actually endemic to Española, such as the waved albatross, the Hood mockingbird, and the Española lava lizard.

There are two Visitor Sites on Española, Gardner Bay and Punta Suárez. If I had the option, I would prefer to visit Punta Suárez in the afternoon, during and after the return flights of the sea birds (from their fishing trips).

Gardner Bay – Situated on the northeastern portion of Española, Gardner Bay is a swimming and snorkeling site, with a beach that faces the islet of Gardner-near-Española. You'll have a wet landing amidst a large colony of sea lions. The Visitor Site at Gardner Bay is basically a beach, and there is no trail per se; it is considered an open area. Many visitors stay in one location, admiring and photographing the sea lions at close range. This seems to be the logical thing to do, especially since (and regrettably) many of the Guides sit on the sand and either read a book or talk with other Guides. What happens, though, is that you could miss seeing a Galápagos hawk at close range or a pair of American oystercatchers, Galápagos doves, 3 species of Darwin's finches, the endemic Hood mockingbird, yellow warblers, lava lizards, and marine iguanas. Do as you wish, but be aware of the possibilities.

Gardner Bay is an excellent place to check out your snorkeling equipment (especially for those who flew in to San Cristóbal, as this will be your first full day). Once your check-out is complete, however, the really good snorkeling is off Tortuga Rock, the islet in the distance that, oddly enough, looks like a *tortuga* (turtle).

Punta Suárez – Forming the western tip of Española, Punta Suárez offers the tourist a great abundance of wildlife, especially sea birds, and is one of my favorite Visitor Sites. The National Park Service has recently built a landing dock, so what was once a tricky wet landing is now a relatively easy dry landing, although the *panga* may encounter some chop on its long journey through the breakers. You will marvel at the skill of the *panga* driver. Pay particular attention to protecting your camera equipment from the spray.

After your landing, it will be difficult to concentrate on the Guide's introductory comments, due to all the natural distractions. Aside from the sea lions, you will be approached by the endemic Hood mockingbird, and (especially in the afternoon) red-billed tropicbirds will be winging their way back and forth. The marine iguanas on Española are among the largest in the Galápagos and are brightly colored throughout the year; on other islands, these would be called "seasonal breeding colors." The lava lizards are also above average size, and the female's red throat coloring is pronounced.

Once on the trail you will soon approach a series of tall rock formations on which a colony of masked boobies is generally found. After you continue on, nesting blue-footed boobies will most likely be everywhere on and off the trail. These are the type of scenes you envisioned when your decision was made to visit the Galápagos Islands.

What comes next is even more dramatic, for you will soon approach an open area that forms the home (typically from the end of March through December) to the entire world population (estimated at about 15,000 couples) of waved albatrosses – large, strikingly beautiful birds. You really don't want to leave this area, but you will have to move on, walking along the high cliffs of the southern shore, where the skies are full of sea birds. Finally, before you head back, you will come to a spectacular blowhole, loudly roaring and spouting forth a foamy spray almost 75 ft in the air.

Your tour will take about 3 hours (less if visiting from a Cruise Ship); you'll wish you could stay longer.

Unique Photo Opportunities: This is the place to let loose with the film, so make sure you have plenty in the camera bag when you go ashore. This is an ideal area for video as well. You'll have wonderful opportunities to photograph nesting blue-footed boobies at close range, possibly (depending on the season) even getting a few shots of their dance performance (see Photo #46). Then there are the dramatic poses of the masked boobies, their white body plumage beautifully set off against the grey rocky cliffs. This will be your best chance at photographing masked boobies (see Photo #45). Occasionally, the blue-foots and the masked boobies abandon their eggs, which are then preyed upon by the scavenging Hood mockingbirds, their long, thin bills being well suited for this purpose. This scene is worthy of documentation (see Photo #55). The brightest colors are the Christmas red and green of the marine iguanas, often jumping out at you (the colors – not the iguanas); these shots turn out especially brilliant on an overcast day or when taken late in the afternoon (see Photos #32-33).

If the waved albatrosses are in town (typically April-December), you will go through a lot more film, including shots of them feeding their overgrown, down-covered youngsters and their ritualized courtship displays (perfect for video). When you reach the cliff walk, you can start panning the camera, as the red-billed tropicbirds will be everywhere in the sky. Sometimes the lighting is just right to accent their long streaming tail feathers (see Photos #26-27). Then there's the blowhole, great for wide-angle photography and video (especially when back-lit).

Those are the sure shots. You might also be fortunate enough to get some pictures of a Galápagos hawk and/or perhaps a yellow-crowned night heron; both are frequently seen on Española.

FLOREANA (CHARLES)

Located directly south of Santa Cruz and west of Española, Floreana is also somewhat isolated, being a 4-5 hour cruise from either of its neighbors. The combination of nutrient-rich soil and an adequate water supply make Floreana an island of abundant plant life. This fact was not lost on the centuries of settlers who chose to live and farm on Floreana, giving the island a rich human history (some would call it infamous – see the History section of Chapter II).

There are three official Visitor Sites on Floreana – Punta Cormorán, the Devil's Crown, and Post Office Bay – as well as one unofficial site, the Wittmer Residence on Black Beach.

Punta Cormorán – Forming the northern tip of Floreana, Punta Cormorán is one of the most interesting Visitor Sites in the islands, with an emphasis on plant life and shore birds. Your first lesson will be in geology, however, as the tour begins with a wet landing on a beach with "green sand." Olive green that is, for these are olivine crystals, volcanically-derived silicates of magnesium and iron.

The trail soon leads to a brackish lagoon, where there are usually a few flamingos at the far end, often too far for good photos. The lagoon is also home to white-cheeked pintail ducks and common stilts (and occasionally other shore birds, including western sandpipers, sanderlings, semipalmated plovers, and phalaropes). Surrounding the lagoon are several of the steep, *palo santo*-covered hills that dot Floreana; the stark, grey color and the twisted, usually barren branches give an eerie feeling to this island, whose history is mysterious enough.

The tour continues across the neck of the point to a beach on the other side. Along the way, your Guide will point out a rich variety of plants, including the hairy morning glory, cutleaf daisy, *Lantana,* leather leaf, *palo verde* & *palo santo* trees, passion flower, and *Scalesia.* The endemic *Lantana* is being threatened by the introduced *Lantana,* brought to the islands in 1938 as an ornamental for a family garden; it has now spread over several thousand acres.

The beach at the far end is composed of fine, white sand particles; appropriately enough, it is referred to as "Flour Beach." This beach was formed of coral, finely-digested and excreted by the pencil sea urchin and parrotfish. Here you can often see sting rays feeding right off the shoreline, floating in and out with the wave action. If your feet are in the water, shuffle rather than lifting them; you do not want to step on a sting ray! Listen to your Guide for complete instructions. Also, listen to your Guide for instructions regarding how close you can approach any female sea turtle(s) that crawl up on shore – not to lay eggs but rather to rest up between mating episodes.

Unique Photo Opportunities: You'll want to get at least one documentation shot of the green beach formed of olivine crystals. There are several good photo opportunities at the lagoon, including the flamingos, shorebirds, wide-angle surreal vistas of the *palo santo* trees (see Photo #51), and the cracked lagoon bottom, visible during dry seasons (see Photo #29). This is also one of the best opportunities to take some pictures of the plant life; if you have a macro lens, this is the ideal time for it. If there's an opportunity for shots of the sea turtles, you'll need a polarizer to cut out the reflection of the water. Also, the beach will provide your best chance of seeing and photographing a few ghost crabs as they peek out of their burrows; you have to be as fast as the ghosts to get this shot. For the birders in the audience, be on the lookout for the Galápagos flycatcher and the dark-billed cuckoo on the walk to and from Flour Beach.

Devil's Crown – The Devil's Crown, located just off Punta Cormorán, is said to offer the best snorkeling in the Galápagos (although it tends to be overcrowded at times and is not my favorite Site). In fact, the only way to see the Crown is by water; it is termed a Marine Visitor Site, and no landings are allowed. Sometimes referred to as Onslow Island, this is an almost completely submerged volcano, and erosion has transformed the cone into a series of jagged peaks; as a result, this Site really does look like a devil's crown.

You will typically get to snorkel at Devil's Crown right after visiting Punta Cormorán. The *panga* will take you over to the Site and will remain in the area while you snorkel. This is a necessary safety factor, as the currents here can be very strong. Listen to and heed your Guide's advice and cautions! There are hammerhead sharks that occasionally can be seen just outside Devil's Crown. They are not dangerous, and it is considered safe to swim in the same area; generally, they are well below you and will leave the area as soon as people get in the water.

Unique Photo Opportunities: Snorkeling in the inside of the Crown should provide an excellent opportunity to put your underwater camera through its paces. There is some coral here and many of the colorful fish that you would expect to find around such formations. Be careful not to touch or step on the coral. Unless you're a pretty good free-diver, the waters on the outside are too deep for good photography.

Post Office Bay – Located at the northern end of Floreana, just to the west of Punta Cormorán (see the Map), Post Office Bay is not the most scenic of the Galápagos Visitor Sites, but certainly one of the most famous (see the section on History in Chapter II). For here is where the Post Office Barrel was placed and put into use in the late 18th century by English whaling vessels; soon the American whalers were using this "post office" as well. The idea was for the crew of the outbound ships to deposit any mail for home in the barrel; inbound whalers would then pick up any mail that was destined for their part of the world. You are invited to do the same – leave a post card or two, and pick up any mail from your home area, which you can then post when you get back. This system is typically at least as fast as the regulation postal service, which says a lot about both distribution systems.

Your visit to Post Office Bay will begin with a wet landing. After the trip to the Barrel Post Office, several tours take a short walk to look at the remains of a Norwegian commercial fish drying and canning operation that was started in 1926 and abandoned after a couple of years. A lava tube that extends to the sea is also visited.

You may have some snorkeling time before or after your land visit.

Unique Photo Opportunities: You have to get at least one shot of the Barrel Post Office. This is also a good spot for a "here we are" picture.

Black Beach – By special arrangement, small groups may visit the Wittmer Pension (some Day Trip programs arrange to spend the night there) and meet its famous residents (see the History section in Chapter II). The tour begins with a dry landing at a cement pier and a short walk through the small settlement of Puerto Velasco Ibarra (consisting of mostly administrative buildings).

If you've read your history, this is a visit you won't want to miss. Discuss this possibility with your Tour Operator before the trip and with your Guide at the beginning of your cruise (so that the necessary requests and plans can be made). The Wittmer Pension is the "administration headquarters" of the Post Office Barrel, as well as the official post office for the community, and one of the Wittmers will cancel-stamp your post cards with one or more of the various seals and emblems (there are currently four) of this famous and unusual post office. Other items for sale include Floreana T-shirts and signed copies of the book, **FLOREANA,** by Margret Wittmer (see the Literature section).

Recently, the Wittmer family has begun to offer guided tours of their original settlement in the Highlands of Floreana; the tour requires about 2 hours and has a fixed price per group. Aside from providing a unique look at an important part of Galápagos history, the Floreana Highlands is the only place that the medium tree finch is found.

Unique Photo Opportunities: As of this writing, Margret Wittmer (in her mid-90s) is still occasionally meeting the public and will sometimes consent to pose for a photo.

SAN CRISTOBAL (CHATHAM)

San Cristóbal is the easternmost island in the archipelago.The principal town of Puerto Baquerizo Moreno is the capital of the Galápagos Province; the administration offices and a major Ecuadorian Navy facility are located here, as well as one of the two major airports linking the Galápagos to the mainland. The airport is run by SAN AIRLINES, an affiliate of SAETA.

There are also several Visitor Sites on and around San Cristóbal, including Cerro Brujo, Frigatebird Hill, El Junco Lake, Kicker Rock, Lobos Islet, Playa Ochoa, Sapho Cove, and a new Natural History Interpretation Center in Puerto Baquerizo Moreno.

Puerto Baquerizo Moreno – Located just off the southwestern tip of San Cristóbal, Puerto Baquerizo Moreno is the second largest town in the Galápagos, with a population of 6000. With the recent opening of the major airport (which now has almost as many flights per week as Baltra), it is hoped that local tourism will expand. Indeed, the town would like to take some of the tourist dollars away from Puerto Ayora. But this won't be easy; this is a workingman's town and isn't really oriented (or visually appealing) to many tourists. Most visitors that spend the night here bypass the town altogether, going from the airport to the Grand Hotel, located on an isolated beach on the other side of town. Even the name, Puerto Baquerizo Moreno, is a bit difficult for most tourists. And the name of the town's port, Wreck Bay, is somehow not as cheerful-sounding as Academy Bay.

But the final page of this story has yet to be written. Puerto Baquerizo Moreno, the capital of the Galápagos, has a lot going for it. There are some progressive people in town, and changes are being made, including a growing number of tourist activities (trips to the Highlands, diving, etc). The profile of the main street is slowly developing a more modern look, with a few attractive shops and restaurants. Tourism will certainly increase starting in 1998, with the completion of a beautiful Natural History Interpretation Center. I would imagine that every boat that operates out of San Cristóbal will begin to offer tours of this attractive educational facility to their passengers. And more boats may begin to operate out of San Cristóbal because of the Interpretation Center.

Unique Photo Opportunities: You can get some excellent sunset shots from the beach at the Grand Hotel.

Cerro Brujo – An on-shore version of nearby Kicker Rock, Cerro Brujo is a very striking, eroded tuff cone. The area has a bit of history attached to it as well, as this was one of the first sites visited by Charles Darwin. Captain FitzRoy also climbed to the top of the tuff cone in order to scout out the nearby reefs. Your visit begins with an easy wet landing on a beautiful white coral sand beach. Here you can take a leisurely walk, seasonally viewing brown pelicans, blue-footed boobies and swallow-tailed gulls, in addition to sea lions and marine iguanas. Near the end of the beach, there are lagoons where you can usually find some shore birds. The beauty of this dramatic area can also be experienced by *panga,* where you can explore a tunnel that goes all the way through the eroded rock formation. The visit is capped off with what is normally your first snorkel of the trip; the area is protected and is a good equipment/skills check-out site.

Unique Photo Opportunities: As a visit to Cerro Brujo will usually be on the first day of your Galápagos tour, this will be an excellent time to check out your photo and video equipment. The striking contrast of the tuff formations against the sky can be heightened by the use of a polarizing filter. You should be able to get some excellent wide-angle shots, especially if you take a *panga* ride around the point. Sometimes you can see Kicker Rock (see below) right through the tunnel, with all sorts of creative ways of capturing this scene on film.

Frigatebird Hill – Situated just outside Puerto Baquerizo Moreno, Frigatebird Hill is one of only two Visitor Sites (N. Seymour is the other) where one can see nesting colonies of both species of Frigatebirds (the "great" and "magnificent"). The tour is usually capped off with a stop and swim at the beach, Playa Mann.

El Junco Lake – Located in the Highlands, this is the only sizable fresh water lake in the Galápagos. This Visitor Site is reached by bus or van, and is about a half hour drive from Puerto Baquerizo Moreno. Along the way, you will pass through several Vegetation Zones and the farming community of El Progreso; the settlement has a rather notorious history, dating back to the 1880s, related to the cruel treatment of the workers by its founder, Manuel Cobos (see the History section in Chapter II).

The cavity of the lake is the caldera of an extinct volcano. El Junco is fed by rain water, and the volume varies with the season; it may not be advisable to visit this Site during the rainy season (January-April) because of possible muddy conditions. Incidentally, the name El Junco is not associated with pollution or Chinese boats, but is Spanish for "sedge," which is found along the edges of the lake.

Birders should take note that, aside from the cultural part of a trip to the Highlands of San Cristóbal, this is the best opportunity to see the endemic Chatham mockingbird.

Unique Photo Opportunities: In general, the orientation is the misty view and the birds. You may want a documentation shot of the infamous (at least in Galápagos history) settlement of El Progreso.

Kicker Rock (León Dormido) – Located about an hour and a half to the northeast of Puerto Baquerizo Moreno, Kicker Rock is a remnant of a vertical tuff cone formation, abruptly rising almost 500 ft from the ocean (see Photo #9). Erosion has split the rock and given it its characteristic shape, which some see as a shoe, the origin of the name Kicker Rock. Others see it as a sleeping sea lion, or *León Dormido* in Spanish.

Although not an official Visitor Site (there is no landing area), Kicker Rock is cruised around by most tour boats that are based out of San Cristóbal. Due to its proximity to the San Cristóbal Airport, Kicker Rock is visited on either the first or the last day of most tours. Aside from the beauty of the formation itself, one can usually see several blue-footed boobies, masked boobies, and frigatebirds on the cliffs as well as sea lions along the shore.

Unique Photo Opportunities: This is a great opportunity for wide-angle shots of these unusual formations from several perspectives, including kneeling down and shooting straight up. Some of the best sunrise/sunset shots are taken from the boat with Kicker Rock in silhouette (see Photo #59).

Lobos Islet – Situated less than an hour's ride from Puerto Baquerizo Moreno, Lobos Islet is a seasonal nesting location for the blue-footed booby. There is no annual schedule for their presence, however. This, combined with the rough, rocky terrain, makes Lobos one of my least favorite Visitor Sites. If you feel that you might have difficulty with the walk, skip this land tour.

Playa Ochoa – Due to its proximity to the San Cristóbal airport, Ochoa Beach is sometimes used for the first visit of the trip, and a very good one at that. After a relatively easy wet landing (sometimes more difficult January-April if there are swells from the north), your first sea lion colony (usually a small group) awaits you on the beach. Behind the beach, there is a tidal lagoon, where you can usually spot some shore birds. The rare Chatham mockingbird can also occasionally be seen here.

Ochoa Beach serves as an excellent place for your Guide to check out your snorkeling skills and equipment and to offer instruction as required.

Punta Pitt – Forming the northeast point of San Cristóbal, Punta Pitt is a tuff formation that serves as a nesting site for many sea birds, including blue-footed, masked, and red-footed boobies, frigatebirds, swallow-tailed gulls, and storm petrels. Punta Pitt is considered by many to be a first class Visitor Site. Your tour at Punta Pitt begins with a wet landing; the seas can be a bit rough here at times, so protect your camera equipment.

Unique Photo Opportunities: This is the only location, except of course for Tower (Genovesa) Island, to see and photograph red-footed boobies. There are several good birding photo opportunities on Punta Pitt.

Sapho Cove (Puerto Grande) – Sapho Cove is located on the west coast, near Kicker Rock (see the Map). This well-protected cove has been used as a safe anchorage by sailing ships for hundreds of years. Today it is used by local fisherman to refit their boats and as a swimming area for tourists. There is a wet landing on the beach.

SANTA FE (BARRINGTON)

The island of Santa Fé is located in the southeastern portion of the archipelago, between the towns of Puerto Ayora (on Santa Cruz) and Puerto Baquerizo Moreno (on San Cristóbal). It's about a 2 hour cruise from Puerto Ayora and about 3 hours from Puerto Baquerizo Moreno. Santa Fé is another volcanic uplift (see the description of Mosquera in the Central Island section).

Your tour begins with a wet landing (on the northeastern portion of the island) at a beach known for ornery sea lion bulls. The trail has recently been redone by the Park Service, making it much easier to traverse. The main attraction here is the opportunity to find and observe one of the few remaining land iguanas of the species (*Conolophus pallidus*) endemic to Santa Fé Island. Some of these land iguanas can be 5 ft. long and have a beautiful golden-yellow color that shows off the scales to advantage, almost like a knight's mail (see Photo

#36). Also, the spines along its back are very pronounced. In the same area, you'll also see a forest of giant prickly pear cactus. The height is an adaptive mechanism to protect them from the land iguanas and giant tortoises (now extinct on Santa Fé).

After your tour, swimming and snorkeling often follow. Be cautious about the somewhat-aggressive sea lion bulls (that are known to frequent this area) in the water.

Unique Photo Opportunities: The yellow coloring makes the endemic Santa Fé species of land iguana the most photogenic; avail yourself of this opportunity. You will also want a documentation shot of the giant prickly pear cactus trees (see Photo #53). Have a person stand in front for a size comparison. Also, there are some great panoramic views, including your boat in the harbor.

THE NORTHERN ISLANDS

The majority of the boats do not visit the northern portion of the archipelago during a 1 week tour; notable exceptions include the Cruise Ships and some of the better yachts. Almost all 10 day and 2 week cruises visit Tower (Genovesa), the only northern island with Visitor Sites. Marchena Island is a Marine Diving Site only, and Pinta is "off-limits."

TOWER (GENOVESA)

Located in the northeast portion of the Galápagos (less than half a degree north of the equator), Tower is an outpost for many sea birds (as Española is in the south). Perhaps this is why they are two of my favorite islands to visit. The visit, however, is not an easy one for the captain and crew. First, it is a tiring 8-10 hour all-night cruise from Puerto Ayora, Santa Cruz Island. Second, the entrance to Darwin Bay is extremely narrow as well as shallow (being part of the outer rim of a volcanic crater) and must be negotiated during daylight hours, preferably at high tide.

Interestingly, there are no land reptiles on Tower, only very small marine iguanas. This is attributed to the direction of the ocean currents, which evidently wouldn't have carried the terrestrial animals here.

Note: The island has two Visitor Sites (see below), although the National Park has deemed Prince Philip's Steps to be sensitive to the impact of tourism and (as of this writing) allows only boats with a capacity of 16 (or less) passengers to visit; thus, the larger boats (including the Cruise Ships) only visit Darwin Bay.

Darwin Bay – As mentioned above, the anchorage at Darwin Bay, located on the southern portion of the island (see the Map), is actually the caldera of an extinct, partially-eroded volcano, with the surrounding cliffs forming the inner portion of the rim. While the origin of the name Tower is not known, one can imagine it had something to do with these towering cliffs. The tour will be a long, fairly-easy walk, but it is usually hot and dry here, so you may want to carry some water.

After a wet landing on a coral beach, the trail begins in an area where there are several swallow-tailed gulls. Often, they nest along the trail, and the Guide will warn you to be careful as you walk. As you walk back from the beach, there is a mixture of *Opuntia* cactus and mangroves. This is actually a rich intertidal zone, and you can find a wide diversity of animal life, including juvenile yellow-crowned night herons, lava gulls, nesting red-footed boobies (in the mangroves), and even fiddler crabs. Soon, you begin to walk on the edge of a dense "forest" of salt bush, where you will find more red-foots as well as great frigatebirds. The trail continues past a beautiful tide pool area. In fact, the entire area including the trail becomes a tide pool at high tide; for this reason, and whenever possible, the Guides try to arrange this visit at low tide. From here on, the trail becomes somewhat difficult, traversing *aa* lava until you reach a cliffside, with a commanding view of the bay. The view sometimes includes a few Galápagos sharks.

Unique Photo Opportunities: You'll have some excellent opportunities at photographing the endemic swallow-tailed gull; make sure you focus tightly on the red eye-ring. The red-footed boobies also make wonderful subjects. There usually tends to be bright sun on this part of the tour, thus washing out the beautiful facial coloring of the red-foots, so I prefer to get close-ups on the other Visitor Site, Prince Philip's Steps. The great frigates are also great subjects, especially during February-May, when the males are courting and have their large, bright-red gular sacs inflated, hoping to attract a female flying overhead. This scene makes for great video as well, with the audio portion picking up the male's high-pitched, turkey-like, "I'm available" call. Whether you're shooting video or using a still camera, take off the polarizing filter to capture the green iridescent sheen on the male's back, as iridescence is a reflected color (and would be absorbed by the polarizer).

Prince Philip's Steps – This tour begins with a fantastic *panga* ride along the base of the cliffs. During the ride, you can look directly up and see one redbilled tropicbird after the other trying to make a precise landing in their nest (usually a crevice on an overhanging ledge). Squadrons of frigatebirds are seen flying back and forth in their endless piratical pursuits. Red-footed boobies are perched on branches of *palo santo* trees which seem to grow out of the cliffs. And you haven't even stepped ashore yet.

Your *panga* ride continues until you reach the landing area, located near the eastern tip of Darwin Bay (see the Map). As the *panga* slows to land, you may notice a few fur seals in the water or resting on the shore. A dry landing is made at the base of a steep rock staircase named Prince Philip's Steps, in honor of His Majesty's royal visit in the 1960s. Although the climb is steep, the National Park has recently constructed a handrail, making the ascent quite manageable. You'll be at the top within a minute; go ahead and time it!

Once at the top, a trail enters an open area where nesting masked boobies and great frigatebirds are found. This is also a good place to see Galápagos doves and sharp-beaked ground finches (also called "vampire" finches – ask your Guide for the origin of this name). Soon, a wooded area begins, a forest of dwarf *palo santo* trees, in which a colony of red-footed boobies is perched. Eventually the woods give way to an open lava field near the western coast.

Storm petrels are usually seen here in great numbers, sometimes in the tens of thousands. Although the petrels seem to be aimlessly swarming, if you let your eyes follow a single individual, you will eventually see it land and enter its home (a small crevice in the lava or part of a lava tube). It is able to locate its home by a very acute sense of smell. If you look very carefully (with the aid of binoculars) you will often spot something else looking very carefully – a short-eared owl – lurking on the lava field in search of its next fill-up of petrel.

Unique Photo Opportunities: Have a couple of rolls of film handy and your telephoto lens on during the *panga* ride; the sea birds flying overhead offer seemingly-endless shooting opportunities. The *palo santo* forest is the best place for red-footed booby photos, including close-ups of their feet and face. The facial colors are incredibly beautiful and intricately complex; slow film is in order, as one of these shots will most probably be a blowup!

THE WESTERN ISLANDS

Very few of the boats visit the western islands of Fernandina and Isabela during a 1 week tour. The Cruise Ships and some of the yachts do travel to Tagus Cove, Isabela and Punta Espinosa, Fernandina as part of their weekly itinerary. However, for an extensive trip along the entire length of Isabela, including an optional climb to the rim of one of the volcanoes, a 2 week Galápagos Island tour is required. And highly recommended!

The western islands have a pristine, untouched quality that you won't find in the other regions of the Galápagos. This is most evident as you sail along the western coast of Isabela and through the narrow Bolívar Channel separating the island from Fernandina. These islands are still volcanically active, and fumaroles of steam and gas venting from the distant volcanoes can be seen from the boat. The fact that you only meet perhaps one other boat during your entire visit to the western islands only adds to the unique sense of adventure that is felt in this part of the archipelago.

The western islands receive a double dose of upwelling (from both the Humboldt and Cromwell Currents). As a result, there is cool nutrient-rich water, and the marine life is abundant – including penguins, flightless cormorants, and the largest population of whales in the Galápagos. Going on-deck at night and viewing the southern sky as well as the numerous large bioluminescent particles in the water (that seem to remain "on" for several seconds) is quite the experience. A trip to the western islands definitely rounds out and completes a tour of the Galápagos.

FERNANDINA (NARBOROUGH)

Fernandina is just over a 100,000 years old and is the youngest of the Galápagos Islands. Volcanically it is also the most active, with eruptions still occurring every few years, most recently in 1995 (a spectacular event, viewed in awe by many visitors). In 1968, the crater floor (4 miles by 3 miles across) collapsed about 1000 ft, a geological event of "most significant" status in Galápagos recorded history. This event was accompanied by hundreds of earthquakes, and fumes of ashes were gas-propelled 15 miles into the air.

There is only one Visitor Site on Fernandina – Punta Espinosa.

Punta Espinosa – Punta Espinosa is a wonderful Visitor Site – my favorite one in the Galápagos! Located on the northeast portion of Férnandina, across the channel from Tagus Cove, Isabela, it is a narrow point of land (more like lava and sand) extending out from the base of the Fernandina Volcano. Your tour begins with a dry landing, and you may spot a few penguins from the *panga* on one of the rocky islets that dot this part of the coast. Due to several geologic uplifts, the dock is at landing level only during high tides, and other landing sites are used at lower tides. Once ashore, you proceed to the tip of the point across a sandy area which serves as a nesting site for the marine iguana (seasonally, during the first half of the year). The nests can be spotted as holes in the sand, and care must be taken not to step on them, or on the numerous creatures themselves. Indeed, Fernandina has the largest colony of marine iguanas in the Galápagos.

As you near the tip of the point, you will pass a large colony of sea lions. There are several territories encompassing both sides of the point, and the loud barks of several resident bulls blend with the hard pounding of the surf to add a dimension of sound to the experience. Starting in this area, and continuing out to the tip, are the flightless cormorants, nesting on the open rocks just above the high tide line. Occasionally, an adult will come out of the water bearing a piece of seaweed for the nest.

After walking the point for about a half hour, you retrace your steps almost to the landing area and continue on to a second trail which winds its way through a lava field. The recent volcanic activity is obvious from all the fissures, so watch your step. In fact, the land here is very fragile, and care must be taken to stay on the trail. While the lava flow has obliterated much of the vegetation on Fernandina, several pioneering plants can be observed, including clumps of lava cactus. If you visit Punta Espinosa at low tide, your tour will probably include a visit to the tide pool area, just past the lava field. This is a great place to sit and watch; there usually is something very special going on – sea lion pups interacting, sea turtles, rays, shore bird activity, etc. After your visit, you will probably snorkel at one of several locations, depending on the waves and currents. This is one of my favorite snorkels, with good to excellent chances for seeing penguins, flightless cormorants, sea turtles, and (at low tide) marine iguanas feeding on algae.

Unique Photo Opportunities: The sea lions are most photogenic when silhouetted against the high waves. I was able to spot two bulls standing at the edge of their territories and barking "not one step further" warnings at each other (see Photo #18). This is one of the few locations to photograph the flightless cormorant. The classic shot is taken after they exit the water as their atrophied wings are spread to dry the feathers (see Photo #57). If you are able to get close to a cormorant, position yourself the best you can to get a gleam of reflected light in the eye, which is a beautiful turquoise color. This is also my favorite spot for iguana photos, with several sitting together, regally posed, with their "arms" around each other – the **"GOOD FELLAS"** shot! One of my other favorites is a lava lizard sitting on the head of a marine iguana, a scene that happens more often than you would think. Finally, there are several wide-angle vista opportunities, with the dramatic shield volcano of Fernandina in the background.

ISABELA (ALBEMARLE)

With over 1800 square miles (more than half the land surface area in the archipelago), and about 80 miles in length, the seahorse-shaped Isabela is the largest island in the Galápagos. This wasn't always the case, as originally there were six islands, each with an active volcano. The extensive lava flows from the six volcanoes (Alcedo, Cerro Azul, Darwin, Ecuador, Sierra Negra, and Wolf) joined together and formed what is today Isabela. Five of the six volcanoes (all but Ecuador) are still active. The Wolf Volcano is the highest point, at 5600 ft.

There are several Visitor Sites on Isabela, including Punta Albemarle, Elizabeth Bay, Punta García, Punta Moreno, Tagus Cove, Punta Tortuga, Urvina Bay, and the town of Villamil. Two of the volcanoes, Alcedo and Sierra Negra, are also Visitor Sites.

Punta Albemarle – Located at the northern tip of Isabela (forming the horns or raised ears of the seahorse), Punta Albemarle was used as a radar base by the U.S. during World War II. As one sails past, the abandoned water tanks can be viewed through a pair of binoculars. Often that's all that will be seen, as very few boats land here, due in part to the rough surf. The waters in this region seem to be very productive, and there are excellent chances for seeing whales here. So if you're passing by during the day, keep your collective eyes open!

Elizabeth Bay – Elizabeth Bay is situated on the west coast, about a third of the way up, at the narrow Perry Isthmus (6 miles wide). This is a Marine Visitor Site; landings are not permitted. The tour is a *panga* ride that begins with a visit to a few rocky islets (called "the Marielas") where a colony of penguins is usually found. The penguins prefer the cooler waters of the western portion of the archipelago, and the greatest part of their population is found in this area. Flightless cormorants and giant marine iguanas are also seen. The largest marine iguanas in the Galápagos are found on Isabela, due to the upwelling activity which produces plentiful marine iguana food – algae.

The tour continues as the *panga* enters a narrow cove, lined with large red mangrove trees. Here, marine turtles, rays, and shore birds can be seen.

Unique Photo Opportunities: This is one of the best areas for penguin photos. There is limited lighting around the rocky caves where they are seen, and since most penguins are spotted early or late in the day, high speed (ASA 400) film is recommended. The backgrounds are beautiful, with the Alcedo Volcano to the north, the Sierra Negra Volcano to the south, and Fernandina across the water.

Punta García – Punta García is located on the eastern coast, across the Isabela Channel from James Island. Except for early in the morning, the dry landing is not an easy one. Sometimes not a very dry one either. All things considered, this is not my favorite Visitor Site, but it is the only opportunity to visit Isabela (and to see flightless cormorants) without sailing around to the western shore.

Unique Photo Opportunities: Aside from the lava flows, the subject here is the flightless cormorant (see the section above on Punta Espinosa, Fernandina

Island). Take extra care in protecting your camera and photographic equipment on the usually-rough *panga* ride.

Punta Moreno – Situated on the southwest portion of Isabela, Punta Moreno is often the first western island Visitor Site for boats approaching from the south. The tour begins with a *panga* ride along the beautiful rocky shores where penguins and shore birds, including great blue herons, are usually spotted. The *panga* then enters a grove of mangroves, where oysters can be seen at the base of the trees. After a dry landing, a difficult trek begins that traverses the sharpest lava rocks in the islands. This is another tour to skip if you're not up for a rough hike. Also, this is a harsh, dry climate, and you may want to pack some water.

While the terrain is rough, this is a recommended tour. The environment is enigmatic; the driest lava fields you will ever see are interspersed with lagoons and small ponds containing abundant wildlife, including a few pintail ducks and flamingos. There are several clumps of lava cactus and other pioneering plants here, but a species of *Scalesia* is also seen, as is the carpenter bee, one of the few insect pollinators in the *Galápagos.* There is verification at every vantage point that the advanced forms were here first and were partially displaced by subsequent eruptions of the Sierra Negra Volcano.

Unique Photo Opportunities: The *panga* ride offers the opportunity of several dramatic seascapes, especially early in the morning. In fact, this is one of the best sunrise areas I've seen in the Galápagos. The *Scalesia* plants here make beautiful subjects, in particular when the bright green is shown in contrast to the stark, black lava.

Tagus Cove – Tagus Cove is located on the west coast, about two thirds of the way up Isabela, across the narrow channel from Fernandina. As soon as your boat enters this protected cove, you can (as they say) "see the writing on the wall." For here indeed are written the names of many ships, some dating back to the 1800s, but unfortunately the majority is recent grafitti (courtesy of Navy vessels for the most part). After a dry landing, you can view the graffiti from a closer distance, where it doesn't look any prettier.

The land tour is a bit strenuous in that a steep climb is involved; some people with difficulty walking may want to remain on the boat. This is also another of those dry areas, and a sip of packed water may be refreshing after the uphill climb. The tour begins at a trail leading to a salt water lagoon. The trail then slopes up the base of the Darwin Volcano, providing a great view of the fragile lava fields, the volcanic formations, and the ocean as well.

My favorite part of this Visitor Site is a *panga* ride along the coast, especially late in the afternoon when the colors are very dramatic. The experience is wonderful, with the beautiful tuff formations & rocky outcroppings with blue-footed boobies, penguins, and marine iguanas. You will approach large caves with invertebrates on the lower walls and brown noddy terns above, and there are usually quite a few pleasant surprises along the way.

Unique Photo Opportunities: As you sail through the Bolívar Channel between Fernandina and Isabela, be on the lookout for whales and whale footprints (see the section on Whales in Chapter III). Several whales travel alone through this passage. The salt water lagoon, sometimes referred to as Darwin Lake, is optically interesting in that the water level looks at times higher and at other times lower than sea level. You may be able to capture both effects on film. The view from the plateau at the end of the trail can provide some dramatic shots, with the rugged volcanic landscape in the foreground and the ocean in the distance. If you take the *panga* ride, use ASA 400 film and bring plastic bags to cover your camera and camera bag. In the afternoon the lighting is very dramatic; the use of a polarizing filter will heighten the emotional tone and contrast of the scene.

Punta Tortuga – Located just north of Tagus Cove on the west coast of Isabela, Punta Tortuga is a bathing beach surrounded by mangroves. This is one of the few sites where the mangrove finch (one of the two tool-using finches) can be found in the Galápagos.

Urvina Bay – Urvina Bay is situated on the west coast of Isabela at the base of the Alcedo Volcano. In 1954, almost 4 miles of its coastal seabed, marine life and all, were dramatically and suddenly uplifted about 15 ft. This event is associated with an eruption of the Alcedo Volcano. The coastline was driven three-quarters of a mile further out to sea, forever exposing giant coral heads and stranding marine organisms on what was now the shore. The marine remnants and coral skeletons, some of them waist-high, are visited after a wet landing on the beach. The landing can be a bit rough, so protect your photographic equipment.

Urvina Bay is also a nesting site for the brown pelican and flightless cormorant. Giant marine iguanas are also seen in this area along the coast, which you will visit prior to the uplifted marine relics. On the extensive inland hike (carry water, and wear long pants to protect your legs from the thorn bushes) you will also see a few large land iguanas. Occasionally, a tortoise or two can also be seen.

Note: Your Guide will remind you that it is illegal to take any of the marine remnants, including the deteriorating coral formations. Remember, if everyone took a little piece, in a short time there wouldn't be much left.

Unique Photo Opportunities: Aside from documenting this unusual geologic event, there are several surreal scenes of the uplifted marine skeletons that you will want to put on film. If the flightless cormorants are nesting, the scene is usually a wonderful photo/video opportunity. Long lenses are usually required, as you probably won't get closer than 15 feet.

Villamil – The town of Villamil is located on the southeastern coast of Isabela. Villamil was founded in 1897 by Antonio Gil as the center of a lime-producing operation (achieved by burning coral). During the same time period, a second town called Santo Tomás was located a few miles inland. Santo Tomás, named for the volcano next door (now generally called Sierra Negra), was formed as a small-scale sulfur operation, mined from the crater. A coffee plantation was also established. The combined population of the two towns is about 1000 people, and their principal source of income is fishing. There has recently been an attempt to promote tourism, with the opening of a small plane airport (which doesn't seem to be very practical, as most residents can't afford the service, and most tourists are already on a boat). Also, to really increase tourism, the conservation ethic of the locals will have to be raised a few notches. Aside from Villamil being the center for illegal fishing, as well as legal, traditional fisheries, the once-beautiful sandy streets are fairly polluted. Hopefully, this will change in the future.

On a more positive note, the *Galápagos National Park Service* has recently opened a Tortoise Breeding and Rearing Center located just outside the town of Villamil (to protect and increase the endangered populations of giant tortoises in southern Isabela). This Center is very well designed, the setting is very attractive, and the tortoises have ample space & shade. A must visit if you're in Villamil for a tour of the Sierra Negra Volcano (see below).

Adjacent to Villamil are several lagoons where flamingos and common stilts are usually seen; these are nesting areas from November-April, but the birds also feed here for a good portion of the year. There are also some very beautiful beaches that, along with the lagoons, are said to be among the most significant migratory bird viewing areas in the Galápagos.

There are visitor accommodations in Villamil, often used by tourists preparing to take the trip up the Sierra Negra Volcano (see below).

Unique Photo Opportunities: This is an excellent opportunity to photograph the common stilt, a most graceful and elegant bird; sometimes a few branches in the foreground can help accentuate these qualities (see Photo #56). Actually, I have found the lagoons here to be the most opportune as well as dramatic areas in the islands to capture many of the shore birds on film, including flamingos, whimbrels, and occasional migrants.

Sierra Negra Volcano – Located in the southern portion of Isabela, the Sierra Negra Volcano is below the Perry Isthmus and above the Cerro Azul Volcano. Sierra Negra is considered to be the oldest and largest volcano on Isabela, with its caldera measuring about 5 miles by 6 miles across. A full day trip to the rim of Sierra Negra is available as an option to some of the 2 week Galápagos tours.

The tour begins at Villamil where a rented vehicle takes the group to Santo Tomás. From here, the 3-7 hour round-trip to the caldera can be made on foot or by horseback. The tour continues around the rim of the caldera until the Volcán Chico area is reached, a series of craters with fumaroles (columns of volcanic steam and gas) rising into the air. This area last erupted in 1979, but that event was not as dramatic as the month-long eruption of 1963. The site of vast sulfur deposits (vented from the fumarole of the "Sulfur Volcano," as it is called) is also visited. Along the way, you will usually be able to see vermillion flycatchers, Galápagos martins, whimbrels, egrets, Galápagos hawks, and possibly the dark-billed cuckoo. At the end of the walk, you will be rewarded with an incredible panoramic view of Isabela, including the Perry Isthmus and the east/west coast lines.

Your very full day tour will usually also include a visit to the Tortoise Breeding and Rearing Center, located just outside the town of Villamil, and the lagoons in the town itself.

Note: The weather is often overcast and misty. Rain gear is always advised. The comfort level is actually higher when it is overcast, as you will eventually ascend through the *garúa* (mist) into clear, sunny, and often hot weather. If it is sunny down below, you are in for one hot day.

Unique Photo Opportunities: The scenery of the Highlands, the fumaroles, and the misty environment combine to present many photographic opportunities – often spectacular and quite beautiful, sometimes surreal, probably dramatic, always unique, and quite often all the above. Your camera gear should be packed securely and in a plastic bag as well. In fact, if you are doing this excursion by horseback, you may consider leaving your long lenses on-board the boat. Even though the vista shots are incredible, you still may not want to take your good camera; instead you can just pack a point-and-shoot or disposable camera (they are available with 3 X 10 panoramic views). This precaution is just to avoid the possibility of your good camera's electronics getting jostled into amnesia on the horseback ride.

Alcedo Volcano – The Alcedo Volcano is centrally located and just north of the Perry Isthmus. Aside from Sierra Negra, Alcedo is the oldest and largest of the volcanoes on Isabela, with the caldera measuring about 4 miles by 5 miles across. There are several steaming fumaroles, often used by hikers as a landmark, with the largest of these steam and gas vents called "the Geyser." The main attraction on Alcedo is the tortoises, over 4000 of them – the largest population in the Galápagos. They are in the wild, not in holding pens.
    Note: At this time, there is bad news to report on Alcedo. The population of tortoises described above is very much in danger, as their habitat is rapidly disappearing along with their food. Disappearing before our eyes (and those of the tortoises) as introduced goats are denuding almost all the vegetation. These goats have crossed the Perry Isthmus (once considered a virtually impassable lava field) from southern Isabela, where they were introduced by man. They have reproduced rapidly, and their numbers on Alcedo are reckoned in the multiple tens of thousands.
    Due to this continuing crisis, the Visitor Site at the Alcedo Volcano has been closed since 1995, as the National Park and Darwin Station have been conducting an intensive goat eradication program. Some success has been made, but there is a long way to go. The *Charles Darwin Foundation* needs all your help and support to wage this difficult battle and save these tortoises; for details, see the section on Growth, Tourism, and Conservation in Chapter II.
    Depending on the success of this program, the Visitor Site at Alcedo may be reopened in the future. If so, typically only those on 2 week Galápagos tours will have the opportunity to make this arduous trek, as a 2-3 day trip to the rim of Alcedo is recommended (due to the physical exertion required). It is a long 6 mile climb (4-6 hours), part of it over steep, rugged terrain. So you have to be physically fit. And have a strong back, because you'll have to pack 25-35 pounds up the volcano. Unlike the hike to Sierra Negra, there is no nearby town to rent horses or hire porters to carry the camping equipment, food, and water (one-half gallon per person per day minimum). In addition, most Tour Operators require passengers to supply their own sleeping bags, backpacks, water bottle, and flashlight. Eating/cooking utensils, food, and tents are usually provided.
    To complicate things further, it's best if all the passengers go on the trek. Those that stay behind must remain on the boat for the duration of the hike; they

cannot even take a walk on the beach (because the legally-required Guide is elsewhere, climbing the side of a volcano). The result is that the Tour Operator can have problems putting the trip together, because while some of the prospective passengers may be avid hikers, usually some are not, and the rest "aren't sure."

The Alcedo Volcano climb begins early in the day (around 4:00 a.m.) with a wet landing at Shipton Cove on the east coast of Isabela. The approach trail is fairly easy, a gradual incline over smooth pumice (porous lava – basically road construction material). The final ascent, however, is very steep, the terrain is very uneven, and the unmarked "trail" is overgrown with shrubs. The last few hundred feet can take over an hour to negotiate. The rim is reached early in the afternoon, before the severe heat of the day. After a light lunch and a well-earned rest, camp is made. Once the tents are pitched and the gear stowed, a trek part way round the rim is made (without most of the weight). After the return to camp, the gas stove is lit, and dinner is under way. The fare will probably be freeze-dried mountaineering food (perhaps *fettuccine Alcedo*). No matter, it will be delicious. As your Guide will point out, no campfires are permitted.

The following day brings a sunrise you don't want to miss. In your mind, you will want to savor the experience at this location, the edge of a still-active volcano, a special place on earth where few people have set foot. Breakfast will be followed by a more extensive hike along the rim. The views are wonderful in every direction. In addition to the tortoises, there are several Galápagos hawks, vermillion flycatchers, and Galápagos martins in the area. Those on a 2 day Alcedo trip will then break camp and head back down (about 4 hours to the beach). All trash has to be packed out. If you're making a 3 day Alcedo trek, you get to experience another night on the rim.

Unique Photo Opportunities: I can think of no better way of describing the photographic opportunities that await the visitor to the Alcedo Volcano than to refer the reader to the opening pages of Tui de Roy's inspiring book, **GALAPAGOS: ISLANDS LOST IN TIME.** Softly-lit tortoises immersed in pools of mud and rain with several fumaroles in the distance, a hawk spreading its talons to land while a storm builds over the caldera – one photo after the other perfectly captures the images of Alcedo. You and I can do our best and capture our own images as we see them. It's mostly a matter of being there with a camera in hand and a positive-thinking eye.

THE OUTER ISLANDS

The outer islands of Darwin (Culpepper) and Wolf (Wenman) are, as they say, off the scale; they are located way to the northwest, separated from the other islands by about 100 miles. There are no Visitor Sites on Darwin and Wolf, although their waters offer the best and most challenging diving in the Galápagos (see the section on Diving Tours in Chapter IV).

LITERATURE

This section is divided into categories of essential ("must"), recommended, and background (or reference) reading. Some of these publications are becoming a little easier to find in the U.S., especially in travel-oriented bookstores, but there is still a reasonably good chance that your local, friendly bookshop will have to place a special order for you.

Once in Quito, you will want to visit **Libri Mundi** (located at Juan León Mera 851), without a doubt the best bookstore in Ecuador; they have a comprehensive selection of Galápagos literature. While **Libri Mundi** has a smaller branch in the arcade mall of the Hotel Colón, the main store is just a few blocks away from the major hotels.

Many of these books are also available through **Galápagos Travel,** the publisher of the book you are reading; call (800) 969-9014 to confirm availability, price and delivery, and/or to place an order.

MUST READING

I consider the following books and published material to be "must reading" for those wanting to learn as much as possible about the Galápagos prior to, during, and after touring the islands. Many of these books will allow you to more fully comprehend what the Naturalist Guide (and/or Tour Leader) is pointing out, and you will thus be able to ask more advanced questions. You will also be able to identify more species and behavioral characteristics on your own. Finally, you'll be free to tune out some of the tour lecture (to the extent that you are familiar with the material being discussed) and concentrate on picture taking.

THE BEAK OF THE FINCH, Jonathan Weiner, 1994. New York: Alfred Knopf. Easy-to-read, this is one of the most significant and enlightening books on evolution since Darwin's **Origin of Species.** The author presents a very personal account of the research on Darwin's finches conducted by Peter & Rosemary Grant. The Grants have been studying the finches on the island of Daphne Major in the Galápagos since 1973. During this time, they witnessed and thoroughly documented evolutionary changes in the finches – a truly significant scientific achievement. The second half of the book is quite thought-provoking, as Weiner puts the Grants' findings into the context of contemporary evolutionary research and thought. *Winner of the Pulitzer Prize for Nonfiction in 1995, this book is very highly recommended to everyone as must reading.*

A FIELD GUIDE TO THE FISHES OF GALAPAGOS, 3rd Edition, Godfrey Merlin, 1988. Quito, Ecuador: Libri Mundi. An indispensable identification guide; the color illustrations are superb. Available in Quito and the Galápagos. *There is usually a race for this book after a Galápagos snorkeling session "to see what we saw."*

GALAPAGOS: A NATURAL HISTORY GUIDE, M.H. Jackson, 1993. Calgary: University of Calgary Press. This is, without a doubt, the most comprehensive natural history guide to the Galápagos Islands, including well-written chapters on evolution & ecology, plant life, reptiles, sea birds, land birds, native mammals, intertidal & marine life, and conservation. In addition, the first 3 chapters give the reader an environmental, historical, and scientific background to the Galápagos. Both a General Index and Species Index are provided as well as a complete checklist of plants and animals. *Of all the books, this is the most important. Buy this book as soon as you can, and take it with you!*

A GUIDE TO THE BIRDS OF THE GALAPAGOS ISLANDS, Isabel Castro and Antonia Phillips, 1996. Princeton, NJ: Princeton University Press. Recently published, this compact 5" x 8" book is currently the only field guide to the Galápagos avifauna – many of which are endemic to the archipelago. Isabel Castro has worked for the *Charles Darwin Research Station* in the Galápagos, and her comprehensive descriptions include up-to-date details, including more behavioral information than birding field guides typically provide. *If you're serious about bird identification, bring this book with you.*

GUIDE TO THE VISITOR SITES OF THE PARQUE NACIONAL GALAPAGOS, 3rd edition, Alan Moore, Miguel Cifuentes, and Tui De Roy, 1996. Galápagos: *Servicio Parque Nacional Galápagos.* A concise guide to all touring areas, including maps and principal attractions (plants & animals). Bilingual – a real practical way to learn Spanish words and phrases pertaining to the wildlife of the Galápagos. This newly-printed 3rd edition is most welcome, as this excellent book had been out of print for several years. *Available only in mainland Ecuador and the Galápagos; buy it as soon as you can find it.*

THE NEW KEY TO ECUADOR AND THE GALAPAGOS, David Pearson and David Middleton, 1996. Berkeley: Ulysses Press. Recently published, this is a very comprehensive guide for touring mainland Ecuador. The information is very complete and up-to-date. All the detail you could want – crisp analysis, informative background descriptions, good maps, multiple day sample itineraries, day trip options and thorough Tour Operator contact info. *This is an excellent book, essential for those who will be spending some time in mainland Ecuador.*

PLANTS OF THE GALAPAGOS ISLANDS, Eileen Schofield, 1984. New York: Universe Books. This handy pocket-sized book is the best field guide to the flora of the Galápagos Islands. Illustrated by the author, this book will help you identify the unique and unusual plants of the Galápagos.

REEF FISH IDENTIFICATION: GALAPAGOS, Paul Humann, 1993. Orlando, FL: New World Publications. This comprehensive, easy-to-use guide is an excellent source for identification of Galápagos marine creatures. In addition to over 250 exceptional I.D.-quality photos, the guide offers information on behavior, distribution, distinctive features, and different phases of Galápagos fishes, as well as an index to marine mammals and reptiles. *An invaluable field guide and a must for all serious snorkelers & divers.*

THE STARS: A NEW WAY TO SEE THEM, H.A. Rey, 1980. Boston: Houghton Mifflin. Absolutely the best, easiest-to-read guide to the stars. It's also relatively inexpensive. The book is also a great beginner's astronomy text, with clear explanations of the seasons, the zodiac, time & time zones, planets, light-years, and even normally-difficult concepts such as celestial latitude (declination) & longitude (right ascension). The illustrations and sky charts are also excellent. For the Galápagos night sky, refer to Calendar Chart 15, "The Sky As Seen From Any Place Between Latitudes 10° North and 10° South." *If you're a star gazer or even "just interested in the stars," buy this book and take it with you.*

RECOMMENDED READING

DARWIN, Adrian Desmond and James Moore, 1991. New York: W.W. Norton. There have been a lot of Darwin biographies written in the last few years, but this is widely acknowledged as the definitive one. **Darwin** is a monumental work (808 pages), opening the doors for us to contemplate the full panorama of Victorian science within a very turbulent social and political climate. In this context, we see the full development of Darwin's thoughts on transmutation (evolution) by natural selection, his inner struggle on when and how to communicate his ideas, and the emotional & physical toll he paid nearly every day. The subtitle for this book is most apt – **The Life of A Tormented Evolutionist.** *If you have a serious interest in Darwin and the history of science, get this book, take your time reading it, and let it all sink in.*

ECUADOR & THE GALAPAGOS ISLANDS: A TRAVEL SURVIVAL KIT, Rob Rachowiecki, 1992. Berkeley: Lonely Planet Publications. A good, readable guide to Ecuador, including hotels, restaurants, shopping, and touring in all regions of the country; there are complete sections on Quito and Guayaquil. *Written for the backpacker/outdoor adventurer. The information on the Galápagos is of the summary variety.*

THE ENCHANTED ISLANDS: THE GALAPAGOS DISCOVERED, John Hickman, 1985. Dover, NH: Tanager Books. An excellent human history of the Galápagos, from the Incas, through the whaling and buccaneer era, the days of Darwin, and up to modern day tourism, including issues of conservation.

FISHES OF THE PACIFIC COAST, Gar Goodson, 1988. Palo Alto, CA: Stanford University Press. This guidebook will familiarize you with the fishes of the

Pacific coast including the Galápagos Islands. Each species is shown in full color along with a thorough guide to identification and description of behavioral traits. The book also illustrates the differences between a juvenile, adult, and breeding stage of the same fish. *Inexpensive and very informative.*

FLOREANA, Margret Wittmer, 1989. Shropshire, England: Anthony Nelson Ltd. Margret Wittmer has written her own firsthand version of the mysterious deaths and disappearances that took place on Floreana Island during the 1930s (see **The Galápagos Affair** below). **Floreana** (translated from the German *Postlagernd Floreana*, published in 1959) also chronicles Margret Wittmer's 60 years on Floreana Island. The book is available throughout Ecuador and the Galápagos. *Those that visit the Wittmer Cafe and Pension on Floreana may have the opportunity of getting the book autographed by Mrs. Wittmer and/or a member of the family.*

GALAPAGOS: A TERRESTRIAL AND MARINE PHENOMENON, Paul Humann, 1988. Quito, Ecuador: Libri Mundi. Distributed in the U.S. by Publishers Group West, Emeryville, CA. Paul Humann has been leading dive trips to the islands for many years; this is the best collection of underwater photographs (194 full color plates) of the Galápagos archipelago. *Highly recommended and back in print.*

PORTRAITS OF GALAPAGOS, Tui De Roy and Mark Jones, 1990. Quito, Ecuador: The Roving Tortoise. The latest work by Tui De Roy, author of the classic, **Galápagos: Islands Lost in Time** (see the Background and Reference Material section below). A collection of beautiful photos of the islands' fascinating wildlife, including an intimate description of each photograph. *Available in the U.S. through Galápagos Travel.*

SPANISH AT A GLANCE: PHRASE BOOK & DICTIONARY FOR TRAVELERS, 1984. Hauppauge, NY: Barron's Educational Series. This is everything you need to learn the basics of Spanish. You get a pocket-sized situation phrase book/dictionary and a cassette tape (to get the sound of the language). The comprehensive 200 page phrase book is broken up into several sections including Most Frequently Used Expressions, Slang, Colloquialisms, Passport and Customs, Hotel Services, Getting Around Town, Eating Out, Meeting People, Shopping, Driving a Car, Telling Time, Weather, etc. The examples are very useful and easy to learn. *Recommended for those who want to make a serious effort at learning Spanish while they are in South America.*

SPANISH IN 10 MINUTES A DAY, Kristine Kershul, 1988. Menlo Park, CA: Lane Publishing. Part of a *Sunset Series,* this is a great book for those with no Spanish whatsoever. As the title suggests, a brief (yet consistent) daily session will quickly give you a feel for the language, the confidence to make the effort and say a few words, and the motivation to continue learning. *Recommended for beginners.*

VOYAGE OF THE BEAGLE, Charles Darwin, 1845. London: John Murray. Garden City, NY: Doubleday. Chapter XVII, GALAPAGOS ARCHIPELAGO, is truly fascinating while lounging on the boat, whereas it may seem a bit dull if read before you leave. *Take a copy of this chapter with you!*

WHALES, DOLPHINS, AND PORPOISES, Mark Carwardine, 1995. New York: DK Publishing. I've used a lot of whale identification books, and this is by far the best. The illustrations are numerous and are incredibly well done. There are even drawings of action sequences, including breaching and diving, which help in the identification. Often, there are squares showing color variations, which are also quite useful. *While cetaceans are not usually the highlight of a Galápagos trip, this book is highly recommended as a guide to whales throughout your world travels.*

BACKGROUND AND REFERENCE MATERIAL

Several of the following books are listed as "out of print." They may still be available through your local library and/or "used book/book search" dealers.

A CENTURY AFTER DARWIN'S DEATH, Dieter and Mary Plage, January, 1988. *National Geographic,* Vol. 173, pp. 123-145. A good photographic and written essay, which serves as an excellent introduction to the Galápagos. Back issues of *National Geographic* are available at most libraries.

DARWIN'S ISLANDS: A NATURAL HISTORY OF THE GALAPAGOS, Ian Thornton, 1971. New York: Natural History Press. An important work and for many years the only natural history guide to the Galápagos.

ECOLOGY AND EVOLUTION IN DARWIN'S FINCHES, Peter Grant, 1986. Princeton, NJ: Princeton University Press. Peter Grant and his students have conducted extensive research studies on the Darwin's finches, including the actual mechanics of natural selection. There are 16 chapters in all, dealing with general characteristics, patterns of morphological variation, adaptation, and speciation. Generalizations are also made to evolutionary dynamics of other species. *This is the definitive text on the Darwin's finches. Recommended for birders, ornithologists, and anyone seriously interested in evolutionary theory.*

THE ENCANTADAS, Herman Melville, 1854. First published as a serial in *Harper's Monthly,* this tale of the Galápagos subsequently appeared in its entirety as part of a collection of Melville short stories called **The Piazza Tales,** published in 1856 by Dix and Edwards, London. Melville spent several years on New England whaling ships, and the rich narrative expressed here (as well as in **Moby Dick**) was acquired firsthand. Never one to hold back an opinion, Melville vividly describes the harsh environment of the Galápagos in terms of a hell on earth, complete with fiery eruptions, demonic animals, and islands that are little more than heaps of ashes.

EVER SINCE DARWIN, Stephen Jay Gould, 1977. New York: W.W. Norton. One of several excellent books by the great evolutionary biologist, Steven Jay Gould; each book is a thematic compilation of his monthly essays in *Natural History* magazine.

FLORA OF THE GALAPAGOS ISLANDS, Ira L. Wiggins and Duncan M. Porter, 1971. Palo Alto, CA: Stanford University Press. *This is a thorough text, the complete reference guide to the Galápagos plant life.*

EXPLORING TROPICAL ISLES AND SEAS: AN INTRODUCTION FOR THE TRAVELER AND AMATEUR NATURALIST, Frederic Martini, 1984. Englewood Cliffs, NJ: Prentice-Hall, Inc. Stimulating descriptions on several relevant topics, including life on an island, the tropical environment, and marine reptiles and mammals. The chapter on marine fishes is fascinating, beginning with a description of "what exactly a fish is" and then functionally classifying groups of fishes as Generalists, Speeders, Maneuverers, Wrigglers, Commandos, Grazers, and Advertisers. *Highly recommended and, unfortunately, out of print.*

THE GALAPAGOS AFFAIR, John Treherne, 1983. New York: Random House. During the 1930s the island of Floreana was the scene of a real-life Agatha Christie mystery (unsolved to this very day) that could easily carry the title of "Death in Paradise." John Treherne offers a complete and fascinating account of this who-done-it. *Unfortunately, this book is out of print, but is available at many libraries.*

GALAPAGOS: DISCOVERY ON DARWIN'S ISLANDS, David Steadman and Steven Zousmer, 1988. Washington, DC: Smithsonian Institution Press. Produced by the Smithsonian Institution, this book is more than the coffee-table image it reflects at first glance. Steadman's writing is based on first-hand knowledge and insight gained by his extensive research in the Galápagos. The illustrations are beautiful, many of them full page color plates, with a complete description of the animal on the facing page. *Long out of print, although this unique book still shows up in mail order catalogs.*

GALAPAGOS FISHES: A COMPREHENSIVE GUIDE TO THEIR IDENTIFICATION, Jack S. Grove and Robert S. Lavenberg, 1997. Palo Alto, CA: Stanford University Press. Jack Grove has years of experience in the Galápagos as a Naturalist Guide and, more recently, as a Tour Leader. Jack also just received his doctorate degree. Recently published, this scholarly text containing over 2300 drawings and reviewed by 75 ichthyologists, has been over 10 years in the making.

GALAPAGOS: ISLANDS LOST IN TIME, Tui De Roy Moore, 1980. New York: Viking Press. Tui has spent almost all her life in the Galápagos; her love for these islands and the countless days she has spent observing and documenting its wilderness and wildlife is shared with the reader in an inspiring manner. This book, conveying the feel of the Galápagos like no other, is a collection of what are generally considered to be the most beautiful photographs ever taken of the islands accompanied by a sensitively-written text. *Unfortunately the publisher has long ago decided to take this highly-sought-after book out of print. It can still be found through book-search dealers, but usually at a hefty price.*

GALAPAGOS: ISLANDS OF BIRDS, Byron Nelson, 1968. New York: William Morrow. An in-depth look at the behavior patterns of the Galápagos sea birds. Byron Nelson and his wife actually camped out on Española (Hood) and Tower (Genovesa) Islands for a year, when (prior to tourism) it was still possible for an author to do so.

GALAPAGOS: WORLD'S END, William Beebe, 1924. New York: Dover Publications. Beebe, a renowned biologist and explorer, led a scientific expedition to the archipelago sponsored by the *New York Zoological Society*; his book paints a romantic account of the voyage. Without sacrificing technical accuracy, this book was (during its day) a blend of popular science and adventure travel at its best. It quickly became a best seller, inspiring many to follow in Beebe's footsteps. *Good background reading!*

KEY ENVIRONMENTS: GALAPAGOS, Edited by Roger Perry, 1984. Oxford, England: Pergamon Press. A comprehensive summary of the scientific knowledge of the flora and fauna of the Galápagos archipelago. There are 19 chapters, each written by a scientist who has conducted important research in areas of specialization, including geology, oceanography, terrestrial plants, inshore fish, giant tortoises, sea birds, land birds, iguanas, and sea lions.

THE ORIGIN, Irving Stone, 1980. New York: Doubleday & Co. A fascinating biography of Charles Darwin, the most famous and significant evolutionary biologist we have known. But many of us do not know much about Darwin himself or the extent of his accomplishments. Also, why did it take Darwin almost 25 years to publish **Origin of Species**? And why didn't he ever take a second voyage? Irving Stone answers these questions and many more in a well-researched narrative account that traces Darwin's life and achievements, including his prolific writings. Stone also captures Darwin's moods, his constant battle with illness, his family life, and his friendships/professional relationships with the leading scientists of 19th century England. *A captivating book that is difficult to put down. For some reason, the publisher didn't have this difficulty, and The Origin is now out of print.*

ON THE ORIGIN OF SPECIES, Charles Darwin, 1859. London: John Murray. Garden City, NY: Doubleday. A classic; the ideas set forth in this work remain today as one of the major breakthroughs in scientific thought, and led the way for over 150 years of biological research.

MY FATHER'S ISLAND: A GALAPAGOS QUEST, Johanna Angermeyer, 1989. New York: Viking Penguin. A beautifully written book, **My Father's Island** is a true story about the author and the summers of her early adolescence, which were spent in the Galápagos. It is in the rustic setting of these enchanted isles that Johanna begins the search for her identity and her past. For it was here that her father Hans somehow died in the 1940s. Hans was one of four Angermeyer brothers who sailed for the Galápagos in 1935, leaving the politics of Germany behind them. As Johanna matures, she learns more of the bittersweet details. Under the tutelage of her aunts and uncles, she also learns the details of island life in a beautiful yet arid and often harsh environment. The book is especially relevant for the traveler, as the offspring of the Angermeyer family now rank among the best captains of the touring yachts that sail the waters of the Galápagos archipelago. *An absolutely wonderful book to read while you're touring the islands, but the publisher won't let you do that very easily – out of print since 1995.*

GENERAL INDEX

TOUR OPERATIONS INDEX